THE KNOWING ORGANIZATION

How Organizations Use Information to Construct Meaning, Create Knowledge, and Make Decisions

SECOND EDITION

Chun Wei Choo

New York   Oxford

OXFORD UNIVERSITY PRESS

2006

Oxford University Press, Inc., publishes works that further Oxford University's
objective of excellence in research, scholarship, and education.

Oxford   New York
Auckland   Cape Town   Dar es Salaam   Hong Kong   Karachi
Kuala Lumpur   Madrid   Melbourne   Mexico City   Nairobi
New Delhi   Shanghai   Taipei   Toronto

With offices in
Argentina   Austria   Brazil   Chile   Czech Republic   France   Greece
Guatemala   Hungary   Italy   Japan   Poland   Portugal   Singapore
South Korea   Switzerland   Thailand   Turkey   Ukraine   Vietnam

Published by Oxford University Press, Inc.
198 Madison Avenue, New York, New York 10016
http://www.oup.com

Library of Congress Cataloging-in-Publication Data

Choo, Chun Wei.
  The knowing organization : how organizations use information to construct meaning, create
knowledge, and make decisions / Chun Wei Choo.--2nd ed.
      p. cm.
  Includes bibliographical references and index.
  ISBN-10: 0-19-517677-4 (cloth : alk. paper)
  ISBN-10: 0-19-517678-2 (pbk. : alk. paper)
  ISBN-13: 978-0-19-517677-3 (cloth : alk. paper)
  ISBN-13: 978-0-19-517678-0 (pbk. : alk. paper)
1. Communication in organizations. 2. Decision making. 3. Knowledge, Sociology of. I. Title.
  HD30.3.C46 2005
  658.4'5--dc22   2005004302

Printing number: 9 8 7 6 5 4 3 2
Printed in the United States of America
on acid-free paper

To Bee Kheng,
Ren Min, and Ren Ee

CONTENTS

PREFACE

What is the *knowing organization*? At one level, the knowing organization possesses information and knowledge so that it is well informed, perceptive, and enlightened—descriptions that may be found in the *Oxford English Dictionary*'s entry for "knowing." At a deeper level, the knowing organization uses its information and knowledge to create a special advantage, allowing it to maneuver with intelligence, creativity, and occasionally cunning. This book suggests that such an organization is well-prepared to sustain its growth and development in a dynamic environment. By sensing and understanding its environment, the knowing organization is able to anticipate and adapt early. By marshaling the skills and expertise of its members, the knowing organization is able to learn and innovate. By defining decision rules and values, the knowing organization is primed to take timely, purposive action. At the heart of the knowing organization is its management of the information processes that underpin sense making, knowledge building, and decision making.

Purpose and Approach

This book brings together the research in organization theory and information science in a general framework for understanding the richness and complexity of information use in organizations. Research in organization theory suggests that organizations create and use information in three arenas. First, organizations interpret information about the environment in order to construct meaning about what is happening to the organization and what the organization is doing. Second, they create new knowledge by converting and combining the expertise and know-how of their members in order to learn and innovate. Finally, they process and analyze information in order to select and commit to appropriate courses of action. We combine these perspectives into a model of how organizations use information to adapt to external change and to foster internal growth. The knowing organization model looks at how people and groups work with information to accomplish three outcomes: (1) create an identity and a shared context for action

ix

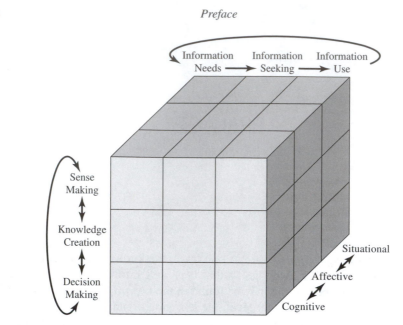

FIGURE P.I. The Knowing Organization Framework

and reflection, (2) develop new knowledge and new capabilities, and (3) make decisions that commit resources and capabilities to purposeful action.

Research in information science on information-seeking behavior suggests that when people seek and use information, they are influenced by a number of cognitive, affective, and situational contingencies. Thus, different types of cognitive gaps lead to the activation of different information behaviors to bridge those gaps. Affective and emotional states influence the preferences and modes of information seeking. Characteristics of the work or problem situation determine the ways that information is used and assessed to be helpful (or otherwise). We use this multi-tier approach to analyze information seeking and use in the organization's sense-making, knowledge-building, and decision-making processes. The general structure of our discussion is shown graphically in Fig. P.1.

Audience

As a text, this book may be useful in courses that focus on information management, knowledge management, organizational communications, information studies, and information systems management. The first edition has served as a text in graduate and executive courses at the University of Amsterdam's PrimaVera Program, TIAS Business School at Tilburg University, Copenhagen Business School, and of course the Faculty of Information Studies at the University of Toronto. The book has also sparked interest in consultants and practitioners who want to know what current research has to offer to help them help organizations.

By presenting in a single volume a survey and synthesis of the state of our knowledge about organizations as social information systems, the book should be relevant to researchers and students in the fields of information management and organization theory and to people managing and working in organizations who share a common desire to acquire a clearer understanding of how organizations turn information into insight, innovation, and an impetus to act.

Overview of the Content

The book is divided into seven chapters. Chapter 1 sets the scene with brief introductions to theories of organizations as sense-making communities, knowledge-creating enterprises, and decision-making systems. It makes the case that these three apparently divergent points of view are in fact complementary pieces of a larger canvas, and that the information behaviors described in each model coalesce into a richer explanation of the nature of information use in organizations.

The recent years has seen a blossoming of research in information-seeking behavior. Chapter 2 surveys the large body of work in this fast-growing field. We define information-seeking behavior as the patterns of behavior that people display when they experience information needs, make choices about where and how to look for information, and reflect or act on the information they see. Conceptually, then, information-seeking behavior consists of (1) information needs, (2) information seeking, and (3) information use, each of which is influenced by a number of cognitive, affective, and situational dimensions. We draw these elements together in an integrative model of human information-seeking behavior, which we apply in subsequent chapters to explore the structure and dynamics of information use by actors and groups in organizations.

Chapter 3 takes a closer look at the first of our three modes of strategic information use—sense making. We view sense making as a process where individuals look at elapsed events, bracket packets of experience, and select particular points of reference to weave patterns of meaning. The result of sense making is an enacted environment that is a reasonable and socially credible rendering of what is going on. The central problem in sense making is how to reduce ambiguity and develop shared meanings so that the organization may act collectively. In sense making, information use tends to be shaped by the existing mental structures or cognitive schemas of organizational members. Sense making in organizations can also be a political arena for "sense giving" and "sense contesting," especially when the organization is facing consequential but unfamiliar changes in a complex environment.

Chapter 4 examines how an organization creates and makes use of new knowledge. An organization possesses three kinds of knowledge: tacit knowledge embedded in the expertise and experience of individuals and groups; explicit or rule-based knowledge codified in organizational rules, routines, and procedures; and cultural knowledge expressed in the assumptions, beliefs, and norms used by members to assign value and significance to new information or knowledge. We examine three ways that an organization can create new knowledge by (1) converting between its tacit and explicit knowledge; (2) building up and refreshing its core capabilities; and (3) transferring and sharing the knowledge that exists in different parts of the organization. In knowledge creation and use, the ability to share and find information—between groups in the organization or between organizations—is an important part of information seeking. There are two distinctive requirements: information has to negotiate boundaries inside and outside the organization; and information sharing often takes place in social networks that are built on trust and cooperation.

Chapter 5 discusses how decisions are made in organizations. All decisions are about finding and choosing courses of action in order to attain some goals. The difficulty of making a decision then depends on how clear the goals are and how well we know about methods that can achieve the desired goals. All decision situations in organizations may therefore be characterized by these two basic dimensions: goal uncertainty and procedural uncertainty. Depending on the level of goal and procedural uncertainty, organizational decision making may be analyzed using the rational model, process model, political model, or anarchic model. Organizations attempt to control the creation and use of information by establishing decision premises, rules, and routines for different types of decision situations. These premises and rules define what information is needed, where to collect it, and how it is to be evaluated in order to arrive at a decision. Depending on the decision-making mode, information seeking can be "satisficing" (finding a good-enough alternative); politically motivated (gathering information to support a position); or process driven (extensive search for a solution to a consequential problem).

The three preceding chapters looked at sense making, knowledge creation, and decision making, one process at a time. Chapter 6 has a different purpose: it analyzes the pathways that connect the domains of meaning, knowing, and acting, and considers how these interactions can promote but also prevent learning in organizations. The chapter examines the *Challenger* and *Columbia* space shuttle accidents in 1986 and 2003 in order to reveal the dynamics between sense making, knowledge creation, and decision making that can impede learning in any organization. The analysis of the two accidents show that sense making driven by beliefs and past actions can be a way of seeing *and* a way of not seeing problems and risks. Moreover, knowledge creation can be compromised when vital tacit knowledge is not transferred, and when knowledge selection and use is controlled by organizational agendas. Finally, repeated patterns of decision making can entrench rules and premises, induce overconfidence, and lower decision vigilance.

The two accidents examined in Chapter 6 suggest that there are inherent features in the way organizations use information that can, against the best of intentions, impede learning and change. These challenges will loom even larger as organizations operate in increasingly complex and uncertain environments. In Chapter 7, we turn to an organization that has accomplished what might at first seem to be an impossible task—the elimination of a deadly disease in the WHO Smallpox Eradication Program. We observe how organizational vision, human ingenuity, and an openness to learning and new ideas combined to make this accomplishment possible. The smallpox program was also a triumph of information management. Information needs were clearly defined, information gathering was thorough and efficient, and information use was managed so that field results were analyzed in time to influence the course of action.

We end the book with a few observations. Decision making attracts much attention because it is closest to the taking of action. At the same time, decision making depends on sense making—we need to know "what is going on and why" before we are able to decide "what is to be done." In a highly dynamic and diverse environment, where different stakeholders move quickly to offer their own interpretations of ambiguous events and issues, organizations realize that constructing meaning has become a new strategic element of organizational life. While sense making constructs the shared context for collective action, knowledge creation expands the horizon of organizational capabilities that cradles innovation. Efforts to enhance knowledge creation would need to focus simultaneously on creating the enabling conditions and providing the enabling tools to support knowledge sharing and use. Ultimately, the knowing organization is a way of thinking about how organizations learn that focuses on the information behaviors that undergird learning. We are still in the early stages of this intellectual journey—our first goal is better understanding, as a necessary step toward better practice.

Changes in the Second Edition

Three of the seven chapters in the second edition are essentially new. Chapter 6 ("A Tale of Two Accidents") and Chapter 7 ("Knowing and Learning in Organizations") are written specially for this edition. Chapter 4 ("The Management of Learning: Organizations as Knowledge-Creating Enterprises") has been expanded to twice its length in the first edition. Chapter 2 ("How We Come to Know: Understanding Information-Seeking Behavior") has been augmented significantly with recent research. Each chapter now ends with a concise summary of the most important messages of the chapter. Many more case studies and organizational examples have been included.

Acknowledgments

The research and preparation of a book draws upon the support, advice, and encouragement of many old friends and colleagues. A new book also provides an occasion—a calling card, if you will—for making new friends and creating new collaborations. In the category of old friends, I would like to thank my colleagues at the Faculty of Information Studies in the University of Toronto who share an interest in at least some aspect of information management: Ethel Auster, Wendy Duff, and Lynne Howarth. The FIS Library staff has been nothing short of heroic in responding to my requests for books and papers. A few colleagues were brave or perhaps generous enough to allow me to work with them in research projects that contributed in one way or another to the book: Brian Detlor of McMaster University, Pierrette Bergeron and Lorna Heaton of the University of Montreal, Marlene Scardamalia of the University of Toronto, and France Bouthillier of McGill University. It has also been a special honor to have had the opportunity to learn from so many talented PhD students, including Don Turnbull, Anu MacIntosh-Murray, Christine Marton, Herman van den Berg, Mary Cavanagh, Scott Paquette, Colin Furness, Cindy Gordon, and Anabel Quan-Haase, to name but a few.

In the category of new acquaintances, I am delighted to have become friends and collaborators with Rik Maes, Ard Huizing, and Toon Abcouwer, all of the University of Amsterdam's PrimaVera Program; Pieter Ribbers of the TIAS Business School in Tilburg University; Maija-Leena Huotari and Pertti Vakkari of the University of Tampere in Finland; Ricardo Barbosa, Rodrigo Baroni, and Silvio Popadiuk of the Federal University of Minas Gerais and Mackenzie Presbyterian University in Brazil; and Alex Byrne and Joyce Kirk of the University of Technology Sydney. Over the years, students of the classes I presented at the University of Toronto, the University of Amsterdam (I+M EMIM), Tilburg University, and elsewhere have through their participation helped to sharpen the ideas presented here.

Among the many who have commented on and caused me to think about the material in the book I would especially like to acknowledge Russell Ackoff, Joel Alleyne, Max Boisot, Paul Bouissac, Stephen Dembner, Joachim Goldberg, Pal Horsle, Wiggo Hustad, Ray Johnston, Rene Jorna, Esko Kilpi, Dorothy Leonard, Hubert Saint-Onge, Deb Wallace, and Tom Wilson. Special thanks to Noe Urzua (Oxford University Press, Mexico) and Armando Rossi (SENAC, SP), for making possible Spanish and Portuguese editions of the book. Finally, a note of appreciation goes to John Rauschenberg, my editor at Oxford University Press in New York, for his enthusiasm in supporting this project.

Chun Wei Choo
Faculty of Information Studies
University of Toronto
Toronto, Canada
http://choo.fis.utoronto.ca
January 2005

C H A **1** T E R

THE KNOWING ORGANIZATION

For love of anything is the offspring of knowledge, love being more fervent as knowledge is more certain, and certainty springs from a thorough knowledge of all those parts which united compose the whole.
   —*Leonardo da Vinci, c. 1510*

The *knowing organization* presents an information-based view of organizations, a model of how organizations use information to adapt to external change and to foster internal growth. Specifically, the model looks at how people and groups in organizations work with information to accomplish three outcomes: (1) create an identity and a shared context for action and reflection, (2) develop new knowledge and new capabilities, and (3) make decisions that commit resources and capabilities to purposeful action. The use of the adjective *knowing* is deliberate. Most dictionaries define *knowing* as possessing private exclusive knowledge (as in "a knowing smile"); being aware and alert; cognitive, intelligent, reflective; and intentional, deliberate, purposeful (as in "a knowing intervention"). Our use of *knowing* to describe organizations embraces all these meanings. The use of *knowing* instead of *knowledge* also underscores our view that knowledge is the result of collective action and reflection, and not simply the acquisition of things and objects that somehow "contain" knowledge.

How *do* organizations use information? This question is much harder than it sounds. Information is an intrinsic part of nearly everything that an organization does, so much so that it fades into the background and its particular role becomes invisible. Yet the question is not facetious. Without a clear understanding of the organizational and human processes through which information becomes selected and expressed as insight, knowledge, and action, an organization is unable to thrive and grow in an increasingly complex environment. In this chapter, we preview the principal ways in which an organization uses information and suggest how these processes are interconnected to enable learning and adaptation.

Studies of organizations emphasize three distinct arenas in which the creation and use of information play a strategic role. First, organizations use information to make sense of changes in their environment. Organizations thrive in a dynamic, uncertain world. A dependable supply of materials, resources, and energy must be secured. Market forces and dynamics modulate the organization's performance. Fiscal and legal structures define its identity and sphere of influence. Societal norms and public opinion constrain the organization's roles and reach. Changes in the environment continuously generate signals and cues. Unfortunately, these messages are ambiguous and are compatible with multiple interpretations. As a result, a crucial task of management is to discern the most significant changes, interpret their meaning, and develop appropriate responses. The short-term goal of sense making is to construct shared understandings that allow the organization to continue to act and function; the longer-term goal is to ensure that the organization adapts and continues to thrive in a dynamic environment.

The second arena of strategic information use is when organizations generate new knowledge. Knowledge is dispersed throughout the organization and exists in different forms and venues. Individuals develop an informal kind of knowledge that is derived from practice and experience, but which cannot be expressed easily as formulas or propositions. Although it is personal and hidden, organizations are very interested in this knowledge because it is the source of creativity and innovation, without which organizations cannot create new knowledge. At the same time, organizational knowledge is not the same as a simple aggregation of individual knowledge. Over and above personal expertise, there is knowledge based on what the organization believes about itself (identity, purpose), its capabilities, and its environment (communities, markets). There is knowledge embedded in the physical goods it produces and in the rules and routines that it has learned over time. An organization exists because of its ability to integrate and channel these sets of knowledge into activities and outcomes that are meaningful and valuable. An organization grows when it is able to continuously refresh its knowledge and extend its capabilities.

The third arena of strategic information use is when organizations search for and evaluate information in order to make decisions. In theory, this choice is to be made rationally, based upon complete information about the organization's goals, feasible alternatives, probable outcomes of these alternatives, and the utility of these outcomes to the organization. In practice, decision making is muddled by the jostling of interests among stakeholders, the biases and idiosyncrasies of individual decision makers, information being hard to find, and the lack of time or resources. Despite these complications, an organization must keep up at least an appearance of reasoned behavior if it is to sustain internal trust and maintain external legitimacy. Although decision making wants to be complex and messy, organizations control the decision process by giving it some degree of order and structure. Ultimately, decisions are vital because they lie closest to action: all organizational actions are initiated by decisions, and all decisions are commitments to action. Herbert Simon and his associates have maintained that management *is* decision making, so that the best way to analyze organization behavior is to analyze the structure and processes of decision making.

I. A PREVIEW OF THE KNOWING ORGANIZATION

Although they are often approached as distinct and separate organizational information processes, the central thesis of this book is that the three arenas of information use—sense making, knowledge building, and decision making—are in fact highly interconnected processes, and that by analyzing how the three activities invigorate each other, a more complete view of organizational information use emerges.

As a preview, we can visualize sense making, knowledge building, and decision making as representing three layers of organizational information practices, with each inner layer building upon the information created in the outer layer (Fig. 1.1). Information flows from the external environment (outside the circles) and is progressively assimilated and focused to enable organizational action. First, information about the organization's environment is sensed and its meaning is constructed. This provides the context for all organizational activity

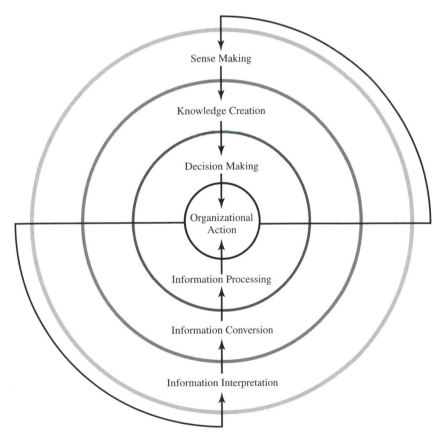

FIGURE 1.1. The Knowing Organization

and guides both the knowledge-creation and decision-making processes. Knowledge resides in the minds of individuals, and this personal knowledge needs to be converted into knowledge that can be shared and applied. Understanding and knowledge forms the basis for action, and the organization chooses a course according to its aspirations and capabilities. Organizational action changes the environment and produces new streams of experience for the organization to adapt to, so the cycle of learning is continuous.

During *sense making,* the principal information process is the interpretation of cues and messages about the environment. Members must choose what information is significant and should be attended to; they form possible explanations from past experience; and they exchange and negotiate their views in an effort to collectively construct an interpretation. During *knowledge creation,* the main information process is the conversion of knowledge. Members share their personal knowledge through dialogue and discourse, and articulate what they intuitively know with the help of analogies, metaphors, and stories. During *decision making,* the key information activity is the processing of information about available alternatives in order to select one that can achieve desired objectives. Members are guided by premises, rules, and routines that structure their search for information and evaluation of alternatives. All three modes of information use—interpretation, conversion, and processing—are dynamic, social processes that continuously constitute and reconstitute meaning, knowledge, and action.

The organization that is able to effectively integrate sense making, knowledge creation, and decision making may be described as a *knowing organization.* The knowing organization possesses information and knowledge so that it is well informed, mentally alert, and aware of threats and opportunities. Its actions are based upon a shared understanding of the organization's context and aspirations, and are leveraged by the available knowledge and skills of its members. Thus, the knowing organization possesses information and knowledge that confers a special advantage, allowing it to maneuver with intelligence, creativity, and occasionally cunning. By managing information resources and information practices, it is able to

- sense and respond to a changing environment, but also shape and influence changes in the environment that are advantageous;
- extend its base of knowledge and capabilities, but also unlearn old assumptions and beliefs;
- make decisions that are sometimes rational and sometimes creative in order to meet increasingly complex challenges.

In the subsequent sections, we will examine each of the three information-use processes that animate the knowing organization. We will see how the different perspectives illuminate different aspects of organizational information behavior, and we will also see how some of the interactions between the processes bind them into a larger whole.

II. SENSE MAKING

Sense making is induced by changes in the environment. These changes generate streams of messages and cues. Unfortunately, the messages are equivocal in that they are open to multiple interpretations. The issue is not that we need more information, but what does the information we are getting mean? Thus, the principal information activity is to resolve the *equivocality* of information about the organization's environment: What is happening out there? Why is this taking place? What does it mean? This sense making is done retrospectively, since we cannot make sense of events and actions until they have occurred and we can glance backward in time to construct their meaning. Current events are compared with past experience in order to construct meaning: "the goal of organizations, viewed as sensemaking systems, is to create and identify events that recur to stabilize their environments and make them more predictable. A sensible event is one that resembles something that has happened before" (Weick 1995, p. 170). Weick suggests that an organization makes sense of its environment through four sets of interlocking processes: ecological change, enactment, selection, and retention (Fig. 1.2).

As shown in Figure 1.2, sense making begins when there is some change or difference in the organizational environment, resulting in disturbances or variations in the flows of experience affecting the organization's participants. This *ecological change* requires the organization's members to attempt to understand these differences and to determine the significance of these changes. In trying to

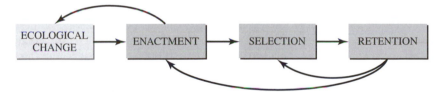

	Enactment	Selection	Retention
Information inputs	• Raw data from the environment	• Equivocal data from enactment • Enacted interpretations that worked before	• Enacted environment from selection process
Processes	• Bracket raw data • Create features in the environment to attend to	• Select plausible interpretations based on "best fit" with past understandings	• Store enacted environment as product of successful sense making
Information outcomes	• Equivocal data as material for sense making	• Enacted, meaningful environment	• Interpretations available for use in future sense making

FIGURE 1.2. Sense-Making Processes in an Organization (Adapted from Weick 1979b)

understand the meaning of these changes, an organization may take some action to isolate or bracket some portion of the changes to attend to.

The first step in the sense-making process is enactment. In *enactment,* people actively construct the information they attend to in two ways. First, they selectively bracket, isolate, and highlight information, paying attention to some messages and ignoring others. They label, categorize, and connect together information about actors, events, and outcomes. Second, they intrude into the environment and create new features in order to help them make sense of the environment. For example, an organization might introduce new messages or actions in the environment and then focus their sense making on these activities (e.g., distribute a discussion document, hold a special meeting, create a website). When managers enact the environment, they "construct, rearrange, single out, and demolish many 'objective' features of their surroundings. . . . they unrandomize variables, insert vestiges of orderliness, and literally create their own constraints" (Weick 1979b, p. 164). The result of this enactment is a smaller set of data that is still equivocal. The enactment process segregates possible environments that the organization could clarify and take seriously, but whether it actually does so depends on what happens in the selection process.

In the *selection* process, people look at the information they have enacted and try to answer the question, "What is going on here?" They overlay the new data with interpretations that have worked before in explaining similar or related situations in the past. Interpretations that have proven sensible in explaining previous situations are now superimposed on the current raw data to see if they could provide a reasonable interpretation of what has occurred. Interpretations are selected that provide the best fit with past understandings. The information outcome of selection is a set of cause-and-effect explanations that render the environment understandable and meaningful. These explanations have to plausible, but they need not be the most accurate nor the most complete. The selection process therefore reaches into the past to extract history and select a reasonable scheme of interpretation.

In the *retention* process, the products of successful sense making are retained for future use. The product of organizational sense making is an enacted environment: "a sensible rendering of previous events stored in the form of causal assertions, and made binding on some current enactment and/or selection" (Weick 1979b, p. 166). As we have seen, the enacted environment is based on the retrospective interpretations of actions or events already completed. It is like a historical document, stored perhaps as stories, explanations, and beliefs or as a map of relationships between events and actions. In these forms, interpretations are remembered and made available for future cycles of enactment and selection.

In the sense-making view, the reason for the existence of an organization is to produce stable interpretations of equivocal data about environmental change. Although the entire process operates to reduce equivocality, some equivocal features do and must remain so that the interpretations may be usefully compared with new data in future sense making. Indeed, organizations can continue to learn only if they maintain a balance between flexibility and stability in their rendering of a meaningful context for organizational action.

	"83 percent of people file their tax forms; 17 percent do not."		
	Enactment	*Selection*	*Retention*
Organization X	17 percent do not file their taxes. A lot of people do not pay their taxes. A lot of people are dishonest scofflaws.	People won't pay unless we come down hard on them. Create a special collection agency.	People cannot be trusted: "law and order."
Organization Y	83 percent do file. Most people file their taxes. Most people are honest, law abiding.	People will pay if we make it easy for them. Simplify the collection process.	People can be trusted: "make it simple."

FIGURE 1.3. Sense-Making Example (Adapted from Leonard and Swap 1999, p. 130)

Fig. 1.3 contrasts how two organizations make sense of the same phenomenon in their environment. The phenomenon is indicated by the message that "83 percent of people file their tax forms; 17 percent do not." In the enactment phase, organization X (top row, Fig. 1.3) brackets the information that "17 percent do not file their taxes" and makes the observation that "a lot of people do not pay their taxes." In the selection phase, X overlays this data with the cause-and-effect explanation that "people won't pay unless we come down hard on them." In the retention phase, X retains this interpretation with the belief or idea that "people cannot be trusted" to file their taxes, and that some form of intervention is needed for "law and order." Organization Y (bottom row, Fig. 1.3) arrives at different conclusions. During enactment, Y brackets the cue that "83 percent do file" and that therefore "most people file their taxes." During selection, Y chooses the explanation that "people will pay if we make it easy for them." The interpretation it retains is that "people can be trusted" to file their taxes, and that when creating the collection process, the idea is to "make it simple."

This example illustrates how different organizations operating in the same environment can make different sense of their common environment. Even when they are looking at the same issues or trends with the same information, they arrive at different answers to the question of "what's going on." They arrive at different interpretations because they bracket and highlight different features of the environment; they use different labels and language to describe and discuss what they are noticing; they construct meaning by relying on their beliefs and their past actions. The way organizations make sense of events and trends thus depends on their beliefs and the history of actions they have taken.

An important corollary of the sense-making model is that organizations behave as interpretation systems:

Organizations must make interpretations. Managers literally must wade into the swarm of events that constitute and surround the organization and actively try to impose some order on them. . . . Interpretation is the process of translating these events, of developing models for understanding, of bringing out meaning, and of assembling conceptual schemes. (Weick and Daft 1983, p. 74)

What is being interpreted is the organization's external environment, and how the organization goes about its interpretation depends on how analyzable it perceives the environment to be and how actively it intrudes into the environment to understand it. Equivocality is reduced by managers and other participants who discuss ambiguous information cues and construct a common interpretation of the environment.

III. KNOWLEDGE CREATION

According to Nonaka and Takeuchi (1995), organizations need to develop the capacity to continuously create new knowledge. Knowledge creation is achieved through managing the relationship between tacit and explicit knowledge, and through designing social processes that generate new knowledge by converting tacit knowledge into explicit knowledge. Tacit knowledge is personal knowledge that is hard to formalize or communicate to others. It consists of subjective know-how, insights, and intuitions that comes to a person after having worked on an activity for a long period of time. Explicit knowledge is formal knowledge that is easier to transmit between individuals and groups. It may be coded in the form of formulas, instructions, procedures, rules, and so on. The two categories of knowledge are complementary. Tacit knowledge, while it remains closely held as personal know-how, is limited in its usefulness to the organization. On the other hand, explicit knowledge does not appear spontaneously, but must be nurtured and cultivated from the seeds of tacit knowledge.

Nonaka and Takeuchi (1995) suggest that the production of new knowledge involves "a process that 'organizationally' amplifies the knowledge created by individuals and crystallizes it as a part of the knowledge network of the organization" (p. 59). The basis of organizational knowledge creation is therefore the conversion of tacit knowledge into explicit knowledge and back again. Nonaka and Takeuchi (1995) identify four modes in which new knowledge is created through conversion between tacit and explicit knowledge: socialization, externalization, combination, and internalization. We outline these processes, using examples from Nonaka and Takeuchi's analysis of how Matsushita, one of Japan's largest consumer electronics conglomerate, developed an automatic home bakery product in 1985.

Socialization is a process of acquiring tacit knowledge through sharing experiences. Tacit knowledge is transferred from an experienced person to another person by the two working side by side, sharing the same work and social setting. As apprentices learn the craft of their masters through watching, imitating, and practicing, so do new employees of a firm learn their jobs through on-the-job training and mentoring activities. In 1985, Matsushita decided to develop its automatic home bread-making machine. Its goal was to design a home bakery that produced bread which tasted at least as good as that found in the supermarkets.

One of the secrets of making good bread was in kneading the dough. Although the software team could program the motor to emulate kneading motions, the bread that was produced did not taste good enough. An early problem was how to emulate the dough-kneading process, a process that takes a master baker years of practice to perfect. To learn this tacit knowledge, the head of the software development team, Ikuko Tanaka, decided to volunteer herself as an apprentice to the head baker of the Osaka International Hotel, who was reputed to produce the area's best bread. After a period of imitation and practice, she observed that the baker was not only stretching but also twisting the dough in a particular fashion ("twisting stretch"), which turned out to be the secret for making tasty bread.

Externalization is a process of converting tacit knowledge into explicit concepts through the use of abstractions, metaphors, analogies, or models. The externalization of tacit knowledge is the quintessential knowledge-creation activity and is most often seen during the concept creation phase of new product development. Externalization can also be triggered by dialogue or collective reflection. Returning to the Matsushita case, Tanaka could not specify in engineering terms the "twisting stretch" motion she had learned from the master baker. Nevertheless, she was able to communicate this tacit knowledge to the engineers by creating the mental concept of "twisting stretch," and by indicating the power and speed of the kneading propeller in order to imitate this motion. For example, Tanaka would say, "make the propeller move stronger" or "move it faster," and the engineers would make the necessary adjustments through trial and error.

Combination is a process of creating explicit knowledge by finding and bringing together explicit knowledge from a number of sources. Thus, individuals exchange and combine their explicit knowledge through telephone conversations, meetings, memos, and so on. Existing information in computerized databases may be categorized, collated, and sorted in a number of ways to produce new explicit knowledge. The Matsushita home bakery team drew together eleven members from different specializations and cultures: product planning, mechanical engineering, control systems, and software development. The "twisting stretch" motion was finally materialized in a prototype after a year of iterative experimentation by the engineers and team members working closely together, combining their explicit knowledge. For example, the engineers added ribs to the inside of the dough case in order to hold the dough better as it is being churned. Another team member suggested a method (later patented) to add yeast at a later stage in the process, thereby saving the cost of a cooler otherwise needed to prevent the yeast from overfermenting in high temperatures.

Finally, *internalization* is a process of embodying explicit knowledge into tacit knowledge, internalizing the experiences gained through the other modes of knowledge creation into individuals' tacit knowledge bases in the form of shared mental models or work practices. Internalization is facilitated if the knowledge is captured in documents or conveyed in the form of stories, so that individuals may re-experience indirectly the experience of others. Matsushita's home bakery product turned out to be a great success. It sold a record 536,000 units in its first year, topped the list of Mother's Day gifts, and was featured in a 1987 issue of

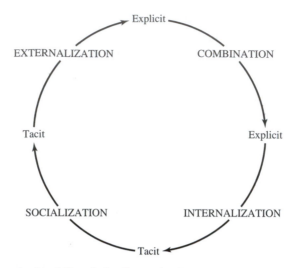

FIGURE 1.4. Organizational Knowledge Conversion Processes (Nonaka and Takeuchi 1995)

Fortune magazine. The success story was disseminated throughout Matsushita by word of mouth and in-house publications, changing employees' perceptions about the potential of home appliances and inspiring them to develop other innovative products. The new tacit knowledge being internalized was that Matsushita could develop a product by interfacing directly with customers and by pursuing quality without compromise. This inspired Matsushita to launch a new grand concept labeled "human electronics" to develop more innovative consumer products that would enhance the quality of human life using electronics.

As shown in Fig. 1.4, the four modes of knowledge conversion follow each other in a continuous spiral of knowledge creation. Knowledge creation can begin with individuals working on a tough problem who develop some insight or intuition on how to solve it. This tacit know-how may have been gained from a knowledgeable person through socialization. However, as long as the knowledge stays tacit, the organization is unable to exploit it further. In the Matsushita example, the master baker's kneading technique had to be converted into explicit knowledge that was available to everyone in the team so that it could be used to design the kneading motor. Drawing out tacit knowledge requires taking a mental leap and often involves the creative use of a metaphor, an analogy, or a story. To turn a tentative idea into a viable product, the organization needs to wrap the idea with operational and production features that make it useful and cost effective. Adding these features require the organization to find and combine complementary expertise to make the new product operational. This is one reason why cross-functional teams can be effective in new product development, as was in the Matsushita case. Finally, the experience of creating and applying the new knowledge is assimilated and internalized as new practices and mental models that provide the ground for more cycles of knowledge creation.

Nonaka describes the dynamics driving his model of knowledge creation as follows:

> Organizational knowledge creation, as distinct from individual knowledge
> creation, takes place when all four modes of knowledge creation are
> "organizationally" managed to form a continual cycle. . . . First, the *socialization*
> mode usually starts with the building of a "team" or "field" of interaction. This
> field facilitates the sharing of members' experiences and perspectives. Second, the
> *externalization* mode is triggered by successive rounds of meaningful "dialogue."
> In this dialogue, the sophisticated use of "metaphors" can be used to enable team
> members to articulate their own perspectives and thereby reveal hidden tacit
> knowledge that is otherwise hard to communicate. Concepts formed by teams can
> be combined with existing data and external knowledge in a search of more
> concrete and sharable specifications. This *combination* mode is facilitated by such
> triggers as "coordination" between team members and other sections of the
> organization and the "documentation" of existing knowledge. Through an iterative
> process of trial and error, concepts are articulated and developed until they emerge
> in a concrete form. This "experimentation" can trigger *internalization* through a
> process of learning by doing. Participants in a "field" of action share explicit
> knowledge that is gradually translated, through interaction and a process of
> trial-and-error, into different aspects of tacit knowledge. (Nonaka 1994, p. 20,
> italics mine)

IV. DECISION MAKING

In an ideal world, rational decision making would require a complete search of available alternatives, reliable information about their consequences, and consistent preferences to evaluate these outcomes. In the real world, such demands on information gathering and processing are unrealistic. Instead of a comprehensive, objective rationality, Herbert Simon suggested that decision making in organizations is constrained by the principle of *bounded rationality:*

> The capacity of the human mind for formulating and solving complex problems
> is very small compared with the size of the problems whose solution is required
> for objectively rational behavior in the real world—or even for a reasonable
> approximation to such objective rationality. (Simon 1957, p. 198)

What constitute the bounds that limit the capacity of the human mind for rational decision making? Simon identifies three categories of bounds: the individual is limited by his cognitive and mental capacities; by the extent of knowledge and information possessed; and by values or conceptions of purpose which may diverge from organizational goals (Simon 1976, pp. 40–41, 241). It is because individual human beings are limited in their cognitive ability that organizations become necessary and useful instruments for the achievement of larger purposes. Conversely, the organization can alter the limits to rationality of its members by creating or changing the organizational environment in which the individual's decision making takes place. Simon proposes that the organization influences its members' behaviors by controlling the *decision premises* upon which decisions are made, rather than controlling the actual decisions themselves (Simon 1976, p. 223). A fundamental problem of organizing is then in defining the decision premises that form the organizational environment: "The task of administration is so to design this environment that the individual will approach as close as practicable to rationality (judged in terms of the organization's goals) in his decisions" (Simon 1976, pp. 240–41).

Organizations specify two types of decision premises. First, there are value premises that determine what the decision maker perceives as "good, desirable, or valuable" in an alternative. Examples of value premises might include high profit margins, cost efficiencies, or environmental friendliness. Value premises allow the decision maker to select one future outcome or alternative as being preferable to others. Second, factual premises determine what the decision maker perceives as "factual, relevant" information to a decision situation. Thus, certain items of information are typically required in order for a decision to be made (e.g., information about a client, sales data, facts about a location). Factual premises allow the decision maker to derive statements about an observable world that are verifiable or true and that are relevant to the decision at hand.

Another consequence of bounded rationality is that the organizational actor *satisfices* when making decisions—selecting a course of action that is satisfactory or good enough rather than seeking the optimal solution. To satisfice is to be satisfied with a sufficiently good alternative ("sufficiently satisfactory"). The difference has been likened to searching a haystack to find the sharpest needle in it and searching the haystack to find a needle that is sharp enough to sew with. A course of action is satisfactory if it exceeds some acceptable criteria. March and Simon believe that "most human decision making, whether individual or organizational, is concerned with the discovery and selection of satisfactory alternatives" (1993, p. 162). Satisficing standards can change with experience. If the search for alternatives has been accomplished with little effort, these standards may rise over time. Conversely, when even satisfactory solutions are hard to find, standards for judging and accepting solutions may be lowered!

The *search* for alternatives is simplified in three ways. First, search is *problemistic,* in that search is driven by the appearance of a problem, so that there is little proactive search, and search stops when the problem goes away. Second, search is *localized* and takes place near the appearance of the problem symptoms, and near to past experience or recent solutions. Third, search is *sequential* with respect to goals: search pursues one goal at a time, different goals at different times, and not all the goals at the same time. Briefly, then, search is motivated by the occurrence of a problem, is concentrated near the symptoms or an old solution, and reflects the training, experience, and goals of the decision maker.

Decision premises, satisficing, and simplified search together form the basis of how organization design *performance programs* that structure the decision-making process. Performance programs define rules and procedures that specify who has authority to decide; what information is to be obtained; where to look for the information; who gets to participate or be consulted; what criteria is to be applied; and so on. Performance programs thus reduce the need for extensive search or for weighing many alternatives at the same time, and simplify the choice process by developing standard responses to defined situations.

Performance programs or *decision routines* lie at the heart of organizational decision making and serve a number of valuable and visible functions. Decision routines reflect what the organization has learned from experience about how to deal with recurrent situations—organizations remember by doing, and action and decision routines become part of the organization's procedural memory. Planning, budgeting, and project evaluation procedures allow internal groups to compete for resources based on criteria and procedures that are open and nominally fair. Routines also allow the organization to project legitimacy externally to its community and stakeholders, since an organization following rational decision routines may be construed to have attempted to behave responsibly and accountably. At the same time, critics of standardized procedures blame them as the cause of organizational stasis and inertia. Over-rigid routines can block organizational learning, stifle creativity, and forfeit organizational flexibility.

Organizational decision making is rational in spirit (and appearance) if not in execution: the organization is intendedly rational even if its members are only boundedly so. The key features of organizations as decision-making systems are shown in Fig. 1.5. Organizations seek rational behavior in terms of actions that contribute to their goals and objectives. Unfortunately, the decision behavior of individual members are constrained by their cognitive capacity, information, and values. In the light of bounded rationality, organizations reduce uncertainty and complexity by specifying decision premises and designing decision routines. In the bounded rationality model, decision behavior is still rational (with respect to organizational goals), but it is a more prescribed, regulated rationality that is guided by decision premises and routines.

For an illustration of how decision premises can mold organizational behavior, consider how Intel allocated its expensive manufacturing resources in the 1970s and 1980s. In those years, when Intel was actively manufacturing dynamic DRAM (dynamic random access memories), EPROM (erasable programmable read-only memory), and microprocessors, all three product divisions shared

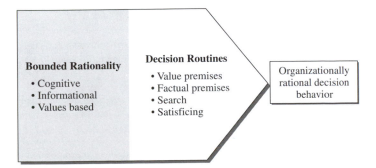

FIGURE 1.5. Organizational Decision Making

wafer fabrication plants. Sharing was possible because wafer fabrication plants could initially be converted to manufacture one of the three classes of products. The decision premises and routines that were employed in this resource allocation process have been summarized as follows:

> product division managers would get together monthly to decide on how to load the factories based on the rule to maximize margin-per-wafer-start. Deciding which type of product to put on a wafer at the start of the sequence of production steps was a key decision. The adoption of this rule reflected the fact that Intel's businesses were characterized by high asset intensity (and hence low asset turnover), and return on sales was important for profitability. (Burgelman 2002, pp. 65–66)

> The sales department would bring to this meeting its forecast shipments by product, and accounting would bring a rank ordering of those products by gross margins per start. The highest-margin product would then be allocated the production capacity needed to meet its forecast shipments. The next-highest-margin product would then get the capacity it needed in order to meet its forecast shipments, and so on, until the product line with the lowest gross margins were allocated whatever residual capacity remained. Gross margins per wafer start, in other words, constituted the values of the organization that were used in this critical resource allocation decision. (Christensen and Raynor 2003, p. 219)

In this example, we can see how the value premises ("margin-per-wafer-start"), factual premises ("sales and margins forecasted"), and decision rules ("highest-margin product allocated first") are combined to structure the decision process by which Intel assigned its manufacturing resources.

V. TOWARD THE KNOWING ORGANIZATION

There seems to be much that separates the three models of organizational information use (Table 1-1). The sense-making model sees the organization as trying to interpret an equivocal environment. Members look back on their actions and

TABLE 1-1. Three modes of organizational information use.

Mode	Central Idea
Sense Making	Environmental change → Interpret equivocal messages by enacting interpretations → Meaningful context for action. Information is interpreted.
Knowledge Creating	Knowledge gap → Convert and combine tacit and explicit knowledge → New capabilities, innovations. Information is converted.
Decision Making	Decision situation → Search and select alternatives guided by premises, rules → Goal-directed action. Information is evaluated.

experiences and enact or construct their own perceptions of the environment. Sense making is retrospective in that people can only try to understand what they have already done or what has happened. The outcomes of sense making are enacted environments or shared interpretations that construct the context for organizational action. The knowledge-creating model sees the organization as continuously tapping its knowledge to solve tough problems. Different forms of organizational knowledge are converted and combined in continuous cycles of innovation. The outcomes of the process include the development of new products as well as new capabilities. The decision-making model sees the organization as a rational, goal-directed system. Decision makers search for alternatives, evaluate consequences, and commit to a course of action. Because individuals are limited in their ability to search and process information in a completely rational manner, decision premises and rules reduce the uncertainty and complexity of the choice-making process. The outcome of decision making is the selection of courses of action that are intended to enable the organization to achieve its goals.

Of the three models, the rational decision-making framework is probably the most influential and widely applied. Yet there are some perplexing behavior patterns common in organizations that do not seem to fit this view. People gather information ostensibly for decisions but do not use it (Feldman and March 1981). They ask for reports but do not read them. Individuals fight for the right to take part in decision processes, but then do not exercise that right. Policies are vigorously debated but their implementation is met with indifference (March and Olsen 1976). Managers observed in situ seemed to spend little time in making decisions but are instead most often engaged in meetings and conversations (Mintzberg 1973; Kotter 1982). Such findings seem to suggest that decision making, apart from being an occasion for making choices, is also "an arena for developing and enjoying an interpretation of life and one's position in it. A business firm is a temple and a collection of sacred rituals as well as an instrument for producing goods and services. The rituals of choice tie routine events to beliefs about the nature of things. They give meaning" (Cyert and March 1992, p. 236). In other words, organizational life is not just about choice but also about interpretation, and the process of decision making must embrace the process of sense making even as it examines the behaviors of choice making. In their introduction to the 1993 edition of their 1958 classic, *Organizations,* March and Simon wrote:

> Some contemporary students of meaning in organizations would go further to assert that it is interpretation, rather than choice, that is central to life. Within such a view, organizations are organized around the requirement to sustain, communicate, and elaborate interpretations of history and life—not around decisions. Decisions are instruments to interpretation, rather than the other way around. Although we think an interpretive perspective yields important insights into organizations, we would not go that far, even in retrospect. But we suspect that a 1992 book on organizations, even while reaffirming that there is a real world out there to which organizations are adapting and which they are affecting, would need to pay somewhat more attention than a 1958 book did to the social context of meaning within which organizations operate. (March and Simon 1993, p. 18)

In the sense-making model, the enacted environment is an outcome of the meaning-construction process and serves as a reasonable, plausible context for action. However, once the environment has been enacted and stored, people in the organization now face the critical question of what to do with what they know—these are what Weick (1979b) has called "the consequential moments." Furthermore, the shared interpretations are a compromise between stability and flexibility—some equivocal features do and must remain in the stored interpretations, so that the organization has the flexibility to adapt to a new and different future. People in organizations are therefore "people who oppose, argue, contradict, disbelieve, doubt, act hypocritically, improvise, counter, distrust, differ, challenge, vacillate, question, puncture, disprove, and expose. All of these actions embody ambivalence as the optimal compromise to deal with the incompatible demands of flexibility and stability" (Weick 1979b, p. 229).

Where decision premises in the decision-making model control organizational choice making, shared beliefs and experiences in the sense-making model constrain the ways that people in an organization perceive their world. Both phenomena are aspects of *premise control,* and premise control becomes a useful concept that links sense making to decision making (Weick 1995, p. 114). The central concern of sense making is understanding how people in organizations construct meaning and reality, and then exploring how that enacted reality provides a context for organizational action, including decision making and knowledge building.

Commenting on the rational decision-making model, Nonaka and Takeuchi (1995) argued that this information-processing view has a fundamental limitation. For them, the decision-making model does not really explain innovation. The decision-making view is essentially conservative, where decision premises and performance programs are designed for control, and search simplifications inhibit radically innovative solutions. On the other hand, "when organizations innovate, they do not simply process information, from the outside in, in order to solve existing problems and adapt to a changing environment. They actually create new information and knowledge, from the inside out, in order to redefine both problems and solutions and, in the process, to re-create their environment" (p. 56).

The key to innovation is in unlocking the personal, tacit knowledge of the organization's members. For Nonaka and Takeuchi, tacit knowledge has two dimensions: the technical dimension and the cognitive dimension. The technical dimension is about the practical know-how of doing a task. The cognitive dimension consists of "schemata, mental models, beliefs, and perceptions" that "reflect our image of reality (what is) and our vision for the future (what ought to be)" (Nonaka and Takeuchi 1995, p. 8). These implicit models shape the way people in an organization perceive the world around them—they create a shared understanding of what the organization stands for, where it is headed, what kind of world it wants to live in, and how to help make that world a reality. An organization's leadership should create a *knowledge vision* that "defines the 'field' or 'domain' that gives corporate members a mental map of the world they live in and provides a general direction regarding what kind of knowledge they ought to seek and create" (p. 227). Just as decision premises and shared beliefs link sense making with decision making, this knowledge vision and shared views about the organization and its world link sense making with knowledge creation.

Although they adopt contrasting perspectives and grapple with different aspects of organizational behavior, the three modes of organizational information use act on and react to each other. Sense making constructs enacted environments or shared interpretations that serve as meaningful contexts for organizational action. Shared interpretations help configure the organizational intent or knowledge vision necessary to give direction to the knowledge conversion processes in knowledge creation. Knowledge creation leads to innovation in the form of new products and new capabilities. When it is time to select a course of action in response to an enactment of the environment or as a result of knowledge-derived innovation, decision makers apply rules and premises to make choices and to commit resources.

VI. THE KNOWING CYCLE

Having examined each of the three processes of sense making, knowledge creation, and decision making, we now look at the interactions between these processes and consider some implications for information management and practice. These interactions are introduced in Fig. 1.6 and discussed in this section.

In sense making, organizations look at their changing environments and ask the questions "What is going on in the environment?" "What does it mean?" The

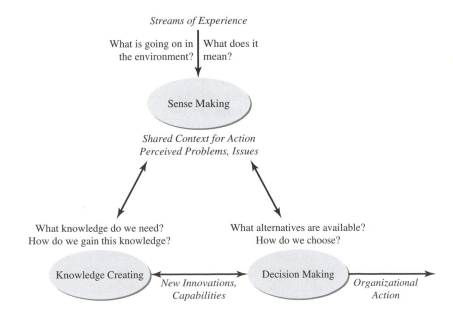

FIGURE 1.6. The Knowing Cycle

answers depend on how people in organizations selectively notice, highlight, and connect events, actions, and outcomes. What they notice and how they make sense of that which they notice is driven by their beliefs and actions. *Beliefs* are about categories that are used to label events and actions, as well as the cause-and-effect assumptions that are used to link events and outcomes. *Actions* refer to the path of action the organization is on and includes what the organization has done in the past, what it is currently doing, and what it wants to do in the future. Action here also refers to features that the organization has enacted or created in the environment to help it understand developments. Beliefs and actions combine so that organizations actively construct and interpret the environment they attend to by selectively highlighting and connecting events, and by enacting new features to help them understand the environment.

The outcome of sense making is an ongoing series of enacted interpretations about the organization and its environment that constructs a shared *context for action,* a frame of reference for creating knowledge and making decisions. This shared context includes beliefs and interpretations about the identity and purpose of the organization, and forms the frame of reference for perceiving problems and opportunities. It is against this shared background that certain problems and issues are brought into focus—problems or concerns that the organization needs to work on.

Sense making is a way of seeing but also a way of *not seeing*. Thus, we may not notice things that we have no categories for or that are not part of our cause-effect expectations; or we may choose not to notice things that contradict our past actions or undermine the validity of our current projects. A case of obsolete shared interpretations seemed to have afflicted General Motors in the early 1980s. According to Mitroff and Linstone (1993), GM for many years had used the following retained assumptions to enact its competitive environment: "GM is in the business of making money, not cars"; "Cars are primarily status symbols—style is therefore more important than quality"; "The American car market is isolated from the rest of the world"; "Energy will always be abundant and cheap"; and so on. These assumptions were badly out of step with the reality of the new American automobile industry at that time. By 1985, GM was last in the industry in terms of product quality, manufacturing efficiency, and new product design (Ingrassia and White 1994).

Effective decision making depends on sense making—we need to know what's going on and why before we can decide what is to be done. Making "good" sense becomes as crucial as making the right moves. In today's fast-changing, complex environment, making sense of the environment, understanding what is happening, becomes a harder and more important challenge. Most of the time, organizations are not conscious of how they are making sense of their environments until they encounter situations when they have been surprised or when they see events that fail to make sense. The suggestion here is that organizations can preempt these surprises by introducing a degree of alertness and discipline in the ways that they try to construct explanations. Thus, organizations need to be conscious of their beliefs and to be able to question them. They need to design interventions that probe the environment to test their assumptions and to collect information to clarify ambiguous situations. They need to be mindful about over-relying on past experiences to construct meaning. They need to re-gard interpretations as tentative, temporary accounts that may have to be revised. They seek information actively for the purpose of revising and updating their interpretations, rather than focusing on information that confirms their beliefs and actions.

Given the importance of sense making, it is something of a puzzle that most discussions of information management do not examine sense making explicitly. A notable exception is Maes (2004). In developing a comprehensive framework for information management, Maes suggests that while the use of technology introduces a new *syntax* and the business of the organization constitutes the *pragmatics* of a given problem, it is the use of information in sense making that defines the *semantics* of interpreting, communicating, and working on a problem. In information management, there are two views of the role of information: the economic perspective sees information as a business resource, while the socio-constructivist perspective sees information as a social construction that is the result of sense making. Maes (2004) believes that it is important for information management as a discipline to recognize that both perspectives are necessary and complementary. Thus, information management can no longer confine itself to the delivery of information but is increasingly concerned with the ways that information is utilized, so that "information management is transforming into a *management of meaning*" (Maes 2004, p. 14).

Sense making constructs a shared context for action as well as brings into focus problems and issues that the organization needs to work on. When the problem situation is novel or unfamiliar, the organization may find that it lacks the knowledge or capability to solve a problem or exploit an opportunity—it faces a knowledge gap. The organization may then embark on knowledge creation. When the problem situation is *sufficiently familiar,* the organization may apply its existing rules and protocols to search for alternatives and select an appropriate course of action—it then faces a decision gap.

Knowledge creation is thus driven by the questions "What knowledge do we need?" "How do we gain this knowledge?" The creation and use of organizational knowledge simultaneously engages both tacit and explicit knowledge. The model developed by Nonaka and Takeuchi (1995) emphasizes the conversion between the tacit and explicit (the socialization and externalization modes in their model), but it also highlights the combination that is necessary in bringing that new knowledge into meaningful application (the combination and internalization modes in their model).

This simultaneous, ongoing engagement of the tacit and explicit in organizational knowledge creation and use poses some interesting challenges. Organizations that focus only on managing explicit knowledge—capturing and codifying knowledge in databases or as written cases and practices—may find that their efforts to build up a stock of knowledge have inadvertently left out the personal and contextual elements that are needed to make knowledge from one person useful and useable to another. Other organizations contend that all knowledge is tacit, inside a person's head, and there is not much that an organization can do about that. Yet as long as knowledge remains inside a person's head, the organization is limited in its ability to identify that knowledge and to make it available to problems that other groups are working on. Knowledge and expertise becomes isolated, dispersed. Knowledge flows in person-to-person interactions, but only a small number of people are privileged to participate in these exchanges.

A more inclusive approach would encompass the tacit and explicit dimensions of organizational knowledge. Knowledge creation and use is an extended process that typically requires both finding or determining the existence of knowledge on some subject matter and connecting with the sources or authors of that knowledge to bring it to bear on tough problems. We need to codify certain aspects or features of an organization's knowledge in order to find it again, and in order to assess its initial match with a new problem. We also need to recognize that once a promising set of ideas is found, the utilization of this knowledge to solve difficult problems often requires face-to-face interactions to understand the context, adapt to local conditions, and establish trust. Perhaps an important insight of the Nonaka and Takeuchi model is to respect the dynamic interplay that is inherent between the tacit and explicit knowledge of an organization, and to manage this interplay in a way that honors the special nature of tacit knowledge, even as the organization is implementing systems to make knowledge more accessible and available.

The result of knowledge creation can be new capabilities or innovations (products or prototypes). These expand the range of options that is available for decision making. However, they also introduce new uncertainties: capabilities are unpracticed, innovations are untested, so decision making can become riskier. Knowledge creation can result in sustaining or disruptive innovations (Christensen 1997; Christensen and Raynor 2003). A sustaining innovation targets demanding, high-end customers with better performance than what was previously available. Whether an innovation is sustaining is not just a function of technological sophistication: some sustaining innovations are incremental improvements, others are breakthroughs. A disruptive innovation, on the other hand, does not attempt to bring better products to established customers in existing markets. Instead, it introduces products that are not as good as those currently available but that nevertheless offer benefits that appeal to new or less-demanding customers—benefits such as being simpler to use, more convenient, less costly, and so on.

When it comes to deciding about allocating resources to support innovations, sustaining and disruptive innovations interact differently with organizational values or decision premises used to make these choices. Sustaining innovations tend to be consonant with existing decision premises about profit margins and returns, so current rules and premises may be applied. Disruptive innovations, however, are dissonant with current decision premises since they do not offer improved margins relative to current cost structures. If they are to move ahead, disruptive innovations need a different set of decision value premises:

> An organization's values are the standards by which employees make prioritization decisions—those by which they judge whether an order is attractive or unattractive, whether a particular customer is more important or less important than another, whether an idea for a new product is attractive or marginal, and so on. . . . Sustaining-technology investments fit the values of the leading companies, because they promise improved profit margins from better or cost-reduced products. On the other hand, . . . because disruptive products typically promise lower gross dollars per unit sold and cannot be used by the best customers, disruptions are inconsistent with the leading companies' values. Established companies have the resources—the engineers, money, and technology—required to succeed at both sustaining and disruptive technologies. But their processes and values constitute disabilities in their efforts to succeed at disruptive innovations. (Christensen and Raynor 2003, pp. 188, 190)

Knowledge creation may result in fundamentally new products for which no historical precedent is available to assess the potential. Further sense making may then be necessary: the firm probes and enacts the environment in order to construct a plausible picture of who the users might be and what they would use the innovation for. Minnesota Mining and Manufacturing Company (3M) is a company whose history is decorated with stories of talented individuals who were able to invent new products or modify existing products that address latent consumer demand. A laboratory technician named Dick Drew invented masking tape and Scotch tape. John Borden, a sales manager, created a dispenser for Scotch tape with a built-in blade. More recently, Art Fry invented the Post-It sticky notepads. Fry sang in the church choir and wanted markers to stick to the pages of selected hymns that could be peeled off after use without damaging the hymn books. He used a weak adhesive that had been developed four years earlier to produce self-sticking sheets of papers. Following a gut feeling that there would be many other uses for the sticky notes, Fry single-handedly built a machine that would successfully apply the adhesive onto paper. Fry said, "Even though I felt that there would be demand for the product, I didn't know how to explain it in words. Even if I found the words to explain, no one would understand" (Nonaka and Takeuchi 1995, p. 138). Fry distributed samples to 3M employees, and in a short time a large number of unanticipated uses for the sticky notes were discovered. The development of new product ideas has become a strong tradition at 3M, and researchers can spend up to 15 percent of their work time, or roughly one day a week, "pursuing their own dreams." 3M seems to be a company that recognizes that the seeds of innovations grow in the personal, tacit knowledge of creative individuals.

As noted earlier, when the problem situation is *sufficiently familiar,* the organization activates its existing rules and procedures to search for alternatives and select an appropriate course of action. Instead of a knowledge gap, it perceives a decision gap that can be met by applying past learning captured in organizational rules and protocols.

Decision making is thus driven by the questions "What courses of action are available?" "How do we choose?" Organizations reduce the complexity and uncertainty of decision making by specifying decision premises, rules, and routines that collectively define what decision makers attend to, where they search, and how they select alternatives. Value-based decision premises determine what qualities will be valued in an alternative and its consequence. Value premises thus constitute *selection rules*. Factual premises determine what facts are important and need to be established in a decision situation. Factual premises thus constitute *attention rules*. Value and factual premises supply the parameters that guide the search process. Search takes place in decision routines—performance programs that specify where to obtain needed information, where to search for solutions, who to ask, what questions to ask, and so on. Decision routines thus embody *search rules*. To summarize, organizational decision making may be construed as information behavior that follows rules for search, attention, and selection.

Firms can use relatively simple rules to make strategic decisions (Eisenhardt and Sull 2001; Burgelman 2002). Eisenhardt and Sull (2001) found that firms cope with uncertainty in chaotic environments by applying simple rules to make strategic decisions. For example, when Cisco first adopted an acquisitions-based strategy, its decision rule was that it could acquire companies with at most 75 employees, 75 percent of whom were engineers. At the Danish hearing-aid company Oticon, executives would pull the plug on a product in development if a key team member left for another project. Yahoo!'s managers lived by four product innovation rules: know the priority rank of each product in development, ensure that every engineer can work on every project, maintain the Yahoo! look in the user interface, and launch products quietly. Burgelman (2002) observed that "simple" decision rules often contain a great deal of information and learned wisdom. In Section IV ("Decision Making"), we discussed his analysis of how Intel allocated chip fabrication resources to its product divisions. Intel's use of the rule "assign fabs to maximize margin-per-wafer-start" effectively brought together information about profitability, return on sales, technological competence, and manufacturing efficiency in order to make decisions about which fabrication facilities to allocate to which product divisions.

Decision making as rule-following behavior creates a stable, orderly environment inside the organization: the organization signals its rationality and maintains its structures of authority and legitimacy. At the same time, decision making as rule following can create undue caution and inertia in the face of risky innovations and alternatives. March (1988) noted that "when faced with risky alternatives, managers do not simply assess risk as part of a package of exogenously determined attributes, but actively seek to redefine alternatives, looking for options that retain the opportunities but eliminate the dangers" (p. 4). Even when risk is not a dominant element, there are certain types of innovations (disruptive innovations) that are dissonant with existing decision rules and premises and are therefore disadvantaged in current choice and evaluation procedures. Thus, while decision rules and premises apply past learning, they can also block new learning. Just as beliefs and enactments in sense making constitute a way of seeing and not seeing, decision rules and premises constitute a way of learning and not learning.

The allocation of attention and the execution of search lie at the center of organizational decision making (March 1988). The organizational knowing model suggests that this allocation of attention already begins in the sense-making activity, in the way beliefs and meanings are constructed and problems or issues are brought into the foreground. Weick (1995) noted that just as decision making is based on premises, sense making is based on beliefs and shared experiences: "where decision premises in the decision making model control organizational choice-making, shared beliefs and experiences in the sense-making model constrain the ways that people in an organization perceive their world. Both phenomena are aspects of *premise control,* and premise control becomes a useful concept that joins sensemaking with decision making" (p. 114). Value and factual premises in decision making are derived from or influenced by beliefs and interpretations enacted through sense making.

Decision making is the focus of managerial activity because it is closest to the taking of action. At the same time, the context in which decisions happen can be extended or constrained by the outcomes of knowledge creation. The range of decision alternatives, as well as the quality and innovativeness of these alternatives, all depends on the knowledge-creating capability of the firm. While new knowledge represents a potential for action, it is decision making that transforms this potential into a commitment to act, by formally endorsing a plan of action and by allocating resources to pursue it. Knowledge creation produces new capabilities that are still untested and innovations whose market acceptance may be hard to predict ("How many people will want to buy the home bread-making machine that Matsushita was building?"). Through its decision rules and premises, an organization attempts to manage risk and uncertainty by specifying search, attention, and selection criteria.

The model presented in this section provides a structure and language that can be used to think about information use in organizations. Real life itself is always richer and more complex than our models of it: a terrain is never the same as a map which relates to it. A map is a simplified representation of reality, but it does highlight key features of the terrain, show the big picture, help us see where we are, and warn us about gaps and obstacles. The model also does not imply a particular sequence or order. Instead, the three processes are interconnected, and there are many possible "pathways" along which the model might play out. The initial impetus for change and adaptation might be in decision making (e.g., when institutionalized decision rules do not appear to work anymore); knowledge creation (e.g., when new innovations or capabilities become available); and of course sense making (e.g., when threats or opportunities are perceived).

VII. THE KNOWING CYCLE IN ACTION

To illustrate how the interplay between the three processes of sense making, knowledge creating, and decision making can enable an organization to act intelligently, we examine the Royal Dutch / Shell Group of companies and its use of scenario planning during a particularly uncertain period of the organization's history.

The Royal Dutch / Shell Group is a century-old group of companies that has shown adaptiveness in anticipating and reacting to dramatic changes in its global environments. In the early 1970s, Shell was able to discern differences between Iran and Saudi Arabia (while everyone else perceived the Arab oil nations as a homogenous cartel) and thus anticipate the shortages that led to the 1973 oil shortage, which caused the price of oil to escalate from $2 per barrel to $13 per barrel in a year and a half. Oil prices continued to rise from 1973 onward, and most oil companies believed that the trend would persist. Shell, however, perceived that oil demand had been overestimated because consumers and industries had learned to be much more energy efficient since the 1973 crisis. In 1981, Shell was able to sell off its excess reserves (while other companies were stockpiling following the Iran-Iraq war) before the glut caused the price collapse. In 1983, by recognizing the demographic and economic pressures on the Soviet Union (while Western politicians saw only an evil communist empire), Shell was able to anticipate perestroika and the appearance of a man like Gorbachev who would bring about massive economic and political restructuring. Arie de Geus, head of planning of Shell for more than three decades, observes that "Outcomes like these don't happen automatically. On the contrary, they depend on the ability of a company's senior managers to absorb what is going on in the business environment and to act on that information with appropriate business moves" (de Geus 1988, p. 70).

Being a large multinational corporation with interests all over the world, Shell faces a daunting task as it attempts to *make sense* of its highly complex and equivocal environment. Shell uses scenario planning as a means of reviewing experience and building mental maps (Galer and van der Heijden 1992). A *scenario* is an internally consistent account of how the business environment is developing. By using multiple scenarios, it is possible to make sense of a large number of diverse but intersecting factors in the environment. In this way, scenarios become tools for organizational perception, broadening the collective vision of the organization. Managers in most Shell companies "are trained to pay attention to world events, visualize what might happen next, and (in Shell parlance) 'adjust their mental maps' according to what they perceive. Then they base decisions on those mental maps, instead of on top-down policy" (Kleiner 1989, p. 7). *Mental maps* are stored interpretations retained from experience that people turn to first when trying to interpret new signals from the environment. Shell's scenario-planning approach developed alternative stories about the future to stimulate its managers to re-examine their assumptions and to "think the unthinkable."

In trying to construct plausible interpretations of the external environment, Shell's planners differentiate between two types of driving forces—*predetermined variables* and *key uncertainties*—a process that is analogous to *enacting* the environment. Predetermined variables are what managers in the organization perceive to be reasonably predictable factors (based on an analysis of, for example, demographic data). They are used to set the boundaries of future scenarios. On the other hand, key uncertainties refer to those forces in the environment that are hard to predict, have high levels of ambiguity, but can create the most serious consequences for the decisions that may be taken by the organization. In scenario planning, participants bracket these variables for closer attention, connecting them and other factors into cause-and-effect narratives about possible futures. In selecting a reasonable interpretation, Shell's managers and planners plot out two or three scenarios and use them in extended conversations with managers to converge on a shared representation of the environment and a consensus on what Shell is to be in that new environment (van der Heijden 1996; Kleiner 1994).

Shell has evolved scenario planning into a system for *creating knowledge* that involves both the internalization and the externalization of knowledge. The objective of scenario planning is not to predict the future but to reveal the nature and dynamics of the driving forces that are shaping the environment. Insight about driving forces is derived from both hard, analytical data and soft, intuitive hunches. Such knowledge is made explicit by weaving them into storylike scenarios of how these forces could interact to produce outcomes. Some of the scenarios would appear to contradict long-standing trends and may be difficult to accept initially. Provoked by the ideas in the scenarios, Shell managers spend many hours in face-to-face dialogue trying to understand the driving forces and how they may need to adjust their own mental models to take account of them. This conversion from explicit knowledge in the form of stories to tacit knowledge in the form of updated mental models is related to the process of *internalization* that Nonaka and Takeuchi described. Pierre Wack, one of the architects of Shell's scenario approach, describes the process:

> Scenarios deal with two worlds: the world of facts and the world of perceptions. They explore for facts but the aim at perceptions inside the heads of decision makers. Their purpose is to transform information into fresh perceptions. This transformation process is not trivial—more often than not it does not happen. When it works, it is a creative experience that generates a heartfelt "Aha!" from your managers and leads to strategic insights beyond the mind's previous reach. . . . It happens when your message reaches the microcosms of decision makers, obliges them to question their assumptions about how their business world works, and lead them to change and reorganize their inner models of reality. (Wack, cited in Kleiner 1989, p. 13)

To construct scenarios, Shell needed to be able to tap into the personal insights and experiences of its managers who work in different countries all over the globe. It was important for knowledge sharing that managers operating in vastly different environments be encouraged to put forth candidly their concerns and perspectives. Extended conversations and special questions are employed to draw out the personal, tacit knowledge of managers and planners and *externalize* the knowledge into formal scenarios which facilitate the creation of a shared interpretation of external developments (Wack 1985). Planners use an interviewing method with trigger questions and feedback which uncover the mental models, assumptions, and critical concerns of managers (van der Heijden 1994). Examples of the trigger questions include "What two questions would you most want to ask an all-knowing oracle?" and "Ten years from today, you are reading a newspaper story about the organization's demise, what would you expect to see?"

Managers' assumptions and concerns, together with the planners' projections, are then melded into a few scenarios that managers can use to deepen their understanding and uncover possibilities for action.

This internalization of new knowledge derived from scenario analysis induced managers to consider new strategic options to prepare for the eventualities that their analysis indicated might develop. For example, in the 1970s, Shell managers were able to use their knowledge about the possibility of an oil shortage to initiate *innovations* that would help them weather the crisis. Crude oil varies by geographical region, so that a refinery engineered to process crude from one source would not necessarily be able to handle crude from another source. Shell's innovation was "to convert its refineries so they could switch from Kuwait oil to Saudi or Iranian oil, or back again, depending on what was available and what product mix was needed at any moment" (Kleiner 1989, p. 11).

Over time, Shell evolved a "planning as learning" system in which the insight and knowledge gained through scenario planning are able to propagate through various levels of organizational *decision making*. The highest level of global planning is the responsibility of the Committee of Managing Directors (CMD), which is generally composed of eight managing directors who have both functional and regional responsibilities (called *spheres of influence*). The CMD is described as being "like a small debating society, where the directors discussed global issues around the world" (van der Wyck and Hesseling 1994, p. 43). Shell's Group Planning Cycle begins with the first stage of developing scenarios for the review of the CMD. The second stage is the Business Planning Cycle (formerly known as the Programming and Investment Review). In this stage, the CMD issues short-term guidelines derived in part from the global scenarios, called *premises* in Shell, that would help sectors, regions, and countries produce their business plans and subsequently their financial budgets. Shell saw the objective here "as implementing strategies in terms of specific medium-run actions, the assessment of financial and human resources required and, most importantly, how much to commit to which action and when" (van der Wyck and Hesseling 1994, p. 48). The third and final stage is Appraisal, in which the CMD monitors and reviews implementation and short-term targets. Graham Galer and Kees van der Heijden, long-time members of Shell's Group Planning, summarized the cycle thus:

> In Shell, scenario planning, understood as "corporate perception," is a means of internalizing and reviewing experience. Strategic planning workshops are a device for inferring conclusions, while business planning, project planning and budgeting are the means for planning new steps and taking action. Business appraisal provides feedback from the results of action. (Galer and van der Heijden 1992, p. 12)

At the operating company levels, more-focused scenarios are developed to address a particular business issue concerning, for example, a market or an investment. In contrast with the global scenarios, these focused scenarios are generated quickly in one-day workshops and are created by the managers themselves (van der Wyck and Hesseling 1994). Workshops are well structured, following predefined rules and a six-step routine: agree on objectives and purpose; identify most important and uncertain business variables (the critical uncertainties); write story lines; create the scenarios; assess implications for business; and agree on follow-up action.

Galer and van der Heijden (1992) illustrate the benefit of the scenario-based learning approach with the experience of one Shell operating company ("opco"):

> For example, in one Shell opco scenarios were used to make managers face the realities of an unstable political and economic regime, to prepare them for inevitable changes, to handle great uncertainty during the change process and to develop a joint vision of emerging as a strong player in a new world. This was done over a five-year period and helped among other things in changing the market profile away from profitable traditional businesses towards potential new markets and making the company financially robust for an uncertain future. (p. 9)

Shell's ability to make strategic sense of environmental signals and to integrate its learning with its planning and decision-making processes helped the group become one of the world's top-performing oil companies. In the 1970s, Shell's position did not seem strong—it did not have the huge Saudi Arabian reserves of Exxon, Chevron, Mobil, or Texaco, nor the exclusive relationship that Gulf or BP had with Kuwait. From a position of the least profitable of the seven large oil companies, Shell moved ahead to become the world's most profitable oil company in the late 1980s.

VIII. SUMMARY

- The "knowing organization" is a model of how organizations use information to adapt to external change and to foster internal growth. It looks at how people and groups work with information to accomplish three outcomes: (1) create an identity and a shared context for action and reflection, (2) develop new knowledge and new capabilities, and (3) make decisions that commit resources and capabilities to purposeful action.

- In sense making, people in an organization actively construct the environment they attend to, based on their actions and beliefs: they selectively highlight and connect information; they enact or create new features to help them understand the environment.

- Sense making constructs a shared context for action (and for thinking and talking about what is to be done).

- Sense making brings into focus problems, opportunities, and issues that the organization needs to work on.

- Sense making is a way of seeing but also a way of not seeing: we may not notice things that we have no categories for, that are not part of our expectations, or that contradict our beliefs and actions.

- Organizational knowledge is different from individual knowledge: in addition to personal, tacit knowledge, an organization also makes use of explicit knowledge and cultural knowledge.

- In knowledge creation, an organization converts between and combines its different types of knowledge to develop new capabilities and innovations.

- Knowledge creation can extend the range of options available for decision making. It can also introduce options that require new sense making to understand.

- The knowledge-based advantage of an organization is temporary and fragile. The organization needs to continuously expand and refresh its knowledge-creation capabilities.

- Decision making in organizations is structured by rules, premises, and routines.

- Decision premises are value based or factual. Value premises specify what qualities or criteria are important in evaluating alternatives. Factual premises specify what facts are important and need to be established in a decision situation.

- Decision making commits the organization to a course of action.

- Decision making is a way of learning but also a way of not learning: decision premises and rules encode and apply past learning, but they can also block new learning.

- Sense making constructs the *context,* the frame of reference for knowledge creation and decision making. Knowledge creation expands organizational *capabilities* and introduces innovations. Decision making converts beliefs and capabilities into *commitments* to act.

2

HOW WE COME TO KNOW:

UNDERSTANDING

INFORMATION-SEEKING BEHAVIOR

When action grows unprofitable, gather information; when information grows unprofitable, sleep.
>—*Ursula K. Le Guin,* The Left Hand of Darkness, *1969*

Information is a name for the content of what is exchanged with the outer world as we adjust to it, and make our adjustments felt upon it.
>—*Norbert Wiener,* The Human Use of Human Beings: Cybernetics and
>   Society, *1967*

Increasingly, America is the attention-deficit nation, moving to ever sharper sound bites and smaller quanta of meaning. Citizens live in a blizzard of information without wisdom, content without context, and are being pulled a million ways by tech toys and a zillion cable channels and the multitudinous blogs. A white noise of data is the ambient soundtrack to our lives.
>—*John Swartz,* New York Times, *December 26, 2004*

Information needs arise when the individual recognizes gaps in his or her state of knowledge and ability to make sense of an experience. Information seeking is the process in which the individual then purposefully searches for information that can change his or her state of knowledge or understanding. Information use occurs when the individual selects and processes information or messages which lead to a change in the individual's capacity to make sense of the experience and to act or respond in the light of that new understanding. Information seeking and use is part of a larger human and social activity through which information becomes useful to an individual or group. Information seeking and use is situated action, so that the way the process develops depends on changing conditions in the individual's context of information use, and this in turn depends on the changes in the context induced by the individual's actions. Although information seeking and use is a dynamic process that often appears disorderly, we suggest that there is underlying structure in the ways people look for and use information. Our goal in this chapter is to develop a model to analyze information-seeking behavior in a systematic manner. We begin with a survey of the long history of information needs and uses studies, highlighting the research focus and scope of these studies. The ensuing sections develop general, multiperspective models of information-seeking behavior.

I. INFORMATION NEEDS AND USES RESEARCH

The study of how people behave as they seek and use information has a long history in information science, going back as far as the year 1948. At the Royal Society Scientific Information Conference of that year, two studies were presented: one on the information-seeking behavior of over 200 British scientists in government, university, and private research institutions, and the other on the use of the London Science Museum Library. The earliest studies were mostly sponsored by professional associations that were designing their information programs to respond to the explosion of scientific information and new technology or initiated by librarians or administrators of information centers or laboratories who needed data to plan their services. Information needs and uses studies grew significantly when government organizations began to support a number of studies on diverse groups, particularly scientific and technical groups who were receiving funds from government agencies such as the U.S. Department of Defense and NASA. Over a fifty-year history, it is possible to count thousands of studies that in some significant way investigated the information needs and uses of particular groups of people. Case (2002) observes that the very wide range of studies may be organized by occupational category (scientists, engineers, social scientists, humanities scholars, health care providers, managers, journalists, lawyers), social role (e.g., citizens, consumers, patients, gatekeepers), and demographic group (according to age, race, socioeconomic status, and other attributes). The seeking and processing of information is central to many social systems and human activities, and today, the analysis of information needs and uses has become an increasingly important component of the research in disciplines such as cognitive psychology, communication studies, diffusion of innovations, information retrieval, information systems, decision making, and organizational learning.

What may be gleaned from decades of research on human information seeking? What are the goals and assumptions that have framed past research? What are some of the main findings? And what unifying perspectives have emerged? To answer these questions, it may be helpful to attempt to map the research terrain by locating past studies according to their scope and content, using the map to detect movement toward promising destinations. Fig. 2.1 plots a selection of important studies on information needs and uses along two axes that indicate research orientation and research scope.

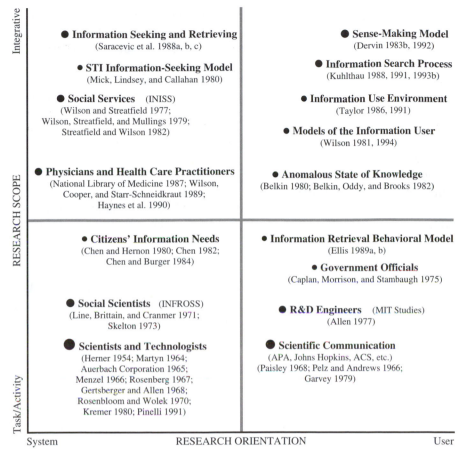

FIGURE 2.1. Information Needs and Uses Studies

The horizontal axis of the map in Fig. 2.1 indicates the *research orientation* of the studies, which can range from being system oriented to being user oriented (Dervin and Nilan 1986). A *system orientation* views information as an external, objective entity that has a content-based reality of its own which is independent of users or social systems. Information exists a priori, and it is the task of the user to locate and extract the desired information. Each document or record contains information "about something," and that something may be objectively determined. Indeed, it is this specification of content that makes it possible to represent, organize, and store information. The term *systems* here includes social structures, practices, and communities that exist for sharing and disseminating information; tools, services, and agencies that facilitate access to information; as well as computer-based information systems that allow information to be searched and retrieved. System-oriented research has therefore examined how information flows through these social systems, and how tools and services may be developed to simplify information access and enhance information sharing.

A *user orientation,* on the other hand, views information as a subjective construction that is created internally in the minds of the users. While a document or record may be defined or represented as being about something or some topic, the user wraps this objective content in an interpretive envelope so that the information therein becomes meaningful, and it is this combined package of content plus interpretation that users find valuable and useable. Information value thus resides in the relationship that the user constructs between herself or himself and a given piece of information. Thus, information is only useful when the user has infused meaning in it, and the same piece of objective information can be given quite different subjective meanings by different individuals. Whereas system-oriented research generally looks at what takes place in the information environment external to the individual in terms of tools, services, and practices, research with a user orientation would also examine the individual's internal cognitive and psychological needs and preferences and how they affect information-seeking and communication patterns.

The vertical axis of the map indicates the *research scope* of the studies, which can range from being task directed to being integrative. *Task-directed* research focuses on particular activities that form part of the information-seeking process. A significant number of major studies had focused on information-seeking activities, such as fact finding, literature searching, use of computer-based information systems, and use of online database services, and on particular communication activities such as conferences or information-sharing channels in a workgroup. Common research goals are to analyze the internal and external information sources that are used by defined groups of people, the interaction with information systems, and the formal and informal modes of information sharing and communication within professions or organizations. Perceptions and attitudes toward information, information seeking, and information sources are often also examined in order to account for preferences and patterns in information behaviors.

Integrative research, in contrast with task-directed research that focuses on particular information activities, embraces the entire process of information seeking and use. Its scope includes understanding the situation or context leading to the recognition of information need, examining the information-seeking or retrieval activities, and analyzing the use of information for problem resolution, decision making, or sense making. The assumption is that the study of information seeking should extend into an analysis of why information needs arise and how the needs are perceived, represented, defined, and experienced. It also becomes important to study how information obtained is put to use, to understand how the information helps the user, and to assess the outcomes of its use, including its impact, benefits, and contribution to some notion of effectiveness or performance. Integrative research views information seeking as a dynamic, ongoing process that is constituted both by the actions and needs of the individual, and by the social and physical features of the environment in which the individual gathers and uses information.

In the map of Fig. 2.1, four categories of information needs and uses studies are differentiated according to their research orientation and scope. We present below a small number of representative studies in order to give a sense of the work in each category. Overall, there is a general movement toward research that focuses on individual users and on building general models of information seeking. Examining the development of the cognitive approach to information retrieval, Ingwersen (1999) distinguishes two periods: the 1977–91 period that can be characterized as user- and intermediary-oriented; and the 1992–2000 period, "when the approach turns into a holistic view of all the interactive communication processes that occur during information transfer" (p. 3). (Comprehensive surveys of information needs and uses studies may be found in the *Annual Review of Information Science and Technology:* Menzel 1966; Herner and Herner 1967; Allen 1969; Lipetz 1970; Crane 1971; Lin and Garvey 1972; Martyn 1974; Crawford 1978; Dervin and Nilan 1986; Hewins 1990. See also Case 2002.)

System-Centered, Task-Directed Studies

These studies are placed in the lower-left-hand quadrant of the map of Fig. 2.1. Many of the earlier studies were largely concerned with the objective attributes of the information sources, channels, and systems utilized by particular groups of users in obtaining the information they require for scientific research or problem solving. For example, the U.S. Department of Defense in 1964 initiated a large-scale study of 1,375 scientists and engineers selected from among 120,000 working for the department. Respondents were asked to recall their most recently completed tasks and to enumerate the "chunks" of information used to accomplish these tasks. The study found that in 52 percent of the searches, the first source used was a local source (typically a colleague); 42 percent of the information chunks consisted of performance characteristics and specifications; and there was little discrepancy between the depth of information desired and that obtained (Auerbach Corporation 1965; Menzel 1966; Bates 1971). Another large-scale study examined the information-seeking patterns of 1,900 scientists and engineers in four very large U.S. corporations and 1,200 Institute of Electrical and Electronics Engineers (IEEE) members by asking participants to report on a recent instance of receiving information and on the sources of information utilized (Rosenbloom and Wolek 1970). A main conclusion was that the work of scientists involved to a greater extent the use of external information sources, while the work of engineers, with its operational focus, emphasized the use of internal sources. In more than half the cases examined, useful information was obtained from activity that was labeled "competence building" or was pointed out by others, and not from the outcome of specific searches.

One of the most comprehensive and unified studies of scientific communication and information use was the American Psychological Association's Project on Scientific Information Exchange in Psychology (Menzel 1966). In its first five-year period (1963–68), 22 reports were produced covering nearly every aspect of information use among psychologists, including information exchange activities associated with the attendance of conventions, the use of various types of information channels, and the effects of innovations in information exchange. One interesting innovation was the prepublication of papers that were to be presented at the annual APA convention. The studies found that, among other effects, the prepublication of papers stimulated greater audience participation, and that authors of prepublished papers were likely to delay or eliminate subsequent publication (Herner and Herner 1967). Today, it has become the norm to publish a set of conference proceedings before the conference takes place. While the numerous studies are too rich to be summarized briefly, one of their major contributions has been to elucidate the differences in information and communication needs that exist among different disciplines, and to enable the professional societies to introduce or modify information channels and services that would best suit their members (Allen 1969).

In the United Kingdom, a study of the Information Requirements of the Social Sciences (INFROSS) was launched in 1969. The study surveyed over 2,500 British social science researchers and focused mainly on information needs and uses as related to references, indexes, abstracts, library catalogs, and bibliographies and on the use of books and libraries. The study concluded that the state of information services for social scientists was underdeveloped and identified major deficiencies, such as the lack of review articles, translation services, and services oriented to practitioners (Line 1971). Formal bibliographical tools such as abstracting and indexing services were not well used, and British social scientists did not seem eager to use them regularly. INFROSS did have a successful outcome: the study induced many U.K. universities to introduce social sciences information services along the lines of those already established for the physical sciences.

System-Centered, Integrative Studies

These studies are in the upper-left-hand quadrant of the map of Fig. 2.1. While still focused primarily on information sources, systems, and services, many of these studies also extend their scope to include the broader context of the users' work or organizational settings, personal preferences, and information-use situations. An important study of the information needs of social service workers in the United Kingdom began in 1975 at the University of Sheffield as Project INISS (Information Needs and Information Services in Local Authority Social Services departments). Its basic goal was to understand the information needs of staff in social services departments and to design information services that would best respond to these needs. By observing the communication activities of staff in five departments, the study was able to relate the information behavior of the social services workers to their personal, work, and organizational characteristics. Staff strongly preferred personal, oral communications such as face-to-face meetings or telephone conversations; their workday was highly fragmented so that most communication episodes were of short duration; and the functional specialization of the departments suggested specialized information services (Wilson and Streatfield 1977). The study led to the introduction of a number of successful innovations, including training courses, book collections chosen by office staff, abstracts bulletins, and indexes of expertise.

Mick et al. (1980) attempted to develop a generalized model of the environmental and situational variables (as distinct from individual attributes) influencing the seeking of scientific and technical information by scientists and engineers. By analyzing the information behavior of scientists and engineers working in a variety of organizational settings and environments, they identified key variables in five areas: perception of management attitudes toward information, general information orientation, specific task orientation, demographics, and perceived attributes of information sources. A number of hypotheses were tested on how these variables would influence information needs, access to information, and information satisfaction. The study revealed a few key organizational variables that management can control or modify in order to enhance the utilization of scientific and technical information.

A major research effort to define a comprehensive model of information seeking was that undertaken by Saracevic et al. (1988a, b, c). The goal of the large-scale, multiyear project was to formally enumerate all the important elements that would characterize information-seeking and -retrieving activities. Forty users and 39 searchers took part in the study; 40 questions were searched, each by 9 searchers. The proposed general model of information seeking and retrieving consisted of seven major events (with their accompanying classes of variables in parentheses): (1) user has a problem which needs to be resolved (user characteristics, problem statement); (2) user seeks to resolve the problem by formulating a question and starting an interaction with an information system (question statement, question characteristics); (3) pre-search interaction with a searcher, human or computer intermediary (searcher characteristics, question analysis); (4) formulation of a search (search strategy, search characteristics); (5) searching activity and interactions (searching); (6) delivery of responses to user (items retrieved, formats delivered); (7) evaluation of responses by user (relevance, utility) (Saracevic et al. 1988a, p. 164). Analysis of the empirical data showed that "the suggested models tested well, that is, the elements suggested by the models had by and large a significant relation with retrieval outcome" (Saracevic et al. 1988c, p. 213). For example, the context of a question was confirmed to be important, including the background leading to the question being asked and the intended use of the information to be retrieved. Different types of questions—classified according to their clarity, specificity, complexity, and so on—may be expected to have different retrieval performance levels. Cycles in searching tended to improve outcome, since intermediate results may be reviewed and search strategies refined accordingly.

User-Centered, Task-Directed Studies

These studies are in the lower-right-hand quadrant of the map of Fig. 2.1. As part of MIT's Research Program on the Management of Science and Technology, a number of studies on the information transfer behaviors of scientists and engineers were conducted by Thomas Allen and his associates over a ten-year period (1963–73). The studies included the comparative evaluation of 33 project teams working on matched pairs of projects, and the analysis of communication networks in 13 research laboratories (Allen 1977). In the matched case method, Allen took advantage of the U.S. government's practice of awarding contracts to two or more laboratories simultaneously to perform the same design studies. Pairs of such projects were monitored, and the government agencies provided evaluations of each laboratory's performance. These evaluations were then related to the use of information channels by the individual laboratories. At the same time, respondents were asked to track their use of information week by week through "solution development records." Each week, respondents would estimate the probabilities of acceptance of a number of alternative solutions that would address a problem. Changes in the relative probabilities were then related to information channels and inputs. An interesting finding was that the choice of information channel or source was based on the cost associated with using the channel, balanced against the value or payoff expected of that source. Cost in this case is multifaceted and includes such important elements as physical accessibility and psychological cost (since asking for information is admitting ignorance, implying a loss of face or stature). Payoff is indicated by the technical quality or reliability of the source. In the communication network studies, Allen and associates identified the role of "technology gatekeepers" in introducing new information into the organization through a two-step process (that is, indirectly through the gatekeeper). Gatekeepers read more widely (including more refereed journals), continuously maintain a broad range of personal contacts, and can translate external information into terms that the average technologist in the organization can understand. The studies also found that increased communication between R&D projects and laboratory staff, as well as increased interaction outside the project, were strongly related to problem-solving performance (Allen 1977, p. 122).

William Garvey, one of the heads of the American Psychological Association's Project on Scientific Information Exchange in Psychology, carried over the project's approach to examine information use in other scientific disciplines when he moved to the Johns Hopkins Center for Research in Scientific Communication. These studies adopted a psychological perspective of scientific communication which emphasized

> the interaction between the scientist and his environment (a major element of this
> environment being other scientists). Each scientist brings to each situation a
> particular cluster of psychological attributes (personality, skills, style, experience,
> habits, etc.), which, combined with specific circumstances in the research process,
> gives the individual scientist a predisposition to perceive and detect, to assimilate,
> to associate, etc. what is happening with his research at any given moment. . . . his
> style, subjectivity, bias, etc. all play a part in his detection, selection, retention, and
> use of information encountered in the search. (Garvey 1979, p. 4)

It was precisely this variation in observation, selection, and interpretation among different individual scientists that allowed science to progress. The Johns Hopkins studies concluded that the scientific enterprise functioned as a social system, and that a key feature of the social system was the highly interactive process by which scientific communication took place.

Caplan, Morrison, and Stambaugh (1975) investigated the use of social science research information in the formulation of government policy. Two hundred and four upper-level employees in the executive branch of the U.S. federal government self-reported 575 instances of the use of social science information. The study found that the political implications of research findings appeared to override all other considerations in determining whether the information is used or not. The nature and extent of information use were also influenced by the cognitive styles of the respondents. Three styles were identified: those with a "clinical" style could analyze both the scientific or objective internal logic of an issue as well as its value-laden or ideological implications; those with an "academic" style concentrated on the internal logic of issues; and those with an "advocacy" style tended to ignore internal logic but dealt mainly with political considerations.

Information Needs and Uses Studies: Research Contributions

Information needs and uses studies have added significantly to our understanding of how people seek information. An abundance of field data has been collected and analyzed about the channels, methods, and sources used by various groups of scientists, technologists, professionals, government officials, citizens, and others as they seek information. Innovations were introduced to promote information exchange and simplify information access, including the prepublication of conference papers, customization of tools to help users locate and retrieve information, development of current awareness services, and so on. Data collection and analysis often leveraged upon methodologies from multiple disciplines, such as the critical incident technique to analyze information-receiving episodes, structured observations to log information activities, action research to introduce new tools or services, and special interviewing techniques to uncover users' information needs in greater detail.

In terms of theory construction, a number of general observations may be made:

1. Information needs and uses need to be examined within the work, organizational, and social settings of the users. Information needs vary according to users' membership in professional or social groups, their demographic backgrounds, and the specific requirements of the task they are performing.

2. Users obtain information from a wide range of formal and informal sources. Informal information sources, including colleagues and personal contacts, are frequently as important as and sometimes more important than formal information sources such as the library or online databases.

3. A large number of criteria can affect the selection and use of information sources. Research has found that many groups of users prefer sources that are local or close at hand, which are not necessarily the best regarded. For

these users, the perceived accessibility of an information source is more important than its perceived quality.

(Choo and Auster 1993, pp. 284–85)

While the number of user studies continued to proliferate, there was a growing unease about the lack of progress toward building up a core of theoretical knowledge about information needs and uses. Generalization was thought to be difficult because many studies were limited to groups of users with special information requirements and on their interactions with specific information channels, systems, and tools. There were no agreed-upon definitions for the concepts of information needs, information use, and other important variables. This lack of a common framework made it difficult to compare and combine research findings, so much so that many user studies existed as isolated case studies and collections of empirical data which were peculiar to specialized and often small groups of users. Several studies also had a strong system focus, concentrating on the utilization and performance of selected information sources, information systems, and communication channels—users' needs and use of information retrieved were not examined in-depth.

User-Centered, Integrative Studies

Over the years, information needs and uses studies have progressively broadened their research orientation and research focus. On the horizontal axis of research orientation (Fig. 2.1), studies have moved from an orientation that is primarily *system-centered* (in which information is objective, resides in a document or system, and where the main issue is to how to get at this information) to an orientation that is also *user-centered* (in which information is subjective, resides in the users' minds, and is only useful when meaning has been created by the user). On the vertical axis of research scope, research has shifted from concentrating on particular information *tasks* or activities, such as literature searching, fact-finding, or communications in a workgroup, to studies that go beyond the information-seeking activity itself by trying also to understand something of the personal, organizational, and social *situation* in which the information need arose and in which the acquired information will be put to use.

These user-centered, integrative studies represent a relatively recent development and are placed in the upper-right-hand quadrant of the map of Fig. 2.1. An early call to examine information seeking from the point of view of the user (rather than that of the document or the information system) was made by Belkin (1980). People in problematic situations who are looking for information experience inadequacies in their state of knowledge—"inadequacies in a state of knowledge can be of many sorts, such as gaps or lacks, uncertainty, or incoherence, whose only common trait is a perceived 'wrongness'" (Belkin 1980, p. 137). Belkin named this condition an Anomalous State of Knowledge (ASK). The ASK hypothesis implies that information seekers are often unable to specify their information needs since they cannot readily express what they do not know or what is missing.

Information retrieval systems that depend on users precisely specifying their information needs a priori are therefore unlikely to work well. Instead, the ASK hypothesis suggests that the information system should be designed to assist users in discovering and representing their knowledge of a problem situation, especially the anomalies which prevent specification of need. Belkin and his colleagues used a free-form interviewing technique that allowed users to describe problem situations with unstructured statements. The situation description was analyzed by computer according to statistical word occurences and word associations in the text. A graph network was then drawn that represented the user's ASK. The same statistical profiling is used to represent each document in the database. Finally, the system applied different mechanisms to match the user's ASK structure with the word-association structures representing the documents in order to retrieve documents that would be relevant to the problem situation (Belkin et al. 1982).

Tom Wilson of the Department of Information Studies at the University of Sheffield (United Kingdom) is a strong advocate of a user-centered approach to analyzing information needs and information-seeking behavior. Adopting a phenomenological perspective, Wilson sees individuals as constantly constructing their own social worlds from the world of appearances around them. Information needs arise from these attempts to make sense of the world. Information seeking is "almost always frustrated in some degree because of the division between the meanings embedded in information systems and the highly personal meaning of the information-seeker's problem" (Wilson 1994, p. 32). He proposes a model in which information needs arise out of a work setting and the roles the individual plays in social life, including work roles. Personal needs may be physiological, affective, or cognitive. Work roles and personal needs are influenced by the work setting, which have sociocultural, politico-economic, and physical dimensions. As a result, in order to properly study information needs,

> our concern is with uncovering the facts of everyday life of the people being investigated; by uncovering those facts we aim to understand the needs that exist which press the individual towards information-seeking behavior; by better understanding of those needs we are able better to understand what meaning information has in the everyday life of people; and by all of the foregoing we should have a better understanding of the use and be able to design more effective information systems. (Wilson 1981, p. 11)

Wilson continues to develop his information-seeking model. Wilson (1997, 1999) is a recent synthesis, drawing significantly from research in health communication studies and consumer behavior. In this model (Fig. 2.2), information need is the root cause of information-seeking behavior, and the person-in-context remains the focus of analyzing information needs. As information needs can be difficult to define, an alternative is to focus on psychological stress and coping as an *activating mechanism* for information seeking. In the health information field, stress and coping can lead to a cognitive state of attention or avoidance (orientation or turning away from the threat), and to information behaviors of monitoring (preferring high information inputs to reduce arousal and stress) or blunting (preferring less information) (Krohne 1993; Miller and Mangan 1983). Whether

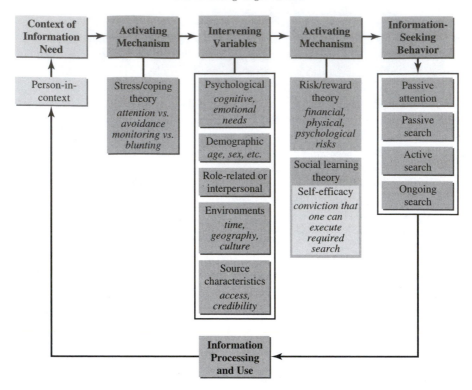

FIGURE 2.2. Information-Seeking Model (Wilson 1997)

the perception of an information need leads to information seeking depends on a number of *intervening variables* that could act as inducements or impediments to information-seeking behavior. These variables may be psychological (e.g., cognitive and emotional need), demographic (age, sex), role-related or interpersonal, environmental or situational (time available, national culture), and source characteristics related (source accessibility and credibility). Another set of activating mechanism can affect information seeking: risk/reward theory that weighs the financial, psychological, and physical costs of undertaking a search for information; and social learning theory, which embodies the concept of *self-efficacy*—the conviction that one can successfully execute the behavior required to produce the desired outcome (Bandura 1977). Finally, four modes of information-seeking behavior are identified: passive attention (such as listening to the radio); passive search; active search; and ongoing search (Wilson 1997, 1999).

II. FRAMEWORK FOR ANALYZING INFORMATION-SEEKING BEHAVIOR

The study of information-seeking behavior crosses many disciplines, including cognitive psychology, communication studies, diffusion of innovation theory, information economics, information retrieval, information systems, organization theory, and social anthropology. At the same time, this diversity presses for a unifying perspective that would bring coherence to the bounty of research on how humans seek and use information. While information often has a physical manifestation such as a document or record, the context and meaning of the information therein are created afresh each time it is taken up by a user. Information is fabricated by individuals, who cut new cloth from the fabric of their past experience and tailor the cloth according to the exigencies of the particular situation in which the information is to be used. A general model of information use must consider the range of human experience that is information seeking: the thoughts, feelings, actions, and social and physical setting in which these interactions are played out. Our starting position is that the information user is a sentient, cognitive actor; that information seeking and use is a dynamic process extending over time and space; and that the context of information use determines in what ways and to what extent the received information is useful.

Following Wilson (1999), we adopt the term *information-seeking behavior* to refer to the patterns of behavior that people display as they recognize information needs, make choices about where and how to look for information, and reflect or act on the information they see. Conceptually, information-seeking behavior consists of (1) information needs, (2) information seeking, and (3) information use. In this chapter we are primarily interested in purposeful information-seeking behavior, that is, the individual requires information in order to move from the current state to a desired end state. Movement may be problematic because the individual lacks the knowledge or means to do so. The individual first becomes aware of or recognizes a problematic situation and perceives *information needs* in terms of goals and values; important entities and their attributes, relationships; facts that need to be established; and so on. *Information seeking,* then, is the process where the individual looks for information in order to change her state of knowledge. During information seeking, typical behaviors include identifying and selecting sources; formulating a query, question, or topic; extracting information; evaluating the information found; and extending, modifying, or repeating the search. *Information use* is the selection of relevant messages from the information encountered during the search and the processing of the information so that it leads to a change in the state of the individual's knowledge or capacity to act.

From an economic analysis of organizations, Huizing and Bouman (2002) identify three generic information problems that can inhibit any process of information seeking and exchange: "(1) the relevant questions have to be posed unambiguously, (2) reliable information sources have to be found, and (3) the information acquired has to be interpreted and translated to a unique social practice" (p. 186). We may relate these generic problems to the recognition and expression of information needs, information seeking, and information use. Huizing and Bouman (2002) go on to analyze four structures that can reduce the informational costs associated with these problems. In a *market* structure, an organization allows information seeking and exchange to be determined by information demand and supply forces. In an *organized market,* the focus is on providing help to find reliable information sources (by, for example, creating communities of practice). In an *extended market,* the organization guides information asking by clarifying and specifying information needs (by, for example, designing a search engine that verifies what the user means). Finally, in a *firm* structure, the organization addresses all three information problems, including the facilitation of information interpretation in order to promote information use (by, for example, providing standardized best practices).

Saracevic (1997) proposes a stratified model of information retrieval that identifies three levels on the user side of the interaction: the cognitive, affective, and situational levels. The *cognitive* level refers to how people use cognitive structures to interact with texts and their representations in information resources. At this level, we are interested in relevance inferences, effects of or changes in the state of knowledge, and other cognitive processes or results. The *affective* level refers to users' intentions as well as the beliefs, motivations, feelings, desires, urgency, and so on that accompany intentionality. The *situational* level concentrates on effects on tasks or problems at hand, changes in the problem, the use of information to resolve a problem, and the like. While Saracevic (1997) was modeling the information retrieval interaction between user and computer system, we suggest that the stratified approach may be extended to analyze information-seeking behavior in general.

In the next section, we amplify the needs-seeking-use model by examining the cognitive, affective, and situational dimensions of information behavior. Our approach is shown in Figs. 2.3a and 2.3b. In the ensuing chapters of the book, we

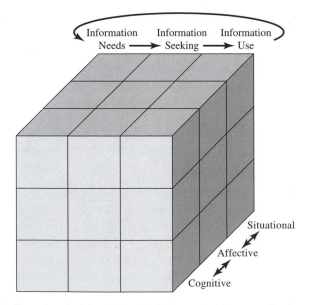

FIGURE 2.3a. Information-Seeking Cube (1): A Theoretical Framework of Information-Seeking Behavior

		Information needs	*Information seeking*	*Information use*
Cognitive	Anomalous states of knowledge Sense-making gaps Cognitive styles			
Affective	Uncertainty Stress Self-maintenance			
Situational	Task complexity Situational complexity Information use environment			

FIGURE 2.3b. Information-Seeking Cube (2)

will use this framework to analyze how people in organizations seek and use information.

III. COGNITIVE, AFFECTIVE, AND SITUATIONAL DIMENSIONS OF INFORMATION-SEEKING BEHAVIOR

Cognitive Dimensions of Information-Seeking Behavior

In information science, an influential attempt to model information needs was the concept of Anomalous States of Knowledge (ASK), introduced in Belkin (1980) and Belkin et al. (1982). We discussed ASK earlier in this chapter, and here we note its assumption that information behavior is mediated by cognitive states of knowledge about users themselves and about the entities that the users are interacting with, such as an information system or another person. Although problem statements can be elicited from users to model their information needs, these information needs are not identified easily or precisely, and they change over time as they are updated and compared to earlier states of knowledge.

Sense-Making Metaphor

Dervin (1983a, b, 1992, 2003) has been active in developing and applying a sense-making metaphor to analyze how people perceive information needs as cognitive gaps. In the sense-making metaphor, the person is moving through space and time, taking steps through experiences (Dervin 1992). A new step is taken in each new moment. Even though the step may be a repetition of past action, it is a new step because it takes place at a new moment in space and

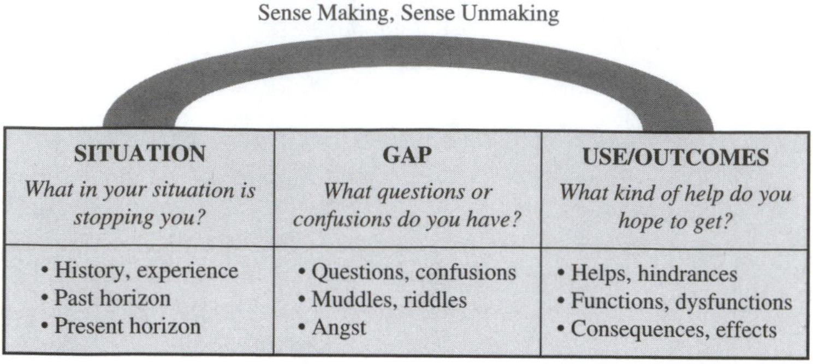

Sense Making, Sense Unmaking

SITUATION	GAP	USE/OUTCOMES
What in your situation is stopping you?	*What questions or confusions do you have?*	*What kind of help do you hope to get?*
• History, experience • Past horizon • Present horizon	• Questions, confusions • Muddles, riddles • Angst	• Helps, hindrances • Functions, dysfunctions • Consequences, effects

FIGURE 2.4. The Sense-Making Metaphor (Adapted from Dervin and Frenette 2001)

time. Movement is accompanied by the person continually making sense of her actions and the environment. For as long as the person is able to construct meaning, movement ahead is possible. However, from time to time, movement is blocked by a perceived discontinuity. The person is stopped in a situation where movement forward is prevented by the perception of some kind of cognitive gap. The person has run out of internal sense and needs to create new sense. The person defines the nature of the gap and, based on this interpretation, selects tactics to bridge the cognitive gap. Finally, the person crosses the cognitive bridge she has constructed in order to continue on the journey. The essence of the sense-making approach is understanding how the individual defines a gap situation and attempts to bridge the cognitive gap. Information seeking and use is analyzed in terms of the triad *situation → gap → use,* exemplified by these questions (Fig. 2.4): (1) What in your situation is stopping you? What is missing in your situation? (2) What questions or confusions do you have? (3) What kind of help do you hope to get? (Dervin and Clark 1987). The results of field studies applying the sense-making approach show that gap-defining and gap-bridging strategies account for individual information behavior better than factors such as system characteristics, message content, or user demographics.

More than 40 different sense-making studies have been conducted over two decades in a number of institutions, such as the California State Library, National Cancer Institute, and Ohio Department of Health, and within a range of populations, including blood donors, cancer patients, college students, computer software users, immigrants, and library users (Dervin and Nilan 1986; Dervin 1992, 2003). The principal research methodology is the micro-moment timeline interview. Each respondent is asked to reconstruct a situation in terms of the events and steps that make up the timeline development of the situation. The respondent then describes each step in detail in terms of how the respondent saw the situation, the gap, and the help wanted. A general finding of these studies is this: The ways in which people *perceive their cognitive gaps* and the ways that they *want information to help* are good predictors of their information-seeking and -use behaviors. Better yet, the ways in which people perceive their cognitive gaps and the ways in which they want information to help can be coded into universal categories that are applicable across different groups of information users:

> Much of the quantitative work of sense-making studies, to date, has also focused on developing generic categories to describe needs, barriers, and helps wanted—categories which are universal in the sense that they pertain to gap-bridging and gap-defining across situations while at the same time they capture important aspects of particular situations. Across studies, these category schemes have stabilized. (Dervin 1992, p. 75)

For example, a set of categories, labeled *situation stops,* has been developed to describe the ways in which humans see their way ahead being blocked. These situation-stop or gap-defining categories include the following (adapted from Dervin 1992):

Decision stop:
where the human sees two or more roads ahead;

Barrier stop:
where the human sees one road ahead but something or someone stands on the road blocking the way;

Spin-out stop:
where the human sees self as having no road;

Wash-out stop:
where the human sees self as on a road that suddenly disappears;

Problematic stop:
where the human sees self as being dragged down a road not of his or her own choosing

Other situation categories:
that depend on how the human judges perceptual embeddedness (how foggy is the road), situational embeddedness (how many intersections are on the road), and social embeddedness (how many people are also traveling).

People who perceive themselves as being in these situation gaps will ask questions in their attempts to bridge the gap. A second set of categories has been developed to relate these gap-bridging questions to the timing and location of events; understanding causes; projecting outcomes; and identifying characteristics of self, others, events, and objects. Finally, to capture how people put the information obtained to use, a third set of help categories has been developed: creating ideas, finding directions or ways to move, acquiring skills, getting support or confirmation, getting motivated, getting connected to others, calming down or relaxing, getting pleasure or happiness, and reaching goals.

In summary, the sense-making metaphor analyzes information needs as gap perceptions, information seeking as gap-bridging strategies, and information use

TABLE 2-1. Sense-making model (Dervin 1992).

Situation and information help categories	
Situation	*Information help*
• Decision stop • Barrier stop • Spin-out stop • Wash-out stop • Problematic stop • Perceptual embeddedness • Situational embeddedness • Social embeddedness	• Creating ideas • Finding directions • Acquiring skills • Getting support • Getting motivated • Getting connected • Calming down • Getting pleasure • Reaching goals

as the help obtained in crossing the gap. Research applying the approach has discovered general categories by which people perceive and bridge their cognitive and information gaps and has found that the way the individual perceives a gap is a good predictor of how the individual will go about bridging the gap and wanting the information to help.

Cognitive Styles

An individual's cognitive style and preferences influence the manner in which information is sought, processed, and utilized. A number of methods and instruments have been developed to differentiate personality types as well as the cognitive and information preferences that characterize each type. One of the most widely used personality assessment instruments is the Myers-Briggs Type Indicator (MBTI) classification, which is derived from the work of Carl Jung (Bayne 1995). MBTI analyzes personality types based on four pairs of traits, traits that also highlight differences in the ways that people seek and use information:

> *Introversion versus Extraversion: Introverts draw mental energy from themselves whereas extroverts draw energy from others.*
> *Sensing versus "Intuiting": Sensing types rely on information perceived through their five senses. Intuitive types rely more on patterns, relationships, and hunches.*
> *Thinking versus Feeling: Thinking types use information to make logical decisions based on objective criteria. Feeling types depend on personal values to decide between right and wrong.*
> *Judging versus Perceiving: Judging types move quickly to closure by making use of the available information. Perceiving types keep their options open by taking their time to gather sufficient information.*

These four pairs of attributes are combined to create a matrix of 16 person-ality types. Each personality type is expected to display distinctive styles and preferences when processing and using information, as summarized above.

Other cognitive style variables that have been examined include field dependence and adaptation-innovation styles. Field-dependent individuals tend to respond uncritically to environmental cues, whereas field-independent individuals orient themselves correctly in spite of environmental cues (Witkin and Goodenough 1981). In Kirton's adaptation-innovation theory (Kirton 1989), adaptors support existing frames of reference and attempt to improve an existing system, while innovators are more prepared to challenge existing paradigms and try to reconstruct the system. When innovators select and use information, they are more likely than adaptors to explore new elements and generate new mental models.

Affective Dimensions of Information-Seeking Behavior

Cognitive needs are draped in affective responses so that they are as much felt as they are thought about. Recent research in neurobiology shows that emotions play a crucial role during information seeking and processing by directing attention to potentially important new or confirmatory information, and by marking out options that, based on past experience, could be dangerous or favorable (Damasio 1999; LeDoux 1996). Information-use studies recognize that information needs are both affective and cognitive in origin, so that emotional responses often regulate information seeking by channeling attention, pointing out doubt and uncertainty, indicating likes and dislikes, and motivating effort.

Uncertainty in Information Seeking. In information science, Kuhlthau has done important work on the role of affect in information-seeking behavior. Her studies of the information-seeking behaviors of library users and college students found common patterns in the users' experience as they search and use information (Kuhlthau 1991, 1993a, 1993b, 2004). She postulates that the information search process is composed of six stages: initiation, selection, exploration, formulation, collection, and presentation (Fig. 2.5). Each stage in the search process is characterized by the user's behavior in three realms of experience: the affective (feelings experienced), the cognitive (personal knowledge, thoughts relating to tasks, and content of encountered information), and the physical (actions taken). During *initiation,* the user first recognizes a need for more information. Feelings of uncertainty and apprehension are common. Thoughts center on contemplating the problem and relating it to past experience. Actions involve discussing possible topics and approaches with others. During *selection,* the user identifies the general area or topic to be investigated. Feelings of uncertainty are replaced by optimism and a readiness to search. Thoughts are on choosing a topic most likely to "succeed" and best able to satisfy the criteria of personal interest, information available, and time allocated. Actions involve seeking background information on the general topic area. During *exploration,* the user expands

Tasks	Initiation	Selection	Exploration	Formulation	Collection	Presentation
Feelings (Affective)	Uncertainty	Optimism	Confusion/ Frustration/ Doubt	Clarity	Sense of direction/ Confidence	Satisfaction or disappointment
Thoughts (Cognitive)	Vague ⟶ Focused					
					⟶ Increased interest	
Actions (Physical)	Seeking relevant information ⟶ Exploring				Seeking pertinent information Documenting	

FIGURE 2.5. Information Search Process (Adapted from Kuhlthau 2004, Fig. 5.1, p. 82)

personal understanding of the general area. Feelings of confusion and doubt may increase. Thoughts are on becoming sufficiently informed and oriented in order to formulate a focus or a personal point of view. The fourth stage of *formulation* is the turning point of the process in which the user establishes a focus or perspective on the problem that can guide searching. Feelings of uncertainty fall as confidence rises. Thoughts become clearer and more directed. During *collection,* the user interacts with information systems and services to gather information. Confidence increases and interest in the project deepens. With a clear sense of direction, the user is able to specify and look for particular, relevant information. In the final stage of *presentation,* the user completes the search and resolves the problem. There is a sense of relief, accompanied by satisfaction if the search is thought to have gone well or disappointment otherwise. Thoughts are on closing the search with a personal understanding of the issues investigated. Kuhlthau's extended field work on college students and library users found that the participants' feelings and thoughts matched those predicted by the model. However, at the task or action level, most participants began to gather information before they had explored background or developed a focus or perspective. In most stages of the search process, the dominant activities were information gathering and attempting to complete the search.

Central to Kuhlthau's model of the information search process is the notion that uncertainty—experienced both as a cognitive state and an affective response—rises and fall as the search process progresses. Kuhlthau states this formally as a "principle of uncertainty for information seeking":

> Uncertainty is a cognitive state that commonly causes affective symptoms of anxiety and lack of confidence. Uncertainty and anxiety can be expected in the early stages of the information search process. The affective symptoms of uncertainty, confusion, and frustration are associated with vague, unclear thoughts about a topic or question. As knowledge states shift to more clearly focused thoughts, a parallel shift occurs in feelings of increased confidence. Uncertainty due to a lack of understanding, a gap in meaning, or a limited construction initiates the process of information seeking. (Kuhlthau 2004, p. 92)

The implications of the uncertainty principle are elaborated in a set of six corollaries (Kuhlthau 1993a, b). (1) Information search is a process of constructing understanding and meaning. The user constructs meaning from the information encountered, and in doing so, moves from uncertainty and vagueness to confidence and clarity as the search progresses. (2) The formulation of a focus, guiding idea, or point of view is the pivotal point in the search process. Formulation is an act of thoughtful reflection, the result of relating and interpreting the information encountered in order to select a defined area to concentrate searching on. Unfortunately, many users bypass the formulation activity altogether, beginning to gather information without first forming a sufficiently clear focus. (3) Information encountered may be redundant or unique. Redundant information fits into what the user already knows or believes in and is readily recognized to be relevant or not. Unique information is new and extends knowledge, but it may not match the user's constructs, requiring reconstruction. Too much redundant information leads to boredom, while too much unique information causes anxiety. (4) The range of possibilities pursued in a search is influenced by the user's mood or attitude toward the search task. A user in an invitational mood would tend to take more expansive, exploratory actions, while a user in an indicative mood prefers conclusive actions that lead to closure (Kelly 1963). Computer-based information systems assume an indicative mood, and therefore try to provide information with speed and specificity. In reality, a user's mood changes during the search process, from perhaps an invitational, exploratory mood in early stages to a more indicative mood as the search progresses. (5) The search process is a series of unique, personal choices based on the user's predictions or expectations about what sources, information, and strategies will be effective or expedient. Thus, users make predictions or develop expectations about the sources used or not used, the sequence of source use, and the information selected from the sources as relevant or irrelevant. Relevance is not absolute nor constant but varies considerably from individual to individual. (6) The user's interest and motivation levels grow as the search progresses. Interest is higher in later stages when the user has defined a search focus and has enough understanding of the topic to become intellectually engaged. Interest may also be enhanced by introducing the notion of fun and play, but most information systems ignore this need.

In summary, the cognitive gap or uncertainty that drives the information search process is accompanied by distinct emotional states. In the early stages of information search, uncertainty or lack of understanding causes affective symptoms of anxiety, confusion, frustration, and doubt. As the information search progresses, feelings shift toward increased confidence and satisfaction if the search has been successful. These affective states motivate and direct the individual's information-processing and information-use experience. Affective responses influence, and are influenced by, the user's ability to construct meaning, focus the search, balance redundant and unique information, manage moods and expectations, and deepen personal interest in the search.

Stress in Information Seeking. Wilson (1997) suggests that uncertainty and its affective symptoms constitute a state of stress that the individual must cope with. For example, research in health information seeking has contrasted "monitors," who prefer high levels of information input to cope with a stressful event and suffer less psychological arousal when they have the information, with "blunters," who prefer less information and suffer greater arousal when they receive a high information input (Miller and Mangan 1983). Wilson also examines the relationship between information needs and coping by applying Krohne's (1989) model of coping. When an individual's intolerance of uncertainty is high but the intolerance of arousal is low, the individual copes through "constant monitoring." On the other hand, when both uncertainty intolerance and arousal intolerance are high, the individual engages in "fluctuating coping."

Drawing from social learning theory, Wilson (1997) suggests that the construct of self-efficacy or sense of personal mastery (Bandura 1977) may influence information seeking. Thus, Bandura postulates that an individual's belief or feeling about his or her own effectiveness would affect whether the individual even tries to cope with situation. Wilson reasons that since a strong feeling of self-efficacy or personal mastery about using a source would lead to a more extended and intensive use of that source, doubt about one's capacity to use a source properly would lead to that source not being used, even if the source might be perceived to contain relevant information.

Self-Maintenance. Here, self-maintenance refers to the tendency for people and groups to maintain self-image and self-identity. People are more likely to use information that confirms or supports their existing cognitive structures. They use information selectively to avoid conflict or regret; to maintain self-image; and to enhance status or reputation. At the affective level, we may expect that when people process information, they avoid using information that will arouse strong, negative emotions in others or in themselves. When they confront information that contradicts their existing beliefs and assumptions, they experience a sense of conflict or tension. People reduce or relieve this *cognitive dissonance* (Festinger 1957) by one of several defensive maneuvers, such as avoiding the new information, rejecting its validity, explaining away the differences, reconstructing new cognitive structures, and so on.

Argyris (1994) explains how in the name of maintaining "morale" and "considerateness," people in organizations often censor and control their use of information. When facing problems presenting potential threat or embarrassment, they often reason and behave defensively. Argyris argues that this form of defensive reasoning serves no purpose except self-protection, although the people who use it rarely acknowledge that they are protecting themselves. Instead they believe they are protecting the group, the department, the organization, all for the sake of being positive.

Argyris (1994) describes a company that applied Total Quality Management (TQM) techniques to help its 40 supervisors identify nine areas for improvement. Much to the satisfaction of management, the resulting initiative met its goals one month early and saved more money than was anticipated. In conversations with the supervisors, Argyris was told several times how easy it had been to identify the nine areas since the supervisors had known where the worst inefficiencies were for the past three to five years. Although they had the information for many years, the supervisors never acted on it. When asked why, they cited the blindness of management, rivalry between departments, and a corporate culture that avoided getting others into trouble for the sake of correcting problems. The responsibility for fixing the problem areas and the blame for not doing so always lay elsewhere. Argyris observes that although the supervisors believed they were using the rigorous methods of TQM, their actual information practices were driven more by affective, defensive routines. Thus, they gathered data selectively, postulated only nonthreatening causes, and tested explanations in self-serving ways. Argyris suggests that people learn this procedure over time, supported by *affective norms* such as being "caring" and "thoughtful."

The underlying reason for such behavior is psychological and has to do with the mental and affective strategies that people learn early in life for dealing with emotional or threatening issues. In stressful situations, people depart from their espoused theory of action based on rational principles and commitments and instead behave according to a theory-in-use that is quite different. While espoused theories vary widely, most theories-in-use have the same four governing values,

> All of us design our behavior in order to remain in unilateral control, to maximize winning and minimize losing, to suppress negative feelings, and to be as rational as possible, by which we mean laying out clear-cut goals and then evaluating our own behavior on the basis of whether or not we've achieved them. The purpose of this strategy is to avoid vulnerability, risk, embarrassment, and the appearance of incompetence. (Argyris 1994, p. 87)

Situational Dimensions of Information-Seeking Behavior

In this section, we highlight three major situational dimensions that can affect information-seeking behaviors significantly: task complexity, situational complexity, and information-use environment.

Task Complexity. We may expect the complexity of the task or the uncertainty of the task environment to influence information seeking. A complex task consisting of numerous interdependent task elements that can behave and interact unpredictably may require more information gathering and processing. Similarly, a task environment marked by volatility and turbulence may induce greater information scanning. Task complexity depends on the knowledge, tools, and techniques that are used to transform inputs into organizational outputs. Perrow (1967) describes how this task technology is defined by two underlying task characteristics: task variety and task analyzability. Task variety is the frequency of unexpected and novel events that occur in the conversion process. Task analyzability is the extent to which the conversion process is analyzable and can be controlled by set procedures or standard practices. Thus, in organizations that apply technology with high task variety and where the task is not analyzable, large amounts of information are used to handle exceptions and rich information media are used to resolve unanalyzable issues.

In a comprehensive review of task complexity, Campbell (1988) identifies four fundamental attributes of complex tasks. These include the presence of (1) multiple potential paths to arrive at a desired end state, (2) multiple desired end states to be attained, (3) conflicting interdependence among paths to multiple desired outcomes, and (4) uncertain or probabilistic links among paths and outcomes. Using these attributes, Campbell classifies tasks into five types:

1. simple tasks: single desired outcome, a single solution scheme, no conflicting interdependence or uncertainty;

2. decision tasks: crafting a solution that best satisfies multiple and potentially conflicting outcomes; each desired outcome involves a separate information processing stream;

3. judgment tasks: emphasis on resolving conflict and uncertainty in information associated with the task;

4. problem tasks: finding the best solution scheme from among multiple possible schemes, which satisfies a single, well-defined desired outcome; group members have to be able to configure the problem in various ways in order to achieve the best outcome;

5. fuzzy tasks: have very little focus, and members expend most of their effort on understanding and structuring the problem; information load, diversity, conflict, and uncertainty are all part of fuzzy tasks.

Vakkari (1998) analyzes a set of studies on the effects of task complexity on information source use. He finds a similarity in the conceptualization of task complexity along the dimensions of the degree of predeterminability of information requirements, procedures, and outcomes of a task. The studies indicate that as the task becomes more complex, a greater number of sources are used, and a greater quantity of information is processed subsequently. The use of both personal and documentary external sources increases with task complexity. Moreover, a study by Bystrom and Jarvelin (1995) found that increasing task complexity led to the use of more general-purpose sources, with a reduced share of problem- and fact-oriented sources.

Situational Complexity. We may expect information needs to be shaped by the complexity of the situation in which the information is to be utilized. Situational complexity increases when many actors and entities are involved, and when these agents interconnect and interact in complicated and unpredictable ways. A specific instance of situational complexity is perceived environmental uncertainty, a variable that represents the external environment's perceived complexity and changeability. The external environment may be divided into sectors, such as the customer, competition, technological, regulatory, economic, and sociocultural sectors (Choo and Auster 1993). Perceived environmental uncertainty is conceptualized as lack of information about environmental factors; lack of knowledge about the outcome of an action; and inability to assess how environmental factors affect success or failure (Duncan 1972). Empirical studies found that information scanning increases with perceived environmental uncertainty, and that the scanning tends to be focused on market-related sectors, with information on customers, suppliers, and competitors appearing to be the most important (see, for example, Ghoshal 1988; Lester and Waters 1989; Choo 1993; Olsen, Murthy, and Teare 1994).

Information-Use Environment. Information behavior may be defined as the sum of activities through which information becomes useful (Taylor 1991). The usefulness or value of information is based not only on subject matter or how well the information content matches a query or topic, but also on the requirements, norms, and expectations that are contingent upon the user's work and organizational contexts. These contexts are what Taylor calls *information-use environments* (IUEs), which consist of "those elements that (a) affect the flow and use of information messages into, within, and out of any definable entity; and (b) determine the criteria by which the value of information messages will be judged" (Taylor 1986, p. 24). The elements of the information-use environment may be grouped into four categories: sets of people, problem dimensions, work settings, and problem resolution assumptions (Taylor 1991).

Sets of people share assumptions and attitudes about the nature of their work that act on their information behaviors. These assumptions may be learned formally through education or professional training or assimilated informally

TABLE 2-2. Information-use environments (Taylor 1991).

Sets of people	Typical problems	Work settings	Problem resolution
1. The professions 2. The entrepreneurs 3. Special interest groups 4. Special socioeconomic groups	• Problems are **dynamic** • **Discrete classes of problems** are created by requirements of profession, occupation, social condition, etc. • **Problem dimensions** determine the criteria for judging the value of information	• Organization structure and style • Domain of interest • Access to information • History, experience	• Assumptions about what constitutes the resolution of a problem • **Classes of information use** • **Traits of information** anticipated to resolve problem

through, for example, membership and participation in a group. Taylor identifies four sets of people based on patterns of information behavior (Taylor 1991, p. 222): the professions (engineers, lawyers, social workers, scientists, teachers, managers, physicians, etc.); entrepreneurs (farmers, small businesspeople, etc.); special-interest groups (consumers, citizen groups, hobbyists, political action groups, ethnic cultural groups, etc.); and special socioeconomic groups (information-poor, the disabled, minorities, the elderly, etc.). Demographic and nondemographic characteristics help describe these sets of people. (Taylor was initially most interested in testing his framework by examining the professionals and entrepreneurs.) From the wide range of demographic variables that might be applicable, education appears to be the most significant. Among the nondemographic characteristics, the more important appear to be preferences for channels and media; use of social networks; and attitudes toward new technology, education, risk taking, and innovation. Scientists and engineers, for example, make heavy use of print media such as journals and books, whereas managers prefer face-to-face meetings or telephone conversations. Doctors tend to rely on their social networks of colleagues for information on the efficacy of new drugs. As for attitudes toward information and innovation, scholars and policy makers may value background and context, while teachers and engineers may favor specific information addressing practical concerns.

Problem dimensions are the characteristics of the typical problems that a set of people are concerned with. Taylor asserts that "each of the definable IUEs has a discrete class of problems, spawned by its particular setting and by the exigencies of its profession, occupation, or life style" (Taylor 1991, p. 225). Problems change over time as new information is received and people alter their perceptions. Problems act as surrogates of the information-use environment, and because they encapsulate enough of the more salient demands of the use environment, defining problem dimensions enable information needs to be inferred in a more systematic way (MacMullin and Taylor 1984). MacMullin and Taylor identify eleven problem dimensions that define information need and serve as criteria by which the relevance of information to a problem will be judged. These dimensions position problems as lying on a continuum between each of the following pairs:

Design	*Discovery*
Well-structured	*Ill-structured*
Simple	*Complex*
"Goals are specific"	*"Goals are amorphous"*
"Initial state understood"	*"Initial state not understood"*
"Assumptions agreed upon"	*"Assumptions not agreed upon"*
"Assumptions explicit"	*"Assumptions not explicit"*
"Familiar pattern"	*"New pattern"*
"Magnitude of risk not great"	*"Magnitude of risk great"*
"Susceptible to empirical analysis"	*"Not susceptible to empirical analysis"*
"Internal imposition"	*"External imposition"*

Collectively, these dimensions provide a detailed representation of the information-use environment surrounding problem situations and suggest ways of elaborating information needs that include both subject-related needs and situation-related demands.

Work settings are the social and physical attributes of the organization or unit that a set of people work in—attributes that influence attitudes toward information, the types and structures of information required, and the flow and availability of information. The style and culture of the organization, including its goals and reward and recognition systems, help mold members' perceptions about the role and value of information. The content of the work to be performed, whether it be designing a skyscraper or decoding a software program, will set its own information demands peculiar to the domain. Work setting features such as organizational hierarchy and the location of information sources can affect the flow and availability of information. Perceived accessibility of a source is an important variable governing the decision whether to use the source. Accessibility is a function of source proximity, physical effort required, as well as the psychological cost of using the source. An organization that has specialized in a particular area for many years may become set in its ways and may tend to attenuate the effect of new information. Confident in its history and experience, such an organization may absorb large amounts of information without conceiving the need to rethink its behavior.

Problem resolution assumptions are the perceptions shared by a set of people about what constitutes the resolution of their typical problems. These assumptions guide information seeking and use in several ways. They provide a frame of reference to view and structure problems; and they create expectations about the traits of information required to resolve the problem. For Taylor, the ways in which people view their problems and what they anticipate as resolution constitute a built-in although unconscious means of controlling the amount of information used. Thus, people's perceptions and anticipations indirectly control the breadth and depth of their information search—including the time and effort to spend on searching, where to search, how information encountered is to be filtered, and how much and what kinds of information are required. Managers, for example, do not attempt comprehensive searches or look for optimal solutions. Instead, they search for information locally using familiar sources, often seeking solutions in the vicinity of the problems. Problems are considered resolved when a good-enough solution has been found, that is, a manager "satisfices" as she "looks for a course of action that is satisfactory or 'good enough'" (Simon 1976, p. xxix).

In summary, the information-use environment consists of sets of people who share assumptions about the nature of their work and the role of information in it; whose work is concerned with problems characterized by dimensions that are applied to judge the usefulness of information; whose work settings influence their attitudes toward information as well as the availability and value of information; and whose perceptions about problem resolution regulate the intensity of their information search and their expectations about the kinds of information they need. Taylor suggests that the information-use environment "can become a generalizable model, a fruitful means for organizing, describing, and predicting the information behavior of any given population in a variety of contexts" (Taylor 1991, p. 251).

Normative Information Behavior

A broader and important view of the social context of information seeking is developed by Chatman (1991, 1992, 1996, 1999). Drawing upon her significant body of work studying the information behaviors of the working poor, elderly women, prison inmates, and others, Chatman (2000) creates a theory of normative behavior to describe and analyze information behaviors:

> Normative behaviour is that behaviour which is viewed by inhabitants of a social world as most appropriate for that particular context. Essentially driven by mores and norms, normative behaviour provides a predictable, routine, and manageable approach to everyday reality. Aspects of interest are those things which serve to legitimize and justify values, which embody social existence. (Chatman 2000, p. 13)

Although her analysis is framed in terms of the specific social worlds of her study participants, we feel that many of her arguments are generalizable to the social worlds that are constituted by individual organizational units. Chatman's theory is built on four concepts: social norms, worldview, social types, and information behavior. Social norms create standards to judge "rightness" or "wrongness" in social appearances. Norms give people a way to gauge what is "normal" in a specific context and at a specific time—they point the way to acceptable standards and codes of behavior. Worldview is a collective perception by members of a social world regarding those things which are deemed important and unimportant. Worldview provides a collective approach to assess the importance of information. Social types are "the absolute definitions given to members of a social world." They classify persons, and in doing so, "members of a small world have sensible clues to the ways in which to behave, converse, and share information" (p. 12). The theory consists of five propositional statements:

1. Social norms are standards with which members of a social world comply in order to exhibit desirable expressions of public behavior.

2. Members choose compliance because it allows for a way by which to affirm what is normative for this context at this time.

3. Worldview is shaped by the normative values that influence how members think about the ways of the world. It is a collective, taken-for-granted attitude that sensitizes members to be responsive to certain events and to ignore others.

4. Everyday reality contains a belief that members of a social world do retain attention or interest sufficient enough to influence behavior. The process of placing persons in ideal categories of lesser or greater quality can thought of as social typification.

5. Human information behavior is a construct in which to approach every-day reality and its effect on actions to gain or avoid the possession of information. The choice to decide the appropriate course of action is driven by what members' beliefs are necessary to support a normative way of life.

(Chatman 2000, p. 14)

In commenting on Chatman's model, Pettigrew, Fidel, and Bruce (2001) note that

> Within this framework, individuals strive to represent a positive social type that shares the collective worldview and respects the social norms upheld by other members of the social world. One's efforts at creating and maintaining this social type will affect whether and how one engages in information seeking. If a situation requires information behavior that is inconsistent with the established worldview or contradicts the social type one has established, then the individual is likely either to avoid or to disengage in information seeking or to move to another social world where he or she can engage in the behavior more freely. (pp. 56–57)

IV. INFORMATION-SEEKING BEHAVIOR: INFORMATION NEEDS, SEEKING, AND USE

Having looked at the cognitive, affective, and situational dimensions of information-seeking behavior, we now examine the activities that comprise information seeking itself. Conceptually, information seeking consists of three activities: the recognition of information needs, looking for information, and the use of information. In practice, these stages tend to overlap, so that each activity itself is a microcosm of one or more of the other activities. For example, the clarification of information needs itself requires information seeking and use, the gathering of information switches between sources and strategies as new information is processed, and so on. Nevertheless, a conceptual partitioning into these activities facilitates analysis of the structure and dynamics of information-seeking behavior.

Information Needs

Information needs are often analyzed in terms of a person's cognitive needs—gaps or deficiencies in the state of mental knowledge or understanding that may be represented by questions or topics that could be posed to an information system or source. Satisfying the cognitive need then involves retrieving information whose subject matter matches that of the inquiry. However, because information is sought and used in social situations, information often has to satisfy not just cognitive needs, but also affective or emotional needs (Wilson 1994). While the performance of organizational tasks, including planning and decision making, are the main generators of cognitive needs, "the nature of the organization, coupled with the individual's personality structure, will create affective needs such as the need for achievement, for self-expression and self-actualization. . . . In such a wider view the individual would be perceived not merely as driven to seek information for cognitive ends, but as living and working in social settings which create their own motivations to seek information to help satisfy largely affective needs" (Wilson 1981, pp. 9, 10). Furthermore, information needs do not emerge fully formed but grow and evolve over time. Initially, the individual may experience a vague sense of unease about some general concern or inadequacy in her knowledge. She may or may not embark on information gathering at this point, but she is likely to be sensitive to information encountered about that issue. Gradually she forms an assessment about the importance of that concern and is able to articulate the information gaps that have to be filled in order to develop understanding or enable action. Awareness of an information need does not always lead to search—the individual may decide to accept or suppress the problem. Acceptance or suppression is influenced by the individual's perception of the importance or appropriateness of the problem, her knowledge of the domain, and her assessment of the cost and effort of doing the search (Marchionini 1995). With acceptance, the individual then attempts to understand and define the problem by limiting its boundaries, labeling key concepts and entities, and anticipating what form and format of information is required. By developing a focus and an anticipation of how the information is to be helpful, the person is well prepared to commence information seeking.

In a classic paper, Taylor (1968) suggests that human beings experience four levels of information needs: visceral need, conscious need, formalized need, and compromised need. At the *visceral level,* the person experiences a vague sense of dissatisfaction, a gap in knowledge or understanding that is often inexpressible in linguistic terms. The visceral need may become more concrete and pressing as more information is encountered and its importance grows. When this occurs, the visceral need enters the *conscious level,* where the person develops a mental description of the area of indecision. Such a mental description is likely to be in the form of rambling statements or a narrative that reflect the ambiguity that the person still experiences at this level. To develop a focus, the person may consult with colleagues and friends, and when ambiguity is sufficiently reduced, the conscious need moves to the formalized level. At the *formalized level,* the inquirer is able to construct a qualified, rational statement of the information need, expressed for example in the form of a question or topic. Here the formal statement is made without the user necessarily having to consider what sources or information are available. When the user interacts with an information source or system, either directly or through an intermediary, she may recast the question in anticipation of what the source or system knows or is able to deliver. The formalized question is thus modified or rephrased in a form that could be understood or processed by the information system. In this sense the question finally presented represents the information need at the *compromised level.* Taylor's conceptualization of levels of information need is supported and reinforced in the literature of library and information science, especially in the area of the reference interview (Markey 1981).

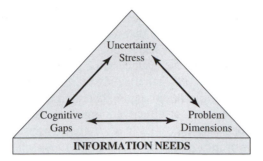

FIGURE 2.6. Information Needs: Cognitive, Affective, Situational Factors

If information needs exist at multiple levels, then satisfying information needs goes beyond just finding information that matches the apparent subject matter expressed in the individual's questions or topic descriptions. A statement of need at the compromised or formalized levels does not retain the nuance and innuendo that give color and complexion to a bald statement of a question. The better that the information found is able to connect with these conscious and visceral needs, the more the individual will feel that the information is pertinent, meaningful, or resonant in a personal way.

Fig. 2.6 highlights some of the major cognitive, affective, and situational factors that shape the perception and experiencing of information needs.

We have seen how information needs have been modeled as *cognitive gaps*: specifically as anomalous states of knowledge (Belkin 1980) and as sense-making gaps (Dervin 1992). Belkin's (1980) treatment of information need as an "anomalous state of knowledge" is analogous to Taylor's representation of information need as visceral and conscious. In both cases, the individual is unable to readily express her information needs since she cannot specify what she does not yet know or what is presently missing. To analyze information needs cognitively, Dervin (1992) uses the metaphor of a person making a journey through life being stopped in gap situations when the ability to make sense has run out. The way that a person perceives the gap is a good predictor of information-seeking and -use behaviors. From a large number of field studies, Dervin is able to identify a number of generic information gaps that people experience. These gaps include decision stops (e.g., when a person faces two or more roads ahead), barrier stops (e.g., when there is one road ahead but the way is blocked), and spin-out stops (e.g., when there is no road ahead). People who perceive themselves as being in these situation gaps will seek information to bridge the gap.

In terms of emotional states, the lack of information and the inability to make sense of or move forward in a situation creates a state of *uncertainty*. Kuhlthau (1993a, b) found that uncertainty causes a number of affective symptoms, including anxiety, apprehension, confusion, frustration, and lack of confidence. Affective responses influence, and are influenced by, the individual's ability to construct meaning, focus information needs, manage moods and expectations, and deepen personal interest in the search. Her "uncertainty principle of information seeking" predicts that feelings of uncertainty and confusion would dominate in early stages of search due to ambiguities in the information need, and that confidence increases as the search progresses. For Kuhlthau, feelings of uncertainty begin to ebb when the individual is able to formulate a focus or theme around which information seeking can then take place. Wilson (1997) suggests that uncertainty and its affective symptoms can constitute a state of *stress*. Individuals cope with the stress in a variety of ways. For example, some prefer large amounts of information and suffer less stress when they have the information, while others prefer less information and suffer greater arousal when they receive too much information.

As for situational demands, people experience information needs as they are engrossed in specific problem contexts. Such contexts are composed of a large number of elements that relate not just to subject matter but also to situational characteristics. For example, the degree to which the situation is new or familiar, simple or complex, and the extent to which participants agree or disagree on assumptions, goals, and options are all likely to influence the nature and intensity of the information need (MacMullin and Taylor 1984). Well-structured problems would require formal, quantitative data, while ill-structured problems need information on how to interpret or proceed. Problems with specific goals would require information that operationalizes or measures the goals, while problems with amorphous goals would first need information to clarify preferences and directions. *Problem dimensions* therefore elaborate information needs and form the criteria by which individuals assess the relevance and value of information.

Information Seeking

Ellis (1989a, b) and Ellis, Cox, and Hall (1993) derive a general behavioral model of information seeking from an analysis of the information-seeking patterns of social scientists, research physicists, and chemists. Their model identified eight generic characteristics that were sufficient to categorize the information-seeking behaviors they observed:

1. Starting: activities characteristic of the initial search for information.
2. Chaining: following chains of citations or other forms of referential connection between material.
3. Browsing: semidirected searching in an area of potential interest.
4. Differentiating: using differences between sources as a filter on the nature and quality of the material examined.
5. Monitoring: maintaining awareness of developments in a field through the monitoring of particular sources.
6. Extracting: systematically working through a particular source to identify material of interest.

7. Verifying: activities associated with checking the accuracy of information.
8. Ending: activities characteristic of information seeking at the end of a topic or a project, for example, during the preparation of papers for publication.

(Ellis 1989b, p. 238; Ellis et al. 1993, p. 359)

We examine each characteristic in greater detail below, amplifying the discussion with related research. *Starting* comprises those activities that form the initial search for information—identifying sources of interest that could serve as starting points of the search. Identified sources often include familiar sources that have been used before as well as less familiar sources that are expected to provide relevant information. The likelihood of a source being selected depends on the perceived accessibility of the source, as well as the perceived quality of the information from that source. Perceived accessibility, which is the amount of effort and time needed to make contact with and use a source, has been found to be a strong predictor of source use for many groups of information users (such as engineers and scientists [Allen 1977]). However, in situations when ambiguity is high and when information reliability is especially important, less accessible sources of perceived high quality may be consulted as well (see for example the environment scanning behavior of chief executives in Choo [1994]). While searching the initial sources, these sources are likely to point to, suggest, or recommend additional sources or references. Following up on these new leads from an initial source is the activity of *chaining*. Chaining can be backward or forward. Backward chaining takes place when pointers or references from an initial source are followed and is a well-established routine of information seeking among scientists and researchers. In the reverse direction, forward chaining identifies and follows up on other sources that refer to an initial source or document. Although it can be an effective way of broadening a search, forward chaining is much less commonly used, probably because people are unaware of it or because the required bibliographical tools are unavailable.

Browsing is the activity of semidirected search in areas of potential interest. The individual often simplifies browsing by looking through tables of contents, lists of titles, subject headings, names of organizations or persons, abstracts and summaries, and so on. Browsing takes place in many situations in which related information has been grouped together according to subject affinity, as when the user views displays at a conference or exhibition or scans periodicals or books along the shelves of a bookshop or library. Chang and Rice (1993) define browsing as "the process of exposing oneself to a resource space by scanning its content (objects or representations) and/or structure, possibly resulting in awareness of unexpected or new content or paths in that resource space" (p. 258). They regard browsing as a "rich and fundamental human information behavior" that could lead to outcomes such as serendipitous findings, modification of information needs, learning, enjoyment, and so on. During *differentiating,* the individual filters and selects from among the sources scanned by noticing differences between the nature and quality of the information offered. For example, social scientists were found to prioritize sources and types of sources according to three main criteria: by substantive topic; by approach or perspective; and by level, quality, or type of treatment (Ellis 1989a, b). The differentiation process is likely to depend on the individual's prior or initial experiences with the sources, word-of-mouth recommendations from personal contacts, or reviews in published sources. Taylor (1986) points out that for information to be relevant and consequential, it should address not only the subject matter of the problem but also the particular circumstances that affect the resolution of that problem. He identifies six categories of criteria by which individuals select and differentiate between sources: ease of use, noise reduction, quality, adaptability, time savings, and cost savings.

Monitoring is the activity of keeping abreast of developments in an area by regularly following particular sources. The individual monitors by concentrating on a small number of what are perceived to be core sources. Core sources vary between professional groups but usually include both key personal contacts and publications. For example, social scientists and physicists were found to track developments through core journals, online search updates, newspapers, conferences, magazines, books, catalogs, and so on (Ellis et al. 1993). *Extracting* is the activity of systematically working through a particular source or sources in order to identify material of interest. As a form of retrospective searching, extracting may be achieved by directly consulting the source or by indirectly looking through bibliographies, indexes, or online databases. Retrospective searching tends to be labor intensive and is more likely when there is a need for comprehensive or historical information on a topic. For some groups or in some situations, the accuracy of the information is critical and requires the activity of *verifying* for correctness or absence of obvious errors. Ellis et al. found that the majority of the chemists they studied attempted to verify all their information, especially sources perceived to be unreliable (Ellis et al. 1993). Finally, Ellis et al. observed that a small number of the chemists performed the bulk of their searching at the end rather than the beginning of a project. Thus, some would return to the literature again at the writing-up stage when they needed to relate their findings to other published work. This is the activity of *ending*.

Although the Ellis model is based on studies of academicians and researchers, susbsets of the categories of information-seeking behaviors may be applicable to other groups of users as well. For example, Sutton's (1994) analysis of the information-seeking behavior of attorneys noted that the three stages of legal research he identified (base-level modeling, context sensitive exploration, and disambiguating the space) could be mapped into Ellis's categories of starting, chaining, and differentiating. The identification of categories of information-seeking behavior also suggests that information retrieval systems could increase their usefulness by including features that directly support these activities. Ellis thought that hypertext-based systems would have the capabilities to implement these functions (Ellis 1989a, b). If we visualize the World Wide Web as a hyperlinked information system distributed over numerous networks, most of the information-seeking behavior categories in Ellis's model are already being supported by capabilities available in common web browser software. Thus, a user could use the browser to reach a search engine to locate sources of interest (starting); follow hypertextual links to related information resources in both backward- and forward-linking directions (chaining); scan the web pages of the sources selected (browsing); bookmark useful sources for future reference and visits (differentiating); subscribe to e-mail-based services that alert the user of new information or developments (monitoring); and search a particular source or site for all information on that site on a particular topic (extracting).

Fig. 2.7 highlights some of the major cognitive, affective, and situational factors that shape information seeking.

The selection of which sources to use is an important component of information seeking. At the cognitive level, people choose sources that are perceived to have the greater probability of providing information that will be relevant, reliable, and helpful to the problem situation at hand—attributes that we may summarize under the label *perceived source quality*. A growing number of studies that examine information seeking by actual users suggest the importance of this concept. Hardy (1982) found that information seekers evaluated sources on the basis of their costs and benefits, and that the quality of the information obtained is a significant factor in this evaluation. Swanson (1987) found that the individual's use of an information channel or source can be explained in part by the individual's attitude or disposition toward that channel, and that the attributed information quality of a channel plays a significant role in this explanation. In a nationwide survey of the information-seeking behavior of U.S. aerospace engineers and scientists sponsored by NASA and the U.S. Department of Defense, Pinelli et al. (1991) found that *relevance* seems to be the single most important determinant of the overall extent to which U.S. aerospace engineers and scientists use these sources. Auster and Choo (1993) discovered that source quality is the most important factor in explaining source use in environmental scanning by CEOs in two industries with high levels of perceived uncertainty (publishing and telecommunications). In the study by Choo, Detlor, and Turnbull (2000) focusing on information technologists and corporate managers, source quality was significantly correlated with the use of many sources, including customers,

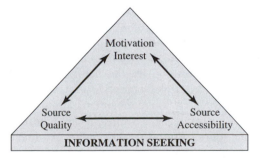

FIGURE 2.7. Information Seeking: Cognitive, Affective, Situational Factors

competitors, external reports, colleagues in same department, internal memos, and internal libraries. Choo and Marton (2003) found a strong, significant relationship between source quality and source usage among women in information-technology (IT) professions and suggested that in an age of information overload, perceived source quality will be an important factor in choosing between information sources.

At the affective level, the individual's degree of personal *motivation and interest* in the problem or topic would determine the amount of effort expended in information seeking. Kuhlthau (1993a, b) describes how initial feelings of anxiety and confusion could be replaced by feelings of increased confidence as the search progresses. If a theme is found to focus the search, the individual becomes more highly motivated. The individual's mood toward the search may also influence the breadth and depth of information seeking—a person in an invitational mood would explore more sources while a person in an indicative mood would seek information that leads to closure or action. If the information found enables the individual to see the problem more clearly and to develop a sense of direction, feelings of optimism and confidence increase as the search progresses. Wilson (1997) postulates that since a strong feeling of self-efficacy or personal mastery about using a source leads to greater source use, doubt about one's capacity to use a source properly would conversely lead to that source not being used, even if the source might be perceived to contain relevant information.

At the situational level, the use of sources is influenced by the *perceived accessibility* of the source. Several classic studies, including those of Rosenberg (1967) and Gertsberger and Allen (1968) that we mentioned earlier in the chapter, have concluded that scientists and engineers selected sources based primarily on their accessibility. After reviewing the concept of perceived accessibility as used in organizational communication, library science, and management information systems, Culnan (1983) observed that in organizational communication, source accessibility has generally been defined as both the social and economic costs associated with acquiring information, whereas in library and information science, accessibility is generally defined in terms of the "physical" costs of use, especially the physical distance of the library from the user. She proposed that perceived source accessibility serve as the unifying concept for the design and evaluation of a wide variety of information systems and services, and defines perceived accessibility as the "expected level of effort required to use a particular information source" (Culnan 1983, 302). She identifies three dimensions of accessibility: gaining physical access to the information source (physical dimension); translating an information need or request into a language that is understood by the source (interface dimension); and being able to physically retrieve the potentially relevant information (informational dimension). Taylor's (1991) conceptualization of the information-use environment identifies perceived accessibility as an important element in deciding whether to use the source. For him, accessibility is a function of work setting features such as the organizational hierarchy and the location of information sources.

Information Use

Perhaps because it is so much a subconscious part of everyday experience, information use as a concept has been difficult to define satisfactorily. To develop our model, we regard information use pragmatically as the individual making a choice or selection of messages from a larger pool of messages to attend to or to act on (Taylor 1986). Presumably, this choice is based on the individual perceiving some meaningful relation between the message content and the task or problem at hand. A discussion of what this "meaningful relation" is about can become very broad, but the important point is that this relation is perceived and determined by the individual, based not only on factors such as the content and form of the message, but also on the individual's knowledge, frame of mind, and life or work situation. The outcome of information use is a change in the individual's state of knowledge or capacity to act. Thus, information use typically involves the selection and processing of information in order to answer a question, solve a problem, make a decision, negotiate a position, or make sense of a situation.

Taylor (1991) proposes a taxonomy of eight classes of information uses, generated by the information need perceived by users in particular situations and derived in part from the classification scheme developed by Dervin (1983b) that was reviewed earlier. The categories are not mutually exclusive, so that information used in one class may also address the needs of other classes.

1. *Enlightenment.* Information is used to develop a context or to make sense of a situation. Information is used to answer questions such as Are there similar situations? What are they? What is the history and experience of Corporation X in making product Y, and how is this relevant to our intent to manufacture Y?

2. *Problem Understanding.* Information is used in a more specific way than enlightenment—it is used to develop a better comprehension of a particular problem.

3. *Instrumental.* Information is used so that the individual knows what to do and how to do something. Instructions are a common form of instrumental information. Under some conditions, instrumental information use requires information use in other classes.

4. *Factual.* Information is used to determine the facts of a phenomenon or event, to describe reality. Factual information use is likely to depend on the actual and perceived quality (accuracy, reliability) of the information that is available.

5. *Confirmational.* Information is used to verify another piece of information. Confirmational information use often involves the seeking of a second opinion. If the new opinion does not confirm existing information, then the user may try to reinterpret the information or choose between sources to trust.

6. *Projective.* Information is used to predict what is likely to happen in the future. Projective information use is typically concerned with forecasts, estimates, and probabilities.

7. *Motivational.* Information is used to initiate or sustain personal involvement, in order to keep moving along on a particular course of action.

8. *Personal or Political.* Information is used to develop relationships and enhance status, reputation, or personal fulfillment. Dervin (1983b, p. 62) associates this information use with phrases such as "Got control," "Got out of a bad situation," and "Got connected to others."

(Adapted from Taylor 1991, p. 230)

Fig. 2.8 highlights some of the major cognitive, affective, and situational factors that influence information seeking.

At the cognitive level, the individual's *cognitive style* and preferences would influence the manner that information is processed and utilized. A number of classifications have been developed to differentiate personality types and cognitive preferences. The Myers-Briggs Type Indicator is a widely used instrument for classifying personality types into 16 categories. Each personality type is expected to process and use information in a distinctive manner. Another cognitive style variable is field dependence. Field-dependent individuals tend to respond uncritically to environmental cues, whereas field-independent individuals orient themselves correctly in spite of environmental cues. Kahneman and Tversky (1982) discovered that when people use information to make judgments they rely on heuristics to simplify information processing. In certain situations, these simplifications can produce errors or biases. For example, to judge whether an event belongs to a category, people rely on mental stereotypes, but they often ignore other relevant information such as the distribution of the categories in the general population. To judge the frequency or likelihood of an event, people over-rely on recent, vivid, easy-to-recall information. To estimate a quantity they make adjustments from an initial anchor or suggestion. Unfortunately, the adjustments are often inadequate.

At the affective level, people avoid using information that arouses strong, negative emotions in others or in themselves. They use information selectively

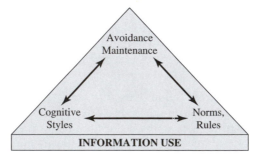

FIGURE 2.8. Information Use: Cognitive, Affective, Situational Factors

to avoid embarrassment, conflict, or regret; maintain self-image; and enhance personal status or reputation. As we discussed earlier, Argyris (1994) observes how people censor their use of information in emotionally charged situations. They do this ostensibly to show "care" and "consideration," but they are in fact acting defensively to "avoid vulnerability, risk, embarrassment, and the appearance of incompetence" (p. 80). Two other examples of affective responses channeling information use are the escalation of commitment (Staw and Ross 1987) and the not-invented-here syndrome (Katz and Allen 1982). In commitment escalation, people continue to evaluate positively and maintain a course of action even when the available information indicates that the action is no longer viable and that withdrawal is necessary to reduce further losses. People persist because they want to save face: they do not want to admit to themselves, much less to others, that they have made an error. In the not-invented-here syndrome, members of a long-standing group reject new information from outside the group. This is because group members have developed strong emotional attachment to their beliefs and past decisions, thereby creating a stable environment that reduces the amount of stress and uncertainty that they need to face. The longer the individuals' membership in a group, the more resistant they become toward outside new ideas and information.

At the situational level, information use is determined by the extent to which norms, rules, and routines structure the task in which the information is utilized. Cyert and March (1992) describe how task performance rules define what information is required and how it is to be used in task execution; records and reports policies define what information is documented and archived; information-handling rules define how information is to be routed and filtered; and planning rules define how information is used to decide about resource allocation. Schein (1997) and Martin (1992) describe the role of organizational culture as establishing a shared framework of assumptions, beliefs, and values for constructing meaning. People use the framework to notice and label actions and events, assign value and significance to developments, and collectively make sense of information. An important part of organizational culture is information politics, and many information-based organizations are struggling with the politics of managing information use. Thus, Davenport, Eccles, and Prusak (1992) found that the most common political model in organizations to be based on information feudalism, where managers act as feudal lords who control information production and use, including what the information means.

Information Use and Types of Relevance

The concept of *relevance* has always been central in the study of information seeking and information retrieval. In recent years, research on relevance suggests that it is evolving into an keystone concept that now includes cognitive, affective, and situational dimensions (see, for example, Schamber 1994; Harter 1992; Saracevic 1996; Cosjin and Ingwersen 2000).

Saracevic (1996, p. 214) distinguishes between five basic types of relevance, or what he refers to as manifestations of relevance. These are (1) system or algorithmic relevance, which describes the relation between the query (terms) and the collection of information objects expressed by the retrieved information object(s); (2) topical-like relevance, associated with aboutness; (3) pertinence or cognitive relevance, related to the information need as perceived by the user; (4) situational relevance, depending on the task interpretation; and (5) motivational or affective relevance, which is goal oriented. *System or algorithmic relevance* can be defined as "how well the topic of the information retrieved matches the topic of the request. A document is objectively relevant to a request if it deals with the topic of the request" (Harter 1992, p. 602). Algorithmic relevance is applied in the evaluation of information retrieval systems, to determine how well a query representation matches the contents of retrieved information objects. *Topical-like relevance* is understood as aboutness, an intellectual assessment of how an information object corresponds to the topical area required and described by the request for information. An observer, either an assessor or a user, makes the subjective relevance assessment. *Pertinence* represents the intellectual relation between the intrinsic human information need and the information objects as currently interpreted or perceived by the cognitive state of an assessor or user (Borlund 2003). It goes beyond "topic-relatedness" to satisfying some personal, visceral need of the individual (see our discussion of Taylor's levels of information needs earlier). *Situational relevance* is the usefulness of the viewed and assessed information objects based on their relationship with the work task at hand underlying the information need as perceived by the user. Situational relevance is a highly context dependent as well as a potentially dynamic type of relevance. Wilson (1973) introduced the concept of situational relevance as the relation between an information object and the information recipient's individual and personal view of the world and his or her situation in it (Wilson 1973, p. 458). An information object is situational relevant if it brings about a change in the information recipient's view of his or her situation, whether the change (of knowledge structure[s]) comes from the topic or the potential utility. *Motivational or affective relevance* describes the relation between the intents, goals, and motivations of the user and the information objects. In short, the intents, goals, and motivations are what make users search for information, carry out information retrieval, and assess relevance of the retrieved information objects. In summary, we see the emergence of relevance as a multidimensional construct and the growing acceptance that relevance should be judged in relation to the information need rather than the information query or request (Borlund 2003). Our discussions here suggest that the ramification of relevance into its cognitive, affective, and situation related dimensions is an important step in helping us understand information-seeking behavior.

An Integrative Model of Information-Seeking Behavior

We bring together our discussion of information needs, seeking, and use, as well as their cognitive, affective, and situational dimensions, in an integrative model shown in Fig. 2.9. As shown in the top triangle of the figure, people experience information needs when they perceive gaps in their state of knowledge or their

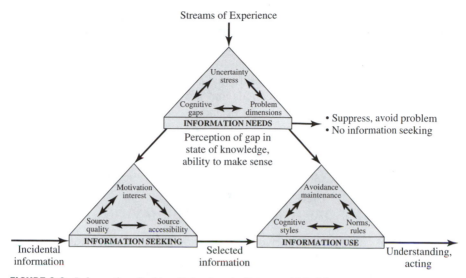

FIGURE 2.9. Information-Seeking Behavior: An Integrated Model

ability to make sense. The experiencing of information needs does not inevitably lead to information seeking. An individual may respond to information needs in one of three ways. First, the individual may choose to suppress this information need by, for example, avoiding the problem situation, so that no information seeking ensues. Second, the individual may search his or her own memory for information that can address the need. Again, no external information seeking occurs. Third, the individual may decide to bridge the gap of knowledge or understanding through purposive information seeking. Purposive information seeking is directed toward the goal of solving a problem, making a decision, or increasing understanding. The individual identifies possible sources, differentiates and chooses sources, makes contact with them, and interacts with the sources to obtain the desired information. Purposive information seeking is depicted by the left-hand triangle in Fig. 2.9.

Even as purposive information seeking is going on, information is also being acquired "incidentally" through the individual's habitual information-gathering routines. Wilson and Streatfield (1977) suggests that everyone maintains a set of habits or routines for keeping his or her internal mental model up to date. Such routines could include, for example, scanning the mass media, conversations with friends and colleagues, and personal observation. Although these activities are not directed at addressing specific information needs, useful information is often encountered in this incidental manner.

As shown in the right-hand triangle of Fig. 2.9, information use is the stage of the model when the individual acts on the information found to, for example, answer a question, resolve a problem, take a decision, negotiate a position, or make sense of a situation. The set of information that is eventually attended to is a very small subset of the total information that is received. How this information is processed and put to use depends on the cognitive style and preferences of the individual, the emotional responses that accompany information processing, and the organizational or social context surrounding information use. The outcome of information use is a change in the individual's state of knowledge or awareness, allowing the individual to make sense or take action. The actions and interactions of multiple individuals and groups generate new experiences. New experiences create new ambiguities and uncertainties, so that the cycle of information needing, information seeking, and information use is always in motion.

V. MULTIFACETED MODELS OF INFORMATION-SEEKING BEHAVIOR

In a survey of conceptual frameworks in information behavior, Pettigrew et al. (2001) contrasted three types of approaches to theory development: cognitive approaches, social approaches, and multifaceted approaches. In *cognitive approaches,* the focus is on individual attributes, including the states and structures of knowledge that mediate information-seeking behavior. Prominent examples of cognitive models would be Belkin's concept of anomalous states of knowledge and Dervin's sense-making metaphor, both of which were discussed earlier in the chapter. *Social approaches* analyze the social contexts of information seeking in order to "address information behavior phenomena that lie outside the realm of cognitive frameworks," emphasizing "the meanings and values associated with social, sociocultural, and sociolinguistic aspects of information behavior" (Pettigrew et al. 2001, p. 54). The work of Chatman on normative information behavior, also examined earlier, would be an important example of this approach. Whereas the cognitive approach considers the concept of information need as being central, the social approach does not: instead it is through the social context, interaction, and discourse that information behavior occurs (Fidel et al. 2004). *Multifaceted approaches* recognize the complexity of information seeking in the real world and attempt to study this complexity by applying multiple perspectives that may include the cognitive, social, system, and other points of view. The information-seeking model presented in the last section would be one example. Recent research adopting this approach would include the work on information mosaics (Solomon 1999), information horizons (Sonnenwald et al. 2001), the information-seeking and mediated searching model (Spink et al. 2002), and cognitive work analysis (Fidel et al. 2004). We introduce each of these models below.

Solomon (1999) uses the concept of *information mosaics* to understand how individuals define their lives and worlds during the situations where they collect information. Solomon constructed information "mosaics" by recording the information- and task-related actions of individuals (work planners in a public agency, college students, professionals planning travel) in chronological sequence using colored sticky notes arranged on a large table top. The resulting mosaic is then used to analyze the rules and resources that are relevant to individuals in connection with their organizational roles, their current tasks, and the history of their work processes. Thus, information mosaics "represent the action of *doers*—not just users—in connection with their tasks, roles, knowledge, and other situational or contextual aspects" (Solomon 1999, p. 152). Solomon considers this approach an extension of Chatman's (1999) theory of life in the round, where context shapes a person's definition of what information is as well as appropriate ways of seeking and using it. He emphasizes the difference here between a research focus that is limited to just information seeking, which expresses a professional ideal and applies a model developed for scientists and engineers, and a broader view that includes the individuals' interactions with a variety of social and technological systems that they find situationally relevant.

Sonnenwald's (1999) framework for human information behavior suggests that within a context and situation is an *information horizon* in which we can act. The information horizon of a particular individual encompasses a variety of information resources that may include social networks, documents, information retrieval tools, and experimentation and observation in the world. Information horizons, and the resources they include, are determined socially and individually. For example, one's perception about the value of a resource and thus its position within the information horizon is influenced by the opinions of one's peers about that resource. Information horizons can change as we interact with others and learn of their opinions. For example, a department head may recommend a report to an employee, thus adding that resource to the latter's information horizon when the head has a positive influence. Information behavior is constructed amidst a flow of reflections and evaluations of changes in self, others, and their environment. In order to increase our understanding of human information behavior, we need therefore to attend to the following: decisions made and activities undertaken during the information-seeking process; when and why information resources, including individuals, are accessed (and not accessed); relationships or interconnectedness among information resources; individual preferences and evaluation of information resources; the proactive nature of information resources; and the impact of contexts and situations on the information-seeking process. Sonnenwald et al. (2001) applied the information horizon method to map and analyze the information-seeking behavior of lower socio-economic students.

In a multipart series of papers, Spink et al. (2002) reported the development of an integrated *model of information seeking and mediated searching*. Their project, jointly supported by the British Library and the U.S. National Science Foundation, investigated the processes of mediated online searching for nearly 200 clients at the University of North Texas and the University of Sheffield. The theory development uses Wilson's problem-solving model (Wilson 1999) to explain why people engage in information seeking: information seeking is directed at the goal of the resolution of the problem and possibly the presentation of the solution. In moving through each of the stages of problem identification, problem definition, problem resolution, and solution presentation, uncertainty must be reduced by engaging in successive interaction episodes with information sources. A user's successive interactions may be analyzed in terms of relevance judgments, uncertainty reduction, and the problem-solving stage. With Wilson's problem-solving process as the overarching framework, the new model includes Kuhlthau's search process model (1993a, b) and Ellis's (1989a, b) behavioral characteristics, which are seen as applying to search activities at any stage of the problem-solving process. The Ellis and Kuhlthau models are viewed as closely related, especially if a stage process is imposed on Ellis's characteristics. Thus, the activities of chaining and monitoring described by Ellis are seen as a deeper specification of the collection stage in Kuhlthau's model (see discussions of both models in earlier sections). The project also attempted to relate the measure of uncertainty at different problem-solving stages to the set of affective variables identified by Kuhlthau as accompanying the search stages she had defined. The results showed that the feelings variables were closely intercorrelated, with the most highly intercorrelated variable being "disappointed/pleased." This result was interpreted as expressing a general affective state that varies between positive and negative (Wilson et al. 2002). Finally, the project tested a number of hypotheses linking two sets of cognitive styles and problem-solving and related information-seeking behavior. The two cognitive styles were field dependence/independence (Witkin and Goodenough 1981) and holist/serialist learning styles (Pask 1976). Field-independent individuals are better at structuring and analytic activity and at differentiating experiences from their backgrounds when compared with field-dependent individuals. Holists adopt a global approach to learning, examining interrelationships between several topics and building up a broad conceptual overview, while serialists use a local learning style, concentrating on one topic at a time. The results suggested that field-independent researchers were more analytic and active than their field-dependent counterparts. Holists engaged more in exploratory and serendipitous information behavior than serialists.

Fidel et al. (2004) propose *cognitive work analysis* as a framework to study information behavior on the job. Cognitive work analysis views human-information interaction in the context of human-work activities and examines dimensions relating to the environment; work domain; organizational structure; task analysis in terms of the work domain, decision making, and the strategies that can be used; and the actor's resources and values. When applying the framework,

> One considers the work activities, their organizational relationships, and the constraints of the work place that impact the activities. One also takes into account the actors' cognitive and social activities and the values that guide them as well as their priorities and personal preferences when they perform a task on the job. This interaction between work and human actors is mediated through the task an actor performs, the decisions she makes, and the strategies she uses to solve problems. Because actors often collaborate with one another to do their work in the modern work place, collaboration among actors is an important aspect of this human-work interaction. (Fidel et al. 2004, p. 942)

Thus, cognitive work analysis is a holistic approach that focuses simultaneously on the task that actors perform, the environment in which it is carried out, and the perceptual and cognitive attributes of the people who typically do the task. Fidel and her associates have applied the framework to study information behaviors of engineers at Boeing and Microsoft.

VI. SUMMARY

- *Information-seeking behavior* refers to the patterns of behavior that people display as they recognize information needs, make choices about where and how to look for information, and reflect or act on the information they see. Conceptually, information-seeking behavior consists of (1) information needs, (2) information seeking, and (3) information use.

- *Information needs* arise when the individual recognizes gaps in his or her state of knowledge and ability to make sense of an experience.

- *Information needs* do not emerge fully formed but evolve over time. In a classic paper, Taylor (1968) suggests that human beings experience four levels of information needs: visceral need, conscious need, formalized need, and compromised need.

- *Information seeking* is the process in which the individual purposefully searches for information that can change his or her state of knowledge.

- Ellis (1989a, b) and Ellis et al. (1993) identified eight general characteristics of *information-seeking behaviors:* starting, chaining, browsing, differentiating, monitoring, extracting, verifying, and ending.

- *Information use* occurs when the individual selects and processes information which leads to a change in the individual's capacity to make sense or to take action.

- Taylor (1991) identifies eight categories of *information use:* enlightenment, problem understanding, instrumental, factual, confirmational, projective, motivational, and personal or political.

- Research has found that information needs, seeking, and use are influenced by a number of cognitive, affective, and situational dimensions.

- An important *cognitive dimension* is how people perceive information needs as cognitive gaps where their ability to make sense of a situation has run out. Field research based on the *sense-making metaphor* (Dervin 2003) found that that the way the individual perceives a gap is a good predictor of how the individual will go about bridging the gap and wanting the information to help.

- An important *affective dimension* is how people respond emotionally during various stages of the information search process. Kuhlthau (2004) found that in the early stages of information search, *uncertainty* causes affective symptoms of anxiety and lack of confidence. As the search progresses and knowledge states shift to more clearly focused thoughts, there is a parallel shift toward increased confidence and satisfaction if the search is successful.

- An important *situational dimension* is the *information-use environment* (Taylor 1991). The information-use environment consists of sets of people whose work is concerned with problems characterized by dimensions that are applied to judge information usefulness; whose work settings influence their attitudes toward information as well as the availability and value of information; and whose perceptions about problem resolution affect their information search and their expectations about the kinds of information they need.

- Information needs, seeking, and use, as well as their cognitive, affective, and situational dimensions, are brought together in an integrative model that is shown in Fig. 2.9. In this model:

  1. People experience information needs when they perceive gaps in their state of knowledge or their ability to make sense. They may choose to ignore or suppress this information need, or they may decide to seek information purposefully.

  2. During information seeking, the individual identifies sources, considers their quality and accessibility, and interacts with them to obtain information.

  3. The information that is eventually used is a very small subset of the total information that is encountered. The outcome of information use is a change in the individual's state of knowledge or awareness, allowing the individual to make sense or take action.

3

THE MANAGEMENT OF AMBIGUITY:
ORGANIZATIONS AS
SENSE-MAKING COMMUNITIES

The reasonable man adapts himself to the world: the unreasonable one persists in trying to adapt the world to himself. Therefore all progress depends on the unreasonable man.
    —*George Bernard Shaw,* Man and Superman, *1903*

We do not stumble upon our experiences, nor do we let them flow over us like a stream. Rather, we have to be active: we have to "make" our experiences. It is we who always formulate the questions to be put to nature; it is we who try again and again to put these questions so as to elicit a clear-cut "yes" or "no" (for nature does not give an answer unless pressed for it). And in the end, it is again we who give the answer; it is we ourselves who, after severe scrutiny, decide upon the answer.
    —*Karl Popper,* The Logic of Scientific Discovery, *1959*

Many people believe that the some of the world's best wines are produced in France. Any firm aspiring to become a significant player in the world wine market must consider on what grounds it wishes to be compared with the established cachet of the French wine producers. The anthropologist Mary Douglas provides an interesting account of how the California wineries effectively changed the market environment by creating their own classification system that in turn defined how the Californian wine producers were to make sense of their businesses. Historically, French wine producers have developed a classification system based on geography, with each geographical location maintaining a tradition for a certain quality of wine. For example, within the Bordeaux region are the smaller regions of Médoc, St. Emilion, Graves, Côtes; and within these are the individual chateaux. Médoc uses a classification system derived from the average price fetched by its wine over the one hundred years preceding 1855, and it was this classification that selected the best land for vineyards. The classification divides quality into several levels of a hierarchy: the first, second, third, and fourth growths at the top, the *Cru Bourgeois* at the bottom, and lastly the unclassed growths. Somewhat differently in St. Emilion, quality is checked by a committee, which required that its most celebrated chateaux, the *Premiere Grands Crus,* requalify for their exalted positions every ten years, while lesser chateaux, the *Grands Crus,* had to submit each vintage for tasting. Each chateau therefore produced its own unique wine. By referencing the established labels of quality, "the chateau is not considered as a plot of land so much as a brand name of whose reputation the owner is extremely careful. . . . Naming the wine after the region and the chateau is to condense information that can only be unpacked by connoisseurship. The name encapsulates a tried process, a traditional blend of grapes, a soil, the slope of a valley, and a climate" (Douglas 1986, pp. 105–106). The net result is that the regional classification system erected a monopolistic guild that protected the French wine producers. The chateau and regional names were the property rights of the French producers, and these names could not be transferred or shared by wine producers in California (Californian wines could only go as far as calling themselves Bordeaux-type or Burgundy-type).

The Californian wine producers elected not to pursue a Napa Valley–type classification based on geography that would in any event have had a hard time in challenging the reputed French regions. Instead of a geographical classification, the Californian producers adopted a classification system that was based upon the kind of grape. As a result, each winery could and did produce a range of wine products using several varieties of grape. Douglas observed that among six well-known Napa County wineries, one (Hetz) used twelve kinds of grapes to produce twelve wines, another (Joseph Phelps) used eight grapes, two used five or six grapes, and the remaining two each used three. This diversification extends to methods of viticulture, treatment of the wine at various stages, and techniques of bottling or corking. By acting to implement its own classification, the Californian wine producers were making possible the strategy of diversification where "each winery is seeking a diverse range of specialized wines within a highly diversified market" (Douglas 1986, p. 108). The success of the Californian wine industry leads Douglas to observe wryly that publications like Hugh Johnson's popular *The World Atlas of Wines,* which uses place for explaining French wines, is largely irrelevant to the Californian scene. Although she was writing about how institutions can impose their own classifications on people, Mary Douglas has also described an instance of how organizations can enact their external environment by creating new categories and using these categories to understand and act on their worlds. Rather than passively treating the environment as a given text to be read and interpreted, enacting organizations make sense of the environment by creating or reconfiguring parts of it.

Today's organizations have their eyes fixed on the horizon, watching markets shift from day to day, firms jostle with one another for advantage, technological innovations compete for attention, and government policies draw and redraw boundaries. More than ever, organizations are keenly aware that their ability to survive and grow is determined by their capacity to make sense of or influence their environments and to constantly renew meaning and purpose in the light of new conditions. Adaptability in a dynamic environment presents a twofold challenge, for it requires organizations to be skilled at both sensing and making sense.

Sensing, or noticing potentially important messages in the environment, is problematic because the organization is simultaneously interacting with many different parts of the environment, and because almost every part of the environment is interconnected with other parts in complex and unpredictable ways. Organizations scan the environment broadly in order to be able to recognize trends and issues that will impact the organization significantly. A detailed analysis of the theory and practice of how organizations scan the environment concluded that scanning can be made more effective if it is systematic, thorough, participatory, and integrative (Choo 2002). The core process of scanning is information management—casting a wide information net by involving as many participants as possible to act as sensors and systematically winnowing and aggregating gathered information into a useable knowledge base.

Making sense, or constructing meaning from what has been sensed about the environment, is problematic because information about the environment is ambiguous and therefore subject to multiple interpretations. Forming a plausible interpretation is hard because each person sees different parts of the environment as interesting, depending on the individual's values, position, and experience. Whereas sensing or scanning is gathering sufficient information to reduce environmental uncertainty, sense making involves choosing and agreeing on a set of meanings or interpretations to reduce ambiguity. Unlike scanning, which can be designed as a systematic and structured activity, sense making is inherently a fluid, open, disorderly, social process. The basic mode of sense making is discourse, for it is through talk that organizational members find out what others think, and it is through talk that people persuade and negotiate their points of view. Sense making is further complicated by the possibility that the organization can enter into the environment in order to produce, influence, or modify parts of it (as in the example of the Californian wineries). In a manner of speaking, the organization that actively enacts its environment is involved in giving rather than making sense.

Organizational sense making has been defined in various ways by different researchers. March and Olsen (1976) saw sense making as part of experiential learning in which "individuals and organizations make sense of their experience and modify behavior in terms of their interpretations" (p. 56). Starbuck and Milliken (1988a) observed that "sensemaking has many distinct aspects—comprehending, understanding, explaining, attributing, extrapolating, and predicting, at least. . . . What is common to these processes is that they involve placing stimuli into frameworks (or schemata) that make sense of the stimuli" (p. 51). Sense making is sometimes thought of as belonging to a larger process of organizational adaptation that also includes scanning the environment, interpreting, and developing responses. In this vein, Thomas, Clark, and Gioia (1993) write that sense making "involves the reciprocal interaction of information seek-ing, meaning ascription, and action" and that "each element of this sensemaking process is presumed to have some relationship to performance" (p. 240).

This chapter is divided into five sections. Section I explores the nature of organizational sense making, identifying the properties that distinguish sense making as a unique process. Section II describes the belief- and action-driven processes that result in sense making as well as the behaviors of enactment, selection, and retention that form the sense-making recipe. Section III discusses the cognitive, cultural, and communication strategies that create shared meaning and consensus in organizations so that collective action is possible and purpose-ful. Section IV introduces the idea of a cognitive theory of the firm. Section V focuses on how information is acquired, processed, and used in sense making in terms of cognitive, affective, and situational variables.

I. THE NATURE OF ORGANIZATIONAL SENSE MAKING

Drawing together the various discussions of sense making in the research litera-ture, Weick (1995) identifies seven distinguishing properties of sense making as an organizational process. In his view, sense making is understood as a pro-cess that is

1. grounded in identity construction

2. retrospective

3. enactive of sensible environments

4. social

5. ongoing

6. focused on and by extracted cues

7. driven by plausibility rather than accuracy.

(Weick 1995, p. 17)

Sense making is grounded in identity construction. Sense making is neces-sary for the individual to maintain a consistent self-conception and is often initi-ated when the individual fails to confirm self-identity. The environment is like a mirror into which people project themselves and observe the consequences in order to learn about their identities. This projection is not one-way nor passive, for people simultaneously try to shape and react to the environments they face—even as they deduce their identity from the behavior of others toward them, they also try to influence this behavior. Thus, what the situation means is determined by the identity that the individual adopts in dealing with it.

Sense making is retrospective. The sense-making individual attends to events that have already taken place. She does so from a specific point in time, so that what is occurring at that moment will affect what she is likely to notice as she casts this backward glance. Furthermore, because the event has already elapsed, the individual has to rely on a memory trace of the event, which may or may not be accurate. In retrospective sense making, the main problem is to select a plausible meaning from several alternative meanings in order to make sense of past events. For this, the individual needs values and priorities to clarify what is important and therefore meaningful in the elapsed experience.

Sense making is enactive. In sense making, people in organizations often produce part of the environment that they face. Weick calls this process *enactment.* One way people enact is by breaking up streams of experience into packets which they then label with categories. By bracketing experience, people endow objects and events with cognitive value in their minds, thus providing the raw material for sense making. Another way that organizations enact is to undertake actions that actually result in physical or structural changes in the environment that they are relating to, as in the case of the Californian wineries. Enactment implies that action is a precondition for sense making, as, for example, "when the action of saying makes it possible for people to then see what they think" (Weick 1995, p. 30).

Sense making is social. All sense making is done in social groups of more than one individual. Even when a person appears to be alone, her sense making will take into account the reactions of others not physically present but who will be affected or whose reactions will be important. More often than not, sense making occurs in groups of people engaged in talk, discourse, and conversation which become the media for social construction.

Sense making is ongoing. Sense making never starts or stops but is continuous in the flow of activities and projects that constitute organizational life. From this continuous stream, people isolate packets of experience for labeling and reflection, and the way they do this selection is based on the perceived salience induced by the particular activities or projects they are working on at the time. Although sense making does not stop, it can be interrupted. Interruptions invoke emotional responses which then influence the sense-making process.

Sense making is focused on and by extracted cues. Extracted cues are "simple, familiar structures that are seeds from which people develop a larger sense of what may be occurring" (Weick 1995, p. 50). They provide points of reference or starting nodes from which ideas may be linked and connected into networks of meaning. The extraction of cues is the result of scanning, search, or noticing. The interpretation of cues depends on the organizational context—a context which can bind people to actions, determine the relevance of information, and impose norms and expectations on what explanations are acceptable (Salancik and Pfeffer 1978).

Sense making is driven by plausibility rather than accuracy. People behave pragmatically when sense making, favoring plausibility over accuracy when they construct accounts of what is going on. The reason is that "in an equivocal, postmodern world, infused with the politics of interpretation and conflicting interests and inhabited by people with multiple shifting identities, an obsession with accuracy seems fruitless, and not of much practical help, either" (Weick 1995, p. 61). Besides, whenever organizational action is time constrained, managers would tend to trade off accuracy for speed.

As a terse summary, one may say that sense making is a continuous, social process in which individuals look at elapsed events, bracket packets of experience, and select particular points of reference to weave patterns of meaning. The result of sense making is an enacted or meaningful environment that is a reasonable and socially credible rendering of what is taking place. The central problem in sense making is how to reduce or resolve ambiguity and how to develop shared meanings so that the organization may act collectively.

Sense Making: Weick and Dervin

In information science, Brenda Dervin and her associates have developed an influential model of sense making based on a significant body of theoretical and empirical work. We discussed her model in Chapter 2, where we noted that the model analyzes information seeking and use in terms of the triangle of "situation—gap—use" as posed by these questions: (1) What in your situation is stopping you from moving forward? (2) What questions or confusions do you have? (3) What kind of help do you hope to get? (Dervin and Clark 1987).

There are general similarities between the seven properties of sense making described by Weick and the sense-making metaphor of Dervin. Dervin sees the individual as continually making sense as she moves through time and space in an ongoing life-journey. Weick also sees sense making as ongoing: being continuous in the flow of activities and projects that constitute organizational life (see last section). Dervin then argues that from time to time, movement is stopped in a *situation* by the perception of some kind of cognitive gap. Movement forward is blocked by a gap in the path she is traveling on when she is temporarily unable to make sense of her situation. This is related to Weick's discussion of how in sense making, people focus on extracted cues and seek to maintain identity. The extraction of cues (what information to focus on) depends on the organizational context (or *situation,* in Dervin's terminology). Weick also suggests that sense making is often initiated when the individual fails to confirm self identity.

Dervin observes that information is sought and processed in a manner that is influenced by the individual's perception of the *gap* and how she wants the information to help. This is analogous to Weick's view of sense making as being enactive: people often construct part of the environment that they face by bracketing experience, endowing objects and events with cognitive value in their minds.

The third element in Dervin's model is information *use,* particularly the way that people want the information to help in order for them to bridge the cognitive gap and continue with their journey. This pragmatic quality is also an important aspect of Weick's conceptualization of sense making. He sees people behaving practically when sense making, favoring plausibility over accuracy when processing information.

Two other properties of sense making identified by Weick also find parallels in Dervin's model. First, Weick views sense making as inherently retrospective, where people attend to events that have taken place. Dervin shares this inherently diachronic perspective when she suggests that "Every moment of sense-making is anchored at the intersection of horizons—past (histories, memories, and narratives), present (current conditions, material, and experiential), and future (hopes, dreams, plans, and trajectories" (Dervin and Frenette 2001, p. 239). Second, Weick argues that all sense making is social, even when a person is thinking alone. Again, Dervin's model assumes that "every sense-maker is inherently a social theorist. Ordinary human beings are assumed to be capable of discussing the connections they see . . . between self and others, and between self and society" (Dervin and Frenette 2001, p. 240).

We may attempt a description of organizational sense making using the language of both Dervin and Weick as follows. People encounter a break or gap in the flow of organizational experience that requires new sense to be made. They construct new meaning by selecting from the information available. The information selected depends on their enactment or perception of the cognitive or gap; and this is in turn influenced by their retrospective recall of past experience and by the particular conditions or extracted cues that define the current gap. Information use is pragmatic: the ability to move forward is often sufficient or even more important than securing the most-accurate information.

How Managers Think

Over a period of three years, Isenberg (1984, 1986a, 1987) studied the thinking processes of managers by analyzing data from many sources: managers' think-aloud protocols collected while they were at work, managers' and students' think-aloud protocols in solving a business case, in-depth interviews with managers, and on-the-job observations. Eighteen senior managers, including three chief executives and thirteen divisional general managers from ten corporations, were studied in depth, with an additional number of senior managers participating in the interviews only. Overall, the studies led Isenberg (1986a, b) to conclude that managers develop plausible, as opposed to necessarily accurate, models of their situations, and that managers develop and efficiently use knowledge structures that guide how they recognize, explain, and plan. *Plausible reasoning* is a central thinking process for managers because they function in an environment of continuous change and uncertainty, and they are often required to act in order to ensure the ongoing viability of the organization. Isenberg gives an instance from his field observations:

> For example, one general manager received a phone message from a product expediter in a sister division that purchased products from the general manager's own division. The general manager surmised that the expediter could have been calling for one of two reasons: to say something about either price or delivery time

on a specific production run. The surmise was based on previous experience
with the particular expediter, knowledge that the run was late, and the general
manager's impression that he had never interacted with the expediter around any
other issue. Before returning the call, the general manager walked by his marketing
manager's office and asked a marketing person why he thought the expediter
called. He received the answer "Price." The general manager then returned the call.
Note that the reasoning process rapidly limited the number of hypotheses for the
general manager to test and that although the answer constituted a weak test of his
hypothesis, the answer considerably increased the manager's certainty with
minimal effort and minimal risk. The increase in certainty was enough for him
to go back and return the phone call with an idea already developed and for how
to discuss price with the expediter. It is this latter point that is the critical one:
plausible reasoning helps the manager increase his or her certainty to the point of
feasible action. (Isenberg 1986a, p. 247)

Again, there are close similarities between the enactment process and the
model of plausible reasoning developed by Isenberg (1986a, b). Like Weick,
Isenberg emphasizes that managerial thinking and action are not separate or sequential activities. Rather than thinking first before doing, many managers think
while doing, so that thinking is inextricably tied to action in what Isenberg has
called *thinking/acting cycles* (Isenberg 1984). This allows managers to act when
information or understanding is incomplete, and furthermore, by reflecting on the
results of their action, managers can often derive new insight and reduce uncertainty. Based on his field studies, Isenberg conceptualized the plausible reasoning
process used by managers in planning and implementing action as a sequence of
four steps:

1. The manager needs to develop a different understanding of a phenomenon, often due to an experience of surprise.

2. The manager tries to take advantage of the data he or she already has in
   order to speculate about the new situation. Each speculation is tested
   against data and assumptions that already exist, and the search for new
   data at this point is confined to search in long-term memory.

3. A very selective external search for information is engaged in, particularly in order to confirm one or more of the speculations, although dis-
   confirmation may also occur. The goal of the search at this point is to
   achieve a degree of certainty that will allow the manager to proceed
   to step four at minimal cost and minimal risk.

4. The manager engages in action in the face of incomplete but tentative understanding of the situation and uses the feedback of his or her actions to
   complete the understanding.

(Isenberg 1986a, pp. 247–48)

As we shall see, these steps fit well with the enactment-selection framework
proposed by Weick that we introduce next.

II. ORGANIZATIONAL PROCESSES
OF SENSE MAKING

In this section, we describe the processes by which organizations make sense of their environments, their identities, and their actions. We begin with a discussion of the enactment process by which people in organizations bracket experience, select meanings, and retain sensible interpretations. We then illustrate the enactment process with a case study of the Scottish knitwear industry. The ensuing subsections discuss two other sets of organizational sense-making processes that are complementary: belief-driven processes and action-driven processes.

Sense Making as Enactment, Selection, Retention

Weick (1979b) encapsulates the main sense-making recipe in the question: "How can I know what I think until I see what I say?" (The quote is from Graham Wallas's *The Art of Thought,* in which the author wrote "The little girl had the making of a poet in her who, being told to be sure of her meaning before she spoke, said: 'How can I know what I think till I see what I say?' " [Wallas 1926, p. 106].) The recipe suggests that people in organizations are continually engaged in talk in order to find out what they are thinking and to construct interpretations of what they are doing. The recipe is executed in connected sequences of enactment → selection → retention. We briefly introduced these processes in Chapter 1, but because they constitute the main routines of sense making, we elaborate here on how they work and illustrate them with an extended example. For each process we examine the inputs, transformation processes, and outcomes (Table 3.1).

Enactment is the process by which individuals in an organization actively create the environments which they face and which they then attend to. The

TABLE 3-1. The sense-making recipe (Adapted from Weick 1979b).

	Information Inputs	*Processes*	*Information Outcomes*
Enactment	• Raw data from the environment	• Bracket raw data • Create features in the environment to attend to	• Equivocal data as raw data for sense making
Selection	• Equivocal data from enactment process • Enacted interpretations that worked before	• Select plausible interpretations based on "best fit" with past understandings	• Enacted, meaningful environment
Retention	• Enacted environment from selection process	• Store enacted environment as product of successful sense making	• Interpretations available for use in future sense making

enactment process begins as a result of noticing some change or discrepancy in the flow of experience. (Weick [1979b] included another process that precedes enactment called *ecological change,* which refers to breaks or changes in the flow of experience that provide the occasion for sense making.) Raw data about these environmental changes form the input to the process. Individuals isolate some of these changes for closer attention by bracketing and labeling portions of the experience or by taking some action to create features of the environment to attend to. In this way, people construct, reconfigure, highlight, as well as over-look many "objective" features of their surroundings. Often, people "actively *put* things out there that they then perceive and negotiate about perceiving. It is that initial implanting of reality that is preserved by the word *enactment*" (Weick 1979b, pp. 164–65, italics in original). The output of enactment is a set of equiv-ocal, uninterpreted raw data that supplies the base material for the other sense-making processes.

Enactment does not take place in a social vacuum. Organizations influence what people notice in their actions and talk; they define assumptions and cate-gories that people treat as part of their own beliefs. To the extent that enactment is guided by retained assumptions and routines, sense making is a conservative force, what Weick (2001, p. 176) calls an "infrastructure of organizational inertia." Studies in information seeking have also noted a strong inclination for people to notice and emphasize information that confirms prior understandings. Despite these tendencies, organizational actions do often lead to unanticipated effects, and it is these surprising consequences that provide the impetus for new ways of seeing and noticing.

Selection is the process by which people in an organization generate answers to the question "What's going on here?" (Weick 1979b). What the selection process chooses are the meanings that can be imposed on the equivocal data from the enactment process. Possible meanings come from meanings and interpreta-tions that have proven sensible in the past, as well as from "patterns implicit in the enactments themselves" (Weick 1979b, p. 175). Past interpretations are used as templates that are laid over current data in order to reveal plausible configurations. Selection, based on an assessment of the degree of fit, is necessary because many of the possible meanings would be inapplicable or inconsistent with the current data. The result of the selection process is an enacted environment that is mean-ingful in that it provides a cause-and-effect explanation of what is taking place.

The use of the label *selection* here is deliberate: it is intended to suggest an evolutionary dynamic in the way enacted interpretations compete for fitness with past understandings. In organization theories based on evolutionary models, "selection occurs when an external environment of financial resources and com-petitors sorts among variations in organizational forms and retains those that make more efficient use of resources. In sense making, selection occurs when an enacted environment of plausible stories from the past sorts among variations in current accounts of enactments and retains those that best fit with prior understandings of plausibility" (Weick 2001, p. 237). Just as some variations in organizational forms make better use of economic resources and thrive, some variations in accounts of enactment make better use of preexisting understandings of plausibility and survive: "In both cases, selection involves editing, pruning, winnowing. In both cases, there is an editor in the form of scarce resources, the scarcity being either financial resources or meanings judged to be plausible" (p. 237).

Retention is the process by which the products of successful sense making, that is, enacted or meaningful environments, are stored so that they may be retrieved on future occasions as possible meanings to be imposed on new equivocal situations. Retained meanings are stored as enacted environments that are "a punctuated and connected summary of a previously equivocal display" (Weick 1979b, p. 131) or as cause maps, often in narrative form, that "identify and label variables, and connect the variables in causal relationships" (p. 132). These retained meanings become the source of organizational culture and strategy and the basis of individual identities and continuities.

Significantly, a certain amount of ambiguity is preserved in these stored meanings. Signals about changes in the environment are filtered through enactment and selection so that some messages are overlooked, others forgotten. The residual ambiguity allows people, when enacting new changes, to "notice some of what was previously overlooked and overlook some of what was previously noticed" (Weick 2001, p. 305), thereby reconfiguring the information space for new learning.

Weick (2001) argues that it is important for organizations to hold their retained meanings lightly, especially in a changing world that is hard to know, much less predict. While retained meanings provide useful guidance from the past in order to start action, past guidance needs to be tempered with alertness toward the unusual and the unexpected. Thus, sense making is also a constant "struggle for alertness":

> The struggle is with the temptation to normalize unusual events, the temptation to
> search for confirmation rather than disconfirmation, the temptation to feel that one
> has experienced it all and there are no surprises left. The premium in business
> organizations on "aggressive confidence" tends to dull alertness and to encourage
> imposing the same sense on a changing world. It's tough to discount hard-won
> lessons of experience. Tough, but necessary. (Weick 2001, pp. 357–58)

Organizations need to be mindful of the bias to base *both* selection and enactment on past meanings: using interpretations that have worked before and acting in ways that have worked before. Weick (2001) suggests that an alert, flexible use of retained knowledge occurs when past meanings guide either selection or enactment, but not both.

We can now see how the sense-making recipe of "How can I know what I think until I see what I say?" is mirrored in the enactment-selection-retention sequence—enactment may be compared with "saying" or doing; selection with "seeing"; and retention with "thinking" or remembering. Thus: "How can I know what I think [retention] until I see [selection] what I say [or do = enactment]?" The three processes interact so that they amplify or attenuate the salience of changes in the environment and accelerate or constrain the processing of information cues that influence the choice of meaningful interpretations and the retention of enacted meanings. Weick sees the enactment-selection-retention sequence as both a recipe for organizing and a recipe for sense making:

> read as a recipe for organizing, we could say that when something unexpected occurs and there is an *ecological change,* people often *enact* something, *select* portions of the enactment to take seriously, and *retain* some meaning of what they enacted. Subsequently, they may then apply or alter what they retain in their next enactments and selections. Read as a recipe for sensemaking, we could say that when people in an *ongoing social setting* experience an interruption, they often *enact* something, *retrospectively* notice meaningful *cues* in what they previously enacted, interpret and retain meaningful versions of what the cues mean for their individual and collective *identity,* and apply or alter these *plausible* meanings in subsequent enactment and retrospective noticing. (Weick 2001, p. 95)

Sense Making in the Scottish Knitwear Industry

In the mid-1980s, Scottish knitwear manufacturers accounted for nearly half of total British exports in knitted outerwear and enjoyed significantly higher profitability levels than other British knitwear producers (Baden-Fuller et al. 1987). The Scottish knitwear manufacturers included companies such as Ballantyne, Cooper & Rowe, Dalkeith/Jaeger, Lyle & Scott, and Pringle, which produced knitted outerwear under their own brand names using high-quality Scottish or cashmere yarn. They manufactured knitwear by combining various colored yarns into a garment whose size and shape were determined on the knitting machine. This labor-intensive technique produced "fully-fashioned" knitwear and was quite different from the "cut-and-sew" technique which allowed larger scales of production but resulted in lower-quality products and more unused yarn so that it was unsuitable for the expensive cashmere material. The 1980s saw all the companies greatly extending their product ranges, with most producers each manufacturing thousands of varieties of sweaters. Although a few of the larger firms had small internal design departments, all the firms hired outside design consultants to help create new products. Independent agents who received commissions brokered the sale of the finished garments to retail stores all over the world. These agents were contractually barred from representing other competing brands of knitwear. Retail stores were typically large department stores and specialty boutiques which sold classic, expensive clothing to the carriage trade. Through extensive interviews with top managers from more than a third of the Scottish knitwear manufacturers located in the border region of Scotland, Porac, Thomas, and Baden-Fuller (1989) were able to uncover some core beliefs underlying the mental models used by the top managers to understand their firms' competitive environment. One set of beliefs concerned how the firms established their own distinctive *market identity,* while another set determined how they dealt with other parties in the *transactional network* (the producers, agents, retailers, and consumers).

Making Sense of Market Identity. Sense making was the process by which the firms studied, discovered, or invented their self-identities, their collective identity, and the perceived identities of their customers and competitors. The firms defined their business as the production of top-quality cashmere pullover and cardigan sweaters and perceived that their customers were individuals in the top 2–5 percent income bracket of any given country (Porac et al. 1989). Three managing directors expressed this belief thus (quoted in Porac et al. 1989, p. 406):

> We're top-end. We're not interested in Marks & Spencer's or anybody other than the top 2 per cent in any country.

> If people are looking for knitwear, the top 5 per cent, we are the segment they will look to.

> We are in the market where customers imply they want the best. Pure and simple. People must want the best.

This emphasis on exclusiveness and high quality also colors their perception of the competition (quoted in Porac et al. 1989, p. 407):

> Quite honestly, there is not a lot of competition. The Italian industry is a different industry from ours. The Asian industry is a different industry from ours. . . . Basically it's pullovers and cardigans. It's classic type garments. In my opinion, it is quite clearly defined that people expect to buy the best cashmere pullovers from Scotland.

> The majority of our competitors are either within our own group, or within our own town. . . . We don't try to be high fashion like the Italians. We call ourselves "classical elegance."

The collective market identity shared by the group of knitwear manufacturers was therefore based on the following core beliefs: that they made the best cashmere knitwear in the world, that their customers were high-income earners who bought premium quality, and that they had no significant competition from outside the group because of their unique capabilities. Their collective competitive strategy was to focus narrowly on a small segment of the market that wanted established quality and classical appeal. This strategy was evolved rather than the result of deliberate planning or detailed market research, as we shall see.

Enacting the Transactional Network. The transactional network consists of the producers, agents, retailers, and customers who make up the value-chain of the knitwear business. The highly interdependent and mutually reinforcing relationships between these groups constrained the generation and flow of information as well as the exploration of meanings and choices. As a result, the transactional network also became an enactment network through which participants created and confirmed a shared interpretation of their competitive position. The Scottish knitwear producers secure contracts with retail shops through agents. Agents are selected because their non-knitwear product representations fit in well with the "classical elegance" image that the Scottish manufacturers wish to project. Selected agents then negotiate with retail shops that sell classically designed clothing. These retail shops are in turn patronized by customers whose tastes are inclined toward traditional knitwear products. Notice how the participants in this transactional network preselect each other as compatible business partners and by doing so mutually reinforce and sustain the collective belief that the Scottish knitwear manufacturers sell garments of classical elegance. The self-defining and self-reinforcing interactions of the network clearly illustrate the dynamics of the enactment-selection-retention sequence of the sense-making recipe:

> The self-definition as a producer of "high quality fully-fashioned knitwear" leads to the selection of agents selling classically designed clothes, who are suppliers of shops merchandising classic garments to consumers with a limited range of preferences for "classical elegance." Market cues from consumers are filtered back through informal network channels and provide the Scottish firms with information primarily about preferences for variations on classically designed garments. Such filtered information is assimilated into the existing business definition, and focuses the attention of managers on a limited set of possible product offerings. In doing so, both the business definition and the competitive space it implies are reinforced, and the Scottish firms use their finite psychological and material resources to compete with each other in the fully-fashioned classic knitwear sector. (Porac et al. 1989, p. 409)

Enactment takes place as the producers, agents, retailers, and customers act and think together to bracket, label, and influence their environment and experience. Labels used to bracket salient experience included phrases used by the managers such as "friendly competition," "Scottish quality," "classical elegance," "crowd in Hong Kong that manufactures for Ralph Lauren," and so on. Enactment is ongoing as it feeds on filtered information generated by like-minded others in the transaction network. Selection takes place when the participants choose and maintain the interpretation that has been sensible for that industry for many years—that they are in the business of selling high-quality knitted outerwear to discerning high-income customers. Retention takes place as the participants continue to store, retrieve, and reapply interpretations that they have enacted to make sense of any changes in their business environment. For example, the Scottish manufacturers have historically used the traditional but labor-intensive methods of hand finishing, partly because they produced high-quality sweaters, but also because the manufacturers had available a pool of workers skilled in hand finishing. Unfortunately, hand finishing was not as efficient as the more modern manufacturing techniques that were increasingly being adopted by many domestic and foreign competitors to produce lower-cost garments. In deciding to continue with the use of the less-efficient method of hand finishing, the Scottish manufacturers were re-selecting and retaining their enacted interpretation that they were producers of high-quality knitwear that were sold to customers wanting premium quality garments. The sense-making cycle invoked here shows that enactment is the result of the simultaneous blending of action making and meaning making.

Belief- and Action-Driven Processes

Given that each individual sees different parts of the environment as interesting and overlays different interpretations on that data, the question is, How do people in organizational groups link their thoughts and perceptions so that some form of collective action is possible? Weick (1995) suggests that organizations achieve this through belief-driven processes *and* action-driven processes:

> Sensemaking can begin with beliefs and take the form of arguing and expecting. Or sensemaking can begin with actions and take the form of committing or manipulating. In all four cases, people make do with whatever beliefs or actions they start with. Sensemaking is an effort to tie beliefs and actions more closely together as when arguments lead to consensus on action, clarified expectations pave the way for confirming actions, committed actions uncover acceptable justifications for their occurrence, or bold actions simplify the world and make it clearer what is going on and what it means. In each of these cases, sensemaking involves taking whatever is clearer, whether it be a belief or an action, and linking it with that which is less clear. These are fundamental operations of sensemaking. Two elements, a belief and an action, are related. The activities of relating are the sensemaking process. The outcome of such a process is a unit of meaning, two connected elements. And the connected elements are beliefs and actions tied together by socially acceptable implications. (Weick 1995, p. 135)

Belief-Driven Processes. Belief-driven processes are those in which groups of people negotiate meaning around an initial set of sufficiently clear and plausible cues and predispositions by connecting more and more small pieces of information into larger structures of meaning (Table 3-2). When cues appear "similar" in their fit with each other and with existing frames of reference, the process is likely to be one based on expecting. When cues and beliefs are contradictory, the process may be based on arguing. *Arguing* is a process by which people move from one initial idea to the selection of another through reasoned discourse that involves drawing inferences from existing beliefs and justifying those inferences in the face of other competing claims (Brockeriede 1974). This process of developing, presenting, comparing, and evaluating explanations in a group often leads members to discover new explanations or to deepen their insights on existing ones. Arguing provides people with a socially acceptable procedure to debate the ambivalence and contradiction that is inherent in most issues. Arguing as reasoned debate does not imply flaring tempers and pounding

TABLE 3-2. Organizational sense-making processes.

Belief-Driven Processes ↕ **Action-Driven Processes**	**Arguing**	Growing meaning by connecting the contradictory
	Expecting	Growing meaning by connecting the similar
	Committing	Creating meaning to justify actions high in choice, visibility, and irrevocability
	Manipulating	Creating meaning to explain actions taken to make things happen

fists, the occurrence of which would in fact undermine discussion. The most common forum for the work of arguing is in meetings. Schwartzman (1987, 1989) views meetings as "sense makers" that define and represent the social entities and relationships that establish meaning and identity for its participants. Arguing as sense making allows people in organizations to resolve or reduce ambiguity, discover new goals, enhance the quality of available information, and clarify new ideas.

Expecting is the other belief-driven process by which people in organizations apply beliefs as expectations to guide and constrain the selection of salient information and the choice of plausible interpretations. Whereas arguments typically are tentative proposals that need to be elaborated or tested with others, expectations are often more strongly held than arguments, and people tend to be more interested in confirming than in contradicting them. In many cases, expectations can have a powerful effect on the way individuals filter information and interpretations, so much so that self-fulfilling prophecies become a fundamental act of sense making (Weick 1995). Initially, prophecies provide the minimal structures around which new information can coalesce. People then actively connect data with their prophecies based on the beliefs that they hold. In doing so, people tend to seek out confirmatory evidence, ignore or devalue contradictory news, and cling on as far as possible to their initial hypotheses. Expecting and expectations thus provide people with a sense of stability and social order and with a set of cognitive structures within which they can find and construct meaning.

Action-Driven Processes. Action-driven processes are those in which groups of people grow webs of meaning around their actions, commitments, or manipulations by creating or modifying cognitive structures that give significance to these behaviors (Table 3-2). Two kinds of action can drive sense making: committing actions for which a person or group is responsible and manipulating actions taken by a person or group that make an actual change in the environment (Weick 1995). *Committing* becomes important if, in situations when behaviors and beliefs contradict each other, it is easier to change the beliefs than the behaviors. Behavior becomes binding and hard to change when the behavior is explicit (evidence exists that the act took place), public (witnesses saw the act), and irrevocable (act is irreversible) (Kiesler 1971). Furthermore, if the person was also seen to have performed the action deliberately, with substantial effort and few external demands, then the act occurred because the person chose to do it and is therefore responsible for it. Commitments form a convenient framework for organizing information and perceptions. An instinctive reaction is to pigeonhole incoming information according to whether it supports the committed action, opposes it, or is irrelevant to it. In this way, committing influences sense making by directing attention, noticing new features, and selecting data.

Manipulating is the other action-driven process by which people in the organization take actions that lead to changes in the environment that in turn become some of the constraints for their own sense making. Common methods of manipulation include constructing desirable niches, negotiating domains, forming coalitions, educating clients and employees, advertising to potential clients and customers, and resolving conflicts (Hedberg, Nystrom, and Starbuck 1976). Manipulating brings clarity to sense making, since by making things happen, people can latch on to these created events and explain them as a way to make better sense of what is taking place. Whereas committing makes new sense by justifying the action itself, manipulating does the same by explaining the meanings of the consequences of the action taken.

The belief- and action-driven processes of sense making are compared in Table 3-2. Arguing is a belief-driven process that grows meaning by connecting and resolving contradictory information and perceptions. Expecting also uses beliefs embedded in anticipations or prophecies to grow meaning by connecting and selecting information that is compatible with expectations. Committing is an action-driven process that creates meaning through justifying actions that have been taken which are deliberate, visible, and hard to reverse. Manipulating creates meaning by explaining the consequences of actively intruding into and changing the environment. It is clear that both beliefs and actions can serve as reference points for meaning-generation, and that once again the essence of sense making is in the blending together of cognitive structures and active choices to construct reality.

Nantes "Toxic Cloud" Crisis

To understand how actions and beliefs interact in the sense-making process, we look at a case that shows contrasting interpretations constructed by two groups grappling with the same phenomenon: an ominous "fire" at a warehouse containing dangerous chemicals. It illustrates how different groups engage different beliefs and actions in their sense making of the same event, and how the dynamics of information gathering and processing modulate the interplay between actions and beliefs.

On October 29th, 1987, at about 9:15 A.M., workers in a warehouse of the firm SA Loiret and Haentjens, located outside Nantes near the River Loire (France), were trying to deal with smoke coming from stored fertilizers (Vidaillet 2001). The person in charge telephoned the fire service for help, giving the product's code (15.8.22) and reporting the presence of toxic smoke.

What Happened from the Firemen's Perspective. At the fire station, the duty chief dispatched a rescue team to the site. He tried unsuccessfully to identify the product from a technical manual, but the code had changed to 15.822. He concluded that the code indicated danger rather than the product's composition.

The rescue team arrived at the scene, and the fire captain toured the warehouse. He easily identified the product (an agricultural fertilizer). He located a stock of ammonitrates and some fuel tanks. (Ammonitrate, or ammonium nitrate, is a common component of artificial fertilizers. It is also used to modify the detonation rate of explosives, such as nitroglycerin. As a strong oxidant it may cause fire or explosion upon contact with other material. It is also harmful if swallowed or inhaled.) Although ammonitrates can explode, they were stored well away from the fertilizers, in tanks that were well insulated. What the fire captain could not understand was the odd "fire," which produced neither flames nor heat but stagnant smoke. He was reluctant to use hoses due to the risk of polluting the river (as the firemen had done in the 1986 Sandoz accident in Basel). He then telephoned the duty chief at the fire station.

The duty chief recalled what he had learned during a recent training session on nuclear risks and became worried about a major catastrophe. He also refused to use water and feared that the ammonitrates might explode. He warned the authorities about a risk of explosion and suffocation. He called the colonel, his superior, and asked for reinforcements. The time was 10:30 A.M.

When the colonel arrived, he inquired about measurements taken by the antipollution unit, which showed high nitric acid levels and traces of chlorine above the warehouse. Two experts gave contradictory advice: one recommended the massive use of water, the other opposed. The colonel and some of his colleagues favored dowsing the fertilizers. Professor Boiteaux, a well-known expert and chair of toxicology at Nantes University who was contacted by the antipollution unit, also supported using water and thought pollution risks were slight. From that moment on, all action was focused on implementing this solution. At around 4 P.M. the situation was brought under control.

What Happened from the Emergency Committee's Perspective. From 10:30 A.M. onward, an emergency committee was formed at the prefecture. The committee was composed of officials used to solving problems of maintaining public order. They relied mostly on information picked up from the firemen's radio—reacting to news coming in from the firemen but not actively seeking further information. The committee noted the risks of fire and explosion. They believed that it was their responsibility to concentrate on the "cloud" and the risks it presented for the population. Focusing on information about the "toxic cloud" and the projected length of operations, it recommended that people living within one kilometer of the warehouse should stay indoors.

Later that morning, the prefect took charge of the committee. At noon an expert in water problems, who was the president of a federation of environmental associations, expressed her alarm at the risk for the population. At 12:15 P.M., experts from the regional department of industry and research arrived. At 1 P.M., the antipollution unit and firemen informed the emergency committee that a measurement made along the main route of the cloud showed a nitric acid level of 5 ppm (parts per million, a unit of measure). From then on, the committee focused its attention on interpreting the significance of this number. The prefect made a comparison with poison gas during World War I. Some committee members mentioned rules in the quarries that allowed exposure up to 25 ppm.

Meanwhile, the mobile emergency medical service had treated workers and others at the warehouse in the morning. There was evidence of poisoning from inhalation of nitrates, but the team had concluded that there was no danger for the population at large. This important information was not passed on: the medical team did not try to do so and the committee did not attempt to find it out.

Based on the risk associated with the 5 ppm measurement and favorable meteorological conditions, the prefect decided to evacuate seven districts (40,000 persons). At 2 P.M., an orderly evacuation began. At 3:30 P.M., an engineer who had been at the warehouse reported that the products involved were fertilizers and not ammonitrates. Moreover, additional measurements made in two districts exposed to the wind showed very low nitric acid levels (1 ppm and 0.5 ppm). Around 4 P.M., the deputy prefect informed the committee that the fire was almost under control. At 7 P.M., the prefect decided to end the evacuation.

Beliefs, Actions, and Information Seeking. Sense making by the firemen was to a degree action driven: the fire captain checked the warehouse, found the ammonitrates and fuel tanks, assessed their vulnerability, and was anxious about the mysterious cloud. Further action was however constrained by beliefs derived from the Sandoz accident in Basle the year before where dowsing the fire had polluted the nearby river. The duty chief also did not want to use water, based on his belief (influenced by a recent training session) that the accident could become a major catastrophe, with the ammonitrates exploding. This tension between belief and action was finally resolved with the arrival of important new information: the advice of a highly respected expert who had been approached by the antipollution unit and who held a chair at Nantes University. It was then decided to use water to put out the fire.

Sense making by the emergency committee, on the other hand, appeared to be driven more by the committee's shared belief that its main responsibility was maintaining public order and safety. Information seeking was limited and passive. The committee relied on indirect data and there was not much contact with people at the scene of the accident. In the afternoon, the committee focused on the data showing a certain level of nitric acid along the cloud's route. There was growing alarm about the danger to the population, and the prefect decided to initiate the evacuation program at 2 P.M. Two hours later the fire was almost under control, and the evacuation ended soon after. For the emergency committee, the tension between belief ("public safety") and action ("evacuation") was not reconciled because a vital piece of information was not passed along for sense making: the medical team had treated early victims and concluded that there was no danger to the population, at large.

The Nantes accident vividly illustrates how beliefs and actions are simultaneously engaged in sense making and how the availability and use of information can alter the dynamics between actions and beliefs, resulting in divergent interpretations and decisions.

III. SHARED MINDS: CONSENSUS AND CULTURE

A network of shared meanings and interpretations provide the social order, temporal continuity, and contextual clarity for members of an organization to coordinate and relate their actions. As a cognitive framework, it presents criteria for selecting, valuing, and processing information. Where information is lacking or equivocal, shared beliefs and assumptions can fill in the gaps or reduce the ambiguity sufficiently in order for organizations to be able to act. As a framework of meanings and norms, it presents expectations for relating and evaluating actions and results and defines communal identity and commitment to purpose. Although order and stability are essential for concerted action, organizations must also be able to continuously assess the validity of assumptions and beliefs, discover opportunities or threats hidden in new information, and stimulate innovation through inquiry and experimentation. As much as order and stability, organizations need variation and diversity to ensure growth and development. The basic structure of shared meanings needs to be sufficiently open and flexible to provide the space for new ideas to take hold and new responses to be enacted. Research suggests that organizations adopt meaning-making and meaning-sharing strategies to build consensus while accommodating diversity.

Managing Consensus Through Shared Meaning

Given that individuals and groups differ in their histories, values, and sense-making styles, how do shared meanings then emerge from such heterogeneity? While much research is still needed, the available evidence suggests two general strategies that organizations use to achieve an actionable level of consensus: tapping into *shared cognitive structures* or collective knowledge bases that guide the processing of information as well as the making of action; and engaging in *communication behaviors* that establish agreement on action implications but at the same time retain a residual amount of ambiguity to accommodate differing interpretations. As examples of shared cognitive structures, we present research on the concepts of cognitive consensus and industry recipe. As examples of communication behaviors, we discuss the ideas of equifinal meanings and interpretation framing.

Shared Cognition: Cognitive Consensus. Some researchers have suggested that organizations develop a certain level of *cognitive consensuality* that makes possible a reasonable degree of common understanding for collective action. Consensuality in this case does not require complete agreement, but that "individuals have achieved a certain similarity in the way they process and evaluate information" (Gioia and Sims 1986, p. 8). It does imply that "there is a reasonable amount of implicit agreement among organization members as to the appropriate meaning of information or events. This leads to consensual cognitive scripts prescribing behavior and action (which are also implicitly agreed to as appropriate by organizational members)" (Finney and Mitroff 1986, p. 320). In an attempt to determine whether cognitive scripts underlie common organizational events, Gioia, Donnellon, and Sims (1989) analyzed videotaped data collected from 96 simulated appraisals conducted by 24 experienced middle- and upper-level managers interacting with 4 different subordinates drawn from a group of business administration students. The results revealed a common behavioral script that suggested the existence of a consensual cognitive script for enacting the appraisal interviews. The use of consensual structures and scripts still allows for differences in individual behavior based on personal styles and preferences. For example, a general cognitive script in an organization may require that business plans be supported by statistical data and analysis. One manager may choose to prepare the business plan working alone, while another manager may prefer to delegate the plan to subordinates; in both cases, a business plan bolstered by statistical analysis is produced that is in line with the script. The individual managers themselves have in fact superimposed their personal behavioral scripts over the general script of how to prepare statistical business plans: "the result is schemas and scripts superimposed on schemas and scripts—that is, meaning and action superimposed on meaning and action. This complex and interactive set of meanings directs the enactment of behavior by the individual, the group, and ultimately the organization" (Finney and Mitroff 1986, p. 322). At the same time, consensuality and concerted action are enacted for a common purpose: they are necessarily tenuous constructions that are subject to revision or dissolution when the perception of reality changes (Gioia 1986).

Shared Cognition: Industry Recipe. In order to develop meaning and draw conclusions from unclear and uncertain information, members of the organization do not directly use the methods of logical analysis or decision making to process information but must first exercise human judgment and creative thinking to deal with the information uncertainty. From his field study of three industries, Spender (1989) observed that firms in the same industry share a body of knowledge and beliefs that is used to cope with uncertainty. Following Alfred Schutz, who saw individuals using "recipes," or shared patterns of beliefs to make sense of everyday experience, Spender called the shared knowledge the "industry recipe":

> I suggest that the burdens and risks of exercising judgment cause managers to cast around for guidance. I hypothesize that they draw their primary support from other managers operating in the same industry. There is no simple imitation involved here. These managers do not seek support that is substantive, detailed or prescriptive, a specific formula which tells them precisely what to do. They know well enough that other firms are in different circumstances and may well be pursuing different policies. I hypothesize that the imitation is at an extremely intellectual level, a sharing of those judgments which give organizational data their meaning. In this way the managers adopt a way of looking at their situations that is widely shared within their industry. I call this pattern of judgments the industry's "recipe." I argue that the recipe is an unintended consequence of managers' need to communicate, because of their uncertainties, by word and example within the industry. The recipe develops a context and experience bound synthesis of the knowledge the industry considers managers need to have in order to acquire an adequate conceptual grasp of their firms. (Spender 1989, p. 188)

From his study of seven major dairies in London and Manchester in the United Kingdom, Spender identified 14 constructs that composed the dairy industry recipe. For example, the recipe indicates that the dairymen need to increase the volume demand of milk in the distribution network (construct 1. increasing gallonage), that gallonage can be increased by supplying milk to smaller retailers as well as bottled milk buyers who purchase in bulk (2. expanding the business), that friendly relations be maintained with the buyers which are family-owned businesses (3. awareness of other retailers' positions), that gallonage can also be expanded by increasing the length and the number of drop points in the milk rounds (4. improving the rounds), and by increasing either the number of customers or the amount of milk delivered to existing customers (5. increasing the drop density), and so on. For an individual firm, the industry recipe enables collective action while accommodating interpretive variations. While it offers general guidance about what is important and appropriate behavior, the recipe is ambiguous enough for individual firms to adapt to their particular situations and preferences.

Communication Behaviors: Equifinal Meanings. In order to reconcile diversity with coordination, organizations develop communication behaviors that allow members of a group to broaden their ideas to accommodate multiple interpretations that are nevertheless consistent with each other in their behavioral implications. For example, Donnellon, Gray, and Bougon (1986) found that "in the absence of shared meaning, organized action is made possible by the shared repertoire of communication behaviors group members use while in the process of developing *equifinal meanings* for their joint experience. . . . Equifinal meanings, then, are interpretations that are dissimilar but that have similar behavioral implications" (p. 44). Donnellon et al. identified four communication mechanisms for achieving equifinal meanings: metaphor, logical argument, affect modulation, and linguistic indirection. Metaphors can reconcile differences in meaning because they allow people to understand and experience one kind of thing in terms of another, and so give new meaning to their actions and beliefs (Lakoff and Johnson 1980). Logical arguments can be used in situations of disagreement to move another party to agreement through incremental steps. Affect modulation evokes feelings through the use of voice, gesture, and emotion-laden words to cause the redefinition of a situation. Linguistic indirection employs the passive voice and broad or imprecise language to create equivocality and so play down sources of dissent. Donnellon et al. (1986) observed that metaphors are particularly effective in generating equifinal meanings because their vagueness allows the different parties to maintain their own interpretations while providing common ground for communal behavior. The study found that in a simulated organization, members of one department eventually agreed to a strike action as a response to planned layoffs only after the meaning of striking was enlarged through the use of the metaphor "Striking is principled behavior." In the same study, group members used logical argument and affect modulation to garner support for a selected interpretation of another department's actions, while linguistic indirection helped to motivate the search for equifinal meanings.

Communication Behaviors: Interpretation Framing. Just as the process of sharing meaning is a complex communication activity with many patterns of behavior, the concept of shared meaning itself can have more than one dimension. If shared meaning is multifaceted, then collective action can take place as long as there is consensus around one or more (but not necessarily all) of the multiple dimensions. Fiol (1994) suggests that shared meaning can reside in the *content* of the interpretation as well as in the *framing* of the interpretation. Content is reflected in the categories or labels that people use to define what is expressed (e.g., labels such as "threat" or "opportunity"), while framing refers to how people express their viewpoint, regardless of its content. Fiol noted that framing differs in the breadth of the frame (e.g., the number or scope of issues attended to, the number of constituencies or functional areas perceived as relevant) and in the rigidity of the frame (e.g., the degree of certainty conveyed, the stability of opinions over time). While people may maintain diverse interpretations about the content of an issue, they may nevertheless show agreement about how the issue is being broadly framed. Fiol (1994) analyzed how a *Fortune* 100 financial services company made sense of and evaluated a new venture project over a period of two years. The new venture team consisted of 11 managers, ranging from division CEO to group vice presidents, covering functions in finance, law, marketing, operations, and systems. The CEO required that all major communications in the group be recorded in a new venture log, which eventually ran to more than 2,000 pages of entries spread over three volumes, reflecting the three phases of the project. In the first phase that lasted six months, the team failed to see a need for the new venture, especially how it could add to or be integrated with existing products, and decided to reject the proposal. In the second phase (seven months), the new venture idea was reintroduced, this time as a totally new business separate from the division's current offerings. This new form gained the tentative support of top managers in the team, and the idea was then pursued as a "new business proposal." In the third phase (nine months), the subgroups worked to flesh out and operationalize the project. Eventually, "the 'New Business' concept that emerges from the third notebook is almost identical to the idea that the [project] Champion had presented more than a year earlier and that had been soundly rejected" (Fiol 1994, p. 409). Data analysis revealed that over the course of the project, there was a general progression from less to greater certainty about their positions (frame rigidity) and a clear convergence toward the perceived scope of the project (frame breadth) as encompassing internal systems, customer needs, and marketing issues. While there was convergence in framing, team members continued to the end to maintain their divergent perceptions about the controllability of the issues raised (interpretation content), with the subgroups perceiving different levels of control over project outcomes. In the final analysis, it was the agreement on how the new venture was to be framed that provided the unifying premise for the new venture to proceed.

Consensus and Diversity in Organizational Culture

The sharing of meaning in a group based on a common set of beliefs and values that leads to similar patterns of behavior within the group is seen as evidence of the existence of a group culture. Indeed, the sharing of beliefs and behaviors is regarded as the essence of culture: "If there is no consensus or if there is conflict or if things are ambiguous, then, by definition, that group does not have a culture in regard to those things. It may have subcultures, smaller groups that have a shared something, a consensus about something, but the concept of sharing or consensus is core to the definition, not something about which we have an empirical choice" (Schein 1991, p. 246). This view, though not uncommon, is not shared universally by students of organizational culture, and we will also present a more diffracted image of culture that encompasses both consensus and multiplicity.

An Integrated View of Organizational Culture. What then is culture? Schein's (1985, 1991, 1992) definition is well known and germane to our discussion. According to him,

> Culture is:
> A pattern of shared basic assumptions,
> invented, discovered, or developed by a given group,
> as it learns to cope with its problems of external adaptation and internal integration,
> that has worked well enough to be considered valid, and, therefore,
> is to be taught to new members of the group as the
> correct way to perceive, think, and feel in relation to those problems.
> (Schein 1991, p. 247)

In Schein's conceptualization, culture is the result of the organization's efforts to simultaneously adapt to external environments and to manage its internal integration. All groups need to face the tasks of external adaptation and internal integration, and both tasks involve building consensus on collective identity, function, and allowable behaviors. In the process of *external adaptation*, members develop consensus on the core mission and functions of the organization; the specific goals to be pursued; the basic means to be used to attain the goals (including structure, reward, and authority systems); the criteria to be used for measuring results; and the appropriate remedial strategies if goals are not achieved (Schein 1992, p. 52). In the process of *internal integration,* members develop consensus on a common language and conceptual categories to be used so that members can communicate with and understand each other; the group boundaries and criteria for inclusion; the criteria for the distribution of power and status; the norms of intimacy, friendship, and love; the criteria for the allocation of rewards and punishments; and the concepts for explaining the unexplainable (ideology and religion) that members can fall back on to cope with and respond to what they cannot understand (Schein 1992, pp. 70–71). To illustrate the dynamic process by which an organization learns its shared assumptions, Schein outlines this scenario of how organizational culture grows from the seeds of the founder's beliefs:

> Basically the founder of the new group starts with some beliefs, values, and
> assumptions about how to proceed and teaches those to new members through a

variety of mechanisms. What is for him or her a basic reality becomes for the group a set of interim values and beliefs about which they have limited choice. The group then behaves in a certain way based on the founder's beliefs and values, and either succeeds or fails. If it fails, the group eventually dissolves and no culture is formed. If it succeeds, and this process repeats itself, what were originally the beliefs, values, and assumptions of the founders come to be validated in the shared experiences of the group. (Schein 1991, p. 249)

Over time, the learning and validation of a set of shared assumptions becomes constituted in the culture of the organization and provides a shared framework of cognitive, behavioral, and affective responses. Within this framework, members can continuously make sense of and adapt to the external environment and continuously develop and maintain internal relationships among themselves.

A Multiperspective View of Organizational Culture. While Schein's treatment of culture, as a prescription of organization-wide consensus that brings about clarity, stability, and unity of action, is certainly a desirable state of affairs, many organizations in practice do not enjoy the level of integration and consistency that it prescribes. An alternative view suggests that organizational culture should be examined simultaneously through multiple lenses, with each lens bringing into focus special features that are missed by the others. Martin (1992, 2001) proposes that three interpretive perspectives are needed, which she calls the integration, differentiation, and fragmentation views (Table 3-3). The *integration* perspective is defined by organizational members experiencing a high level of consensus, consistency, and clarity. All members share a set of basic assumptions, values, common concerns, or "content themes." These themes are enacted consistently in

TABLE 3-3. Three perspectives of organizational culture (Adapted from Martin 1992, p. 13).

Perspective	*Integration*	*Differentiation*	*Fragmentation*
Consensus (Orientation to consensus)	Organization-wide consensus	Subcultural consensus	Multiplicity of views (no consensus)
Consistency (Relation among manifestations)	Consistency	Inconsistency	Complexity (not clearly consistent or inconsistent)
Clarity (Orientation to ambiguity)	Exclude it	Channel it outside subcultures	Focus on it
Metaphors	Clearing in jungle, monolith, hologram	Islands of clarity in sea of ambiguity	Web, jungle

a variety of cultural manifestations (actions, stories, rituals, jargon, and other symbols); members know what they are to do and why, so that there is no place for ambiguity. In many respects, Schein's (1985, 1992) conceptualization of organizational culture portrays such a unifying, integrative perspective. Instead of a single, seamless culture, the *differentiation* perspective assumes that organizations consist of a number of subcultures based on differences in power, areas of interest, and work or professional practices. Its defining features are that consensus exists only locally within subcultures; inconsistent interpretations of content themes are common; and clarity is preserved within subcultures while ambiguity is channeled outward. The differentiation perspective acknowledges that conflict and power are important elements of cultural behavior and assumes that collective action based on consensus is most likely within subcultures. Finally, the *fragmentation* perspective sees organizations as "webs of individuals" who are loosely and sporadically connected as "new issues come into focus, different people and tasks become salient, and new information becomes available" (Martin 1992, pp. 150–51). The organization lacks a center, and its boundaries are blurred as part-time employees, contractors, suppliers, and customers move in and out of the organization. There is no organization-wide or subcultural consensus; any local consensus is temporary and limited to particular issues. Neither consistencies nor inconsistencies are clear. Constant flux and ambiguity is the rule of the day. In this view, collective action is still possible because individuals form temporary coalitions to tackle specific issues and concerns:

> When a particular issue becomes salient, one pattern of connections becomes relevant. That pattern would include a unique array of agreements, disagreements, and domains of ignorance. A different issue would draw attention to a different pattern of connections—and different sources of confusion. Whenever a new issue becomes salient to cultural members or researchers, a new pattern of connections would become significant. (Martin and Meyerson 1988, p. 117)

Meyerson and Martin (1987) applied the three perspectives to analyze cultural change in the Peace Corps/Africa during the Kennedy and Nixon administrations. From the integration perspective, the volunteers and staff of Peace Corps/Africa during the Kennedy administration were all seen as sharing the same core values espoused by Kennedy and the top administrators—the importance of international volunteer work, altruism, the excitement of living in new environments, and the ability to change the world through their work and ideals. The differentiation perspective focused on the behaviors of several subculture groups, including the top staff (the Africa director, country directors); volunteers assigned to particular countries; and volunteers assigned to specific projects such as sanitation, agriculture, and teaching English. The fragmentation perspective concentrated on the consequences of the short two-year tenures of most volunteers and high turnover of country directors. As a result, "transient issue-specific interest groups" often developed, establishing informal alliances around issues such as an epidemic in a particular country or the relative importance of English instruction. Furthermore, since most volunteers worked in isolated settings,

Peace Corps members had to be tolerant of confusion and to be able to live with ambiguity.

When Nixon became U.S. president, the integration view focused on the new kinds of Peace Corps volunteers he deemed desirable: people with practical skills in construction and farming so that the Corps could do more infrastructure building and less English teaching. The differentiation view saw how environmental factors, including a severe drought that caused famine, outflows of refugees, and changes in several national governments, influenced the composition of subcultures. In addition, new country members, the termination of sanitation projects, and the introduction of drought-resistant crops and irrigation projects all led to new subcultural configurations. The fragmentation view showed temporary alliances coalescing on concerns such as effective education techniques for introducing innovations (new sewage disposal methods, cooking untraditional grains) and political violence in a particular country. Budget cuts in Washington, D.C. and uncertainty about the Corps' future further increased the feeling of anxiety and ambiguity. Overall, the integration view focused on the creation of an organization-wide consensus based on policies initiated by the Corps leadership; the differentiation view focused on local consensus in subcultures formed by people working in the same countries or projects; while the fragmentation view focused on the experiences of individuals who were working in fast-changing and isolated settings.

Martin explains the value of adopting a three-perspective analysis of organizational culture:

> At any point in time, a few fundamental aspects of an organization's culture will be congruent with an Integration perspective—that is, some cultural manifestations will be interpreted in similar ways throughout the organization, so they appear clear and mutually consistent. At the same time, in accord with the Differentiation perspective, other issues will surface as inconsistencies and will generate clear subcultural differences. Simultaneously, in congruence with the Fragmentation viewpoint, still other issues will be seen as ambiguous, generating unclear relationships among manifestations and only ephemeral issue-specific coalitions that fail to coalesce in either organization-wide or subcultural consensus. Furthermore, individuals viewing the same cultural context will perceive, remember, and interpret things in different ways. (Martin 1992, pp. 168–69)

Bounded Ambiguity. In organizations, the diversity of groups and identifications with different communities implies that there is considerable variation in what meanings and values become relevant in different situations. Although inconsistencies and contradictions are inherent features of organizational life, an organization's shared cultural understandings can moderate the confusion that might result from these inconsistencies. Alvesson (2001) proposes the concept of bounded ambiguity,

> in which cultures do not necessarily establish clarity, shared orientations and consensus among broad groups of people, but still offer guidelines for coping with instances of ambiguity without too much anarchy or confusion. Bounded ambiguity may mean broadly shared rules and meanings for how to steer around

tricky issues, e.g., avoid decision-making or involve as many people as possible in a difficult decision. . . . We can thus say that it offers "meta-meanings"—clues for how to deal with tricky meanings. It may also mean a preference for vague, positive-sounding vocabulary, a tolerance for certain, not to say considerable amount of inconsistency and even contradiction without reacting, the use of "mediating myths" between a strong discrepancy between what is preached and what is practised. (Alvesson 2001, p. 166)

Bounded ambiguity does not suggest that organizations avoid experiences of high ambiguity. Rather, the organization can use its shared meanings, preferences, and practices to both acknowledge and reduce ambiguity, mitigating the stressful effects of contradictory and confusing experiences.

IV. TOWARD A COGNITIVE THEORY OF THE FIRM

Our discussion of organizations as noticing, perceiving, and processing information; forming interpretations; and taking action all point toward a cognitive view of organizations. Huff and Huff (2000) advocate the development of a cognitive theory of the firm as a useful addition to economic and behavioral theories of the firm. For them, the defining interest in economic theories is in "output" and "structure," while behavioral theories are primarily focused on "processes" relating to interaction and influence—"the defining word for cognitive theory would be *understanding* or *coherence*" (p. 29, italics in original). A cognitive theory would have four distinctive features:

1. The firm as a social system is a unique site for sense making, learning, and problem solving.

2. Managers (indeed all participants) are *motivated* to understand their own situation and the situation of the collectives that are important to them; human *behavior* is influenced by these sense-making efforts.

3. The articulation of influential, shared goals is difficult; it is influenced by the interpretation, knowledge, and problem-solving abilities of individuals and by understandings shared with others.

4. A firm's environments generate varying stimuli that tend to structure, but be structured by, cognition and action.

(Huff and Huff 2000, p. 30)

In analyzing shared cognitive frameworks within the firm, Huff and Huff (2000) invoke the concept of *epistemic communities* as described by Haas (1992) in his work on how new policies were developed by government agencies (e.g., monetary reform or environmental protection policies). Haas suggests that epistemic communities share (a) norms and principled beliefs that provide a value-based rationale for social action, (b) causal beliefs, derived from their analysis of policy actions and outcomes, (c) notions of validity that define criteria for evaluating information, (d) a common set of practices that direct their professional competence to a set of problems. Huff and Huff (2000) feel that organizations, and especially their top management teams, must be "epistemic communities" of some strength in order to be viable. While individuals have beliefs and inter-pretations that are unique to themselves, they also share many beliefs and under-standings with others. To the extent that beliefs are shared by key actors, the resulting shared cognitive framework then provides the basis for coordinated activity (p. 124).

Ocasio (2001) asks the question "How do organizations think?" and finds that two variants of answer are common in the literature: the shared cognition perspective and top management cognitive perspective (e.g., Fligstein 1990; Hambrick and Mason 1984). (The notion of top management teams as "epis-temic communities" described in the last paragraph would seem to combine both perspectives.) Ocasio sees limitations in either approach and proposes a wider view where organizational cognition is a situated process that crosses many lev-els, including the cognition of individuals, the psychology of groups, and the social dimensions of organizations:

> To understand how organizations think is therefore to understand not only how individuals think but how thinking is situated in organizations, how situations are structured by organizations, and how thinking and situations are embedded in broader social, economic, political, and cultural environments. (Ocasio 2001, p. 41)

An important corollary of this perspective is that organizational thinking persists even when individual participants change. The persistence of thought and action in organizations despite personnel turnover shows that cognition within organizations is socially structured and constituted.

Earlier, Ocasio (1997) has suggested that to explain firm behavior is to ex-plain how firms distribute and regulate the *attention* of their decision makers. Here, attention is defined as the noticing, encoding, interpreting, and focusing of time and effort on both issues (available categories for making sense of the envi-ronment) and answers (available action alternatives). This attention-based view of the firm then implies that

1. What decision makers do depends on what issues and answers they focus their attention on (*focus of Attention*).

2. What issues and answers decision makers focus on, and what they do, depends on the particular context or situation they find themselves in (*situated attention*).

3. What particular context or situation decision makers find themselves in, and how they attend to it, depends on how the firm's rules, resources, and social relationships regulate and control the distribution and allocation of issues, answers, and decision makers into specific activities, communica-tions, and procedures (*structural distribution of attention*).

(Ocasio 1997, p. 188)

In this view, failures of organizational adaptation are failures of enactment, that is, failures to attend successfully to the relevant issues and answers. Ocasio (2001) expands Weick's (1979b) enactment-selection-retention (ESR) framework. For Ocasio, enactment refers to the "focalization of the current perceptual stimuli" as well as the "retrieval in memory of previous cognitions or mental models" (p. 44). Selection reduces equivocality in human cognition by the choice of one among several alternative enactments. Retention involves both transmission and storage. Transmission refers to communication with other participants not involved in the initial process of enactment and selection. Storage occurs at various levels of organizational memory, including individual, group, and institutional memory. Thus, Ocasio modifies Weick's ESR framework and presents the situation-enactment-retrieval-selection-transmission-storage (SERSTS) model as an alternative view of information processing in organizations. Using this model, Ocasio returns to the original question that motivated his study:

> How do organizations think? This [research] gives three interrelated answers. First, organizations think through parallel, decentralized processes of situated enactment, retrieval, selection, transmission, and storage. Organizations think, according to this observation, by organizing the situations in which enactment and selection occurs and by linking the retrieval, selection, transmission, and storage of issues and schemas among situations. Second, organizations think by reducing equivocality through the process of selection and dynamic control. Thinking by individuals and groups in organizations is controlled by the contests for status in organizations, by differential power and prestige of organizational coalitions, and by the logic of appropriateness and common social identification contained in an organization's culture. Finally, organizations think by embedding the components of thinking—the participants, resources, issues, schemas, and space that constitute organizational situations and knowledge structures—into organizational subsystems that regulate the enactment, retrieval, selection, transmission, and storage of the issues, schemas, and mental models that constitute thinking in organizations. (Ocasio 2001, p. 58)

V. INFORMATION NEEDS, SEEKING, AND USE IN SENSE MAKING

The reduction of ambiguity lies at the heart of organizational sense making. When ambiguity is excessively high, organization members lack a clear and stable frame of reference within which their work and behavior have meaning and purpose. When ambiguity is unnecessarily suppressed, organization members feel unduly complacent and unchallenged to learn or innovate. Each organization finds its own balance between ambiguity and certainty, and this locus depends on the business of the organization, its operating environment, its relationships with stakeholders, and the beliefs and values held by its members. Through the sense-making process equivocal information is interpreted and negotiated so that members share some basic understandings upon which collective action can be taken. In this section, we detail the information-seeking and -use processes that constitute sense making and meaning construction in organizations. The sequence of discussion follows the conceptual framework developed in Chapter 2: we examine (1) information needs, (2) information seeking, and (3) information use, each in terms of cognitive needs, affective responses, and situational dimensions (Table 3-4).

Information Needs. During sense making, information needs are unclear. The lack of clarity revolves around two basic questions: In the flood of signals indicating change in the environment, which messages and cues are important and need to be focused on? Given that the information is ambiguous, which interpretation is the most plausible and should be used to understand what the cues mean? The central issue is therefore the management of ambiguity. Whereas uncertainty refers to the lack of information about an issue, ambiguity refers to the equivocality of the information available, where the same information can support multiple and sometimes conflicting interpretations. The lack of information may be addressed by gathering more data that are relevant to an issue, but the lack of clarity has to be met by constructing a plausible interpretation that makes

TABLE 3-4. Information needs, seeking, and use in sense making.

	Information Needs	*Information Seeking*	*Information Use*
Sense Making	• *Needs are unclear* • *"What's happening here?"* • *"Which interpretation to choose?"*	• *Scanning the environment* • *Noticing significant, reliable information* • *Developing interpretations through verbal discourse*	• *Reduce but not eliminate ambiguity* • *Build consensus or shared meanings for collective action*
Cognitive Needs	• Frames of reference • Cognitive profile and degree of bracketing • Types of information needs	• Information quality and clarity • Information reliability and accuracy • Organizational memory	• Schema-driven sense making • Cognitive filtering • Expectations and self-fulfilling prophecies
Affective Responses	• Emotions as markers • Inertia and stress • Cognitive dissonance	• Information richness • Affective moods • Information cultures	• Interpretive orientation • Attributional biases • Equifinal meanings
Situational Dimensions	• Ill-structured problems • Perceived environmental uncertainty • Attention in organizations	• Environmental analyzability • Enacting as information seeking • Access to information	• Sense giving and sense contesting • Commitment to actions • Dominant logic

sense of the noticed information. The initial attempt to reduce ambiguity is to try and fit the information with existing assumptions, beliefs, and expectations.

Information Seeking. Three related activities constitute the information-seeking process in organizational sense making: scanning, noticing, and interpreting. *Scanning* is the sensing activity that precedes sense making, and it involves looking at the external environment in order to see developments that could impact the organization. Specific events or discontinuities are *noticed* and information about them is isolated for closer scrutiny. Such information tends to be equivocal, so the main task then becomes *interpreting* the meaning of noticed events by talking about and negotiating disparate perceptions in verbal discourse. Organizations scan using a variety of information strategies, ranging from the irregular, ad hoc scan to continuous, proactive information gathering as part of an institutionalized scanning-planning system. The information culture of the organization, its dependence on and perception of the environment, and its access to channels that can influence the environment are some of the major factors that affect information-seeking behavior.

Information Use. During sense making, information is processed to reduce situational ambiguity and to develop a consensus of shared meanings that enable organizational members to act. Both are partial objectives—ambiguity cannot and should not be completely removed, and consensus is rarely and need not be universal. By maintaining a residual level of equivocality and accommodating a diversity of interpretations, the organization stays alert and open to change. People in organizations construct networks of meanings by starting from some existing beliefs or some sequence of actions that have been taken. The process may be belief driven (Weick 1995), where organizational members construct meaning by connecting similar pieces of information based on expectations or by connecting contradictory information through argumentation. The process may be action driven, in which case they create meaning to justify visible actions they are committed to, or they create meaning to explain actions they took to make things happen. People in organizations develop shared meanings by tapping into shared cognitive structures in order to establish some level of cognitive consensus that can be the foundation for collective action. Developing consensus is aided by communication behaviors that allow different interpretations to coexist or to be reconciled. The nature and extent of the consensus depends on the properties of the organizational culture, which can simultaneously be integrated, differentiated, and fragmented (Martin 1992).

Information Needs in Sense Making

Information Needs and Cognitive Needs

Cognitive frames of reference. Organizations develop cognitive *frames of reference* to define the boundaries of a domain of inquiry, suggest appropriate methods of inquiry, and allocate significance, value, and priority to information.

These organizational frames of reference consist of "cognitive elements, cognitive operators, and reality tests that select, organize, and validate information" (Shrivastava and Schneider 1984, p. 796). *Cognitive elements* "determine the type of information and data that the organization prefers to use" as well as "represent the intellectual commitments and cognitive interests or motives of inquiry in organizations" (Shrivastava, Mitroff, and Alvesson 1987, p. 96). Some organizations value soft information based on subjective, personal experience, others emphasize objective, formal, quantitative data. Cognitive elements also reflect vocabularies for expressing features important to the organization: an organization stressing service quality would use a vocabulary different from another stressing financial performance. *Cognitive operators* are "methods by which information is ordered and arranged to make meaning and sense out of large amounts of data that organizations continuously receive. . . . They essentially consist of guidelines for perceiving and formulating problems, descriptions of acceptable solutions, and criteria for evaluating solutions" (Shrivastava and Schneider 1984, p. 798). By specifying methods for ordering information, they also specify the acceptable methods for studying organizational problems. *Reality tests* validate the elements of the frame of reference as well as the information that results from organizational inquiry by comparing current situations with critical past experiences. Overall, the frame of reference sets the boundaries of the scope of any organizational inquiry and provides the information-organizing principles that "shape information acquisition and processing patterns in organizations. . . . information selectively enters the system in patterns based on its nature, source, timing, and consistency with cognitive elements. Rudimentary organization is implicit in this selective perception. Cognitive operators classify and categorize information allowing the formation of concepts/constructs" (Shrivastava and Schneider 1984, p. 801).

Cognitive profile and degree of bracketing. The experiencing of information needs is closely related to the bracketing of issues that needs to be worked on or better understood. Whether and how an issue is bracketed in turn depends on the cognitive frames of reference that are activated. Within an organization or a group, members may hold different frames of reference, and they may bracket an issue differently (or perhaps not at all). Ericson (2001) studied a strategic change process at a large Swedish university hospital in a multiyear longitudinal case study and derived two concepts to analyze sense making: the *cognitive profile* of a group and the *degree of bracketing* associated with a set of issues. The cognitive profile of a group is a function of the diversity of cognitive schemas among members of the group and can be heterogeneous or homogenous. The degree of bracketing refers to the number of individuals in a group who do bracket a specific issue: if only a few bracket the issue, then the bracketing degree of the group is low. The degree of bracketing can change over time. For example, in the hospital case study, a number of members of the management team initially did not bracket the structural and financial issues that were driving the change process (the degree of bracketing was low). Over time, the degree of bracketing increased as more team members began to concentrate on the same issue. Ericson (2001) calls this a concentration process and suggests that there is an opposite process of diffusion when an initially noticed issue becomes less salient over time. Similarly, the cognitive profile of a group can become more similar or dissimilar over time (processes of homogenization or heterogenization).

Types of information needs. When we speak of information needs, we generally imply a lack of information. This may be an oversimplification, since the experiencing of information need may be brought about not just by an absence of information, but also by a lack of a frame of reference to make sense of received information. Fig. 3.1 (adapted from Zack 1998) shows four different conditions of information need and information abundance. In the upper-left quadrant, when there is a perceived lack of information, the individual experiences a condition of "uncertainty." A parallel situation is when the individual perceives that there is no usable frame of reference to make sense of the available information: a condition of "ambiguity." Both uncertainty and ambiguity refer to the lack of information. The reverse is when the individual experiences an abundance of information, including unsolicited and unwanted information, in a state of information "overload." There is a fourth condition that arises when there are multiple frames of reference (perhaps introduced by different stakeholders) that could be used to interpret the received information, and it is hard to assess which interpretation is more valid. This would be a condition of "equivocality." When individuals complain of overload, they may also be referring to this form of equivocality. Fig. 3.1 suggests that in conditions of uncertainty and ambiguity, an appropriate response would be to seek more information in order to fill in information gaps or to find a usable frame of reference. In conditions of overload and equivocality, a common response would be to filter information or to select information that is compatible with a particular frame of reference.

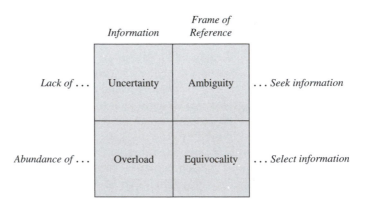

FIGURE 3.1. Types of Information Needs (Adapted from Zack 1998)

Information Needs and Affective Responses

Emotions as markers. As Kuhlthau (1993a, b) has observed, the initiation of the information search process is characterized by feelings of "uncertainty due to a lack of understanding, a gap in meaning, a limited construct" (p. xxiii). Because the human mind prefers order and stability, it experiences feelings of *stress and tension* when confronted with a high level of ambiguity brought about by equivocal information from confusing situations. In recent years, evidence from neuroscience and cognitive neuroscience has clarified the role of emotions in mental processes. A series of studies by Damasio (2003) found that individuals who lost certain classes of emotions due to neurological damage also lost their ability to process information rationally. Damasio suggests that every experience in our lives is accompanied by some degree of emotion. Under the influence of these emotions, "we gradually categorize the situations we experience—the structure of the scenarios, their components, their significance" (Damasio 2003, p. 146). Moreover, some feelings optimize recall while others (extremely painful feelings in particular) suppress recall: "In general, memory of the felt situation promotes, consciously or not, the avoidance of events associated with negative feelings *and* the seeking of situations that may cause positive feelings" (Damasio 2003, p. 178). When facing a new situation, emotion signals focus our attention on certain aspects of the problem. The signals mark options and outcomes with a positive or negative signal that narrow the sense-making space and increase the probability that actions will conform to past experience (Damasio 2003, p. 148). Because the emotion signals are body related, Damasio refers to them as *somatic markers* that can indicate mismatches between the available information and the cognitive categories the individual is using to make sense. Thus, positive or negative emotions can shape information needs by influencing the perception and experiencing of a sense-making situation. For example, managers become personally and emotionally involved during problem recognition:

> managers are not cool and detached observers of their organizational scenes. They are invested in their points of view, policies, and ways of doing things, and they are identified with the fate of their people and their organizations. To contemplate a problem is not a cool mental act but "hot cognition." (McCall and Kaplan 1990, p. 29)

Inertia and stress. An important way that the experiencing of information needs can be blocked is through organizational inertia. Huff and Huff (2000) discuss how *inertia* increases as patterns of interpretation and behavior become increasingly routinized from one time period to another. The source of inertia is at the individual level, where inertia arises from the reuse of schema available in the social setting and developed from the individual's own experience. Huff and Huff (2000) define schemas as units of knowledge that consist of the knowledge itself as well as information about how the knowledge is to be used. By imposing a structure on knowledge or information, schemas allow individuals to function effectively in an otherwise vast and confusing environment. This reliance on available schemas to make sense of the environment grows over time, and the individual becomes increasingly resistant to schema change. Huff and Huff believe "this resistance at the level of individual cognitive processes is the primary source of inertia in organizations. It results not from any active external force but rather from properties inherent to the use of knowledge structures. The very properties that make schema useful sensemaking structures (i.e., efficiency, expectancy) also stand in the way of change" (p. 46). The effect on information needs is that "people attend to schema-supporting evidence, rather than evidence that challenges it" (p. 48). Nevertheless, from time to time, stimuli-attracting attention cannot be interpreted by established schemas, and stress is felt when there is a mismatch between expectations, interpretations, and behavior. Huff and Huff (2000) define *stress* "as a general term describing stimuli that *strain* or cause 'wear and tear' on an individual or larger collective without assuming that the stimuli are noxious or that the results are negative" (p. 49). It occurs when the usefulness or validity of a currently held schema is called into question by unanticipated events that affect the relationship between the environment and the individual or organization. Like inertia, stress also tends to increase over time as signals and stimuli accumulate that suggest a need for new sense-making structures. Unlike inertia, which is internal and invisible, stress is external and highly noticed: "The cumulative resistance to significant, strategic change grows primarily out of gradually accumulating resource commitments and institutional routines, many of which receive little ongoing attention. Cumulative stress, which makes renewal more likely to be sought and accepted, is more often associated with specific events that directly capture individual and group attention" (Huff and Huff 2000, p. 84).

Cognitive dissonance. When sense-making structures fail, people experience psychological discomfort or *dissonance*. Festinger (1957) begins by postulating that pairs of cognition or elements of knowledge can be relevant or irrelevant to one another. If relevant, they are either consonant or dissonant. Two cognitions are consonant if one follows from the other, and they are dissonant if the opposite of one cognition follows from the other. Dissonance is psychologically uncomfortable: it motivates the person to reduce the dissonance and to avoid information that is likely to increase the dissonance. The greater the dissonance, the greater the pressure to reduce dissonance. Festinger uses the example of a habitual smoker to illustrate. A smoker who learns that smoking is bad for health experiences dissonance, since the knowledge that smoking is bad for health is dissonant with the cognition that he continues to smoke. He can reduce dissonance by changing his behavior, that is, stopping smoking. Alternatively, he could reduce dissonance by changing his cognition about the health effect of smoking, that is, believing that smoking does not have a harmful effect on health. Thus, he might believe, for example, that smoking reduces tension and keeps him from gaining weight (adding consonant cognitions); that the health risk from smoking is negligible compared with the danger of car accidents (reducing the importance of the dissonant cognition); and that the enjoyment from smoking is a very important part of his life (increasing the importance of consonant cogni-tions). Cognitive dissonance theory has been applied widely to analyze the inter-play of cognition, motivation, and emotion. The effect on information needs and use is summarized by Harmon-Jones and Mills thus: "Dissonance is aroused when people are exposed to information inconsistent with their beliefs. If the dissonance is not reduced by changing one's belief, the dissonance can lead to misperception or misinterpretation of the information, rejection or refutation of the information, seeking support from those who agree with one's belief, and attempting to persuade others to accept one's belief" (Harmon-Jones and Mills 1999, p. 5).

Information Needs and Situational Dimensions

Ill-structured problems. Information need situations may be described by a small set of problem dimensions, which are "those characteristics that, beyond specific subject matter, establish the criteria for judging the relevance of infor-mation to a problem or to a class of problems" (Taylor 1986, p. 42). Of the eleven problem dimensions that have been identified (MacMullin and Taylor 1984), five are particularly relevant to understanding information needs during sense making: (1) sense-making problems tend to be *discovery* rather than design problems—information for discovery concentrates on a small, detailed set of data perceived to be important in order to discover its meaning; (2) sense-making problems tend to be *ill-structured* and require information on how to interpret or proceed; (3) sense-making problems tend to be *complex,* involving many variables that interact with each other; (4) sense-making problems tend to have *amorphous goals,* so that information is required to clarify preferences and directions; (5) sense-making problems tend to be those in which *assumptions are not agreed* upon. Assumptions may be contradictory or contested, and information is needed to explain underlying perceptions, define terms and concepts, and so on.

Perceived environmental uncertainty. In the research literature of how organi-zations scan their external environments, *perceived environmental uncertainty* is the variable that represents the external environment's perceived complexity and changeability. Duncan (1972) infers two dimensions of the environment that would determine its perceived uncertainty: the simple-complex dimension (the number of environmental factors considered in decision making) and the static-dynamic dimension (the degree to which these factors change over time). Duncan found that decision makers in environments that are dynamic and complex experienced the greatest amount of perceived environmental uncer-tainty. Perceived environmental uncertainty itself is conceptualized as (1) lack of information on environmental factors associated with a decision situation; (2) lack of knowledge about the outcome of a specific decision; and (3) inabil-ity to assign probabilities with confidence on how environmental factors affect success or failure. There is general agreement in the findings of scanning studies that managers who experience higher levels of perceived environmental uncer-tainty tend to do a larger amount of information seeking or environmental scanning (see, for example, Kefalas and Schoderbek 1973; Nishi, Schoderbek, and Schoderbek 1982; Daft, Sormunen, and Parks 1988; Auster and Choo 1993). In terms of information needs, research suggests that the external business environment may be divided into *environmental sectors,* such as the customer, competition, technological, regulatory, economic, and sociocultural sectors (Choo and Auster 1993). Again, there is agreement in the research findings that information scanning tends to be focused on the market-related sectors, with information on customers, suppliers, and competitors appearing to be the most important (see, for example, Ghoshal 1988; Lester and Waters 1989; Choo 1993; Olsen et al. 1994).

Attention in organizations. Ocasio (1997) proposes an attention-based view of the firm that extends Weick's (1979b) concept of organizational enactment of the environment. In this view, which of the multiple enacted environments are selected to shape organizational response is a function of the firm's procedural and communication channels and its attention structures. Ocasio (1997) discusses how attention in organization is structurally distributed: the specific context that people find themselves in, and how they attend to it, depends on how the organization distributes and controls the allocation of issues, answers, and decision makers within specific firm activities, communications, and procedures. Different functions in an organization direct attention to selected issues and answers through localized procedures and communication channels:

> attentional processes of individual and group decision-makers are distributed
> throughout the multiple functions that take place in organizations, with different
> foci of attention in each local procedure, communication, or activity. Each local
> activity within the firm involves a set of procedures and communications, and
> these procedures and communications focus the attention of decision-makers on a
> selected set of issues and answers. (p. 190)

These procedural and communication channels can be formal and informal concrete activities. They include formal and informal meetings, reports (e.g., memos, quarterly reports, customer satisfaction surveys), and administrative protocols (e.g., personnel evaluations, budgetary requests, requests for proposals). They are concrete because they are tangible and have a specific location in space and time. Procedural and communication channels constitute a critical part of the attention structures of the organization and influence the noticing of information needs and the processing of issues that the organization needs to work on.

Information Seeking in Sense Making

Information Seeking and Cognitive Needs

Information quality and clarity. From an information perspective, every change or development in the external environment creates signals and messages that organizations may need to heed (Dill 1962). Some of the signals would be weak (difficult to detect), many would be confusing (difficult to analyze), and others would be spurious (not indicative of a true change). The information seeker would have to attend selectively to numerous signals created by a dynamic environment, interpret often confusing messages, and make sense of cues in relation to existing frames of reference. A basic cognitive need of information seeking in sense making is thus to subjectively increase the *clarity and quality of information* about ambiguous situations. Unfortunately, information rarely comes directly from the scene; more often than not it travels a circuitous route, flowing through many intermediate channels. The risks of failure in gathering reliable information become real:

> Sources of failure are legion: even if the initial message is accurate, clear, timely, and relevant, it may be translated, condensed, or completely blocked by personnel standing between the sender and the intended receiver: it may get through in distorted form. If the receiver is in a position to use the message, he may screen it out because it does not fit his preconceptions, because it has come through a suspicious or poorly regarded channel, because it is embedded in piles of inaccurate or useless messages (excessive noise in the channel), or, simply, because too many messages are transmitted to him (information overload). (Wilensky 1967, p. 41)

Information reliability and accuracy. Because sense-making situations are those in which ambiguity is high and action is consequential, organizational members seeking information may be particularly sensitive to the *reliability* of a source and the *accuracy* of its information. Studies on source use in scanning have found that managers do not just rely on the most accessible sources (a common heuristic that characterized how many groups of users seek information, see Chapter 2), but that they also use heavily sources they perceive to be dependable or authoritative (e.g., Culnan 1983; Auster and Choo 1993). A source is more likely to be seen to be credible when it has a good track record of supplying accurate data, when the individual has used it before, or when another well-regarded source has recommended it. Based on available research,

> the general pattern of source usage for scanning suggests that although managers use a wide range of sources in scanning, they prefer personal sources that communicate information personally rather than impersonal sources that communicate information formally or to broad audiences. This preference for live information from personal sources is particularly strong when seeking information about market-related environmental sectors which are highly fluid and equivocal. There is some evidence to indicate that source selection for scanning is influenced by the perceived quality of the source, and not just its perceived accessibility. (Choo 2002, p. 112)

Since sense making involves overlaying existing meaning structures on the new information, sources that provide access to what sense the organization has made in the past become important in constructing interpretations.

Organizational memory. Interpretations of the past can be embedded in the minds of individuals as well as in systems and artifacts that make up the *organizational memory* (Walsh and Ungson 1991). Walsh and Ungson postulate that organizational memory is held in five "storage bins": individuals, culture, transformations, structures, and ecology. Individuals "store their organization's memory in their own capacity to remember and articulate experience and in the cognitive orientations they employ to facilitate information processing" (Walsh and Ungson 1991, p. 63). As well, individuals maintain their own files and collections of data. Because retrieving from memory is not simply a matter of literal recall but also involves subjective reconstruction, the other components of organizational memory actively modulate the selection and processing of information. Thus, culture "embodies past experience that can be useful for dealing with the future" (p. 63); transformation procedures convert inputs into outputs and so encode the logic and rules of work; structures are the definitions of individual roles "which provide a repository in which organizational information can be stored" (p. 65); and ecology is the physical structure of the workplace that reflects hierarchy and affects the flow of feedback and information.

Information Seeking and Affective Responses

Information richness. A large part of information seeking during sense making is the comparing of experiences and interpretations among organizational members. Since recollections fade with time and the current situation is ambiguous, such information sharing is marked by feelings of doubt and uncertainty. In conversing about ill-defined situations, formal and explicit language is inadequate. Hunches, intuitions, and judgments are better carried through nonverbal rather than verbal channels: "Nonverbal messages are themselves more ambiguous and, very importantly, can be disowned. The use of an ambiguous channel of communication can help a manager convey the subjectivity and nuance of meaning that are crucial in an ambiguous situation" (McCaskey 1982). Organizational members reduce equivocality by using information sources and communication channels of different *information richness:*

> Information richness is defined as the ability of information to change
> understanding within a time interval. Communication transactions that can
> overcome different frames of reference or clarify ambiguous issues to change
> understanding in a timely manner are considered rich. Communications that
> require a long time to enable understanding or that cannot overcome different
> perspectives are lower in richness. (Daft and Lengel 1986, p. 560)

Rich information media use multiple cues, feedback, and language variety. Managers and others will turn to rich information channels such as face-to-face discussions when they are dealing with ambiguous, complex, ill-defined, or conflict-laden situations (Trevino, Webster, and Stein 2000). Face-to-face meetings are the richest information medium because they provide instant feedback, include multiple cues such as voice inflections and body gestures, add a personal touch, and use language variety. The use of rich information media helps participants to interpret a fuzzy situation and come to an acceptable agreement. Because managers must confront ambiguous and conflicting cues about the environment and then create and maintain a shared interpretation among themselves, they use rich media to talk about the environment and negotiate an understanding.

Affective mood. Affective mood can influence the breadth of the information search. Following Kelly (1963), a mood is thought of as "a stance or attitude that the individual assumes which opens or closes the possibilities in a search" (Kuhlthau 1993a, p. 350). A person in an "invitational" mood would search more sources and take more exploratory actions, while a user in an "indicative" mood would prefer a short search that come to a closure quickly. Weick (1995) also suggests that affective states can signal to the individual when information search may be stopped. In his view, since the feeling of order and clarity is an important goal of sense making, information seeking can end once this feeling is achieved.

Information cultures. An organization's values and norms about new information and ideas can have a major influence on the feelings that members have about noticing and sharing information. Westrum (1992) contrasts three types of information cultures in organizations—the pathological, the bureaucratic, and the generative—according to how well organizations "notice" information and deal with failure, new ideas, and responsibility (Table 3-5). In an organization with a generative information culture, new ideas are welcomed, sharing is rewarded, messengers are trained, and inquiry and reflection are encouraged. As a result, we may expect active seeking, sensing, and interpretation of new information. An organization practicing "conscious inquiry" would be able to "make

TABLE 3-5. Information cultures (Adapted from Westrum 1992, p. 402).

	Pathological	*Bureaucratic*	*Generative*
Noticing	Don't want to know	May not find out	Actively seek information
Messengers	Messengers are shot	Listened if they arrive	Messengers are trained
Responsibility	Responsibility is shirked	Responsibility is compartmentalized	Responsibility is shared
Sharing	Bridging is discouraged	Allowed but neglected	Bridging is rewarded
Failures	Failure is punished or covered up	Organization is just and merciful	Inquiry and reflection
New Ideas	New ideas are actively crushed	New ideas present problems	New ideas are welcomed

use of information, observations or ideas wherever they exist within the system, without regard for the location or the status or the person or group having such information, observations or ideas" (Westrum 1992, p. 402). Conversely, as shown in Table 3-5, organizations with pathological and bureaucratic cultures would discourage the noticing and sharing of new information, including information about adverse events that could threaten safety.

Information Seeking and Situational Dimensions

Environmental analyzability. Organizations differ in their modes of scanning-interpretation, depending on their beliefs about the *analyzability* of the external environment and the extent to which the organization *intrudes* into the environment to understand it (Weick and Daft 1983). An organization that believes the environment to be analyzable, in which events and processes are determinable and measurable, would seek to discover the "correct" interpretation through systematic information gathering and analysis. Conversely, an organization that perceives the environment to be unanalyzable would create or enact what it believes to be a reasonable interpretation that can explain past behavior and suggest future actions. An organization that actively intrudes into the environment would allocate resources for information search and for testing or manipulating the environment. A passive organization on the other hand takes whatever environmental information comes its way and tries to interpret the environment with the given information. Four possible modes of scanning-interpretation result: undirected viewing, conditioned viewing, enacting, and discovery (Choo 2001; Aguilar 1967; Weick and Daft 1983). (1) *Undirected viewing* takes place when the organization perceives the environment to be unanalyzable and so does not intrude into the environment to understand it. Information seeking is opportunistic, relying more on irregular contacts and casual information from external, personal sources. (2) *Conditioned viewing* takes place when the organization perceives the environment to be analyzable but is passive about gathering information and influencing the environment. Information seeking is based on passive detection, using internal, impersonal sources, with a significant amount of data coming from records and information systems. (3) *Enacting* takes place when the organization perceives the environment to be unanalyzable but then moves into the environment in order to influence events and outcomes. Information seeking is from external, personal sources and emphasizes feedback about the actions that the organization has taken. (4) *Discovery* takes place when the organization perceives the environment to be analyzable, and it intrudes into the environment to collect information extensively in order to find the correct interpretation. Information seeking is based on active detection, collecting information extensively and intensively through a variety of sources, including internal, impersonal (formal) sources.

Enacting as information seeking. Enacting takes place when the organization moves into the environment in order to influence events and outcomes. Information seeking is via external sources and channels that the organization has created through its intervention, and this may include collecting feedback about the actions that the organization has taken. Enacting organizations "construct their own environments. They gather information by trying new behaviors and seeing what happens. They experiment, test, and stimulate, and they ignore precedent, rules, and traditional expectations" (Daft and Weick 1984, p. 288). Information seeking is focused on the actions that have been taken, and this information is used to reduce equivocality as well as to test hypotheses. One example of enacting would be a firm that introduces and markets a new product based on what it thinks it can sell, rather than waiting for research to assess market demand. Another example would be an organization that actively influences and shapes the attitudes of its shareholders: it may try to "manipulate shareholder perceptions toward itself, environmental issues, or political candidates by sending information to shareholders through various media" (Daft and Weick 1984, p. 290). In today's network economy, organizations are using the World Wide Web as a channel to enact the environment. For example, firms give away products (browser software, open-source code, search engines) to test new products or increase market share; host online forums and communities to promote discussion and drum up support for issues; and create new web sites to disseminate information as well as collect feedback on topics of interest.

Access to information. Within the organization, the flow of information and *access to information* sources influence the information-seeking patterns of its members. McCall and Kaplan (1990) suggest that, at least for managers, there are four important sets of sources: "(a) systems and structures set up to keep them appraised of ongoing events, (b) the people around them who volunteer information and can be approached in search of trouble signs, clues, and missing pieces of puzzles, (c) the values of the organization, which point people in certain directions and define the critical variables in a complex array of possibilities, and (d) the manager's own direct experience" (p. 16). Systems and structures refer to information systems and organizational structure. Although computer-based *information systems* increase the general availability of information, the access to large amounts of data can result in information overload or in users selectively drawing upon the database to find information that supports a desired position while ignoring information that goes against it (Hogarth and Makridakis 1981). *Organizational structures* define information domains within which some sources are accessible while others are not. Hierarchy and specialization also constrain and direct the flow and availability of information. *Other people* within the organization are among the most important and often used information sources, yet their accessibility and willingness to provide information cannot be taken for granted. For example, people are highly sensitive to the way that their information is being received, and the likelihood of passing on information depends on their perception of the effect of the information on the recipient as well as the sender. Subordinates are known to withhold from their superiors information that prejudices their position or, conversely, to expedite information that enhances their cause. As a result, blocking, delaying, hiding, or even distorting information is not uncommon. The *values of the organization* can have pervasive effects on what information is considered relevant; what data are collected systematically; who gets to see the data; and who cares about it (McCall and Kaplan 1990). Thus, a firm stressing customer service as a main organizational value is more likely to recognize, collect, and make available data on service elements. Finally, the manager's own *direct experience* is also important because concrete information based on personal, firsthand experience is more accessible and more vivid to the individual than secondhand information (Hogarth and Makridakis 1981).

Information Use in Sense Making

Information Use and Cognitive Needs

Schema-driven sense making. Organizational members *reduce equivocality* by selectively comparing the information they have on hand with the information they have retained in their mental knowledge structures. Bartlett (1932) introduced the idea of *schemas* as mental structures that control attention and reconstruction of memory by providing a "knowledge base that serves as a guide for the interpretation of information, actions, and expectations" (Lord and Foti 1986, p. 22). Schemas are used to reduce equivocality in a number of ways: "schemas guide the rapid recall of remembered data and solutions, the instantaneous categorization and evaluation of new data, and the default filling in of missing data and solutions via inference" (Isenberg 1986b, p. 252). First, schemas help make inferences about otherwise ambiguous events by suggesting cause-effect explanations. For example, a schema could suggest that an early product announcement by a competitor is intended to preempt similar introductions by others. Second, schemas guide the categorization as well as the normative appraisal of events, people, and objects (Isenberg 1986b). For example, particular organizations such as GM and IBM may be categorized as "prototypical business organizations," and the U.S. automotive industry's difficulties in the 1970s may be construed as cases of complacent management. Third, "schemas fill in missing data by supplying default options" and "they fill in missing solutions to problems through the recall of past instances" (Isenberg 1986b, p. 249). Thus, once a particular schema is activated, the particular features and responses that are part of the schema are easily recalled and preferentially used in the absence of further information. Examples of organizational schemas include the cognitive maps that members infer from their organizational experience (Bougon, Weick, and Binkhorst 1977; Huff 1990; Eden 1992); standard operating procedures; as well as the dominant logic and industry recipes that we discuss in this chapter. Schemas play a vital role in sense making, so much so that "sensemaking will tend to be schema driven rather than evidence driven" (Weick 1995, p. 153). Schemas organize past experience and behaviors into patterns, and in turn provide the "rules" or "guidelines" for future perception and action.

Cognitive filtering. In a classic study of impediments to the use of management information, Mintzberg (1975) identifies one of the main weaknesses as the way that "the brain systematically filters information in line with predetermined patterns of experience" (p. 15). Thus, we tend to perceive information in terms of our own past experiences and may systematically filter out information that is not in accordance with these experiences. Hammond (1973) explains how an individual's cognitive filter affects perception of incoming information: "different people with different filters can be exposed to the same external stimuli and end up with different resultant information in their thought processes. For example, a production and marketing manager might each read the same consultant's report regarding a particular new product and one would 'see' information regarding production and the other marketing. Each has an internal 'cognitive map' that is heavily colored by his experience and role in the organization. Thus what 'clicks' with one person is largely ignored as being irrelevant by the other" (Hammond 1973, p. 6). Sense making also involves seeing a conceptual relationship linking past experiences and information to current problems: "The process of establishing the required relationship has been dubbed by psychologists, 'cueing.' For instance, the recognition that the opening of a new medical clinic is in fact a marketing problem allows all one's previous experiences and knowledge related to marketing to be brought to bear on the problem" (Hammond 1973, p. 6). There are two aspects of cognitive filtering at work here: selective perception and selective cueing. While they reduce cognitive strain and effort, they can also result in rigidities, causing new problems to be considered in terms of previous ones and thereby filtering out relevant information.

Expectations and self-fulfilling prophecies. Because people favor order, consistency, and stability, they tend to cling on to the *expectations* generated by their schemas. This cognitive need is strong and induces a bias for information that confirms expectations, resulting in their selectively using only supportive information while rejecting or distrusting contradictory data (Hogarth 1987). Since sense making is about finding a plausible, believable explanation, a preferential use of confirmatory data according to strong expectations may well be a practical heuristic that allows the individual to construct an interpretation that is sufficiently clear and sufficiently accurate for the purpose at hand (Snyder 1984; Weick 1995). If confirmatory evidence is available or found, the information is selected for processing or retention. This could then lead to the making of inferences or interpretations implied by the expectations. Such an apparent "validation" reinforces the expectations which become even more strongly held. In cases when events and expectations diverge, both events and expectations may be modified to create situations leading to *self-fulfilling prophecies*. Self-fulfilling prophecies operate when initial expectations lead to the taking of certain actions that in turn produce results that reinforce the original expectations. This mutually confirming cycle is self-amplifying:

> as the actions increase in frequency, the original expectation is strengthened, and as the original expectation is strengthened, there is an even further increase in

actions in an ever-increasing, nonlinear cycle. . . . Because of the nonlinear nature
of this circular interaction, the original expectation needs only enough initial
credibility to start the ball rolling. Actions then lead to outcomes that heighten the
original expectation. That is why a weak initial belief can lead to a huge nonlinear
effect. . . . actions that confirm the original belief increasingly amplify the belief.
(Goldstein 1994, pp. 72, 77)

While self-fulfilling prophecies can distort perceptions and outcomes, again
they may be seen as practical strategies by which people make use of the available
information:

self-fulfilling prophecies are a fundamental act of Sense making. Prophecies,
hypotheses, anticipations—whatever one chooses to call them—are starting points.
They are minimal structures around which input can form as the result of some
kind of active prodding. That prodding is often belief-driven, and the beliefs that
drive it are often expectations. (Weick 1995, p. 148)

Self-fulfilling prophecies can also induce equilibrium that block off new information from outside its own self-sufficient structure. Organizations can unblock
information flow by techniques such as connecting workgroups with their environments, questioning differences in beliefs and points of view, contrasting the
original purpose of a group with its current functioning, challenging assumptions
creatively, using nonverbal methods to represent groups and systems, and so on
(Goldstein 1994).

Information Use and Affective Responses

Interpretive orientation. A study by Sutcliffe and Weber (2003) found that the
way senior executives interpret their business environment is more important for
organizational performance than how accurately they know their environment.
The survey data, drawn from 290 managers in 1991, suggest that, of all the factors examined, the executives' "general interpretive orientation" emerged as the
strongest and most consistent predictors of change and subsequent performance.
(According to Weick [1979a], general interpretive orientation refers to a "minimal sensible structure" consistent enough to filter information and focus attention, but loose enough to allow improvisation and speedy adjustment.) In other
words, an *interpretive orientation* can be a source of competitive advantage.
Specifically, the less the top executives in the study felt they were in control of
their environment, the more likely their companies were to change, and the better
they performed (in terms of sales and profit growth). At the same time, positive
expectations (as indicated by responses to questions like "most situations are
positive for the firm" and "there is a lot to be gained from most situations") were
strongly associated with both increased performance and change. Combining
these two traits suggests that an interpretive orientation based on humble optimism is related to positive change and performance. In contrast, perceptual accuracy based on three measures of the environment—volatility or frequency of
important changes, growth trends, and complexity—showed a negative relationship with profit performance. The authors conclude that the task of leaders is to

manage ambiguity and to mobilize action, not to store highly accurate knowledge about their environment. Leaders need to shape their interpretive outlooks, balancing confidence with caution, pessimism with optimism.

Attributional biases in sense making. Wagner and Gooding (1997) found different attributional tendencies at work when people were making sense of their own organizational successes or failures, and when they were explaining organization successes or failures they observe in others. When considering their own outcomes as actors, respondents' sense making showed self-serving inclinations to credit organizational strengths for organizational successes and blame environmental threats for organizational failures. Conversely, as observers, respondents' sense making tended to attribute other organizations' successes to environmental opportunities and explain other organizations' failures in terms of their weaknesses. These actor–observer effects suggest that the attributional biases influencing the sense made of other managers' actions are typically different from those that influence the sense made of one's own managerial activities. Such everyday attributional tendencies form a pattern of managerial sense making that can have negative consequences for organizational success and survival. Moreover, other research has indicated that actors assessing themselves relative to their competition tend to show evidence of overconfidence, either by overrating themselves or by underrating competitors. Wagner and Gooding (1997) suggest that "this tendency may originate in self-serving bias that leads managers to credit themselves and their firms for organizational success and attribute failure to external, environmental factors outside their control, and in actor–observer differences that lead these same managers to discount the success of other managers' organizations by ascribing them to environmental origins even as blame for organizational failure is placed on the organizations and their management" (p. 283).

Affect modulation. When groups and individuals are discussing their interpretations of what is going on, the types of communication behaviors that are invoked can help to relieve tension between the need to preserve self-values and the need to create shared consensus. Thus, Donnellon et al. (1986) found that organizational participants use affect modulation, linguistic indirection, metaphors, and logical argument in their communication strategies to reconcile dissimilar interpretations that nevertheless have common behavioral implications. In affect modulation, participants use voice, gesture, and emotion-laden words to modulate affective responses and cause the reconsideration of a situation. In linguistic indirection, they use passive voice and imprecise or broad language to play down sources of disagreement. In the use of metaphors parties can maintain their own interpretations while creating new meaning.

Information Use and Situational Dimensions

Sense giving and sense contesting. Sense making in organizations can be a political process. As groups and individuals interact, some may attempt to be "sense giving" (Gioia and Chittipeddi 1991); more are likely to be "sense contesting" (Huff and Huff 2000). Thus, new stories may be invented for what the group has been doing, and might do. Such stories construct new causal orders and propose rationales for action. We may expect sense giving and contesting to be more vigorous when the organization is facing consequential but unfamiliar changes in its environment. The more ambiguous or novel a problem, the greater the initial sense-making vacuum and the larger the impetus for parties to fill that void with plausible interpretations that are advantageous to the interests of these parties. A special case may exist in public policy making. A Canadian project on governing in an information society has as its major theme the better use of information: both how to make sense of incoming information from a wide range of sources and how best to communicate with the general public and stakeholders (Rosell et al. 1992). The study concluded that a basic dilemma of the information society is not so much an overload of information as it is a deficit in the capacity to frame and interpret that information, to translate it into useful understanding. In the project, a case study of the relationship of science and technology information to government decision making demonstrated that what was key for governance was not the scientific information per se, but the very different ways in which that information was translated into interpretations by politicians, officials, scientists, the media, interest groups, and so on. A key challenge for governance is the need to create a common language, a community of discourse among those coming from very different perspectives with very different languages and interests.

   In sense-contesting situations, how is shared meaning and action possible? Huff and Huff (2000) suggest that, through social interaction, the individual's original thoughts about the positives and negatives of a situation are homogenized into a smaller set of ideas that are more "actionable" because they more closely coincide with the interpretations of others (Huff and Huff 2000, p. 69). Orton (2000) sees sense making as the gradual development of a loose agreement among organization members about how to link a stream of events with a set of initiatives. Over time, fragmented individual beliefs are transformed into a loose organizational consensus—a "workable version of reality" (Weick 1979a)—that serves as a foundation for organizational action.

Commitment to action. We saw earlier that sense making may be belief driven or action driven. When actions are hard to change, people may instead modify their beliefs. Belief adjustment is more likely when the individual is highly committed to a course of action: "people try hardest to build meaning around those actions to which their commitment is strongest. Commitment, in other words, focuses sensemaking into binding actions" (Weick 1995, p. 156). Individuals are likely to become committed or bound to a behavior when the following situational dimensions apply:

1. the individual's acts are explicit or unambiguous,
2. the behavior is irrevocable or easily undone,

3. the behavior has been entered into freely or has involved a high degree of volition,

4. the act has importance for the individual,

5. the act is public or is visible to others, and

6. the act has been performed a number of times.

(Staw and Ross 1987, p. 52)

Briefly, individuals are likely to be bound to a current course of action when their prior behaviors in pursuing that course have been explicit, freely chosen, visible to others, irrevocable, repeated, and important (Staw and Ross 1987). Behavioral commitment introduces order into the sense-making process by noticing features that justify the behavior and by imputing value to the incoming information. When commitment is strong, individuals notice or look for features in a situation that others may miss in order to have the justification to support the continuance of the behavior. Available information and diverse interpretations are categorized into those that support, oppose, or are irrelevant to the behavior. On the whole, "commitment affects sensemaking by focusing attention, uncovering unnoticed features, and imposing value" (Weick 1995, p. 159).

Dominant logic. Organizations are inundated with information but find it difficult to interpret and act on the flood of information. Organizations are information-rich but interpretation-poor systems awash in raw information that must be channeled and converted into organizational intelligence. Bettis and Prahalad (1995) suggest that organizations use a *dominant logic* to function as an information filter or funnel that focuses organizational attention:

> Organizational attention is focused only on data deemed relevant by the dominant logic. Other data are largely ignored. "Relevant" data are filtered by the dominant logic and by the analytic procedures managers use to aid strategy development. These "filtered" data are then incorporated into the strategy, systems, values, expectations, and reinforced behavior of the organization. (Bettis and Prahalad 1995, p. 7)

The dominant logic is embedded in the shared mindsets, belief structures, and frames of reference that have been developed based on past experience, and which the managers of an organization use to conceptualize the business and make critical decisions (Prahalad and Bettis 1986). IBM, for example, was for many years guided by the dominant logic that computer mainframes are central to its business. This logic was entrenched in IBM's development of business strategies, reward systems, promotion preferences, and resource allocation priorities. (In recent years, with the growing use of smaller computers in client-server networks, IBM has updated the role of large mainframe computers as enterprise "super-servers" capable of supporting numerous clients in large networks.) Bettis and Prahalad (1995) maintain that the dominant logic is an emergent property of the organization as a complex, adaptive system: that is, it is not the property of any particular constituency, but appears as the dynamic result and shared property of the interactions between the various groups and subsystems of the organization.

VI. SUMMARY

- *Sense making* is a continuous, social process in which individuals look at elapsed events, bracket packets of experience, and select particular points of reference to weave patterns of meaning. The result of sense making is an enacted environment that is a reasonable and socially credible rendering of what is going on. The central problem in sense making is how to reduce ambiguity and develop shared meanings so that the organization may act collectively.

- People in organizations make sense of their environments through the processes of enactment, selection, and retention (Weick 1979b).

- In *enactment*, people notice some change in the flow of experience, and they isolate some of these changes for attention by bracketing and labeling parts of the experience or by taking action to create features in the environment to attend to.

- In *selection*, people choose meanings that can be imposed on the data they have bracketed. They draw from past interpretations and select plausible interpretations that provide the best fit with past understandings. The result is an enacted environment that is meaningful in that it provides a cause-and-effect explanation of what is going on.

- In *retention*, the products of successful sense making are stored so that they may be retrieved on future occasions. Retained meanings may be stored as mental maps that identify and label variables and connect them in causal relationships. Retained meanings become part of organizational culture and strategy and the basis of individual and collective identities.

- *Sense making* can be driven by beliefs or actions (Weick 1995).

- In *belief-driven sense making*, groups construct meaning by connecting pieces of information that fit with expectations or by connecting contradictory information through argumentation.

- In *action-driven sense making*, groups create meaning to justify visible courses of actions they are committed to, or they create meaning to explain actions they have taken to make things happen.

- Organizations achieve an actionable level of consensus by creating *shared cognitive structures* that guide the processing of information and by engaging in *communication behaviors* that establish agreement on action implications while accommodating differing interpretations.

- The sharing of beliefs and behaviors among members of a group is the essence of *organizational culture*. Schein (1991) proposes an integrated view of culture as a pattern of shared basic assumptions developed by a group as it learns to cope with its problems of external adaptation and internal integration. Martin (1992) proposes a multiperspective view of organizational culture as being simultaneously integrated, differentiated, and fragmented.

- *Information needs.* In sense making, information needs are unclear with regard to two basic questions: Which messages are important and need to be focused on? Which interpretation is the most plausible and should be used to understand what the messages mean? A special challenge is that the information available is often equivocal—it can support multiple and sometimes conflicting interpretations.

- *Information seeking.* The information-seeking process in sense making consists of scanning, noticing, and interpreting. The information culture of the organization, its dependence on and perception of the environment, and its access to channels that can influence the environment are some of the major factors that affect information-seeking behavior.

- *Information use.* In sense making, information use tends to be shaped by the existing mental structures or cognitive schemas of organizational members. Sense making in organizations can be a political arena for "sense giving" and "sense contesting." Sense giving and contesting can be more vigorous when the organization is facing consequential but unfamiliar changes in its environment.

THE MANAGEMENT OF LEARNING:

ORGANIZATIONS AS

KNOWLEDGE-CREATING

ENTERPRISES

Knowledge and action are the central relations between mind and world.
In action, world is adapted to mind. In knowledge, mind is adapted to world.
When world is maladapted to mind, there is a residue of desire.
When mind is maladapted to world, there is a residue of belief.
Desire aspires to action; belief aspires to knowledge.
The point of desire is action; the point of belief is knowledge.
    —*Timothy Williamson,* Knowledge and Its Limits, *2000*

Knowledge in an organization is revealed in the range of capabilities that the organization possesses as a result of this knowledge: capabilities that enable the organization to act to attain its goals. While most of an organization's knowledge is rooted in the expertise and experience of its members, the organization provides a physical, social, and cultural setting so that the exercise and growth of this knowledge takes on meaning and purpose. Many organizations recognize the importance of knowledge that it has accumulated over time and seek ways to multiply its value. The challenge here is that the same processes that increase the efficiency of knowledge sharing and use can also diminish the impetus for new knowledge creation.

Consider a modern-day consulting firm whose employees move from client to client, helping the client company to solve problems or implement new systems and procedures. Over time, the consultants gain insight about particular industries and accumulate knowledge about the kinds of solutions and implementation strategies that would work well for certain categories of clients. Although this personal knowledge is valuable to the firm, it is also hard to share and transfer. Orlikowski (1988) studied how one such firm wrestled with this dilemma. The firm was one of the top-ranked accounting firms with a large management consulting practice (MCP). MCP's business was to custom-build application software for its clients by sending in project teams who remained and worked on the client site for months or even years to produce a computerized information system. Building software for clients is a complex, knowledge-intensive activity that is fraught with uncertainty. Over its history, MCP created two innovations to manage its knowledge and to control uncertainty—a standardized system development methodology and a suite of computer-aided software engineering (CASE) tools. Orlikowski explains how MCP's standardized methodology ("Modus") came to be:

> When the MCP division first started developing information systems for clients some thirty years ago, the only written "knowledge" of systems development in the Firm was extracted post hoc from the documentation generated for each project. These so-called "client binders" served as the Firm's information expertise about the systems development production process during the initial years of the consulting practice. As the practice grew, some attempt was made to systematize this varied and highly idiosyncratic knowledge. During meetings partners would review the project documentation, trying to extract general procedures, and identify the common factors that made some projects successful, others mediocre, and still others failures. Over time these generalized "rules of thumb" became more extensive and more sophisticated as the MCP division gained more experience. Eventually the informal guidelines about how to run a successful systems development project and what factors constitute good systems practice, evolved into the formal, standardized methodology that "Modus" is today. (Orlikowski 1988, pp. 166–67)

Thus, MCP's system development methodology grew out of the experience of consultants working on projects. By analyzing and reflecting on this practical know-how, MCP partners were able to generalize and formalize a methodology that specified the tasks to be performed at each stage of the system development life cycle and defined standards for documentation, control, scheduling, and project estimation. The institutionalization of a standard methodology was in line with MCP's "one-firm" philosophy that required all partners to follow a common approach in how they dealt with clients' problems and communicated about them. From its earliest days, the firm had espoused a policy of speaking with one professional voice and upholding the official viewpoint of the firm.

The formalization of the "Modus" methodology made possible the next major innovation in MCP's consulting practice—the introduction of a standard set of computer-aided software engineering (CASE) tools, which MCP called "productivity tools," to support and implement the methodology. This integrated tool environment included software to capture system documentation into a data dictionary; project estimating aids; the project control system; screen and report design aids; data and program design aids; installation tools; and prototyping facilities. The tools "implemented the standard software engineering design philosophy and project management method articulated in 'Modus.'" In fact, "the tools were deliberately based on the methodology as it was recognized that production technology logic had to be compatible with that of the production process, else inconsistency and discontinuity would disrupt the systems development process" (Orlikowski 1988, p. 183). The use of the methodology and CASE tool set was thus mutually reinforcing. Moreover, the use of computerized tools projected an aura of professionalism:

> Tools render an image of a room of consultants all seated in front of their personal workstations, all bent over their keyboards, flashing through complicated-looking screens, performing sophisticated cut and paste procedures, and all done to the accompaniment of the reassuring whir of the disk drives, the steady tapping of keys, and the regular sigh of the laser printer emitting its professional-looking documents. It certainly looks industrious. (Orlikowski 1988, p. 403)

As a result of employing the tool methodology, MCP reported savings of 30 percent up to 50 percent in code generation and an elimination of between 50 percent and 70 percent of the systems installation phase. The use of tools "dramatically" increased MCP's profitability. Competitive position was improved by enabling the firm to bring the price of its services down, to lower its bids on contracts, to go after larger projects, and to increase the income contribution of each partner.

Besides productivity and profitability gains, there were other benefits. As a professional services firm, MCP was expected to deliver customized solutions to each of its clients. The software components in the CASE tool set were relatively easy to modify so that they could work well with a client's hardware and software environment. Each client thus received software systems that were customized to its project and technical requirements. At the same time, since the underlying process logic did not change that much from project to project, MCP was able to reuse significant portions of their development outputs:

> With the deployment of productivity tools it is able to adapt a set of system designs and documentation developed for one project for use in selling a similar system to another client. By being able to customize the visible features of the design to the potential client's needs while leaving the essential logic of the systems design intact, the Firm can exploit the power of the tools in saving time by not having to design another system or generate new documentation. It can use the logic of the existing system to customize the labels, change the screen and report headings, change client references in the documentation, and have a new comprehensive systems proposal to present to a potential client. And if the client accepts the proposal and the project gets underway, many of the tools, shells, macros can be directly transferred to the new project site, hence avoiding reinvention of the wheel. (Orlikowski 1988, p. 352)

The firm's standardization of its system development methodology ("Modus") defined a set of vocabulary to refer to concepts such as entity, data item, database, data flow, and so on and a grammar of rules to represent allowable relationships among these concepts. This vocabulary and grammar together constituted a "language of systems development" that was used by consultants to understand and interpret the organizational realities they were trying to automate. By encoding the systems development language into the CASE tools, consultants collaborating or communicating via these tools were required to use the language. The result is that "the uniform language of systems development plays a very significant role in sustaining the one-firm culture, informing the production process of the Firm, serving as the basis for consultants' indoctrination and training, and differentiating the Firm from its competitors" (Orlikowski 1988, p. 341). Thus, MCP's new recruits learned to be systems developers not only by acquiring the skills of programming and analysis, but also by learning to understand and use the language that represented the firm's view of systems development. Recruits spent six weeks in training before their first assignment. They came from all over the world to the Center for Professional Education in the U.S. Midwest to receive instruction from trainers who were specially flown in. The objective of the training was as much to "indoctrinate everyone into our way of doing work" (senior manager's quote) as it was to teach technical skills.

The training program included a simulation of an actual systems development project: "Recruits work in teams and have to conduct the actual installation of a system for a client—usually the order entry system—from detailed design through to the implementation. By all accounts these three weeks are intensive and pressured. During their three week participation in CPS (Computers in our Practice School), the recruits continue their learning of "Modus" begun in the self-study course, and learn the more specific tasks of programming (COBOL) and testing. They worked an average of twelve hours a day, five days a week, and eight hours a day on Saturdays and Sundays. The intent of CPS was to simulate as much as possible the working conditions of real projects" (Orlikowski 1988, pp. 398–99). A staff analyst who had recently completed CPS had this to say: "You go there not for the skills you learn, but for the indoctrination. Spending three weeks in the same room with the same hundred people doing things you can't see the need for—you quickly get to know the way the Firm does things, and realize if that's what you want to do" (quoted on p. 399). The firm's training school also housed a "Cultural Center" with a museum that presented the firm's history through a display of artifacts and memorabilia. An interactive video system allowed users to select and play videotapes of the partners discussing the firm's history, goals, and values.

After the training program, new hires then worked for two years as staff analysts with experienced consultants in project teams at clients' sites where they would do mostly installation tasks such as programming, testing, and documentation. It was during this on-the-job period that new staff learned the skills of business problem analysis and systems design.

Orlikowski's main conclusion was that the use of information technology at MCP increased the level of unobtrusive control and routinized systems development work while improving its productivity and consistency. The technology became an effective medium for facilitating a shared set of meanings among project members, embedding a "language of systems development" that enhanced instrumental action while discouraging reflection on taken-for-granted assumptions. She noted that

> the tools in their design and implementation deskill the functional production tasks of systems development. The requirement for technical skills has been eliminated through the routinization of the tasks, detaching the execution of a task from the knowledge underlying it. The requirement for functional skills has been reduced to some extent through the rationalization of tasks which makes much of the development work an exercise in filling in standardized forms and using abstracted design techniques. Deskilling the tasks has generated a number of unintended consequences that have raised some problems in the Firm. The tools seem to be breeding a generation of relatively unskilled consultants, whose long-term systems development performance is suspect. The tools create among analysts a dependence on tools and a lack of understanding of programming that sometimes hinders project progress. . . . through formalizing, abstracting and reifying tasks, tools limit individual discretion, eliminate creativity and flexibility, generate shallow designs, encourage passivity, and discourage reflectiveness. (Orlikowski 1988, pp. 241, 250)

The formalization of knowledge at MCP had important negative consequences. It increased reliance on standardized tools, reduced the need to apprehend underlying rules, and led to a gradual hollowing out of consultants' skills. This finding has special resonance for organizations seeking technological solutions that will capture and consolidate knowledge: technology increases efficiency and consistency, but often at the cost of new learning and creativity. What starts out as an attempt to use information technology to leverage the firm's core capability may also accelerate the erosion of this capability, turning it into a liability.

I. DATA, INFORMATION, KNOWLEDGE

Knowledge and information are the outcomes of human action that engage signs, signals, and artifacts in social and physical settings. Knowledge builds on an accumulation of experience. Information depends on an aggregation of data. However, knowledge is not simply an accretion of information over time:

> We cannot regard knowledge as simply the accumulation of information in a stockpile, even though all the messages that are received by the brain may leave some sort of deposit here. Knowledge must itself be regarded as a structure, a very complex and quite loose pattern with its parts connected in various ways by ties of varying degrees of strength. Messages are continually shot into this structure; some of them pass right through its interstices without effecting any perceptible change in it. Sometimes messages "stick" to the structure and become part of it. . . . Occasionally, however, a message which is inconsistent with the basic pattern of the mental structure, but which is of such nature that it cannot be disbelieved hits the structure, which is then forced to undergo a complete reorganization. (Boulding 1955, pp. 103–104)

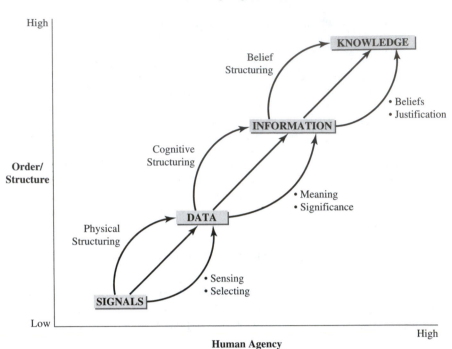

FIGURE 4.1. Data, Information, and Knowledge

Thus, we propose that the transformation of information into knowledge is the result of two complementary dynamics: the "structuring" of data and information that imposes or reveals order and pattern; and the human "acting" on data and information that attributes sense and salience. Fig. 4.1 uses these two dimensions to show the assumed progression of data into information into knowledge.

In the lower left of Fig. 4.1, we start with signals—sights, sounds, and other sensory phenomena to which the human actor is exposed. From the vast amount of signals reaching a person, the actor selects and takes notice of only a small number. This noticing typically involves grouping or delimiting signals into packets of data. Thus, marks on a paper are recognized as words; illuminated pixels on a screen are registered as images. The structuring of signals is physical because it depends on conditions in the material environment (such as lighting, noise) and on technical requirements of the task being performed (such as speed, accuracy). At the same time, which signals are noticed and punctuated into data is influenced by the observer's past learning about parsing of signals, as well as by beliefs about what signals to expect. Data then are facts and messages observed by an individual or group. Data are often elements of larger physical systems (such as books, instrument panels) which give clues about what data to notice and how they should be "read."

In the middle of Fig. 4.1, we show how the observer makes sense of noticed data through a process of "cognitive structuring" which assigns meaning and significance to the perceived facts and messages. What meanings are constructed depends on the schemas and mental models that the actor brings forth to frame, categorize, and contextualize the data. Schemas mediate between sensory experience and intellectual thought: "schema refers to an active organization of past reactions, or past experiences, which must always be supposed to be operating in any well-adapted organic response. That is, whenever there is any order or regularity of behavior, a particular response is possible only because it is related to other similar responses which have been serially organized, yet which operate, not simply as individual members coming one after another, but as a unitary mass" (Bartlett 1932, p. 201). Whereas schemas are concerned with content—they enable the actor to categorize objects and thoughts—mental models are concerned with form—they enable the actor to represent selected data and their relationships to other facts and messages, and thereby make inferences about what the data mean. Mental models (Johnson-Laird 1983) are constructed by individuals using words, images, or both in order to represent data and their relationships in a convenient and accessible manner so that a viable interpretation may be composed and tested. Thus, data become information when the former has been vested with meaning and relevance.

At the top of Fig. 4.1, information becomes knowledge when a human actor forms justified, true beliefs about the world (belief structuring). This view is derived from standard analysis in epistemology that defines propositional knowledge as justified true belief (Audi 1998; Moser et al. 1998). This definition of knowledge specifies three conditions that are individually necessary and jointly sufficient. The belief condition requires that a person who knows that a proposition (which is an object of knowledge) is so believes that proposition. Beliefs are psychological states of the mind: while they may or may not be manifested in overt behavior, they do involve tendencies or dispositions to behave in certain ways under certain conditions. The truth condition requires that a person genuinely knows that a proposition is so only if that proposition is in fact the case. A proposition is true when for example there is a correspondence between the true statement and actual features of the world; or when the statement is "coherent" with some system of other statements (such as one's other beliefs). Since truth is relative, knowledge may vary dramatically from person to person (or from organization to organization), yet there will still be knowledge, in abundance. The justification condition requires that a person must have adequate indication or evidence that a proposition is true. Knowledge is not simply true belief—the justification condition disqualifies true beliefs that are supported only by lucky guesswork.

The treatment of knowledge in organizations is often based implicitly on empiricism—that concepts and propositions claiming to be knowledge are derived from experience and depend for their justification on experience. A related point of view approaches the human actor as a natural phenomenon whose epistemic activity is to be studied using empirical methods ("naturalistic epistemology" [Quine 1969; Kornblith 1994]). For example, Dretske (1981) applies information theory to characterize knowledge as information-produced belief: a person knows that a proposition is so only if some signal conveys this information to that person—information being an object that can be processed and transmitted from one place to another when events at these places are connected by some dependency.

Goldman (1986, 1999) argues that a belief can be justified if it is generated by belief-forming (cognitive) processes that have the reliable capability to arrive at true or correct answers to questions of interest. One such belief-forming practice is *testimony:* the transmission of observed information from one person to others. More generally, it considers observers who decide whether and what to report, and receivers who decide what credence to place in reports they receive. Testimony deals with the most elementary type of factual discourse involving simple reports of observations. Factual discourse often features more-complex speech acts, in which people not only advance a factual claim but present reasons or evidence in support of it. This sort of discursive practice, *argumentation,* places the emphasis on speaker practices rather than hearer practices. Other examples of belief-forming processes include reasoning processes, memory processes, and perceptual processes. A pertinent question becomes just how reliable such a process must be in order that its resultant belief be justified. Since perfect reliability is not required, those processes that sometimes produce error can still confer justification.

How does information in organizations evolve into knowledge? Starting from interpreted information, organizational participants take actions based on construed meaning and import. As they observe and reflect on the outcomes of using different sets of information in a variety of work, social, and personal situations, people discern patterns and form beliefs in order to understand them. Patterns, propositions, and hypotheses are the evolving material of personal and organizational knowledge. While a particular set of information refers to a specific experience, knowledge refers to an accumulation of experiences which has yielded concepts, beliefs, and evidence that sustain these beliefs. Through use, practice, and reflection, information becomes knowledge—in this sense, knowledge is the result of "belief structuring" which leads to a higher level of ordering and understanding than is the case for information (Fig. 4.1). Knowledge supplies beliefs and assumptions that are used to perceive situations or events and to explain cause-effect relationships between actors and actions. Knowledge may be formal and informal, conscious and unconscious, cognitive and affective, prepackaged and situated.

Although an organization certainly possesses beliefs which it perceives to be true, these beliefs are often arrived at through weak belief-forming processes that may not meet the justification condition. Thus, organizations use belief-forming processes that rely on simplifications, individual opinions, or heuristics. Over time, beliefs can become entrenched or protected, so that an organization may continue to act on them unthinkingly or fail to reexamine their validity when new information is available. These behaviors block the acquisition of new knowledge, and this is one reason why organizations are said to be hobbled by learning disabilities.

In organizations, the justification of knowledge as true belief becomes a public process. As individuals bring forth their personal beliefs in the act of sharing knowledge, they are called upon to justify those beliefs in the presence of others. According to von Krogh (1998) such public justification of personal knowledge is a fragile process because of four barriers: the need for a legitimate language to express the knowledge in understandable and acceptable terms; the existence of stories of failure that appear to challenge the personal beliefs; formal procedures that work against the justification process by controlling communications and steps; and the company's prevailing paradigm that seems to disagree with the personal beliefs. Justification may also be a political process, particularly when it involves individuals or groups who are perceived to possess higher power or status, and who can therefore lay stronger claims about the veracity or value of their beliefs.

II. ORGANIZATIONAL KNOWLEDGE

Knowledge in organizations is not monolithic nor homogenous. Individuals, groups, and an organization as a whole all possess knowledge. Thus, there is knowledge unique to each person gained through practice, experience, and reflection. There is knowledge embedded in the physical goods the organization produces and in the rules and routines that the organization adopts. There is knowledge comprising of what the organization believes about itself (identity, purpose), its capabilities, and its environment (communities, markets). Taken together, the knowledge of an organization may be categorized as tacit knowledge, explicit knowledge, and cultural knowledge (Boisot 1998; Spender 1998).

As shown in Table 4-1, *tacit knowledge* is the implicit knowledge used by people in organizations to do their work and to make sense of their worlds. Tacit knowledge is hard to verbalize because it is expressed through action-based

TABLE 4-1. Categories of organizational knowledge.

Tacit Knowledge	• The implicit knowledge used by people in organizations to perform their work and to make sense of their worlds. • Tacit knowledge is hard to verbalize because it is expressed through action-based skills and cannot be reduced to rules and recipes.
Explicit Knowledge	• Knowledge that is codified or made intangible and can therefore be easily communicated or diffused. • Explicit knowledge may be object based or rule based.
Cultural Knowledge	• The shared assumptions and beliefs about an organization's goals, capabilities, customers, and competitors. • The assumptions and beliefs that are used to assign value and significance to new information.

skills and cannot be reduced to rules and recipes. It is learned through extended periods of experiencing and doing a task, during which the individual develops a feel for and a capacity to make intuitive judgments about the successful performance of the activity. *Explicit knowledge* is knowledge that has been codified formally using a system of symbols or made tangible as a physical artifact and can therefore be easily communicated. Explicit knowledge may be object based or rule based. It is object-based when the knowledge is codified in symbolic expressions (words, numbers, formulas) or in tangible assets (equipment, documents, models). Explicit knowledge is rule-based when the knowledge is codified into rules, instructions, or specifications. A large part of an organization's operations is controlled by rules and policies. *Cultural knowledge* consists of the shared assumptions and beliefs about an organization's identity, goals, capabilities, customers, and competitors. These beliefs are used to assign value and significance to new information and knowledge, as well as to give meaning and purpose to the use of organizational knowledge.

While we will be looking at each of these knowledge types in the ensuing sections, it is important to note that all three categories are engaged simultaneously in organizational work. Indeed, the more integrated the three types of knowledge, the greater the capability of the organization to apply and create new knowledge. What then is organizational knowledge, seen as a whole? Tsoukas and Vladimirou provide a thoughtful answer:

> To sum up, knowledge is the individual capability to draw distinctions, within a domain of action, based on an appreciation of context or theory, or both. Organizations are three things at once: concrete settings within which individual action takes place; sets of abstract rules in the form of propositional statements; and historical communities. Organizational knowledge is the capability members of an organization have developed to draw distinctions in the process of carrying out their work, in particular concrete contexts, by enacting sets of generalizations (propositional statements) whose application depends on historically evolved collective understandings and experiences. (Tsoukas and Vladimirou 2001, p. 983)

III. TACIT KNOWLEDGE

Michael Polanyi examines human tacit knowledge by "starting from the fact that *we can know more than we can tell*" (1966, p. 4, italics in original). Tacit knowledge permeates our personal and work lives, enabling us to drive an automobile, enjoy a poem, or deal with familiar problems. In all such cases of personal knowing, "*the aim of a skillful performance is achieved by the observance of a set of rules which are not known as such to the person following them*" (Polanyi 1962, p. 49, italics in original). Tacit knowledge is hard to transfer or verbalize partly because it cannot be expressed as specific rules or elements, and partly because it exists as an emergent quality of knowing something as a whole.

Tacit knowledge may be likened to knowing that is in our action, "implicit in our patterns of actions and in our feel for the stuff with which we are dealing"

(Schön 1983, p. 54). Schön defines this "knowing-in-action" with the following properties:

1. There are actions, recognitions, and judgments which we know how to carry out spontaneously; we do not have to think about them prior to or during their performance.

2. We are often unaware of having learned to do these things; we simply find ourselves doing them.

3. In some cases, we were once aware of the understandings which were subsequently internalized in our feeling for the stuff of action. In other cases, we may never have been aware of them. In both cases, however, we are usually unable to describe the knowing which our action reveals.

(Schön 1983, p. 54)

From her analysis of the work practices of operators in pulp and paper mills, Zuboff observed how operators relied on action-centered skills that are based on tacit knowledge:

> When operators in Piney Wood and Tiger Creek discuss their traditional skills, they speak of knowing things by habit and association. They talk about "cause-and-effect" knowledge and being able to see the things to which they must respond. They refer to "folk medicine" and knowledge that you don't even know you have until it is suddenly displayed in the ability to take a decisive action and make something work. (Zuboff 1988, pp. 71, 187)

Tacit know-how is not limited to technical skills, but is just as important in undergirding the actions of professionals in architecture, engineering, management, psychotherapy, and so on (Schön 1983). Zuboff again provides an example of how bank account officers in the Global Bank Brazil made their credit decisions:

> Our credit decisions have been more related to feeling than to technical skill. For big loans, the officer knows the client and the client's environment. He spends time with that person. They dine together, play golf together. That is why we specialize by industry and company size. This is why the officer comes to know things that are not written. Credit is given by the feeling in one's stomach. (Quoted in Zuboff 1988, p. 164)

Nonaka and Takeuchi (1995) define tacit knowledge in this way: "Tacit knowledge is highly personal and hard to formalize, making it difficult to communicate or to share with others. Subjective insights, intuitions, and hunches fall into this category of knowledge. Furthermore, tacit knowledge is deeply rooted in an individual's action and experience, as well as in the ideals, values, or emotions he or she embraces" (p. 8). They go on to argue that tacit knowledge can be converted to explicit knowledge (and vice versa), and that this process lies at the center of organizational knowledge creation. A number of researchers have questioned this treatment of tacit knowledge. Wilson (2002) stressed that in Polanyi's analysis, "'tacit' means 'hidden', tacit knowledge is hidden knowledge, hidden even from the consciousness of the knower. This is why Polanyi used the phrase 'We know more than we can tell.'" The idea that tacit knowledge can somehow be converted to explicit knowledge suggests to Wilson that "implicit knowledge, which is not normally expressed, but may be expressed, is actually intended here. Implicit knowledge is that which we take for granted in our actions, and which may be shared by others through common experience or culture. . . . Implicit knowledge, in other words, is expressible: tacit knowledge is not, and Nonaka would have saved a great deal of confusion had he chosen the more appropriate term" (Wilson 2002). In a paper titled "Do We Really Understand Tacit Knowledge?" Tsoukas (2003) concludes that tacit knowledge has in fact been greatly misunderstood. Nonaka and Takeuchi's interpretation of tacit knowledge as "knowledge-not-yet-articulated" is "erroneous" because "it ignores the essential ineffability of tacit knowledge, thus reducing it to what can be articulated. Tacit and explicit knowledge are not the two ends of a continuum but the two sides of the same coin: even the most explicit kind of knowledge is underlain by tacit knowledge" (Tsoukas 2003, p. 425).

Nelson and Winter (1982) start also from Polanyi but arrive at a destination different from Nonaka and Takeuchi's focus on the individual as the locus of tacit knowledge. Instead, they view organizational knowledge as being mostly tacit knowledge that is embedded in organizational routines. In their major work on a knowledge-based theory of the firm, an organization's knowledge resides in its memory and is stored primarily in its routines. The routinization of activity in an organization constitutes the most important form of storage of organizational knowledge, so that organizations basically "remember by doing" (Nelson and Winter 1982, p. 99). Most of the operational knowledge in organizations exist at a tacit level, embedded in routines that become the carriers of this knowledge. Here, "routine" refers to "regular and predictable behavioral patterns" that "range from well-specified technical routines for producing things, through procedures for hiring and firing, ordering new inventory, or stepping up production of items in high demand, to policies regarding investment, research and development, advertising, and business strategies about product diversification and overseas investment" (p. 14).

The knowledge expressed in organizational routines is tacit for two reasons. First, routines are ways of doing things that have formed over time: they resemble near-automatic responses that have been internalized by organizational actors who execute them without "conscious awareness" (p. 125). Second, routines are to organizations what skills represent for human behavior: "As in the case of individual skills, the specificity of the behavior involved is simply the obverse of its effectiveness; also, much of the knowledge that underlies the performance is tacit knowledge of the organization, not consciously known or articulable by anyone in particular" (p. 134).

Nelson and Winter suggest three reasons why knowledge used in an organization's operations and practices is likely to remain tacit to a significant degree: "because it cannot be articulated fast enough, because it is impossible to articulate all that is necessary to a successful performance, and because language cannot simultaneously serve to describe relationships and characterize the things related" (p. 82). Speed of communication is a problem when the rate of information transfer is well below the rate needed to actually perform a task. Articulation is a problem when the practical knowledge is limited in "causal depth": that is, enough is known to perform a task without requiring deep theoretical understanding underlying that skill. Relating parts to the whole is a problem when efforts to exhaustively explain details lead to incoherent messages and information overload.

If organizational knowledge resides in its routines, what of the knowledge of the individual? Nelson and Winter explain the relationship between individual knowledge (which also includes tacit knowledge) and organizational knowledge as follows:

> In the sense that the memories of individual members do store so much of the information required for the performance of organizational routines, there is substantial truth in the proposition that the knowledge an organization possesses is reducible to the knowledge of its individual members. . . . But the knowledge stored in human memories is meaningful and effective only in some context, and for knowledge exercised in an organizational role that context is an organizational context. It typically includes, first, a variety of forms of external memory—files, message boards, manuals, computer memories, magnetic tapes—that complement and support individual memories but that are maintained in large part as a routine organizational function. . . . Second, the context includes the physical state of equipment and of the work environment generally. . . . Finally, and the most important, the context of the information possessed by an individual member is established by the information possessed by the information possessed by all other members. . . . To view organizational memory as reducible to individual member memories is to overlook, or undervalue, the linking of those individual memories by shared experiences in the past, experiences that have established the extremely detailed and specific communication system that underlies routine performance. (Nelson and Winter 1982, p. 105)

Nelson and Winter (1982) construct an evolutionary theory of economic change in which organizational routines play the role of organizational genes. Thus, routines as genes are persistent features of the organization that determine its range of possible behavior. They are inheritable in the sense that new "offspring" organizations (such as branch plants or regional offices) possess many of the features of their "parent" organization. They mutate as organizations make adjustments to their routines—sometimes by change, and sometimes as a response to external or internal change. They are selectable in the sense that organizations with certain routines may do better than others, depending on their fit with the environment.

The tension between knowledge that is tacit, embedded in personal skill or organizational routines, and knowledge that is made tangible as a valuable product or service lies at the center of many efforts to somehow "manage" organizational knowledge. As long as skills and expertise remain internalized in the individual, the organization is limited in its ability to parlay that knowledge in some larger, strategic sense. Kogut and Zander (1992) observed that "Unless able to train large numbers of individual or to transform skills into organizing principles, the craft shop is forever simply a shop. The speed of replication of knowledge determines the rate of growth; control over its diffusion deters competitive erosion of the market position. For a firm to grow, it must develop organizing principles and a widely-held and shared code by which to orchestrate large numbers of people and, potentially, varied functions" (p. 390).

The recent history of numerical control machines provides an instance of a somewhat ingenious (some might say disingenuous) way of converting tacit knowledge into explicit computer programs and turning this capability into a competitive advantage (Sabel 1982; Noble 1984). Numerical control machines are machine tools each equipped with a built-in computer that controls its operations and are widely used in many large-scale manufacturing industries. The computer of the numerical control machine has to be individually programmed for each component that the machine is to fabricate. This programming could be done by an engineer coding the operations on a central computer or it could be done by "recording" the activities of a human operator. In Germany and Japan, numerical control users and machine designers opted for the latter, recording the movements and tasks of their most skilled tool operators, in effect externalizing the operators' tacit knowledge and converting it into machine-readable code. The recording process also allowed the operators to make corrections or improvements to recorded sections as they learned to do a particular task more efficiently. In the United States, many managers and engineering departments programmed the numerical control machines themselves, partly because they believed that programming by engineers was superior to machinist programming, and partly because they did not want to be dependent on unionized tool operators should they become the only ones able to run the machines. This difference in the knowledge conversion method has strategic consequences: "nowadays most of the machines are being programmed by less expensive skilled workers rather than by senior engineers who, much more expensively, know both the abstract language of numerical-control programming and the concrete routines of metal-working. This means that now the Japanese and Germans control the international sales of most machine tools, whereas thirty or so year ago the United States was the dominant force in that market. Obviously, someone in the United States made a big mistake in what kind of skill system to build numerical control into" (Stinchcombe 1990, p. 53).

IV. EXPLICIT KNOWLEDGE

Explicit knowledge is knowledge that "can be expressed in words and numbers, and easily communicated and shared in the form of hard data, scientific formulae, codified procedures, or universal principles" (Nonaka and Takeuchi 1995, p. 8). Examples of explicit knowledge include chemical formulae, market forecasts, operations procedures, product specifications, software code, and technical standards. Explicit knowledge may be object based or rule based. Object-based knowledge may be found in artifacts such as products, patents, software code, computer databases, technical drawings, tools, prototypes, photographs, voice recordings, films, and so on. Knowledge is object based when it is represented using strings of symbols (words, numbers, formulas) or is embodied in physical entities (equipment, models, substances). In the first case, the symbols directly represent or codify the explicit knowledge. In the second case, explicit knowledge may be unpacked from the physical object by, for example, reverse-engineering a product, inspecting software code, or analyzing the composition of a substance. Explicit knowledge is rule based when the knowledge is codified into rules, instructions, specifications, standards, methodologies, classification systems, formulas, and so on. A substantial part of an organization's operational knowledge about how to do things is contained in its rules, policies, and directives. (Note the difference between rules and routines. In the previous section, Nelson and Winter [1982] described organizational routines as largely tacit. Here, we say that written-down rules—which may be a component of routines—represent explicit knowledge.)

One important distinction between tacit and explicit knowledge lies in the transferability of the knowledge as well as the mechanisms that accomplish this transfer. Grant (1996a, p. 111) suggests that "explicit knowledge is revealed by its communication. This ease of communication is its fundamental property." On the other hand, tacit knowledge is revealed through its application. If tacit knowledge cannot be codified and can only be acquired through observation and practice, then its transfer between individuals is necessarily slow, costly, and uncertain (Kogut and Zander 1992).

An organization's explicit knowledge may take the form of intellectual assets, which Sullivan (1998, p. 23) defines as

> the codified, tangible, or physical descriptions of specific knowledge to which the company can assert ownership rights. Any piece of knowledge that becomes defined, usually by being written down or entered into a computer, qualifies as an intellectual asset and can be protected. Intellectual assets are the source of innovations that the firm commercializes.

Examples of intellectual assets include plans, procedures, memos, sketches, drawings, blueprints, and computer programs. Intellectual assets may be categorized into commercializable assets and structural assets (Sullivan 1998). Commercializable assets are those that the organization can directly offer in the business or technology marketplace (through, for example, technology licensing or joint ventures). Commercializable assets may in turn be divided into those that are legally protected and those that are not. Legally protected assets are called intellectual property, and this includes, for example, patents, copyrights, trademarks, trade secrets, and semiconductor masks. Unprotected assets that are nevertheless commercializable refer usually to the organization's innovations which are still undergoing development. Structural assets are part of the organization's infrastructure and may include its administrative and technical methods, processes, procedures, as well as role, authority, and reporting structures.

Explicit knowledge codified as intellectual assets are valuable to the organization because they add to the organization's observable and tradable stocks of knowledge. Moreover, because they have been committed to media, ideas may be communicated more easily, increasing the likelihood of discussion, experimentation, and reflection, thereby generating further cycles of knowledge creation and use.

Explicit knowledge serves a number of important purposes in an organization. First, it encodes past learning. Good solutions and methods learned from experience are formalized as rules to avoid reinventing the wheel. Rules and instructions can also be more easily packaged into training programs and tools that help transfer knowledge to new employees. Second, explicit knowledge facilitates coordination between disparate activities and functions in the organization. An organization's tasks are highly interdependent: plans, specifications, contracts, rules, and standards are used to define outputs, reports, and timelines so that the interdependency of an organization's work activities can be properly coordinated. Third, explicit knowledge reduces the information-processing load associated with task performance by stipulating protocols, codes, classifications, and other meaningful informational conventions. Fourth, the use of explicit knowledge allows the organization to signify its professional skill and technical rationality, and so present a self-image of competence, legitimacy, and accountability.

Despite the apparent advantages of explicit knowledge, organizations are concerned that codifying their knowledge will render them vulnerable to the loss of strategically important knowledge. Because explicit knowledge is articulated knowledge, it is often assumed to be readily understood by others and can therefore move more easily outside an organization's boundary, perhaps to competitors or worse. Sanchez (2002) suggests that this assumption may not always be warranted. Even though the knowledge has been made explicit, the receiving organization may experience problems of comprehension and valuation as it tries to understand and appraise the significance of the articulated knowledge. There may be several reasons: firms develop their own languages and vocabularies that others might not understand; different firms possess different levels of technical capability; different firms are at different stages of growth and development; the usefulness of the knowledge depends on its linkages with other knowledge, resources, and capabilities in the originating firm. Given these uncertainties, the assumption that explicit knowledge is fundamentally "less secure" than tacit knowledge may be simplistic.

Explicit knowledge plays a special role in the innovation-decision process. Innovation decision making is an information-seeking and information-processing activity (Rogers 1983, 1995) through which an individual moves from (1) initial knowledge about an innovation through subsequent phases of (2) forming an attitude toward the innovation; (3) deciding to adopt or reject the innovation; (4) implementing the new idea; and (5) confirming the decision. During the knowledge phase, an individual becomes aware of an innovation's existence and gains some understanding of how it functions. An innovation is thus first encountered as an objectification and embodiment of knowledge. Rogers (1983, 1995) calls this software information:

> An innovation typically contains software information, which is embodied in the innovation and which serves to reduce uncertainty about the cause-effect relationships that are involved in achieving a desired outcome (such as meeting a need of the individual). (Rogers 1995, p. 165)

Three types of knowledge are involved in innovation diffusion. First, there is awareness knowledge, which is information that an innovation exists. Second, there is how-to knowledge, which consists of information necessary to use an innovation properly: answering questions such as what quantity of an innovation to secure and how to use it correctly. Third, there is principles knowledge, which is information explaining the principles underlying how an innovation works. Examples are concepts about biology of plant growth which underlie fertilizer adoption by farmers; principles of human reproduction which form a basis for family planning innovations; and basics of germ theory which support vaccination and health campaigns. To accelerate diffusion, all three types of innovation-based knowledge are likely to contain explicit elements in order to promote awareness, visibility, and understandability and to increase the chances of proper use and successful outcomes. Thus, an innovation may be introduced as a physical artifact (e.g., crop fertilizer, birth-control pill) that is accompanied by clearly laid out instructions on its deployment as well as background information on why the innovation works and what the benefits are.

V. CULTURAL KNOWLEDGE

While the classification of organizational knowledge as tacit and explicit is widely discussed, the category of cultural knowledge is less-often encountered. Boisot (1998) attributes this to a "Western bias towards classifying as knowledge only that which can be given a codified and abstract formulation":

> [This] has led knowledge assets—whether embodied in physical objects such as plant and machinery, or in organizational practices such as planning and budgeting systems—to be treated as if they were essentially technological in nature. They are not. They are first and foremost cultural and only then technological. The potential value of a knowledge asset is largely a function of how it is used and in what context. . . . it does not make much sense to talk of knowledge assets independently of the cultures in which they are embedded. It takes culture as operating through institutional structures that must themselves be considered knowledge assets. (Boisot 1998, p. 119)

At the beginning of the chapter, we presented a definition of knowledge as justified true belief. An organization's cultural knowledge thus consists of the beliefs it holds to be true and justifiably so (based on experience, observation,

reflection) about itself and its environment. These beliefs address such fundamental questions as "What kind of an organization are we?" "What is our business?" "Who are our customers, competitors?" "How do we measure success?"
The answers to these questions are in turn used to determine the value and
salience of new knowledge: "What knowledge would be valuable to the organization?" "Which knowledge would be worth pursuing?" "What knowledge are
we able to absorb?"

Briefly then, shared beliefs, assumptions, and norms form the framework in
which organizational members understand their work and its purpose, perceive
problems and opportunities, and assess the value and potential of new knowledge. Collins (1998) highlights two important roles of cultural knowledge: it is
required to understand and use facts, rules, and heuristics; and to make induc-
tions in the same way as others in order to enable concerted action. Cultural
knowledge, by defining the limits and bases of legitimate discourse, also

> constitutes the main conduit for the expression and existence of power, in the sense
> of defining what is legitimized as knowledge in the first place, and who are
> accorded sufficient reputation and status to have their views taken seriously in the
> second place. (Fleck 1998, p. 160)

Fleck's commentary echoes many others. For example, knowledge as power
is a recurrent theme in much of Foucault's work (see, for example, Foucault
1980). Knowledge as paradigm received its most celebrated exposition in Kuhn
(1970), who analyzed how normal science takes place within paradigms that define what kinds of problems are studied, what methods are acceptable, and what
criteria are used to evaluation solutions. In an organization, being aware and
being willing to question foundational beliefs about its identity, purpose, and
environment will allow new knowledge to come to the fore, be noticed, and be
engaged. For many organizations, however, beliefs and values can become so entrenched over time that they are unquestioned or even unquestionable (Argyris
1990).

According to Sackmann (1991, 1992), cultural knowledge in an organization
consists of dictionary knowledge, directory knowledge, recipe knowledge, and
axiomatic knowledge. *Dictionary knowledge* comprises commonly held descriptions, including expressions and definitions used in the organization to describe
the "what" of situations, such as what is considered to be a problem or what is
considered to be success. *Directory knowledge* refers to commonly held practices and is knowledge about sequences of events and their cause-effect relationships that describe the "how" of processes, such as how a problem is solved or
how success is to be achieved. *Recipe knowledge* comprises prescriptions for repair and improvement strategies that recommend what action "should" be taken,
for example, to solve a problem or to become successful. *Axiomatic knowledge*
refers to reasons and explanations of the final causes or a priori premises that are
perceived to account for "why" events happen. Sackman's categories of cultural
knowledge are closely related to the schemas, scripts, cause maps, and basic assumptions that are often associated with discussions of organizational culture.

Garud and Rappa (1994, p. 345) propose that the development of new knowledge based on technology is a socio-cognitive process which rests on three definitions of technology: "technology as beliefs, artifacts, and evaluation routines." Technology development is guided by beliefs about what is possible, what is worth attempting, and what levels of effort are required. Technology as physical artifact specifies the technology's form (such as shape or material of construction) and function (such as uses and applications). Technology as evaluation routines defines testing routines and normative values that "filter data in a way that influences whether or not researchers perceive information as useful. Researchers with different beliefs attempt to sway each other with respect to the routines utilized to judge the technology" (Garud and Rappa 1994, p. 346). Evaluation routines also facilitate communication about the technology and allow the new technology to gain legitimacy in the eyes of researchers. Beliefs, artifacts, and evaluation routines interact with each other to shape the evolution of new technology. Garud and Rappa suggest that beliefs guide the creation of artifacts that in return raise commitment in the technology; beliefs are externalized as testing routines and standards; and routines legitimize and select the form that the technology takes. Overall, an organization's beliefs about what technology or new knowledge is feasible and worth attempting, a part of its cultural knowledge, would influence the direction and intensity of the knowledge development effort, as well as the routines and norms by which new information and knowledge would be evaluated.

In the context of knowledge creating, cultural knowledge plays the vital role of providing a pattern of shared assumptions (Schein 1991) so that the organization can assign significance to new information and knowledge. Cultural knowledge supplies values and norms that

> determine what kinds of knowledge are sought and nurtured, what kinds of knowledge-building activities are tolerated and encouraged. There are systems of caste and status, rituals of behavior, and passionate beliefs associated with various kinds of technological knowledge that are as rigid and complex as those associated with religion. Therefore, values serve as knowledge-screening and -control mechanisms. (Leonard 1995, p. 19)

There are familiar accounts of organizations in which cultural knowledge is misaligned with its efforts to exploit tacit and explicit knowledge. For example, Xerox Palo Alto Research Center (PARC) in the 1970s had pioneered many innovations that Xerox itself was not able to exploit but other companies later commercialized into products that defined the personal computer industry. PARC scientists invented or developed bit-mapped display technology required for rendering graphical user interfaces; software for onscreen windows and windows management; the mouse as a pointing device; the first personal computer, Alto; and early word-processing software, Bravo for the Alto (Smith and Alexander 1988). Xerox did not pursue the commercial potential of these inventions because its identity and business strategy were closely tied up with its experience in the copier market. For example, Xerox believed that it had been successful in the copier market because it was able to control the production or specification of nearly every component of the copier as a tightly integrated system, and because it had developed a leasing scheme for the expensive systems that provided predictable revenue streams. Entering the personal computer market would run counter to these beliefs. Xerox would lose control over the many critical hardware and software components that make up a PC system, and it would have to deal with a complex array of licensing and revenue-sharing arrangements. Thus, the cultural knowledge of Xerox then—its beliefs about what business it was in, and what its key advantages were—did not support the commercialization of the new technologies created at PARC. Many of the researchers working on these innovations subsequently left PARC, taking their knowledge with them.

Cultural knowledge also establishes a framework in which meaningful organizational discourse can take place. Alvesson (1993) suggests that "cultural knowledge represents a prerequisite for the ability to master a particular symbolic and value environment, to decipher the cultural codes and manoeuvre freely in a social setting" (p. 1001). Cultural knowledge in organizations thus plays important roles such as

1. defining a shared language for creating community and social identity;

2. providing a resource for persuasion;

3. giving the organization a profile or intended image;

4. creating legitimacy and good faith about actions and outcomes; and

5. obscuring uncertainty and reducing ambiguity.

(Alvesson 1993, p. 1001)

Organizations are, in a sense, "systems of persuasion," and organizational knowledge work is symbolic action that must be symbolized in talk, action, titles, structures, and cultural objects. Alvesson concludes that in both embracing and moving beyond knowledge work, organizations need

> to develop rhetorical strategies and forms of symbolism in which the distinct claims are brought forward, made clear, credible and competitive, and to develop and control other vital abilities, orientations than those strictly knowledge-related. . . . [This] is also a matter of influencing employees on a broader scale, including securing and developing work and organizational identities. Cultural-ideological forms of control which affect the ways people perceive their work, organizations and themselves and the values, norms and emotion which guide them become a crucial feature. (Alvesson 1993, pp. 1011–12)

It is misleading to approach cultural knowledge as a form of background knowledge where the information is regarded as self-evident, so that the logical steps by which other forms of knowledge have to be justified are not required (Douglas 1975). It is tempting to view cultural knowledge as a stable, relatively static background before which new information and knowledge is perceived and engaged. Douglas (1975) warns that this "stability is an illusion, for a large part of discourse is dedicated to creating, revising, and obliquely affirming this implicit background, without ever directing explicit attention upon it" (p. 4). Thus, cultural knowledge can be as dynamic as tacit and explicit knowledge in guiding the evaluation and use of organizational knowledge.

VI. KNOWLEDGE CREATION

We begin this section with one of the earliest and still influential model of organizational knowledge creation, that developed by Nonaka and Takeuchi (1995). The basic model was introduced in Chapter 1; here we apply the model to analyze knowledge creation in open source software communities and bring the model up-to-date with recent additions made by Nonaka and his associates. We then discuss a model that focuses on how an organization's knowledge-creating activities engender its core capabilities and how these activities could be managed to extend and enhance a firm's capabilities (Leonard 1995).

Knowledge Creation in Organizations

According to Nonaka and Takeuchi (1995), there are two sets of dynamics that drive the process of knowledge creation in organizations: (1) converting tacit knowledge into explicit knowledge; and (2) moving knowledge from the individual level to the group, organizational, and inter-organizational levels. The process grows like a spiral as the interaction between tacit and explicit knowledge takes place dynamically at higher and higher levels of the organization. There are four modes in which organizational knowledge is created through the interaction and conversion between tacit and explicit knowledge: socialization, externalization, combination, and internalization (Nonaka and Takeuchi 1995).

Haefliger and von Krogh (2004) apply Nonaka's framework to analyze knowledge creation in open source software development communities. The open source development process is supported by a number of Internet-based tools, the most important of which include the concurrent versioning system (CVS), mailing lists, and hosting sites. The CVS manages the exchange of program code by providing multiple access to the code base, keeping track of changes to the code, and storing exact copies of previous code states. Mailing lists is the primary communication tool used for discussions and to distribute e-mail to subscribers. Within the hundreds of mailing lists, content is technically focused (on a software module or feature), and messages posted observe a shared netiquette. Finally, hosting sites provide current versions of software for downloading. Members of open source development communities may be divided into four groups: core developers (who do most of the coding, plan version releases, and decide about features and issues); developers with CVS access (who can change official code versions); regular contributors (who contribute code or take part in discussions); and lurkers (who read mailing lists but do not post—they help promote standards and are potential contributors). A programmer wishing to contribute would first identify a project that he would like to work on by browsing through mailing lists and reading about current issues. Having found a project or issue of interest, he can contribute by posting to the mailing list or by submitting code (adding his patch to the overall program code of the project).

In Nonaka's knowledge-creation model, tacit knowledge is transferred through the sharing of experiences in the *socialization* mode. This mode typically requires co-location and face-to-face interaction. Programmers in open source communities are geographically dispersed, rarely meet in person, and have no opportunity to observe each other at work. Nevertheless, Haefliger and von Krogh (2004) suggest that they are able to share tacit knowledge by developing their own reference contexts and making use of information signals contained in their communications and work products. They show how tacit knowledge about, for example, software complexity is transferred using three types of signals or cues: meta-activities, references to a common background, and code patterns. Meta-activity signals concern the amount, quality or timing, or communication or coding. Is there a heated debate about the software module? How many code submissions and corrections did it take to get a feature to work? Is documentation effort centered around one module? Answers to these questions convey a tacit understanding of the obstacles associated with parts of the code and the programming difficulty of certain tasks. References to a common background concern the use of allusions and metaphors drawn from literature that most contributors would have read (such as the publications of Eric Raymond) and the use of jargon from science fiction fandom and hackerdom (such as greatwall, ha ha only serious, Real Soon Now). In mailing lists, jargon, metaphors, and allusions are used to communicate tacit knowledge. Code patterns refer to the structural patterns of program codes. Programmers scrutinize code, looking at how it is written, which algorithms are used, and how it is structured (as there may be several ways to implement a function). By paying attention to patterns and comparing differences across software modules, programmers gain a tacit understanding of software complexity. In addition to these signals, tacit knowledge is also shared in microcommunities, defined as small groups of individuals within an organization that engage in knowledge creation (Haefliger and von Krogh 2004; Nonaka and Ichijo 1997). Open source microcommunities tend to consist of core developers or contributors working on one module or feature. Internet-based contacts can generate social ties, and if two or more programmers have been working on the same problem within a project, they are better able to exchange tacit knowledge.

Externalization of tacit knowledge as explicit knowledge can occur when code is submitted or messages are posted. Haefliger and von Krogh (2004) note that "code is externalized knowledge" (p. 119). Programmers also insert comments into their code and produce documentation for the software. The CVS, by keeping track of version changes, is another source of documentation. In mailing lists, FAQs (frequently asked questions) that bring newcomers up to speed and message threads that discuss issues or problems also constitute forms of externalized knowledge.

Combination of explicit knowledge can take place when contributors read mailing lists or browse submitted code. For example, as they read a mailing list discussing how a new feature may be implemented in different ways, it could trigger the idea for a solution that integrates some of these approaches. Again, as they review code, developers may see connections to work they have done before, adapt their earlier work, and submit it as a new contribution.

Internalization of explicit knowledge is especially important for a newcomer. To become an active contributor, he or she would have to internalize existing code as well as earlier discussions concerning technical issues and obstacles. Newcomers also carefully read project FAQs to gain the general information to accelerate their learning and to enable them to contribute more quickly.

The knowledge-creation model of Nonaka and Takeuchi (1995) was expanded in recent years. The new model proposes a three-layered view of how organizations create knowledge dynamically (Nonaka, Toyama, and Boysière 2001). The first layer is the conversion process between tacit and explicit knowledge through an ongoing cycle of socialization, externalization, combination, and internalization (SECI). The second layer is "ba," roughly meaning "place" but formally defined as "a context in which knowledge is shared, created, and utilized, in recognition of the fact that knowledge needs a context in order to exist" (Nonaka et al. 2001, p. 499; see also Nonaka and Konno 1998). The third layer consists of knowledge assets, which are inputs and outputs of the knowledge-creation process. The three layers need to interact with each in order to generate new knowledge: the knowledge assets of a firm are mobilized and shared in a contextual *ba,* where the tacit knowledge held by individuals is converted and amplified through the SECI process.

We discussed SECI earlier, but the concepts of *ba* and knowledge assets are subsequent additions to Nonaka's theory of knowledge creation. *Ba* is a shared space for interaction, and it can be a physical place (e.g., an office), a virtual space (teleconference), a mental space (shared ideas), or any combination of these. The defining feature of *ba* is that it provides interaction between individuals and between individuals and the environment. There are four types of *ba*. The first type, originating *ba,* describes the space where individuals share feelings, emotions, experiences, and mental models. It is the place where the knowledge creation starts with the sharing of tacit knowledge. This space provides physical, face-to-face contact that promotes the joint exploration and generation of new ideas. The second type, interacting *ba,* is the place tacit knowledge is made explicit and is facilitated through dialogue and the extensive use of metaphor. Here, individuals share their mental models and develop a common understanding of terms and concepts through dialogue and reflection. The third type, systematizing *ba,* is the virtual space where new explicit knowledge is combined with existing explicit knowledge. The new knowledge is organized, shared, and made available to many groups in the firm through the effective use of information technology. The fourth type, exercising *ba,* is the place where explicit knowledge is reinternalized as tacit knowledge through its active and ongoing use in work practices. Activities such as on-the-job training and mentoring stress certain patterns of action and thinking so that they become internalized over time. Each of the four types of *ba* clearly relate to each of the knowledge conversion activities in the SECI layer.

The third layer consists of *knowledge assets* that form the inputs and outputs of the knowledge-creation process. Again, Nonaka et al. identify four types of knowledge assets, where assets are defined as firm-specific resources that the firm uses to generate value. Experiential knowledge assets are the shared tacit knowledge that is gained through direct, hands-on experience. It is shared among members of an organization or between the firm and its customers, suppliers, and partners. Conceptual knowledge assets are explicit knowledge articulated as concepts through images, symbols, and language. Brand equity, product concepts, or designs are examples. Systemic knowledge assets are systematized and packaged explicit knowledge such as patents, product specifications, manuals, and technology standards. Routine knowledge assets are the tacit knowledge that is routinized and embedded within the actions and practices of an organization.

Knowledge-Creating Activities and Core Capabilities

Leonard (1995) develops a knowledge-creation model based on the premise that knowledge-creating activities build up an organization's core capabilities. There is a continuous interaction between the organization's knowledge-creating activities and its core capabilities. While core capabilities are generated by knowledge-creating activities, these activities are also dependent on, and enabled by, current capabilities. The task of management is therefore twofold: to understand what constitutes a core capability and to know how to manage the activities that create knowledge. What are core capabilities? An organization's core capabilities embody proprietary knowledge that is unique to the firm and are superior to those of its competitors. Core capabilities give the firm its distinctive competitive edge, because they have been developed over time and are hard to transfer or imitate. Leonard's analysis focuses on firms whose core capabilities are technology-based, and where "the primary engine for the creation and growth of technological capabilities is the development of new products and services" (Leonard 1995, p. xiii). For these firms, core capabilities consist of (1) people's skills, (2) knowledge embedded in physical systems, (3) managerial systems that support and reinforce the growth of knowledge, (4) values that encourage or discourage the accumulation of different kinds of knowledge. There are clearly parallels between these elements and the tacit knowledge (skills), explicit knowledge (physical systems), and cultural knowledge (values and managerial practices) that we discussed earlier in this chapter. The additional insight here is that the three types of knowledge managed together constitute the core capability of the firm, and that the more tightly integrated the three types of knowledge, the more unique (and sustainable) the organizational advantage.

The dimensions that define a firm's core capability depend on its history of past decisions and activities. An organization must specialize, but as it focuses on one kind of knowledge it means that it is not receptive to or developing others that may be valuable for the firm.

corporations foster certain skills, values, and knowledge bases at the expense of others. By virtue of being excellent in one knowledge domain, an organization is relatively unreceptive to ideas from others. This tendency to pay attention to and collect certain kinds of knowledge at the expense of others is echoed at all levels of the company—by individuals, by project teams, and by functions. (Leonard 1995, p. 60)

Leonard sees this as "the central paradox of a core capability—namely, that *every core capability is also inherently a core rigidity*" (p. 28).

The perplexing paradox involved in managing core capabilities is that they are core rigidities. That is, a firm's strengths are also—simultaneously—its weaknesses. The dimensions that distinguish a company competitively have grown up over time as an accumulation of activities and decisions that focus on one kind of knowledge at the expense of others. Companies, like people, cannot be skillful at everything. Therefore, core capabilities both advantage and disadvantage a company. (Leonard 1995, p. 30)

As long as business conditions remain more or less constant, a firm continues to enjoy the advantages derived from its core capabilities. However, in today's environment, conditions change rapidly, so that a firm's static core capabilities can become a liability, and "managers find themselves fighting the very underpinnings of the firm's success" (p. 30).

How does an organization grow its core capabilities over time? Leonard believes that capabilities expand through the actions of employees at all levels of the organization, and that the crucial task for managers (after understanding what the core capabilities are) is to identify and nurture the kinds of activities that create knowledge that will be absorbed, applied, and retained by the organization and its members. From her study of several technology-based companies, Leonard identifies four knowledge-creating activities: shared problem solving, implementing and integrating new processes and tools, experimenting and prototyping, and importing new knowledge from outside the organization (Fig. 4.2). These are

the key activities that nurture new capabilities and hence open the organization to change. . . . These activities protect the firm against core rigidities, constantly clearing the channels so that the wellsprings of knowledge can flow freely. (Leonard 1995, p. 56)

In the activity of *shared problem solving,* employees with different specializations and problem-solving approaches are brought together so that the diversity of their knowledge and cognitive styles can be channeled toward creative problem solving. According to Leonard, as people become highly skilled, they develop individual "signature skills" that are formed from their specializations, cognitive style approaches to problem solving, and preferences for particular methods or tools. Bringing together people with diverse signature skills to work

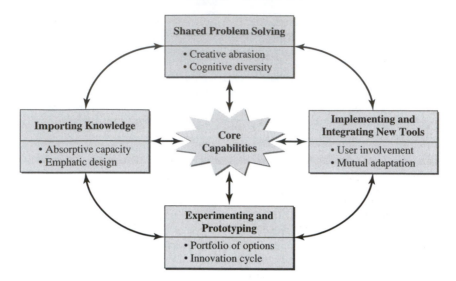

FIGURE 4.2. Knowledge-Creating Activities (Adapted from Leonard 1995, Fig. 1-2, p. 9)

on a problem generates the *creative abrasion* that, when properly managed, can be a source of innovative solutions. (This creative abrasion is not diversity based on gender or race but refers instead to cognitive diversity.) Leonard notes that while nothing productive can come of conflict without compromise or integration, "innovation occurs at the boundaries between mindsets, not within the provincial territory of one knowledge and skill base" (p. 64). To tap this creative energy productively, managers and employees need to develop integrative skills and use techniques such as defining clear shared visions of the project outcome, creating an environment of respect and openness, and constructing prototypes to bridge different realms of specialization.

In the activity of *implementing and integrating new processes and tools,* proprietary knowledge is introduced into process tools and methods that improve internal operation. Leonard (1995) stresses that "the implementation of such tools must be managed as an innovation project" (p. 110) and identifies two key processes: user involvement and mutual adaptation between tools and users. Users should be included in the design and delivery of new tools, since these future users of tools will have critical information that must be integrated during design. At the same time, both the technology and the user environment need to mutually adapt to each other so that users and the new tools complement each other effectively.

Through the activity of *experimentation and prototyping,* the organization creates two new kinds of capabilities. First, continuous and widespread experimentation develops a diverse portfolio of technological options for the organization. Second, the act of experimentation itself "sets up a virtuous cycle of innovation" (p. 114) so that the ability to experiment efficiently and effectively constitutes a competitive advantage. Experimentation needs to be managed to ensure that learning does take place. Failures are a necessary part of experimentation, and the firm should create an environment in which failures are openly examined for their learning potential. Development projects are viewed as experiments, and they contain feedback channels for knowledge to flow back to product developers and project leaders.

In discussing the activity of *importing knowledge from outside,* Leonard distinguishes between external knowledge that is technological in nature and knowledge about the market. Importing technological knowledge depends on the firm's "absorptive capacity"—the ability to recognize the value of new, external information, assimilate it, and apply it. Absorptive capacity can be increased by scanning broadly and continuously for technological opportunity, identifying employees to act as gatekeepers and boundary spanners, and guarding against the not-invented-here syndrome. Importing knowledge about the market presents a challenge when the technology is new and users have needs for which they cannot verbalize a solution. Conventional market research techniques may be of limited use here. Instead, Leonard proposes an "emphatic design" approach which is "the creation of product or service concepts based on a deep (emphatic) understanding of unarticulated user needs" (Leonard 1995, p. 194). This customer knowledge may be obtained by observing actual customer behavior, interacting directly with those who understand the firm's capabilities and potential user needs, and redirecting existing capabilities to new products or markets.

In summary, Leonard emphasizes the continuous interaction between knowledge-creating activities and core capabilities. While core capabilities are created and expanded through knowledge-creating activities, the latter are dependent on and enabled by the organization's core capabilities. The central theme is therefore the creation of knowledge by "managing the interaction between activities pursued in the course of developing new products and processes, and the organization's core technological capabilities" (Leonard 1995, p. 17).

VII. KNOWLEDGE TRANSFER

This section begins with a typology of knowledge transfer methods developed by Dixon (2000), based on her survey of successful methods adopted in a number of organizations. We then discuss a model that analyzes knowledge transfer in an information space defined by the dimensions of codification, abstraction, and diffusion (Boisot 1995, 1998). Finally, we look at the experience of the New United Motor Manufacturing, Inc. (NUMMI), jointly created by General Motors and Toyota to exchange "deeply embedded knowledge."

Knowledge Transfer Near and Far

The sharing of knowledge across boundaries inside an organization is a major challenge in efforts to promote knowledge creation and use. Dixon (2000) notes changes in the ways organizations are thinking about knowledge transfer. She sees three shifts: "from thinking of experts as the primary source of knowledge to thinking that everyone engaged in work tasks has knowledge someone else could use to advantage. . . . from thinking of knowledge as residing with individuals to thinking of [it] as embedded in a group or community. . . . from thinking of knowledge as a stable commodity to thinking of [it] as dynamic and ever changing" (Dixon 2000, pp. 148–49). Following an analysis of successful methods developed by a range of organizations to share knowledge, she concluded that while there was no one universal recipe, there is a systematic way that could be used to select and design an effective knowledge transfer method. The most effective mechanism for sharing knowledge is that which best fits the requirements of the intended recipient, the nature of the task, and the type of knowledge that is being transferred. The determination of fit thus involves asking three questions:

1. Who is the intended receiver of the knowledge in terms of similarity of task and context?
2. How routine and frequent is the task?
3. Is the knowledge tacit or explicit?

(Dixon 2000, p. 169)

Depending on the answers, an organization can transfer knowledge through one of five methods that Dixon has identified: serial transfer, near transfer, far transfer, strategic transfer, and expert transfer. *Serial transfer* focuses on "the knowledge a team has learned from doing its task that can be transferred to the next time that team does the same task in a different setting" (p. 144). One of the best-known examples of serial transfer within a team would be the U.S. Army's use of After Action Reviews (AARs). AARs are held at the end of a team or unit action in order to reflect on what has been learned and to apply these lessons the next time the team performs the same task. Immediately or soon after an important activity, team members meet to review their assignments, identify successes and failures, and look for ways to improve (Garvin 2000). The discussion follows a sequence of four questions: What did we set out to do? What actually happened? Why did it happen? What are we going to do the next time?

Near transfer is replicating the explicit knowledge that a team has gained from performing a frequent, routine task so that other teams doing similar work can use this knowledge. An example would be Ford's Best Practice Replication (BPR) process. BPR was initiated in Ford's Vehicle Operations division, composed of 37 plants that assemble and paint vehicles. Each week, five to eight best practices that apply only to Vehicle Operations are "pushed" via the Intranet to the plants. At each plant, the appointed production engineer (called the Focal Point) is responsible for retrieving the best practices, marking on an online scorecard that is attached to each best practice whether it is adopted, under investigation, previously adopted, not applicable, or too costly. If adopted, the Focal Point calculates and reports costs and savings using standardized algorithms.

Far transfer is making available the tacit knowledge that a team has gained from performing a nonroutine task so that other teams doing similar work in another part of the organization can have the benefit of this knowledge. An example would be British Petroleum's Peer Assist. Peer Assist was conceived as a way for one business unit to call upon another business unit for help, instead of assistance coming from the corporate level. BP has conducted hundreds of Peer Assists across many parts of BP (Collison and Parcell 2001). Some Peer Assists bring in an entire team to help (e.g., one exploration team in the North Sea brought in a team from the Gulf of Mexico, one of the few other places that require drilling in such deep water), others choose individuals from different business units. Peer Assists are appropriate when the problem is a significant challenge, and when the transfer can result in significant business benefits. The assisting team is not expected to say "Here is what we did; you should do it the same way." Rather the issue is "How can what we did be translated into something that is usable in your situation?" (Dixon 2000, p. 91).

Strategic transfer is bringing together the collective knowledge of the organization in order to accomplish a strategic task that occurs infrequently but is highly consequential to the organization. An example would be the U.S. Army's Center for Army Lessons Learned (CALL). The U.S. Army established CALL in 1985 to collect new lessons generated from actual operations as well as training exercises (Thomas et al. 2001). The process begins with senior officers identifying where opportunities for learning exist. Collection teams are formed and sent in with the troops to observe operations in real time and to collect rich descriptions of activities. Reports are sent daily to CALL HQ where assigned analysts and subject matter experts (from inside and outside CALL) work to make sense of the data, devise more questions, and identify lessons learned. Selected lessons are then disseminated to the Training and Doctrine Command or to relevant field units.

Finally, *expert transfer* is providing the specialized knowledge needed by a team that is working on a task beyond the scope of its own knowledge. An early example of expert transfer would be the online technical forums of Buckman Laboratories, a specialty chemical company that provides chemicals to the water treatment, pulp and paper, and leather markets. Buckman's K'Netix Forums function as electronic discussion groups where a member facing a complex requirement from an interested consumer can tap into the collective expertise of the firm by posting questions of the type "Does anybody know . . . ?" Each section of the forums has a section leader appointed as subject expert who answers questions or redirects them, a librarian who checks resources and organizes forum content (creates digests and abstracts, archives discussion threads), and a system operator (sysop) who maintains the section. The use of K'Netix reduced response time to the customer from days and weeks to a few hours or a day or two and increased significantly the percentage of sales from new products that are less than five years old.

Knowledge Transfer in the Information Space

Boisot (1995, 1998) proposes an Information Space, or I-Space, model as a conceptual framework to analyze information flows that constitute the creation and transfer of knowledge. The I-Space is bounded by the three dimensions of codification, abstraction, and diffusion. Within this space, the characteristics and trajectories of an organization's knowledge assets might be mapped according to these dimensions. The key hypothesis of the model is

> that codification and abstraction are mutually reinforcing and that both acting together, greatly facilitate the diffusion of information. . . . the more codified and abstract an item of information becomes, then, other things being equal, the larger the percentage of a given population it will be able to reach in a given period of time. (Boisot 1998, p. 55)

In the I-Space model (Fig. 4.3), the first dimension of *codification* refers to the process that creates perceptual and conceptual categories that facilitate the classification of phenomena. Codification is equivalent to a selection from competing perceptual and conceptual alternatives. By assigning categories to phenomena, uncertainty is reduced, surplus data are shed, and the requirement for data processing is economized. Any task and the knowledge associated with it might be scaled according to the amount of data processing it entails. In the uncodified region of the scale are tasks that require the processing of an infinite number of bits of data (such as riding a bicycle). In the codified region of the scale are simple tasks that need only small amounts of data for their execution (such as

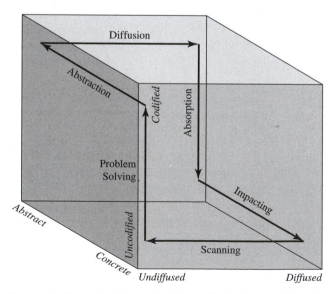

FIGURE 4.3. Knowledge Transfer: Information Space Model (Adapted from Boisot 1998, Fig. 3.3, p. 60)

turning an on-off switch) or structured tasks that follow sequences of instructions (such as using software). Economizing on data processing then involves moving from the uncodified end of the scale toward the codified, from the inarticulate toward the articulate, from the tacit toward the explicit. The effectiveness of codification depends not only on intellectual and observational skill but also on the complexity of the phenomenon that is being partitioned into categories. When performed well, codification facilitates and accelerates information processing.

Whereas codification groups the data of experience into categories, *abstraction* is the process that minimizes the number of categories needed to draw on for a given task. Abstraction is accomplished by revealing the structure and cause-and-effect relationships that underlie phenomena. Both codification and abstraction reduce data processing, but abstraction does so by specifying which categories are likely to be relevant to a given data-processing task. Knowledge can be located on an abstraction scale according to the number of categories that need to be drawn on. In the unabstract or concrete region of the scale would be knowledge based on highly concrete experiences that is mainly perceptual and local in application. In the abstract region of the scale would be knowledge based on abstract thought that is mainly conceptual and broadly applicable. When performed properly, abstraction uncovers causal or descriptive structures and works together with codification to make knowledge even more articulated and hence more shareable.

The *diffusion* of information in I-Space refers to "the proportion of a given population of data-processing agents that can be reached with information operating at different degrees of codification and abstraction" (Boisot 1998, p. 52). Such a population is not limited to individuals inside an organization, but also includes firms, conglomerates, and industries. Diffusibility here is the availability of information to those who want to use it: it is measured with respect to a potential audience for a set of messages being transmitted. Where a knowledge asset is located on the diffusion scale depends on many factors that influence the speed, extent, and trajectory of diffusion. These factors would include the frequency and intensity of interaction within the population; the available means of communication; the sharing of social and cultural codes and contexts; and legal protection and restrictions. Generally, the lower-level technical factors would affect information diffusibility, whereas the higher-level social factors would affect uptake and adoption.

To help assess the degree of codification, abstraction, and diffusion of a knowledge asset, Boisot suggests using questions such as the following:

1. Is the knowledge easily captured in figures and formulae?
2. Does it lend itself to standardization and automation?
3. Is the knowledge generally applicable to all agents whatever the sector they operate in? Is it heavily science based?
4. Is the knowledge readily available to all agents who wish to make use of it?

(p. 65)

The more affirmative the answers to these questions, the greater the degree of codification, abstraction, and diffusion of the knowledge.

The creation and diffusion of new knowledge from personal knowledge to public knowledge can be examined along the three dimensions of codification, abstraction, and diffusion. New knowledge emerges from personal knowledge that is uncodified, based on concrete experience, and undiffused—it lies in the bottom-left-hand area of the I-Space cube. Successive efforts to articulate this knowledge increase its degree of codification and abstraction until it becomes proprietary knowledge. Initially, the knowledge is available only locally (for example, within the organization), or it may be protected by legal restrictions—proprietary knowledge lies in the top-left-hand area of I-Space. However, because it has been made explicit and therefore diffusible, the proprietary knowledge gradually moves into the public domain, finding its way into reports, journals, instruction manuals, newspapers, and so on. Over time, it becomes public knowledge, located in the top-right-hand area of I-Space. Repeated use of this knowledge, often in a variety of settings, results in the assimilation of the knowledge as part of "common sense." Although common sense by definition is widely shared, each individual internalizes and makes use of this common sense differently to create personal intuitions and perceptions. Thus, the cycle is complete as the new knowledge is returned into the tacit domain of personal knowledge.

The I-Space can also be used to analyze the transfer of new organizational knowledge (Fig. 4.3). Boisot (1998, 1995) suggests that the diffusion of new knowledge is likely to follow a particular sequence composed of six phases: scanning, problem solving, abstraction, diffusion, absorption, and impacting.

(1) *Scanning* is the process of identifying threats and opportunities in data that are generally available but where the interpretation or significance of these messages is uncertain. Scanning patterns such weak signals into unique or idiosyncratic insights held by individuals or small groups. (2) *Problem solving* is the process of giving structure and coherence to these insights, for example, codifying them. Much of the initial uncertainty is eliminated as "the new patterns gain a definite form and contour" (Boisot 1995, p. 165). Nevertheless, problem solving that begins in the uncodified region of the I-Space is often risky and conflict-laden (as when, for example, new insights contradict established beliefs of powerful groups). In this phase, the organizational task is "articulating an adapted response to what has been scanned" (Boisot 1998, p. 172). (3) *Abstraction* is generalizing the application of newly codified insights to a wider range of situations. Abstraction involves conceptualizing the new insights by reducing them to their most essential features. In this phase, the response that has been developed in the problem-solving phase is generalized to new classes of problems and opportunities. (4) *Diffusion* is sharing the newly created knowledge, making it available to a wider target audience. The more codified and generalized (abstract) the knowledge, the easier it would be to transfer the knowledge. If a large part of the new knowledge remains uncodified and concrete, then senders and receivers would need to first establish a shared context for the transfer to take place. Forming a shared context can be problematic when the size of the target

population is large. (5) *Absorption* is applying the newly transferred knowledge to different situations in a "learning-by-doing" or a "learning-by-using" mode (Boisot 1998, p. 61). It involves internalizing, or "gaining intuitive familiarity" (p. 175), with the knowledge acquired by using it in different circumstances. (6) *Impacting* is the embedding of abstract knowledge in concrete practices. Embedding can take the form of artifacts, or it could take place through the institutionalization of rules and routines that require or reward certain behaviors. Clearly, absorption and impacting often work together, as it is through repeated doing or using that some abstract principles become internalized.

Boisot calls the full sequence of six processes the social learning cycle. In practice, the shape of the learning cycle would depend on barriers, frictions, or obstacles that limit the flow of information in I-Space. Barriers can take many forms: firms may not scan effectively; many may deliberately prevent diffusion of knowledge through the use of patents; some find it hard to accept and absorb new, ambiguous information; and so on. Barriers such as these would "distort" the trajectory of the cycle, with possible implications for the firm's capacity to learn and adapt.

Cultural Knowledge in Knowledge Transfer: The NUMMI Experience

The movement of knowledge across organizational boundaries can involve tacit, explicit, and cultural knowledge to varying degrees. In a limited number of cases, the transfer can be accomplished through a movement of explicit knowledge (e.g., an equation, a chemical formula). Transfers of such well-defined packages of codified knowledge typically require a substantial amount of collateral knowledge in the receiving organization to decode the new information (in-house engineers and technologies are needed to understand and apply the new equation or formula). In a larger number of cases, the transfer of explicit knowledge is accompanied and facilitated by human experts. Experts interpret the meaning of new information and deal with the detailed questions arising from trying to use the new information in a different situation. Thus, tacit knowledge is necessary to assimilate and apply new explicit knowledge locally. There are important cases when the movement of explicit knowledge even when accompanied by tacit knowledge is not enough: cultural knowledge is also necessary. This is especially so when organizations are trying to learn new practices or systems of work that are woven into organizational networks of roles, relationships, and shared meanings.

In 1963, General Motors opened an automobile assembly plant in Fremont, California, in order to be close to the large and growing market in the West. By 1978, the Fremont plant employed over 7,200 workers. By 1982, the plant was closed. The reasons for closure were clear:

> GM-Fremont was ranked at the bottom of GM's plants in productivity and was producing one of the worst-quality automobiles in the entire GM system. A militant union averaged 5,000 to 7,000 grievances per three-year labor contract.

> The plant was characterized by high use of sick leave, slowdowns, wildcat strikes, and even sabotage. First-line managers were known to carry weapons for personal protection. Daily absenteeism was almost 20 percent, and drug abuse and alcoholism plagued the workforce. There was a climate of fear and mistrust between management and union. (O'Reilly and Pfeffer 2000, p. 182)

In 1983, Toyota and GM entered into a joint venture that reopened the plant, now named New United Motor Manufacturing, Inc., or NUMMI. Toyota's goals were to gain a foothold in the U.S. market, learn about working with U.S. suppliers, and see if their manufacturing and management approaches could work with U.S. employees. GM's goals were to learn about Toyota's production system and to add a small vehicle (the Nova) to its product line. Toyota's production system was the result of a tight integration of tacit, explicit, and cultural knowledge:

> Toyota's knowledge of how to make cars lies embedded in highly specialized social and organizational relationships that have evolved through decades of common effort. It rests in routines, information flows, ways of making decisions, shared attitudes and expectations, and specialized knowledge that Toyota managers, workers, suppliers and purchasing agents, and others have about different aspects of their business, about each other, and about how they can all work together. (Badaracco 1991, p. 87)

At NUMMI, Toyota assumed responsibility for all plant operations, including product design and engineering. NUMMI's management was first headed by Tatsuro Toyoda, son of Toyota's founder. Eighty-five percent of the initial workforce of 2,200 came from the pool of laid-off GM employees. In the first year, NUMMI built almost 65,000 Novas, a car rated by Consumer Reports as one of the highest-quality small cars in the world. Moreover, absenteeism at the plant was down to less than 3 percent, and only a handful of grievances were filed. Within two years, NUMMI was more productive than any other GM plant and had quality that rivaled its sister Toyota plant in Japan. At first, Toyota was concerned that American workers and the United Auto Workers Union would not understand or be willing to follow Toyota production concepts. This fear proved to be unfounded. According to Kan Higashi, NUMMI's second president, he did not see much difference between American and Japanese employees: "We found people here to be capable and flexible," and that "Basically the NUMMI plant is the same as the plant in Japan—only smaller" (O'Reilly and Pfeffer 2000, p. 197). What was different at NUMMI from the previous GM-Fremont plant was the values of trust, respect, and continuous improvement that guided operations and relationships within the plant:

> The NUMMI approach begins with a different set of basic values and assumptions. The underlying belief is that all the people in the plant have a common interest. In a highly competitive global automobile market, success for everyone requires that NUMMI produce the highest-quality car at the lowest possible cost. Doing this will ensure profits for the company and job security for employees. . . . It is a system predicated on the belief in a common fate and one that rests on mutual trust

and respect for the contribution of all members of the organization. (O'Reilly and Pfeffer 2000, pp. 197–98)

Work at NUMMI was organized based on Toyota's lean production system, which sought to utilize labor, materials, and facilities as efficiently as possible. The system was guided by the principles that quality should be assured in the production process itself with no defects overlooked or passed on, and that team members should be treated with consideration, respect, and as professionals. The NUMMI system combined employee involvement and continuous improvement processes. In order to ensure that each job was done in the most efficient way, performance of the work was specified explicitly by sequences or procedures. NUMMI team members themselves were responsible for setting the work standards and continuously improving the job standards for maximum efficiency. NUMMI also used production leveling in an attempt to produce no more vehicles and parts than could be sold. Through production leveling, NUMMI was able to implement just-in-time scheduling and maintain employment stability.

O'Reilly and Tushman (1997) observed that at NUMMI, the organizational culture included norms about continuous improvement and team responsibility. Instead of feeling unmotivated, workers felt a sense of autonomy and responsibility. Instead of feeling monitored, workers "controlled" their own behaviors. In lieu of industrial engineers (there are none at NUMMI; the old GM Fremont plant had 82 industrial engineers), NUMMI workers were trained in industrial engineering techniques and the team itself took on work redesign and improvements. Methods and standards were determined by work teams themselves: workers were taught how to time their own jobs, compare alternative procedures to determine the most efficient one, document the standard procedure to ensure that everyone can understand it, and propose improvements in that procedure. The task of standardized work analysis might be delegated to a team leader or a team member, but everyone could participate in the process. (O'Reilly and Tushman 1997)

In a comparison of the Toyota-GM venture (NUMMI) and Volvo's Uddevalla plant, Adler (1993) noted that

> the Japanese production model explicitly focuses on strategies for organizational learning. Standardization of work methods is a precondition for achieving this end—you cannot identify the sources of problems in a process you have not standardized. Standardization captures best practices and facilitates the diffusion of improvement ideas throughout the organization—you cannot diffuse what you have not standardized. And standardization stimulates improvement—every worker is now something of an industrial engineer. At NUMMI, the skill development strategies for individual workers are managed as a component of this process, rather than as a way of maximizing personal opportunities. As a result, training focuses on developing deeper knowledge, not only of the relatively narrow jobs but also of the logic of the production system, statistical process control, and problem-solving processes. (p. 92)

Although much has been published about Toyota's production system, without the NUMMI experience, GM might have permanently missed the essence of Toyota's management process. Co-practice to learn the system was necessary because the capabilities were "tacit know-how in action, embedded organizationally, systemic in interaction and cultivated through learning by doing" (Doz and Hamel 1997, p. 570). Badaracco (1991) concluded that through NUMMI, GM had the chance to learn firsthand Toyota's collaborative approach to worker and supplier relationships, just-in-time inventory management, and efficient plant operations. For Toyota, the project helped it learn about managing U.S. workers, suppliers, and logistics, and about cooperating with the unions and the state and local governments.

> Scores of GM managers and thousands of workers have worked at NUMMI or at least visited the operation. It would have been much simpler for GM to buy from Toyota the manual *How to Create the Toyota Production System,* but the document does not exist and, in a fundamental sense, could not be written. Much of what Toyota "knows" resides in routines, company culture, and long-established working relationships in the Toyota Group. (Badaracco 1991, p. 100)

VIII. KNOWLEDGE UTILIZATION

This section begins with a view of organizations as knowledge integrators that coordinate, integrate, and combine the organization's specialized skills and capabilities in order to utilize that knowledge (Grant 2002; Kogut and Zander 1992). We then consider communities of practice as social settings in which the use of knowledge is situated, negotiated, and given meaning (Lave and Wenger 1991; Wenger 1998). Finally, we look at the Eureka project in Xerox as a distinctive case of community-based knowledge sharing.

Knowledge Integration

Grant (1996b, 2002) sees organizational capability as the outcome of knowledge integration—the result of the organization's ability to coordinate and integrate the knowledge of many individual specialists. In Grant's view, knowledge creation is an individual activity, and this means that the primary role of an organization is to apply knowledge rather than to create it. More specifically, the organization exists as an institution that "can create conditions under which multiple individuals can integrate their specialist knowledge" (Grant 1996a, p. 112). The fundamental task of an organization is to integrate the knowledge and coordinate the efforts of its many specialized individuals. Whereas Nonaka and Takeuchi (1995) emphasize the creation of new knowledge, Grant stresses the deployment of organizational knowledge, particularly through integration. Whereas Dixon (2000) and others emphasize the transfer of knowledge, Grant (1996a) maintains that transferring knowledge is not an efficient approach to integrating knowledge. The key to efficiency here is to achieve effective integration while minimizing knowledge transfer: that is, to develop modes of communication that integrate knowledge while reducing the time and effort required to transfer knowledge between collaborators.

Grant (2002) identifies four mechanisms for integrating specialized knowledge that economize on communication and coordination: rules and directives; sequencing; routines; and group problem solving and decision making. *Rules and directives* regulate the actions between individuals and can provide a means by which tacit knowledge is converted into readily comprehensible explicit knowledge:

> it is highly inefficient for a quality engineer to teach every production worker all that he knows about quality control. A more efficient means of integrating this knowledge into the production process is for him to establish a set of procedures and rules for quality control. (Grant 2002, p. 139)

Sequencing organizes production activities in a time sequence so that each specialist's input occurs independently in a preassigned time slot. *Routines* can support relatively complex patterns of behaviors and interactions between individuals without the need to specify rules and directives. Organizational routines may be designed to be flexible, permitting individuals to vary their responses and interactions. *Group problem solving and decision making*, in contrast with the other mechanisms, rely on high levels of communication and nonstandard coordination methods to deal with problems that are high in task complexity and task uncertainty. All four mechanisms depend upon the existence of *common knowledge* for their operation. Common knowledge may take the form of a common language between organizational members; commonality in the individuals' specialized knowledge; shared meanings and understandings between individuals; and awareness and recognition of the individuals' knowledge domains (Grant 2002).

In a related perspective, Kogut and Zander (1992) view an organization as a repository of capabilities, capabilities that are "determined by the social knowledge embedded in enduring individual relationships structured by organizing principles" (p. 396). These *organizing principles* establish a common language and set of mechanisms through which people in an organization cooperate, share, and transfer knowledge. They enable sets of functional expertise to be communicated and combined so that the organization as a whole can exist as an integrated community. However, the stability of these relationships and principles induces inertia in the organization's capabilities, making it difficult for the organization to switch to new capabilities (cf. Leonard's concept of core rigidities in the last subsection). Instead, the organization learns new skills by recombining its current capabilities, synthesizing and applying its current and acquired knowledge:

> Creating new knowledge does not occur in abstraction from current abilities. Rather, new learning, such as innovations, are products of a firm's **combinative capabilities** to generate new applications from existing knowledge. By combinative capabilities, we mean the intersection of the capability of the firm to exploit its knowledge and the unexplored potential of the technology. (Kogut and Zander 1992, p. 390)

This view is consistent with Schumpeter's (1934) thesis that innovations generally are combinations of existing knowledge and incremental learning. Kogut and Zander (1992) suggest that the main reason why organizations tend to learn in areas that are related to their present practice is because the introduction and exploitation of innovations occur by building on social relationships that currently exist in the organization, since "a firm's capabilities cannot be separated from how it is currently organized" (p. 392).

While Grant (2002), Kogut and Zander (1992), and others regard organizations as settings for integrating and combining knowledge, Tsoukas (1996) suggests that there may be limits to the extent that organizational knowledge may be integrated. As we have noted, an organization's knowledge is distributed over time, physical and social space, as well as over different groups and individuals. Tsoukas (1996) carries the conceptualization of the firm as a distributed knowledge system further by using a constructionist approach. Organizations are analyzed as "distributed knowledge systems in a strong sense: they are de-centered systems. A firm's knowledge cannot be surveyed as a whole: it is not self-contained; it is inherently indeterminate and continually reconfiguring" (Tsoukas 1996, p. 13). The utilization of organizational knowledge cannot be known by a single agent—no single individual or agent can fully specify in advance what kind of knowledge is going to be relevant, when, and where. There is no "master control room" where knowledge may be centrally managed.

Instead, organizational knowledge is continually constituted and reconstituted through the activities undertaken within the organization. Knowledge is the emergent outcome of engaging in work as social practices that consist of three dimensions: role-related normative expectations; personal dispositions; and local interactions with particular situations (Mouzelis 1995; Bourdieu 1988). First, there are the normative expectations that are associated with the carrying out of an organizational role. Second, personal dispositions are the mental patterns of perception, thought, and action acquired by an individual through past socializations and experiences. Third, local interactions with particular situations arise when normative expectations and personal dispositions interact with specific features and circumstances of the work situation. Whereas an organization may have some control over role-related normative expectations, it has little or no control over members' dispositions or how these dispositions and role expectations play out in particular situations. An organization's knowledge is therefore always emergent and contingent. Moreover, expectations, dispositions, and situations are rarely congruent, so that three elements are separated by gaps. To close these gaps, practitioners exercise their judgment by selecting what they consider to be relevant features from each of the three dimensions and attempting to fit them together.

Viewing the organization as a distributed knowledge system thus refines our perspective of what knowledge management needs to entail:

> Organizations are seen as being in constant flux, out of which the potential for the emergence of novel practices is never exhausted—human action is inherently

creative. Organizational members do follow rules but how they do so is an inescapably contingent-cum-local matter. In organizations, both rule-bound action and novelty are present, as are continuity and change, regularity and creativity. Management, therefore, can be seen as an open-ended process of coordinating purposeful individuals, whose actions stem from applying their unique interpretations to the local circumstances confronting them. . . . Given the distributed character of organizational knowledge, the key to achieving coordinated action does not so much depend on those "higher up" collecting more and more knowledge, as on those "lower down" finding more and more ways of getting connected and interrelating the knowledge each one has. A necessary condition for this to happen is to appreciate the character of a firm as a discursive practice: a form of life, a community, in which individuals come to share an unarticulated background of common understandings. Sustaining a discursive practice is just as important as finding ways of integrating distributed knowledge. (Tsoukas 1996, pp. 22–23)

Knowledge Use in Communities of Practice

Given that organizational knowledge is a tightly bundled package of the tacit, the explicit, and the cultural, how do participants assimilate this knowledge effectively? Lave and Wenger (1991) suggest a process of "legitimate peripheral participation." The process emphasizes that learning takes place through active participation, but that this participation needs to be modified to enhance peripherality and legitimacy. Thus, the novice starts by staying safely on the periphery of practice as a participant observer. Peripherality provides an approximation of full participation that allows learners to engage fully in the actual practice, while at the same lowering the intensity, risk, cost of error, stress levels, and need for close supervision. When she feels sufficiently comfortable or when the mentor feels she is ready, the learner can move from the periphery to the center to engage the task, and then move back out again. In this sense the learner is also a legitimate participant who can move to the center of practice from time to time. Legitimacy gives new learners enough authority to be treated as potential members. Legitimacy can take many forms, for example, being sponsored, being useful, being the right kind of person, having the birth right. Being legitimately on the periphery also means that learners have access to the various modes of communication used by the competent practitioner (mail, meetings, stories, reports) so that they can pick up valuable know-how on technique and nuance.

Instead of treating knowledge as being individually acquired, knowledge in organizations is often tacitly shared by members of social groups: "With individuals, tacit knowledge means intuition, judgment, common sense—the capacity to do something without necessarily being able to explain it. With groups, tacit knowledge exists in the distinct practices and relationships that emerge from working together over time—the social fabric that connects communities of knowledge workers" (Brown and Gray 1995, p. 80). Research suggests that a group holds this tacit knowledge as a community that forms around a shared practice. Members of such *communities of practice* participate in a shared practice informally but legitimately. The community of practice provides a context in which the meaning of objects, problems, events, and artifacts gets constructed and negotiated, and in which people live, work, communicate, and understand the environment and themselves (Brown 1993). Communities of practice emerge naturally from the organization's web of interactions and need not be formally controlled or designed. By reconceiving organizations as comprising communities of practice, working, learning, and innovation are integrated in a unified view (Brown and Duguid 1991).

In a parallel argument, Wenger (1998) sees work practices as social activities that link people through mutual engagement. Workgroups form around these practices, creating communities of practice. Communities of practice emerge of their own accord and tend to self-organize: people join and stay because they have something to learn and to contribute. By sharing and jointly developing practice, communities of practice evolve patterns of relating and interacting with one another. Over time, they develop a common understanding of the meaning and value of their work, as well as a shared repertory of resources that include both the tacit ("war stories," workarounds, heuristics) and the explicit (notebooks, tools, communication devices). Communities of practice therefore constitute historical and social settings that embrace all three categories of organizational knowledge (cultural, tacit, explicit):

> It [a community of practice] includes what is said and what is left unsaid; what is represented and what is assumed. It includes the language, tools, documents, images, symbols, well-defined roles, specified criteria, codified procedures, regulations, and contracts that various practices make explicit for a variety of purposes. But it also includes all the implicit relations, tacit conventions, subtle cues, untold rules of thumb, recognizable intuitions, specific perceptions, well-tuned sensitivities, embodied understandings, underlying assumptions, and shared world views. Most of these may never be articulated, yet they are unmistakable signs of membership in communities of practice and are crucial to the success of their enterprise. (Wenger 1998, p. 47)

Within such communities, knowledge is shared and applied through learning in practice that is composed of the processes of (1) evolving mutual engagement, (2) understanding the nature of the joint enterprise, and (3) developing a shared repertoire (Fig. 4.4). Wenger enumerates the elements of each of these processes:

1. Evolving forms of mutual engagement: discovering how to engage, what helps and what hinders; developing mutual relationships; defining identities, establishing who is who, who is good at what, who knows what, who is easy or hard to get along with.

2. Understanding and tuning their [the joint] enterprise: aligning their engagement with it, and learning to become and hold each other accountable to it; struggling to define the enterprise and reconciling conflicting interpretations of what the enterprise is about.

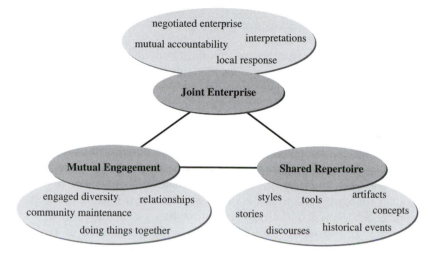

FIGURE 4.4. Knowledge-in-Use: Communities of Practice (Adapted from Wenger 1998, Fig. 2.1, p. 73)

3. Developing their [the shared] repertoire, styles, and discourses: renegotiating the meaning of various elements; producing or adopting tools, artifacts, representations; recording and recalling events; inventing new terms and redefining or abandoning old ones; telling and retelling stories; creating and breaking routines.

(Wenger 1998, p. 95)

Through these processes, a form of group-based tacit knowledge emerges as each member of a community of practice contributes not only his or her own competence, but also involves the competence of others (Wenger 1998, p. 76). These competences may be complementary (as when different members of a team have different roles) or overlapping (as when members have some knowledge of each other's work). When the collective capabilities of a group depend on the interaction between multiple sets of competencies possessed by its members, it becomes more important for members to know how to give and receive help than to try to know everything.

Communities of practice are not self-contained entities: "they develop in larger contexts—historical, social, cultural, institutional—with specific resources and constraints" (Wenger 1998, p. 79). Members define their enterprise by taking into account their position within a broader industry or job system and the influence of the institution that employs them. The enterprise of a community of practice also establishes relations of accountability that answer questions on

what matters and what does not, what is important and why it is important, what to do and not to do, what to pay attention and what to ignore, what to talk and what to leave unsaid, what to justify and what to take for granted, what to display and what to withhold, when actions and artifacts are good enough and when they need improvement or refinement. (Wenger 1998, p. 81)

In developing a shared repertoire, explicit knowledge becomes a source of coherence for a community of practice. The repertoire of a community of practice includes routines, tools, and concepts that Wenger describes as "shared" in order to stress its rehearsed character and its availability for further engagement in practice. Thus, routines and artifacts reflect and encode a history of learning and practice and so provide "recognizable histories of interpretation and usage" that facilitate communication and coordination. At the same time, the shared repertoire of a community of practice also includes stories, symbols, gestures, and ways of doing things. Members use these resources to retain and reintroduce ambiguity in the process of negotiating new meanings and creating new practices. Explicit knowledge therefore has a dual function: it encodes past learning and serves as initial material for the production of new understanding.

Wenger (1998) describes a community of practice that he studied in a medical claims processing center operated by a large U.S. insurance company. Medical claims processing is based on well-structured procedures. Claims processors follow sequences of steps and make use of work objects such as forms, worksheets, computer screens, and manuals. They learn these procedures through formal as well as on-the-job training. However, their learning to use the knowledge embodied in procedures also includes much more:

> What claims processors learn cannot easily be categorized into discrete skills and pieces of information that are useful or harmful, functional or dysfunctional. Learning their jobs, they also learn how much they are to make sense of what they do or encounter. They learn how not to learn and how to live with the ignorance they deem appropriate. They learn to keep their shoulders bent and their fingers busy, to follow the rules and to ignore the rules. They learn how to engage and disengage, accept and resist, as well as how to keep a sense of themselves in spite of the status of their occupation. They learn to weave together their work and their private lives. They learn how to find little joys and how to deal with being depressed. What they learn and don't learn makes sense only as part of an identity, which is as big as the world and as small as their computer screens, and which subsumes the skills they acquire and gives them meaning. They *become* claims processors. (Wenger 1998, pp. 40–41)

Although the claims processors appear to work individually following set procedures, these explicit policies, metrics, training programs, and system designs are often in conflict with the reality of their work. In order to make it possible to meet the demands of the organization, claims processors collectively construct a local practice that allows them to invent and maintain ways of reconciling institutional requirements with the shifting contingencies of actual work situations. The claims processors create a community of practice that functions by (1) resolving contradictions between explicit, institutionalized knowledge and personal, situated actions; (2) supporting a communal memory so that individuals can do their work without having to know everything; (3) helping newcomers to join the community; (4) creating a cultural environment in which the monotonous aspects of the work become part of the rituals, customs, and rhythms of community life.

Community-Based Knowledge Sharing: The Eureka Story

The work of service technicians is vital to the photocopier business of Xerox. It is an important point of contact between the firm and its customers and a primary means of maintaining customer satisfaction and brand loyalty. In the early 1980s, with a shortage of technicians, Xerox decided to use less-skilled and -experienced service staff by moving toward what was called "directive" repair and adjustment procedures. Service instructions would be documented in the form of a decision tree, and technicians need only be trained in using the documentation to be able to diagnose and repair machine failure.

A group in Xerox PARC had a background in artificial intelligence as well as expertise in building programs to diagnose machine faults. In 1991, the group developed a model-based expert system covering one complex module of a particular photocopier that could support a technician in diagnosing repairing problems in this module. The system was shown to some technicians. Here's how the PARC group described the reaction:

> "That's amazing," they said. "Would it really be useful if we had a complete model for the machine?" we asked proudly. "Not really—though it is amazing—rather like a bear dancing. It is surprising to see it do it at all." (Bobrow and Whalen 2002, p. 49)

The research group was surprised by the unenthusiastic response and probed further. It found out that many products (those from Xerox's Japanese partners) did not have full descriptions of their operation. Diagnostic documentation was being produced by inducing faults in machines in a laboratory and then analyzing symptoms. However, the hardest problems in the field were new problems that were not covered by the documentation. This was understandable since photocopy machines operate in a broad range of complex environments. Extremes of temperature, humidity, and dust; vibrations and network interactions; the age of the machine—all these can lead to new failure modes. Moreover, a fault may appear intermittently, making it hard to track down.

The PARC group decided to observe what service technicians actually did in their day-to-day practice by accompanying them on service calls. They saw that when technicians faced a new, undocumented problem that stumped them, they might use their two-way radios to call on a buddy for ideas or turn to the experts (former technicians now serving as field engineers) as part of the escalation process. When tough problems were solved, they would often tell the stories about these successes when they met their peers in the café, the parts depot, or a workgroup meeting.

Eureka in France. A member of the PARC group, a French national (Olivier Raiman), then spent time riding with French technicians to understand if their practices were similar to those in the United States. One interesting observation was that many technicians carried cheat sheets of solutions their workgroup had invented to solve undocumented hard problems. New technicians would ask more-experienced technicians for copies of these cheat sheets.

Through a series of workshops with technicians in France, the PARC research group concluded that a wider sharing of this knowledge across different workgroups would be valuable. The PARC group received the backing of the French service organization—including management and expert field engineers ("tigers")—to try an experiment. An initial database of 100 to 200 tips was created by having the tigers edit and validate the stories volunteered at the workshops, as well as adding tips that the tigers themselves used. Tips were structured simply in terms of symptom, cause, test, and action. Access to the database was via a standard laptop running an easy-to-use program (Colombus) written by the PARC group that included a simple search function.

The experiment was a success, and it was decided to extend the use of technician-invented solutions to the entire French service force. There were two problems: the project needed a distribution and access method that would fit technicians' work practice and a social process to sustain the database so that it had continuing value. For the first requirement, the French Minitel system was chosen as the distribution infrastructure. (Minitel was a nationally deployed system of the French telephone company that consisted of a small keyboard connected to a phone line and a display monitor.)

The second problem was more daunting: service technicians liked the idea that their knowledge could travel beyond their own workgroup but were concerned about several issues: "If they submitted a tip, would it disappear into a black hole? Would they get credit? How would they know they could trust all the tips? And how would they get the right tips at the right time?" (Bobrow and Whalen 2002, p. 51). In workshops and meetings with all the different community members, people came up with solutions to these problems:

- To ensure the quality of each tip, each is warranted by a respected validator known to have expertise on the particular product family. Tigers would oversee the process.

- When a new tip is submitted to Minitel, a message is sent to relevant validators. The validator engages in a dialogue with the submitter to edit and improve the tip, making sure that it is complete and clear. The process is not just an accept or reject decision but is more like a conversation with a respected expert aimed at discovering new solutions. A validated tip would carry the names of both the submitter and the validator.

- New screens (information pages) were added to Minitel to allow service technicians to search the database based on key symptoms in a call record. They could also access at a customer's site if there was a local

Minitel terminal. The organization of the tips was simplified to problem, cause, solution. Service technicians were encouraged to comment and vote on the success of using existing tips as well as to enter new tips.

A major challenge was how to encourage technicians in the field to use the system. A champion from the French tiger group went around the country with one of the PARC staff, talking with each workgroup and explaining how technicians could use this system to help themselves and others. They met with numerous product leaders and helped train the French technicians.

In 1995, the Minitel system was deployed with only three product databases. By the end of the first year, technicians had created over forty databases covering a wide range of products, and more than one new tip was being added each day. The service organization in France went from being an average or below-average performer to being a benchmark performer: its service metrics were better than the European average by 5–20 percent, depending on the product (Bobrow and Whalen 2002).

Eureka in Canada. In June of 1996, the PARC group decided to introduce Eureka to another community. Canada was considered, partly because laptops had been deployed to all Canadian technicians, and partly because the Canadian service force was comparable in size to the French. The PARC group garnered support from one senior manager in Canada and was able to team up with an experienced field engineer who would become a local champion for the development and deployment of Eureka. For the distribution infrastructure, a server-client system was built, allowing a technician to use client software running on a laptop to access a local database that is synchronized with the community database on the server. Tip validation was done by product specialists in each customer business unit, similar to what was done in France. Unlike in France, Canadian service management wanted to continue its financial incentive program for service suggestions, so technicians received a small financial reward for tips. Eureka was successfully launched for 20 products in early 1997. Extensive training of product specialists by the Canadian champion, with the specialists then training service technicians, took place over four months. After six months, Canadian Eureka had become accepted as the technicians' tool (Bobrow and Whalen 2002).

Eureka in the United States. Eureka was rolled out in the United States in 1997 with a pilot program in several locations. Again, where these locations were supported by local champions, the pilot took hold. In 1998, Eureka was distributed generally via CD-ROMs mailed to field managers who were then expected to pass them along to technicians in their workgroups. The PARC group did not favor this "mass distribution" approach but had difficulty persuading U.S. management to adopt the "participatory deployment" strategy that had worked well in France and Canada.

Nevertheless, U.S. technicians were accepting Eureka enthusiastically after they had learned the system. Bobrow and Whalen (2002) cite one technician's remarks as being typical: "In all my years in Xerox, the two best things ever given to us are the (two-way) radios and Eureka." One story was featured in the 1999 Xerox annual report. A technician from Montreal traced a chronic problem with a customer's high-speed color copier to a 50¢ fuse holder and authored a Eureka tip. A technician in Brazil working on a similar problem with the same copier— a problem so severe the customer wanted the machine replaced—discovered this tip during a test run of Eureka, saving Xerox the $40,000 replacement cost. It turned out that demand for Eureka in other countries became so strong that Xerox had to begin distributing the system before it had completed the U.S. deployment.

In early 2001, the tips database had grown considerably as the number of countries using Eureka increased. There were close to 50,000 technician-authored tips, and the number of problems solved using Eureka had increased to nearly 200,000 annually. Solving a problem with Eureka can mean saving several hours of downtime, not having to escalate the problem to experts, or avoiding the replacement of a machine. Xerox reports that the use of Eureka provides many millions of dollars in savings annually and has led to increases in both customer and employee satisfaction.

Lessons Learned

What and where is the valuable knowledge? In the initial stages of the project, Xerox management did not believe that there was much value in what the technicians learned on their own in the field. As part of its "directive repair" strategy, it was more important to ensure that technicians followed the manual than to support them in creating new knowledge. The PARC research group found that the documentation provided only standard solutions to common problems and was of little use in diagnosing and fixing unusual problems that were "not in the manual." The perception that repair work could be highly routinized was inaccurate:

> The practice of experienced Xerox technicians maintaining photocopiers . . . is a continuous highly skilled improvisation within a triangular relationship of technician, customer, and machine. Technical service work is commonly conceived to be the fixing by rote procedure of uniform machines, and routine repair is indeed common. However, individual machines are quite idiosyncratic, new failure modes appear continuously, and rote procedure cannot address unknown problems. Technician's practice is therefore a response to the fragility of available understandings of the problematic situations of service and to the fragility of control over their definition and resolution. Understanding is fragile in that accurate information about the state of the machine is only sometimes available, and the meaning of available information cannot always be found. Control is fragile both because the technicians come to work when the relationship between customer and machine is already askew and because the technicians cannot keep the machines working and the customers satisfied; they can only restore that state after the fall. Work in such circumstances is resistant to rationalization since the

expertise vital to such contingent and extemporaneous practice cannot be easily codified. (Orr 1996, p. 439)

The solutions that technicians invented to overcome difficult, unusual service problems turned out to be knowledge valuable to the firm in improving customer satisfaction and avoiding the cost of service escalation or replacing a machine. Thus, there was a new belief in the importance of drawing on the experience and creativity of frontline employees and the effectiveness of knowledge sharing at the grassroots level.

How is knowledge being shared? How can a process be designed to support this sharing? Service technicians take pride in their work, especially in solving intractable problems that have stumped their peers. They enjoy talking about solutions to hard problems and gaining the respect and recognition of their peers. The Eureka process evolved as a result of consultations with the service technician community. Solutions discovered by field technicians would be submitted as pending tips; tips were validated by respected field engineers; validated tips were distributed with the names of submitters and validators; and technicians commented and voted on their usefulness (see Fig. 4.5). Thus, Eureka works as a knowledge system because it honors the norms of the technicians as a social community—it respects the community norms of peer recognition, trust, respect, and cooperation. Trust is fundamental to Eureka:

> Trust developed further because the knowledge captured was reliable and the system worked. Service technicians trusted the knowledge that was documented in the system and it made a difference in their work and to their customers. There was a great deal of socio-technical systems alignment in Eureka. (Douglas 2001)

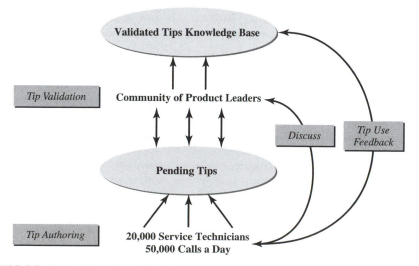

FIGURE 4.5. Eureka Knowledge-Sharing Process

In terms of incentives, Eureka relied more on peer recognition to motivate technicians to share knowledge and contribute to the tips database. Although financial incentives were sometimes included, they tended to be modest, and it was the status and reputation gained from being able to solve hard problems that was the principal inducement for sharing knowledge.

How can people's behavior be changed so that they will use the new system for sharing knowledge? The PARC group recognized early on that building a system did not mean that users will accept and use it. A key factor in the successful deployment of Eureka in France and Canada was the adoption of a participatory implementation approach, described here by members of the PARC group:

> A champion from the French tiger group went around the country with one of our group. They talked with each group about problems with service, and how the [technicians] could use this system to help themselves and others improve. They met with over 60 product leaders, and helped train all 1300 French technicians. Participation was carefully tracked, both in terms of the number of times that the database was referred to, and in terms of the number of new tips entered. There were strong differences among workgroups. While one region may have been high, another of the same size might have quite low usage rates. Revisiting the latter regions, providing some training through examples of use, and reintroducing the purpose of the system helped encourage broader participation. The strategy, then, can best be described as "hands-on participatory implementation," which is a marked contrast to the top-down, cascade model. (Bobrow and Whalen 2002, p. 52)

In contrast, the rollout in the United States followed a top-down, mass distribution strategy, and the uptake was slow. Tom Ruddy, manager of Customer Service Knowledge Programs, noted that

> Eureka had a very slow adoption in the USA—two pilots were actually done in the US, but it took a significant longer time for the USA to embrace Eureka. It was not taking hold in the USA, as Eureka was seen initially as a technology program as there was the belief that there was nothing that the technicians don't already know. What it really took was testimonial video clips of stories of old school hard nosed twenty five years of experienced service technicians to tell their personal stories of how Eureka made a difference to them—hearing the voice of the technicians helped to escalate the belief and value realization. . . . It took more of a marketing approach—value, examples, voice of their peers, benefits to help move the program along. (Ruddy 2001, p. 35)

What is the role of information technology? What constitutes effective technological support for work practice? The PARC research group had started out by building an expert system using artificial intelligence to support service work, based on the assumption that important knowledge had already been captured in the lab. Instead, it found that some of the most valuable knowledge was being invented in the field as technicians grappled with tough problems, and that this knowledge was being shared through "war stories." This suggested to the PARC group that they "could stand the Artificial Intelligence approach on its head, so to speak, with the work community itself becoming the expert system, and with ideas flowing upward from the people actually engaged in work on the organization's frontlines" (Bobrow and Whalen 2002, p. 50).

The telling of war stories by itself does not scale well. While the stories may get told to the dozen people around a water cooler, they would not get shared among the 20,000 service technicians that Xerox had. What was needed a way to share these stories and discoveries more quickly, so that when someone found a solution, it would be made available to the rest of the technicians. Information technology played the crucial role of accelerating and expanding this sharing. Important elements included a distribution infrastructure (initially the French Minitel, then the client-server network in Canada, and now an Intranet); the use of portable laptops; a simple and fast search engine; a standardized format for displaying the content of each tip; easy-to-use templates for submitting tips; and so on, all of which were selected or designed to fit in well with the technicians' work practices.

> Technically, Eureka is a relational database of hypertext documents available online via the Intranet. It can also be viewed as the distributed publishing of local community know-how. In practice, Eureka is an electronic version of war stories told around the water cooler—with the added benefits of a user-friendly search engine, institutional memory, expert validation, and corporate-wide availability. It is a way to simultaneously grow both intellectual capital and social capital. (Douglas 1999, pp. 217–18)

In the end, Eureka's effectiveness is not based on the sophistication of its technology but on its insights about how and why people share knowledge. The system is built on a technological infrastructure that supported existing work activity patterns, as well as a set of social processes and practices that respects the norms of communication and cooperation among service technicians. What made Eureka an interesting story was its distinctive way of marrying the technical with the social—the alignment between technology that enabled distribution and access and the social ties based on trust and peer relations that supported sharing and collaboration.

IX. INFORMATION NEEDS, SEEKING, AND USE IN KNOWLEDGE CREATION

In this section, we consider information seeking and use in the context of knowledge creation, knowledge transfer, and knowledge utilization. Following the framework developed in Chapter 2, we examine (1) information needs, (2) information seeking, and (3) information use in terms of cognitive needs, affective responses, and situational dimensions. A summary of the ensuing discussion is in Table 4-2.

TABLE 4-2. Information needs, seeking, and use in knowledge creation.

	Information Needs	*Information Seeking*	*Information Use*
Knowledge Creation	• *Identify gaps in existing knowledge, capabilities* • *Assign value to new knowledge* • *Information about sources of knowledge, capabilities*	• *Information seeking and information sharing* • *Information crosses boundaries* • *Information flows in social networks*	• *Absorbing new knowledge* • *Exploiting new knowledge* • *Knowledge use as social process*
Cognitive Needs	• Effect of culture and subcultures • Knowledge from customers, partners • Innovation as initiation and implementation	• Stories as carriers of knowledge • Boundary roles • Information stickiness	• Absorptive capacity • Common knowledge effect • Boundary objects
Affective Responses	• Types of emotion in organizational learning • Feelings of uncertainty • Emotive and expert intuition	• Redundant information and uncertainty • Emotional attachment to signature skills • Engagement and safety in sharing information	• Not-invented-here syndrome • Care in organizational relations • Trust in organizations
Situational Dimensions	• Design versus discovery, complex, amorphous • Technology maturity and market alignment • Culture of innovation	• Information politics • Market research or market discovery • Social capital in organizations	• Fair process • Direct and indirect relations • Knowledge institutionalization

Information Needs. In knowledge creation, information needs arise from gaps in the organization's existing knowledge or capabilities. Such gaps may stand in the way of the organization being able to solve a problem or take advantage of an opportunity. To initiate information gathering, the needs pertaining to a problem or opportunity situation have to be identified and elaborated. This process is guided by beliefs and assumptions the organization holds about what knowledge would be advantageous for the organization, which ideas appear to be promising, as well as what levels of effort would be required. These beliefs give shape and direction to the specification of information needs and provide the criteria by which new information and knowledge would be evaluated as they are encountered in information seeking. Gaps in knowledge or capability are usually filled in three ways: by locating expertise within the organization, by developing new capabilities, or by transferring knowledge from outside the organization. An important part of the elaboration of information needs is therefore to discover sources and develop strategies for acquiring specific know-how.

Information Seeking. The ability to share information—between groups in the organization or between organizations—is an important part of information seeking. Information seeking and access has to be able to negotiate boundaries inside and outside the organization. The flow of information often takes place in social networks that are built on trust and cooperation. Generally, information seeking begins by scanning broadly and sharing information extensively, connecting with many internal and external sources. The initial objectives are to assess the state of development of an area, understand the range of possibilities, and identify new opportunities or market needs. At some stage, when the problem is sufficiently defined, information gathering can become more focused and intensive. Two sets of difficulties are commonly encountered in the scanning and focusing of information: the difficulties of sourcing and transferring information from outside the organization or group and the difficulties of retrieving and making explicit the tacit knowledge of the experienced and the expert.

Information Use. Information use is an integral part of assessing, absorbing, and applying new knowledge. The organization evaluates new knowledge in relation to its beliefs about how the application of the knowledge will enhance its competitive position, its interpretations about how the market will react to new products or services, and its expectations about how the new capability supports its longer-term goals and vision. These beliefs are embedded in evaluation routines and norms that determine the usefulness of new information and appraise the value of new knowledge. The use of external knowledge requires the organization to be ready to absorb the new knowledge and to be able to address acceptance issues such as dealing with the not-invented-here syndrome. In either case, the creation, absorption, and exploitation of new knowledge is not just a technical activity but a social process that needs to take into account the culture and context of the organization.

Information Needs in Knowledge Creation

Information Needs and Cognitive Needs

Effect of culture and subcultures. Culture is reflected in values, norms, and practices. At the deepest level, culture consists of values, which are deeply held, tacit preferences about the organization's goals, identity, and modes of operation. DeLong and Fahey (2000) believe that values have the greatest impact on knowledge creation and use. For example, a firm that holds the value that customer interaction is important would be more likely to ask customers questions about product use and satisfaction, to listen carefully to their replies, and to develop relationships over time. Again, values that regard customers as partners are more likely to motivate behaviors that create useful knowledge about customers. Generally speaking, we may expect the values of an organization to influence the way that different aspects of an information need are elaborated and emphasized. Norms are usually derived from values but are more observable in the behaviors of employees. For example, if employees believe that sharing information incurs personal risk and a loss of power, then the social norms governing interaction will not support behaviors needed to create and exchange knowledge. DeLong and Fahey (2000) found that one of the most important consequences of culture is the way it influences assumptions about what knowledge is important. In particular, the subcultures in an organization heavily influence what is perceived as useful, important, or required knowledge for an organization. Subcultures consist of distinct sets of values, norms, and practices of specific groups or units such as R&D, sales, engineering, MIS, different levels of management, and different geographic regions. For example, "R&D's values may seem focused on elegant product features to the detriment of product marketability and profits, while finance appears to value only controlling costs. MIS, on the other hand, may seem concerned only with maintaining strict adherence to its technology standards. . . . Subcultures often lead their members to define important knowledge differently than other groups in the organization" (DeLong and Fahey 2000, p. 117).

Knowledge from customers, partners. Wikström and Normann (1994) distinguish three kinds of knowledge processes in organizations: generative processes, productive processes, and representative processes. *Generative processes* are those in which "new knowledge is created largely in activities which are geared to the solving of problems" (p. 107). First produced in the course of problem solving, generative knowledge is important for increasing the overall pool of knowledge resources in the organization and for providing the organization with capabilities to enter new businesses or bring forth better products. *Productive processes* are those in which new knowledge is accumulated and used by the organization to produce customer offerings. Productive processes thus yield knowledge that is manifest and used. *Representative processes* are those in which the organization conveys its knowledge to the customer, so that its knowledge is made available to customers for their own value-creating processes. Representative processes are increasingly important because organizations are forming cooperative networks to offer products and services that enable customers to create value for themselves. Thus each organization's value-creating processes receive contributions from many different sources, including suppliers, the suppliers' suppliers, its own customers, its customers' customers, and so on (Normann and Ramirez 1993; Wikström and Normann 1994). The flow of knowledge may be drawn as a star, where the organization's value-creating processes are at the hub of many incoming flows of knowledge from many sources. This knowledge may be in the form of new modes of collaboration, training and education, and information sharing through networks of users, suppliers, and others. Each of the three knowledge processes influences the type and content of information needs. In generative processes, information needs are focused on understanding a problem (or an opportunity) so that it can be resolved. In productive processes, information needs are focused on operationalizing new knowledge or information so that it is used in production. Unlike the first two processes, the information needs of representative processes are externally directed: the focus is on the needs of customers, suppliers, and partners in relation to the knowledge and capabilities of the focal organization.

Innovation as initiation and implementation. The innovation process in organizations may be divided into two general stages of *initiation,* which include "all of the information gathering, conceptualizing, and planning for the adoption of an innovation, leading up to the decision to adopt," and *implementation,* which includes "all of the events, actions, and decisions involved in putting an innovation into use" (Rogers 1983, p. 363). During initiation, the organization "sets its agenda" by identifying problems or performance gaps that create a need for innovation or by scanning the environment for new innovations of potential value. The organization then "matches" a problem from its agenda with an innovation to assess how well they are likely to fit. In agenda setting and matching, new information is needed with reference to the organization's intention and core capabilities. During implementation, the organization "redefines" the innovation as it is modified to fit the situation of the organization and the demands of the problem. The organization may also "restructure" how work is organized around the new innovation. During implementation and as the innovation becomes more widely used, information is needed to clarify the interaction between the innovation and other established processes, so that the innovation may be assimilated and eventually "routinized." Stinchcombe (1990) argues that the introduction of an innovation in an organization must be accompanied by the development of a social system that supports the innovation. Information needs therefore are not limited to technical concerns but must also reflect the social and economic requirements that have to be addressed. Stinchcombe (1990) structures the *social requirements of an innovation* around six elements (which he also calls theories), with each element identifying the largely cognitive information needs to be addressed: (1) a core theory of the innovation, or what is technically involved in the design of the innovation; (2) a theory of the investment in the innovation, or what the risks and profits are that justify the innovation; (3) technical costs of the innovation, or what it will cost to produce the innovation; (4) the market or benefits of the innovation, or who will want the goods, at what price, and how the organization can reach them; (5) a theory of the division of benefits, or how benefits are to be distributed, and what promises of future returns can attract investors; (6) a personnel part of the theory, or what the levels of competence, trustworthiness, motivation, and so on are of the personnel involved (Stinchcombe 1990, pp. 167–68).

Information Needs and Affective Responses

Types of emotion in organizational learning. In a literature survey of the positive and negative effects of emotions on individual and organizational learning, Scherer and Tran (2001) suggest grouping emotions into five major classes: approach emotions, achievement emotions, deterrence emotions, withdrawal emotions, and antagonistic emotions. (1) *Approach emotions* refer to affective states such as interest, hope, or joyful anticipation, all of which are likely to increase the motivation and energy to explore and develop a problem or interest. While usually a positive influence, approach emotions can also be dysfunctional, as when the energy is driven mostly by imitation or fashion-following. (2) *Achievement emotions* such as satisfaction, happiness, and pride celebrate success based on accomplishment. Scherer and Tran (2001) note that its effects can be paradoxical: it can reinforce new learning but can also lead to stagnation. (3) *Deterrence emotions* denote anxiety, fear, distress, pessimism, and other affective states that limit the individual's interest and effort in seeking new or more information. Scherer and Tran (2001) write that "emotions of this type can have quite deleterious effects on learning because they often prevent learners from even exposing themselves to new information and experiences, thus vitiating the potential for learning" (p. 386). (4) *Withdrawal emotions* include sadness, resignation, shame, and guilt, again forming a negative context for learning and information seeking. Individuals or organizations characterized by these emotions tend to focus internally rather than externally and lack the necessary energy to pursue new information or ideas. (5) *Antagonistic emotions* may be expressed as anger, irritation, hate, and aggression. Such emotions are usually triggered when an individual experiences obstacles to goal attainment. Antagonistic emotions can divert focus from what is important, limit attentiveness, and redirect energy toward ulterior goals. Scherer and Tran (2001) suggest that "often, a blend of the various classes of emotions is what seems to foster optimal learning" (p. 386). The appropriate "emotional blend" depends on the situation, for example, in periods of rapid environmental change, an optimal climate would be high in approach emotions but tempered by deterrence emotions in order to avoid overshooting.

Feelings of uncertainty. Feelings of uncertainty and doubt are characteristic of the initial stages of information seeking when organizational members are trying to clarify the information needs that should guide their knowledge exploration processes. As Kuhlthau (1993b) has observed, the state of uncertainty about the nature of information needs causes affective symptoms of anxiety and lack of confidence during early phases of the information search. The feeling of uncertainty begins to ebb once the individual is able to formulate some kind of focus or guiding idea which can be used to steer further search. Kuhlthau regards this formulation of a theme as a pivotal point in the search process and suggests that it is an outcome of the individual reflecting thoughtfully on the information encountered thus far in the search. During the first phases of the knowledge-creation process, information needs are progressively answered through information scanning, knowledge sharing, and participative dialogue. By a process of collective reflection, members of a project team develop a shared mental model which can be verbalized into explicit concepts using words and expressions as well as metaphors and analogies. It is through the activities of "sharing tacit knowledge" and "creating concepts" (Nonaka and Takeuchi 1995) that the initial feelings of uncertainty and doubt give way to a heightened sense of direction, confidence, and optimism about what is desirable and achievable. The early feelings of stress and anxiety can be channeled to increase motivation and foster creativity. For example, corporations are known to have tackled hard R&D problems by forming "skunkworks" of small research teams that are set outside the main organization structure and given the mandate to work intensively and uninhibitedly on complex problems and challenging goals.

Emotive and expert intuition. Intuition may play a significant role in situations when information needs are unclear or when a guiding theme does not readily crystallize. Since intuition generally refers to a form of knowing or sensing without the use of rational processes, it is helpful to differentiate between expert intuition and emotive intuition (Simon 1987). Emotive intuition is based on emotional responses, often precipitated by conditions of stress. For example, managers in stressful situations are known to behave in nonproductive ways to allay feelings of guilt, anxiety, and embarrassment (Simon 1987). Expert intuition is based on accumulated knowledge and experience that results in a capability to recognize and retrieve patterns from memory. Leonard (1995) describes companies that make the effort to identify industry experts and technologists who have developed a fine "intuition" of what the market wants now and will need in the future. Such expert intuition is built upon the individual's immersion in a rich and sizeable pool of personal knowledge about customers, competitors, markets, technologies, standards, and so on. Emotions are not absent in the exercise of expert intuition, but they are used to signal to the experts the affective values of current options, affective values which recall their past experience in working with similar options.

Information Needs and Situational Dimensions

Design versus discovery. Information needs may also be clarified by examining the problem dimensions that characterize the situation in which those needs arise. Of the eleven problem dimensions identified by MacMullin and Taylor (1984), four are particularly relevant to understanding information needs in organizational knowledge creation. (1) The problem to be solved can lie on a continuum between *design and discovery*. Design problems may be solved by applying existing knowledge in new ways, while discovery problems may require information and expertise about new technologies and markets. (2) The problem is likely to be *complex,* with many variables interacting simultaneously, so that information is needed to reduce the problem to simpler tasks. (3) The problem's goals are likely to be *amorphous* and challenging, requiring information to give substance and priority to design objectives and preferences. (4) The problem is likely to be of a *new pattern* or unfamiliar, so that information is required to clarify and understand what is possible and what would constitute a significant advance. Generally, because problem solving and knowledge creation often involves thinking broadly and making surprising connections, organizational members can benefit from access to information that goes beyond their immediate operational requirements.

Technology maturity and market alignment. In *new-product development situations,* two sets of factors determine the kinds of information that are needed: "the maturity of the technological design underlying the product line and the degree of alignment between the proposed product line and the current customer base" (Leonard 1995, p. 180). When the *maturity of the technological design* is low, the product will be new to the world, so the developer's questions revolve around whether he or she can solve the problems to make the product work. When the technological maturity is high, the product incorporates incremental improvements to a well-established or "dominant design" (Utterback 1994). When the *market alignment* is high, the product is intended for current customers, so the main issue is understanding what features are most desirable to existing customers. When the market alignment is low, the product is attempting to create a new market, so the major concerns are identifying who the customers will be and how they will use the product. Depending on the degree of technological maturity and market alignment in a particular new-product situation, an organization can adopt the appropriate product definition strategy. For example, when both technological maturity and market alignment are high, explicit customer demands often drive technological enhancements along known performance parameters for current products (Leonard 1995). Conversely, when both technological maturity and market alignment are low, the technology and the market co-evolve together, with technological potential attempting to match or better respond to market need (which may have to be revealed or discovered).

Culture of innovation. Both Nonaka and Takeuchi (1995) and Leonard (1995) observe that much of managing knowledge creation and use involves establishing the conditions that enable those outcomes. Nonaka and Takeuchi identify five enabling conditions. First, since knowledge creation is driven by *organizational intention* or aspirations, the organization needs to clearly conceptualize a vision about what kind of knowledge would be most valuable to realizing the organizational intention and to apply this vision as the principal yardstick for judging the usefulness of new knowledge. Second, organizational members, either on their own or in self-organizing teams, should be given the freedom to act with *autonomy* so that they can motivate themselves to experiment and discover new knowledge. Third, the organization can stimulate the knowledge-creation process by inducing *fluctuation and creative chaos* by, for example, introducing breakdowns of set routines or habitual frameworks, evoking a sense of crisis, and stating ambiguous visions and goals. Fourth, information should be made available to organizational members that goes beyond their immediate operational requirements. *Information redundancy* promotes the sharing of tacit knowledge and the exchanging of ideas. Fifth, according to the principle of *requisite variety,* an organization's internal diversity must match the variety and complexity of its external environment. This implies that organizational members should have prompt access to a wide range of information so they can cope with fast-changing contingencies. There are echoes of these enabling factors in Leonard's discussion of management strategies to support organizational knowledge-building. She emphasizes that organizations need to have a clear understanding of their core capabilities and strategic intent; that members be encouraged to experiment continuously; that creative abrasion is an effective way of parlaying members' cognitive diversity and variety of signature skills; and that group boundaries should be kept porous so that information can be broadly diffused.

Information Seeking in Knowledge Creation

Information Seeking and Cognitive Needs

Stories as carriers of knowledge. War stories, or anecdotes of experience, can be effective vehicles for sharing and transferring otherwise hard-to-articulate collective wisdom. In an ethnographic study of photocopier repair technicians, Orr (1990) found that the technicians used stories to preserve knowledge and to explore it in subsequent diagnoses. In one incident, a sophisticated new machine had been recently installed but had never worked reliably. Changing the component indicated by the error code did not rectify the problem. According to Orr, a dozen stories were exchanged between the assigned technician and the team's technical specialist,

> as the two searched their memories for possible culprits, looking for the key perspective which would integrate their random facts. . . . They are faced with a failing machine displaying diagnostic information which has previously proved worthless and in which no one has any particular confidence this time. They do not know where they are going to find the information they need to understand and solve this problem. In their search for inspiration, they tell stories. (Orr 1990, pp. 176, 178–79)

The shared storytelling eventually developed the correct diagnosis that the initial error code (E053) should not be believed, but this code may then be followed by a second error code (F066) indicating the true source of the failure, a shorted dicorotron. This new insight, not found in the field repair manuals, is then communicated to other technicians as a shorter version of the story. By including technical details and emotional coloring, stories deepen the listener's understanding and affective response, which facilitates subsequent retrieval and evaluation. By providing more details than are necessary, stories also supply additional information that might turn out to be important for a different problem: "the apparent object is to keep all knowledge as closely connected as possible, so that if a new problem connects to any known facts at all, it connects to an understanding of the system with known failures and solutions on which to base a diagnostic strategy" (Orr 1990, p. 184). In this way stories become carriers of knowledge, carriers that can transfer general principles through the telling about particular situations (Brown 1993).

Boundary roles. It is well known that certain individuals perform special roles in the movement and assimilation of information across organizational peripheries. Allen (1977) found that in science and engineering organizations, information from the outside world does not move directly into the organization. Instead, the information flow is indirect and involves two or more steps. External information passes through *technological gatekeepers* who read more, including the more re-search-oriented journals, and who have a broad range of personal contacts both outside and inside the organization which they maintain on a continuing informal basis. It is the gatekeepers who keep their colleagues informed, and who are often consulted about current, external developments. Tushman and Scanlan (1981) noticed a similar phenomenon. Because organizations limit their scope and specialize in certain activities, they evolve local norms, languages, and con-ceptual frameworks. While this specialization increases the efficiency of internal information processing, it also sets up obstacles to information transfer from the external environment. As a result, it becomes necessary to recode information messages at the firm's boundaries. Boundaries can be spanned effectively only by individuals who understand the coding schemes used on both sides of the perimeter, enabling them to recognize significant information on one side and disseminate it on the other side: Tushman and Scanlan name this process *infor-mational boundary spanning.* The phenomenon of information gatekeeping, or boundary spanning, is not limited to scientific organizations but can be found in a wide spectrum of social communication patterns, including voting behavior and the diffusion of innovations (e.g., opinion leaders influencing the voting decisions of friends, and the adoption of innovations such as hybrid seed corn and new drugs). Allen summarizes:

> The phenomenon of the gatekeeper is not an isolated one. Rather it is one example
> of a much more general class of phenomena. There will always be some people
> who, for various reasons, tend to become acquainted with information sources
> outside their immediate community. They either read more extensively than most
> or develop personal contacts with outsiders. A large proportion of these people in
> turn attract colleagues from within the community who turn to them for
> information and advice. (Allen 1977, p. 150)

Information stickiness. The information required for technical problem solving is often hard to acquire and transfer, necessitating significant expenditures of cognitive effort, time, and money. To reflect the costs of information transfer, von Hippel (1994) defines the "stickiness" of a unit of information as "the incre-mental expenditure required to transfer that unit of information to a specified locus in a form usable by a given information seeker" (p. 430). *Information stick-iness* is a function of the attributes of the information itself as well as the attrib-utes and choices made by the information seeker and information providers. Thus, stickiness increases when the information to be transferred is part of the

tacit knowledge of a skilled individual, or when the user is unfamiliar with or un-
trained in acquiring a type of information, or when the provider charges for access to its databases. Information may be made easier to transfer by "unsticking"
the information, as when tacit knowledge is made explicit through narrating or
recording procedures, or when gatekeepers filter and selectively introduce outside information. Information stickiness can also be avoided by changing the
place where the problem solving is done. For example, in the development of information systems, systems developers would do a great deal of work at the user
site to understand the needs of the system to be built. After acquiring this information, the developers return to their firm to design the system. Von Hippel
would argue that a more effective approach would be to move the locus of the
problem-solving effort: the developer and the user could then draw only upon
their own local and idiosyncratic information sets without having to move between locations. Arara, Fosfuri, and Gambardella (2001) highlight how information systems providers increasingly develop system "templates" built quickly
from initial user specifications. Users try out these templates and identify problems or issues. The system is returned to the developers, who make the necessary
adjustments, and the process is repeated until the system is built. "Through these
successive iterations, the users and the producers no longer move the information, but they move the problem-solving activity. Neither party needs to acquire
the sticky information of the other. Each relies on his own information" (Arara
et al. 2001, p. 106).

Information Seeking and Affective Responses

Redundant information and uncertainty. Information seeking in the context of
knowledge creation is likely to be influenced by the individual's attitudes and
preferences about the types of information and the style of information gathering. This may be especially true in the case of sharing information that is based
on personal, tacit knowledge. In Kuhlthau's (1993b) model of the information
search process that we presented in Chapter 2, she drew a few corollaries from
the affective responses of uncertainty and anxiety that characterize stages of the
search process. Among these corollaries, two are particularly pertinent to our
discussion here, and they concern the effects of redundant information and the
searcher's personal choices about how and where to gather information.
Kuhlthau (1993b) observed that *redundant information* fits into what the individual already knows or recognizes, and its relevance and usefulness is easily
judged. Redundant information can therefore build confidence and reduce the
level of uncertainty. Unique information is new and can extend knowledge, but
it may not match the individual's current cognitive framework, requiring the individual to reconstruct meaning and significance. Too much redundant information leads to boredom, while too much unique information causes anxiety.
Nonaka and Takeuchi (1995) define redundant information somewhat differently
and show that it can be used to generate a sense of creative tension. For them,
redundant information is information that goes beyond immediate operational
needs and includes other functional areas that are not one's own. The effect is

that "sharing redundant information promotes the sharing of tacit knowledge, because individuals can sense what others are trying to articulate. . . . redundant information enables individuals to invade each other's functional boundaries and offer advice or provide new information from different perspectives. In short, redundancy of information brings about 'learning by intrusion' into each individual's sphere of perception" (Nonaka and Takeuchi 1995, p. 81).

Emotional attachment to signature skills. Kuhlthau (1993b) noted that the search process is a series of unique, personal choices about what sources and information-seeking strategies will be effective or expedient. Beliefs and expectations about what sources to use or not use, about the sequence of sources to be approached, and about the information selected from the sources as relevant or irrelevant are based on the individual's own experience, training, and cognitive style. Information relevance is therefore a matter of personal judgment and preference. Leonard (1995) makes a similar but more general argument in her discussion of the *signature skills* that people use in problem solving. She observes that the skilled individual becomes emotionally attached to a particular style of problem solving and information seeking, a style by which the individual establishes her own professional identity. Signature skills are the result of three interacting influences—the individual's preferred type of task, preferred cognitive approach to problem solving, and preferred technology (tools and methods) for performing the task. Specialists tend to pursue their signature skills in depth, and the signature skills become "emotionally tied to people's egos and identities" (Leonard 1995, p. 63). This is partly the reason why many experts resist new ideas. Starbuck (1992) attributes this resistance to five factors: clients or peers may view the expert's need to learn as evidence of deficient knowledge; experts account carefully for their use of time and are reluctant to spend it on learning something new or unproven; experts' specialization necessarily reduces versatility and flexibility; experts protect their niches as partial monopolies; and experts' perceptual filters keep them from noticing some social and technological changes.

Engagement and safety in sharing information. A study by Cross et al. (2001) asked 40 managers to reflect on a recent project that was important to their careers and indicate where they obtained information critical to the project's success. The managers overwhelmingly indicated that they received critical information from other people far more frequently than impersonal sources such as their personal computer archives, the Internet, or the organization's knowledge database. The managers also identified the people most important to them as sources and described the relationships with them. Four relational dimensions distinguished effective from ineffective relationships. (1) *Knowledge dimension:* knowing what another person knows and thus when to turn to them. The managers reported that "people they turned to for information provided a critical extension to their own knowledge when the manager had at least a semi-accurate understanding of her or his contact's expertise" (Cross et al. 2001, p. 108).

(2) *Access dimension:* being able to gain timely access to that person. Many critical issues on which outside help or advice is needed often require turnaround within tight time frames. (3) *Engagement dimension:* willingness of the person to engage in problem solving rather than just "dump" information. The person was willing to cognitively engage with the information seeker. This usually means first understanding the other person's problem and then actively shaping what they knew to the problem so that it could be acted on. (4) *Safety dimension:* a degree of safety in the relationship that promotes learning and creativity. Safe relationships encourage more learning, as people are not overly concerned about admitting a lack of knowledge. In safe relationships, people are more willing to take risks with their ideas, often leading to creative solutions. This safety dimension is also evident in the way Lave and Wenger (1991) show that apprenticeship is effective when novices learn through *legitimate peripheral participation.* The novice starts by staying safely on the periphery of practice as a participant observer. When she feels sufficiently comfortable or when the mentor feels she is ready, the learner can move from the periphery to the center to engage the task, and then move back out again. In this sense the learner is a legitimate participant who moves to the center of practice from time to time, and who has access to the modes of communication used by the competent practitioner so that she can pick up know-how on technique and nuance.

Information Seeking and Situational Dimensions

Information politics. The sharing of information is a necessary condition of organizational knowledge creation. Ironically, the more information-intensive that an organization is the less likely it is that its members would share their information freely: "As people's jobs and roles become defined by the unique information they hold, they may be less likely to share that information—viewing it as a source of power and indispensability—rather than more so. When information is the primary unit of organizational currency, we should not expect the owners to give it away" (Davenport et al. 1992, p. 53). From their analysis of more than 25 organizations, Davenport and associates found that the major reason for the inability to create information-based organizations was the failure to manage the politics of information use. Among the organizations studied, five models of information politics were observed: technological utopianism, anarchy, fedualism, monarchy, and federalism (Davenport et al. 1992). The most common political model of information sharing was a form of *information feudalism,* in which individual managers and their departments control information acquisition, storage, distribution, and analysis. Managers act as powerful feudal lords who not only rule over the creation and circulation of information, but also determine the meanings and interpretations that should be attached to information. This fragmentation of information integrity undermines the organization's efforts to consolidate and cross-fertilize its knowledge assets so that the organization as whole can learn and adapt. Instead of feudalism Davenport et al. recommend a form of *information federalism* as being the most appropriate model in today's environment. Federalism recognizes that politics is a necessary and legitimate activity for people with divergent interests to work out a collective purpose and the means for realizing it. Under federalism, managers negotiate among themselves the use and definition of information. Managers bargain with each other to cede some of their information assets in return for producing a larger pool of knowledge that they can tap into and exploit to advantage.

Market research or market discovery. In new-product or new-service development situations, information seeking varies according to how mature the product or service technology is and how well the product or service matches with current customer needs (Leonard 1995). When the new product is an extension of an established product line, an appropriate information-gathering strategy is to make use of traditional market research techniques such as conducting surveys and focus group discussions and interacting with "lead users," "whose present strong needs will become general in a marketplace months or years in the future" (von Hippel 1988, p. 107). When either the technology is immature or the market is likely to be a new or unknown set of customers, traditional market research techniques work less well because no analogous product exists and users and developers cannot easily visualize the new product. In this situation, Leonard (1995) suggests the use of data collection techniques based on "emphatic design," which she defines as "the creation of product or service concepts based on a deep (emphatic) understanding of unarticulated user needs" (p. 194). This deep understanding is achieved by collecting data about actual observed customer behavior, allowing product developers and users to interact directly so that market and technological potential can be assessed, and redirecting existing technical capabilities imaginatively toward new products or services. When neither the technology nor the market is certain, market research and emphatic design techniques are not applicable because it is not clear how the technology will shape the product and who the customers will be. In this situation, new markets are being evolved, and information seeking may involve extrapolating current trends, re-imagining scenarios about the future, and conducting market experiments (Leonard 1995).

Social capital in organizations. Nahapiet and Ghoshal (1998) define social capital as the sum of the actual *and* potential resources embedded within, available through, and derived from the network of relationships possessed by an individual or social unit (p. 243). It thus comprises both the network and the assets that may be mobilized through that network. They identify three features of social capital: structural embeddedness, relational embeddedness, and cognitive dimension. *Structural embeddedness* comes from the properties of the social system and the network of relations as a whole. It refers to the overall pattern of connections between actors: who you reach and how you reach them. Its most important facets are the presence of network ties between actors; network configuration measured in terms of density, connectivity, and hierarchy; and the existence of networks created for one purpose that may be used for another. *Relational embeddedness* describes the kind of personal relationships people have developed with each other through a history of interactions. It focuses on the particular relations people have, such as respect and friendship, that influence their behavior. Its key facets are trust and trustworthiness, norms and sanctions, obligations and expectations, and identity and identification. *Cognitive dimension* refers to those resources providing shared representations, interpretations, and systems of meaning among parties. These resources are of particular importance in knowledge creation and exchange, which often depend on shared language and codes and shared narratives. There are two important consequences of social capital for action. First, social capital increases the efficiency of action. For example, networks of social relations characterized by weak ties or structural holes increase the efficiency of information diffusion by reducing redundancy (Burt 1992). (Weak ties are more distant acquaintances who move in different circles and who are more likely to link to unexpected information than strong ties such as friends and kin [Granovetter 1973]. Structural holes are individuals [or gaps] who are not benefiting from connecting with others and with resources that could be valuable [Burt 1992]. In the statement above, structural holes refer more generally to disconnections or nonequivalencies among players in an arena.) Social capital in the form of high levels of trust also diminishes the risk of opportunism and reduces the need for costly monitoring. The second consequence is that social capital promotes adaptive efficiency, creativity, and learning. Social capital encourages cooperative behavior and information sharing, facilitating the development of new forms of association and innovative organization.

Information Use in Knowledge Creation

Information Use and Cognitive Needs

Absorptive capacity. The ability to recognize the potential value of new, external knowledge, assimilate it, and then exploit the knowledge is vital to the knowledge-creating enterprise. The organization's *absorptive capacity* to evaluate and utilize outside knowledge is largely a function of the level of prior related knowledge that the organization already possesses (Cohen and Levinthal 1990). Absorptive capacity is generated and increased when the organization conducts its own R&D, is directly involved in manufacturing operations, sends its personnel for advanced technical training, and so on. Cognitive research on individual learning suggests that the accumulation and richness of the preexisting knowledge increases the ability to put new knowledge into memory as well as the ability to recall and use it. Thus, learning is cumulative, and learning capability is greatest when what is to be learned is related to what is already known (Cohen and Levinthal 1990). The implication here is that the existence of a diversity of knowledge and knowledge structures possessed by members of the organization would increase the probability of relating new incoming knowledge to what is already known. In practical terms, Cohen and Levinthal suggest that the organization requires an existing internal staff of technologists and scientists who are not only competent in their fields but are also familiar with the organization's idiosyncratic needs, procedures, routines, complementary capabilities, and external relationships. They also note that

> firms may conduct basic research less for particular results than to be able to
> provide themselves with the general background knowledge that would permit
> them to exploit rapidly useful scientific and technological knowledge through their
> own innovations or to be able to respond quickly—to become a fast second—when
> competitors come up with a major advance. . . . we may think of basic research as
> broadening the firm's knowledge base to create critical overlap with new
> knowledge and providing it with the deeper understanding that is useful for
> exploiting new technical developments that build on rapidly advancing science and
> technology. (Cohen and Levinthal 1990, p. 148)

An interesting corollary of the need for an organization to invest in absorptive capacity is that when an organization intends to acquire and use knowledge that is relatively unconnected to its current activities and capabilities, then the organization may need to first work at or invest in creating the absorptive capacity (by, for example, R&D or specialized training) to assimilate and exploit the new knowledge.

Common knowledge effect. In an experiment conducted by Gigone and Hastie (1993), three-person groups were asked to make judgments about the likely performance of students in a course based on six facts or cues (e.g., the student's high school performance, number of classes skipped, standardized test scores). Before the discussion of each student, cues were distributed so that two cues were given to all members (shared information), two cues were given to two members (partially shared information), and two cues were given to only one member (unshared information). The results showed that the influence of an item of information on group judgment was related directly to the number of members who had the item before the discussion. This common knowledge effect is defined as "the more group members who knew an item of decision-relevant information before discussion, the greater the impact of that information on group judgment" (Gigone and Hastie 1997, p. 132). In another experiment, groups considered pairs of students and chose the one who would obtain the higher grade. As before, group members received six cues for each student. Again, the impact of a cue on group choice was related to the number of members who had the cue before the discussion. Only under one cue distribution scheme (out of three) did the discussion of shared cues modify this overall finding, and only rarely was an initial majority opinion reversed by the discussion. Thus, the common knowledge effect was mediated by members' initial opinions. Information pooled during discussion had almost no effect on group judgments. It was as if group members exchanged and combined their opinions but paid little attention to anything else (Gigone and Hastie 1997). Groups wanting to use shared knowledge effectively will need to take compensatory action to counter the common knowledge effect, perhaps introducing procedures to consider all of the information at its disposal, not just the information that members have in common.

Boundary objects. The term *boundary object* was coined to understand how scientists balance different categories and meanings in order to allow them to cooperate without agreeing about the classification of objects or actions. Star and Griesemer (1989) first noticed the phenomenon in a museum, where specimens of dead birds had very different meanings to amateur bird-watchers and professional biologists, although "the same" bird was used by each group. These objects had different meanings in different social worlds but their structure is common enough to make them recognizable in different worlds and act as a means of translation. Boundary objects are defined as

> those objects that both inhabit several communities of practice and satisfy the informational requirements of each of them. In working practice, they are objects that are able both to travel across borders and maintain some sort of constant identity. They can be tailored to meet the needs of any one community. At the same time, they have common identities across settings. This is achieved by allowing the objects to be weakly structured in common use, imposing stronger structures in the individual site tailored use. They are thus both ambiguous and constant; they may be abstract or concrete. (Bowker and Star 1999, p. 16)

Boundary objects arise over time from ongoing cooperation among communities of practice. They embody and represent essential knowledge and can be shared across domains and levels of expertise. For example, experts can produce prototypes or sketches of products as a way of conveying their thoughts about how a product might work and how it should be designed. The prototype has extensive tacit knowledge embedded within it and can serve as a basis for communication, discussion, and elaboration without requiring that the expert articulate a priori all of her thinking about the product design. Through boundary objects, people can see for themselves the way that knowledge is represented and negotiate shared meanings.

Information Use and Affective Responses

Not-invented-here syndrome. The introduction of new knowledge from outside the organization may meet with resistance. One of the most well-known forms that this resistance can manifest itself as is the *not-invented-here (NIH) syndrome,* defined as "the tendency of a project group of stable composition to believe it possesses a monopoly of knowledge of its field, which leads it to reject new ideas from outsiders to the likely detriment of its performance" (Katz and Allen 1982, p. 7). Such behavior may be a natural consequence of individuals who, over time, increase order and stability in their work environments so as to reduce the amount of stress and uncertainty that they need to face. As a result, the longer the individuals' tenure in a group, the stronger their emotional attachment to strategies and decisions that they were (perhaps partly) responsible for, and the more resistant they become toward outside new ideas that upset the familiarity and confidence of their work environments. In their study of 345 R&D professionals working on 50 projects in a large corporate research facility, Katz and Allen (1982) found that project performance increases up to 1.5 years tenure, stays steady for a time, but by 5 years has declined noticeably. The performance decline is best explained by

> a project team's tendency to ignore and become increasingly isolated from sources that provide more critical kinds of evaluation, information, and feedback. . . . Thus, overall performance will suffer when research teams fail to pay sufficient attention to new advances and information within their relevant external R&D community, when technical service groups fail to interact among themselves, or when development project members fail to communicate with individuals from other parts of the organization, particularly R&D, marketing, and manufacturing. (Katz and Allen 1982, p. 16)

Care in organizational relations. Von Krogh, Ichijo, and Nonaka (2000) stress how the ways people interact strongly affect the distribution of tacit knowledge. Their empirical and theoretical work suggests that the concept of "care" describes well the relations that have a positive impact on knowledge creation. Care in organizations is conceptualized as having five dimensions: mutual trust, active empathy (being proactive in seeking to understand the other), access to help (access to knowledgeable persons who are willing to help), lenience in judgment, and courage among members (to experiment, to voice opinion, to receive criticism). These dimensions work together to encourage the sharing of tacit knowledge: "Trust among participants makes it easier to articulate emotional aspects of an experience. Participants extend help to each other in finding new means to convey and share experiences; they practice lenience in judgment; courageously defend their ideas and offer constructive criticism of others" (p. 58). Using these dimensions, organizational relationships can range from high care to low care. Under conditions of low care, individual knowledge creation may be more like a process of *seizing* (everyone out for himself), and social knowledge sharing occurs through *transacting* (swapping documents or other explicit knowledge). When care is high, however, individuals create knowledge through a process of *bestowing* (helping by sharing insights), and groups share or create social knowledge through *indwelling* (living with a concept together). Indwelling is especially important to the sharing of tacit knowledge and creation of new concepts. It involves a shift of perspective: from looking *at* the concept to looking *with* the concept (e.g., moving from formulating a new concept to thinking about how to achieve the desired result). Indwelling requires high care in organizational relationships.

Trust in organizations. Rousseau et al. (1998), in considering a multidisciplinary collection of research papers on trust in organizations, concluded that scholars do appear to agree fundamentally on the meaning of trust. A widely held definition of trust would be that "Trust is a psychological state comprising the intention to accept vulnerability based upon positive expectations of the intentions or behavior of another" (Rousseau et al. 1998, p. 394). There is also agreement across disciplines on two conditions that must exist for trust to arise. The first condition is risk. Trust would not be needed if actions could be undertaken with complete certainty and no risk: risk creates an opportunity for trust, which in turn leads to risk taking. The second necessary condition of trust is interdependence, where the interests of one party cannot be achieved without reliance upon another. Trust then is a psychological state expressed as the willingness to be vulnerable under conditions of risk and interdependence. Trust is not a behavior (such as cooperation) or a choice (such as taking a risk), but an underlying psychological condition that can cause or result from such actions. Trust opens up access to people for the exchange of knowledge and increases anticipation of value through these exchanges (Nahapiet and Ghoshal 1998). Where trust is high, people are more willing to take risks in such exchanges, including an increased willingness to experiment with combining different sorts of information. Boisot (1995) highlights the need for interpersonal trust for knowledge creation in situations of high ambiguity and uncertainty: "When the message is uncodified, trust has to reside in the quality of the personal relationships that bind the parties through shared values and expectations rather than the intrinsic plausibility of the message" (p. 153). There is also a two-way interaction between trust and cooperation—"trust and cooperation: trust lubricates cooperation, and cooperation itself breeds trust" (Nahapiet and Ghoshal 1998, p. 255)—leading to the development of norms of cooperation that group members can rely on to support cooperation and coordination. Mishira (1996) argues that trust is multidimensional, and it indicates a willingness to be vulnerable to another party based upon confidence in four beliefs: (1) belief in the good intent and concern of exchange partners, (2) belief in their competence and capability, (3) belief in their reliability, and (4) belief in their perceived openness. The influence of trust and perceived openness was investigated by Wathne, Roos, and von Krogh (1996), who looked at 62 partner representatives involved in project-oriented cooperative arrangements in 45 Nordic companies. Focusing on partner representatives and their perceptions of the cooperative setting, the study found that perceived openness, trust, richness of the channel of interaction, and prior experience of representatives all had a significant effect on the effectiveness of knowledge transfer, with perceived openness being an especially important factor.

Information Use and Situational Dimensions

Fair process and procedural justice. Nearly every individual possesses unique information that can only be put to use with that individual's active cooperation (Hayek 1945). Kim and Mauborgne (1997) suggest that getting this active cooperation may well turn out to be one of the key managerial concerns. They note that conventional management is based on distributive justice or outcome fairness: when people get the compensation they deserve, they feel satisfied with the outcome and will reciprocate by fulfilling their obligations to the firm. In contrast, the psychology of *fair process,* or procedural justice, "builds upon trust and commitment, trust and commitment produce voluntary cooperation, and voluntary cooperation drives performance, leading people to go beyond the call of duty by sharing their knowledge and applying their creativity" (p. 71). In knowledge work, ignoring fair process creates high opportunity costs in the form of ideas that never surface and initiatives that are never seized. Innovation requires this exchange of ideas, which in turn depends on trust. There are two main reasons why fair process is rare in organizations. The first involves power. Some managers believe that knowledge is power, and they retain power by keeping what they know to themselves and keeping employees at arm's length, with memos and forms taking the place of direct communication. The second reason is the belief that people are concerned only with what's best for themselves. However, "when the process is perceived to be fair, most people will accept outcomes that are not wholly in their favor. People realize that compromises and sacrifices are necessary on the job. They accept the need for short-term personal sacrifices in order to advance long-term interests of the organization. Acceptance is conditional, however, hinged as it is on fair process" (p. 75).

Swift trust. Meyerson, Weick, and Kramer (1996) developed the concept of *swift trust* for temporary groups formed around a common task for a defined life span (e.g., film crews, theater and architectural groups, presidential commissions, senate select committees, and cockpit crews). Because group members are unable to develop expectations of others based on firsthand information, members import expectations of trust from other settings with which they are familiar. Whereas traditional conceptualizations of trust are based strongly on interpersonal relationships, swift trust is based more on cognition, action, and contextual cues. The basis for swift trust include the credibility of the person who formed the group; expectations about individual skills and competence in well-defined roles; membership in professional and social groups that enforce standards of conduct; reputations of group members and their supervisors; and perceived interdependence among members. Thus, conferring swift trust often means rendering judgments more about other individuals' professionalism than their character. Swift trust also relies on action. Evidence of the reasonableness of swift trust is provided by the actions of the temporary group itself, where people often act *as if* trust were in place. Because trust behaviors are enacted without hesitation, reciprocally and collectively, they provide a form of social proof that a particular interpretation of reality is correct: "Thus, by observing others acting in a trusting manner, individuals can infer that such a stance is neither foolish nor naïve. In this respect, each individual enactment of swift trust in the group, no matter how small, contributes to the collective perception that swift trust is reasonable" (p. 186). Group members also adopt hedging behaviors to reduce interdependence and perceived risks: for example, they create backups or documents or software; make sure they have a way out; and identify alternative sources for key resources. Overall, swift trust in temporary groups facilitates the sharing and use of new information by reducing perceived risks.

Direct and indirect relations in knowledge networks. Hansen (2002) analyzed the effects of direct and indirect relations on knowledge transfer and use, based on results of a study of 120 new product development projects in 41 business units of a large electronics company. For indirect relations (i.e., connections through intermediaries), he argues that task teams in focal business units with short path lengths in a knowledge network (i.e., few intermediaries are needed to connect with other units) are likely to obtain more knowledge from other units and perform better than those with long path lengths because of search advantages due to short path lengths. Long path lengths, in contrast, lead to information distortion in the knowledge network, making the search for useful knowledge more difficult. Hansen also argues that a focal unit's direct established relations in a knowledge network bring both positive and negative effects. While they provide immediate access to other business units that possess related knowledge, they are also costly to maintain. They are, therefore, most effective when they help teams solve difficult transfer problems, as when the knowledge to be transferred is noncodified. When there is no transfer problem, they are likely to be harmful for task-unit effectiveness because of their maintenance costs. In summary, direct relations are beneficial to transferring noncodified knowledge, whereas indirect relations are beneficial to the extent that they provide nonredundant information. The transfer benefit of direct relations is less important when that knowledge is highly codified. In these situations, direct interunit relations are not useful for transfer, but they still carry maintenance costs, which take time away from the completion of the project to the extent that team members do not have slack resources to give to maintaining these relationships.

Knowledge institutionalization. Patriotta (2004) notes that in order to make knowledge usable, firms need to incorporate such knowledge in stable organizational devices such as structures, routines, procedures, cognitive maps, and so on. Institutionalization is the process by which human agency and knowledge are progressively delegated to the organization and inscribed into stable structures of signification: "Institutionalization adds two important aspects to the process of knowledge creation. First, it implies an act of social acceptance whereby certain codes, patterns, structures, and practices become progressively taken for granted within a given community. . . . Second, once it has been recognized as valid, knowledge needs to be represented and formalized in order to be transferred and diffused at a corporate level" (Patriotta 2004, p. 181). Through this formalized representation or articulation, controversies recede and legitimate knowledge is "sealed" into organizational "black boxes" (Latour 1987). In addition, Patriotta (2004) suggests that "institutionalization refers to the degree of tacitness of knowledge" (p. 41) because it is a "phenomenological process by which certain social relationships and actions come to be taken for granted" (Zucker 1983, p. 2). This taken-for-granted quality of certain practices and their reproduction in existing institutional arrangements (Powell and Di Maggio 1991) is a source of persistence, which accounts for accumulation and maintenance of knowledge in organizations.

X. SUMMARY

- The knowledge of an organization may be categorized as tacit knowledge, explicit knowledge, and cultural knowledge.
- *Tacit knowledge* is the implicit knowledge used by people in organizations to do their work and to make sense of their worlds. Tacit knowledge is

personal knowledge derived from practice and experience that is hard to verbalize and cannot be reduced to rules or recipes.

- *Explicit knowledge* is knowledge that has been codified formally using a system of symbols or made tangible as a physical artifact and can therefore be easily communicated.

- *Cultural knowledge* consists of the shared assumptions and beliefs about an organization's identity, goals, capabilities, customers, and competitors. These beliefs are used to assign value and significance to new information and knowledge, as well as to give meaning and purpose to the use of organizational knowledge.

- *Knowledge creation.* An organization creates new knowledge through the interaction and conversion between its tacit and explicit knowledge. A cycle of four processes are involved: socialization, externalization, combination, and internalization (Nonaka and Takeuchi 1995).

- *Knowledge creation.* Knowledge-creating activities build up an organization's core capabilities. An organization grows its core capabilities over time by managing four knowledge-creating activities: shared problem solving, implementing and integrating new processes and tools, experimenting and prototyping, and importing new knowledge from outside the organization (Leonard 1995).

- *Knowledge transfer.* The transfer of knowledge across boundaries inside an organization is a major challenge. The most effective mechanism for sharing knowledge is that which best fits the requirements of the intended recipient, the nature of the task, and the type of knowledge that is being transferred. Five transfer methods are important: serial transfer, near transfer, far transfer, strategic transfer, and expert transfer (Dixon 2000).

- *Knowledge transfer.* The transfer of knowledge can be mapped in an Information Space bounded by the three dimensions of codification, abstraction, and diffusion. Within this space, the diffusion of new knowledge follows a particular sequence composed of six phases: scanning, problem solving, abstraction, diffusion, absorption, and impacting (Boisot 1998).

- *Knowledge use.* The fundamental task of an organization is to integrate the knowledge and coordinate the efforts of its many specialized individuals. Four mechanisms for integrating specialized knowledge are rules and directives; sequencing; routines; and group problem solving and decision making (Grant 2002).

- *Knowledge use.* Work practices are social activities that link people through mutual engagement. Workgroups then form around these practices, creating communities of practice. Within these communities, knowledge is applied through learning in practice that is composed of the processes of (1) evolving mutual engagement, (2) understanding the nature of the joint enterprise, and (3) developing a shared repertoire (Wenger 1998).

- *Information needs.* Information needs arise from gaps in the organization's existing knowledge or capabilities. To initiate information gathering, the needs pertaining to a problem or opportunity situation have to be identified and elaborated. This process is guided by beliefs and assumptions the organization holds about what knowledge would be valuable and what knowledge it can absorb and use.

- *Information seeking.* In knowledge creation and use, the ability to share and find information—between groups in the organization or between organizations—is an important part of information seeking. There are two distinctive features: information has to negotiate boundaries inside and outside the organization; and information sharing often takes place in social networks that are built on trust and cooperation.

- *Information use.* Information use is an integral part of assessing, absorbing, and applying new knowledge. The use of external knowledge requires the organization to be at a stage of readiness to assimilate the new knowledge and to be able to address acceptance issues. The exploitation of new knowledge is not just a technical activity but a social process that needs to take into account the culture and context of the organization.

C H A P **5** T E R

THE MANAGEMENT OF
UNCERTAINTY: ORGANIZATIONS
AS DECISION-MAKING SYSTEMS

Reason sits firm and holds the reins, and she will not let the feelings burst
away and hurry her to wild chasms. The passions may rage furiously, like true
heathens, as they are; and the desires may imagine all sorts of vain things: but
judgement shall still have the last word in every argument, and the casting vote
in every decision.
　—*Charlotte Brontë*, Jane Eyre, chapter 19, *1847*

The essence of ultimate decision remains impenetrable to the observer—often,
indeed, to the decider himself. . . . There will always be the dark and tangled
stretches in the decision-making process—mysterious even to those who may
be the most intimately involved.
　—*John Fitzgerald Kennedy, preface to* Decision-Making in the White House *by*
　　Theodore Sorensen, 1963

On October 16, 1962, President John F. Kennedy was informed that the Soviet
Union had installed offensive missiles in Cuba. Located approximately 90 miles
off the Florida coast, the nuclear-capable missiles had the range to strike many
major U.S. cities, including Washington, D.C. The ensuing 13 days of the Cuban
Missile Crisis was the closest the world had come to the brink of nuclear war.
Decision making during crisis situations is always marked by confusion, but a
clearer picture of the Cuban Missile Crisis has emerged recently from analysis
using newly available information, including tape recordings that Kennedy had
made of cabinet meetings during the confrontation (the so-called Kennedy tapes)
(Allison and Zelikow 1999; Blight and Welch 1998; Chang and Kornbluth 1993;
May and Zelikow 1997; Stern 2003).
　　When they were first informed of the installation of Soviet ballistic missiles,
Kennedy and his advisors were stunned and struggled to make sense of why the

Soviet Union would make a move that could bring about nuclear conflict. Four hypotheses were developed that framed the subsequent decision making (Allison and Zelikow 1999). One hypothesis was that the missiles were deployed to defend Cuba against a U.S. invasion. A year earlier, a force of U.S.-trained Cuban exiles had landed at the Bay of Pigs in an invasion attempt that failed disastrously. In November 1961, the United States had authorized Operation Mongoose, a covert plan to instigate internal revolution in Cuba. For the Soviet Union, Cuba was important as the only communist showcase in the Western world. The Soviet position throughout the crisis was that the missiles were there to protect Cuba. Another hypothesis was based on cold war politics. In 1962, American leaders viewed the cold war as a competition against the Soviet Union for global preeminence. The failure of the Bay of Pigs incursion suggested that Kennedy had lacked resolve. The Soviet plan was to present the deployment of missiles in Cuba as a fait accompli, to which the United States would react indecisively and weakly, thereby undermining further the credibility of U.S. commitments to other nations. A third hypothesis was that the Soviet Union was attempting to redress a strategic imbalance of missile power between the two countries. In 1962, the U.S. strategic nuclear arsenal (180 intercontinental ballistic missiles, 12 Polaris submarines, 630 long-range bombers) was significantly larger than that of the Soviets (20 ICBMs, 6 submarines that could launch ballistic missiles, 200 bombers). Moreover, the United States and NATO had installed Thor and Jupiter ballistic missiles in the United Kingdom, Italy, and Turkey. Deploying ballistic missiles in Cuba would fix the imbalance in one bold move. Khrushchev thought that "it was high time America learned what it feels like to have her own land and her own people threatened" (Khrushchev 1970, p. 494). The fourth hypothesis was that the missiles in Cuba would be used to pressure Western forces to withdraw from Berlin. In 1945, Berlin was divided into zones of occupation among the Allied forces (including Americans and the Soviets). After the division of East and West Germany, the Western sectors of Berlin became a capitalist city located deep inside a communist state. In the spring of 1962, Khrushchev faced a looming problem in Berlin: two deadlines that he had set for Western forces to withdraw had already lapsed, East Germany was impatiently urging tougher Soviet action, and Khrushchev's own credibility was ebbing. Khrushchev's deployment of missiles in Cuba would make sense in this context. If the Americans tried to bargain, Cuba would be traded for Berlin. Since Berlin was more important to the Soviets, this would be a win for Khrushchev. If the Americans attacked or blockaded Cuba, this would be an excuse for Khrushchev to do the same to Berlin. Either scenario would have Khrushchev winning. The Berlin hypothesis was at the center of the predicament confronting Kennedy. According to transcripts of the meeting tapes, the U.S. president had explained to the Joint Chiefs of Staff on October 19 that "our problem is not merely Cuba, it is also Berlin. And when we recognize the importance of Berlin to Europe, and recognize the importance of our allies to us, that's what has made this thing be a dilemma for three days" (May and Zelikow 1997, p. 176).

Following the discovery of the missiles, a special committee of the National Security Council was formed that met regularly with Kennedy to deliberate on options and scenarios. This group, the Executive Committee (ExComm), included Lyndon Johnson (vice president), Dean Rusk (secretary of state), Robert McNamara (secretary of defense), Douglas Dillon (secretary of the treasury), Robert Kennedy (attorney general), General Maxwell Taylor (chairman, Joint Chiefs of Staff), John McCone (director, CIA), George Ball (under secretary of state), McGeorge Bundy (special assistant for national security affairs), Theodore Sorensen (special counsel to the president), and Llewellyn Thompson (U.S. ambassador-at-large) (Stern 2003). The ExComm evaluated six major alternatives before finally selecting a course of action that combined elements of several options. The six alternatives were

1. do nothing;

2. apply diplomatic pressures;

3. make a secret approach to Castro;

4. invade Cuba to remove missiles and Castro;

5. launch air strikes to destroy the missile sites;

6. impose a U.S. blockade of Cuba.

Doing nothing was not an option acceptable to Kennedy, as it would weaken his reputation and standing. Diplomatic actions considered were sending a secret ultimatum to Khrushchev demanding missile removal and working through the UN or the Organization of American States for a diplomatic resolution. Dean Rusk suggested going to Castro directly, warning him that the Soviets would sell him out for Berlin. The Joint Chiefs of Staff wanted an invasion to eliminate what they saw as a communist threat close to the United States, but this was seen as a costly, risky last resort. More preferable was an air attack to destroy the missile sites, an option that Kennedy favored at the outset and kept alive. An air strike also has disadvantages: it could escalate, kill Russians working at the sites, leave some missiles undestroyed, and the United States could be accused of doing a "Pearl Harbor" on a small nation. The sixth alternative was an indirect military action in the form of a blockade. First suggested by McNamara, it was later combined with the "ultimatum" approach by Thompson (ambassador-at-large) and Dillon (secretary of the treasury). The blockade would be the vehicle for delivering the ultimatum to remove the missiles. There would be no negotiations, and not complying would precipitate direct U.S. military action. This hybrid approach was eventually chosen, with the important change that the "blockade" would be called a "quarantine" since the former is legally an act of war.

On October 22, 1962, Kennedy announced in a televised speech that offensive missile sites were being built on Cuba, and that the following steps would be taken:

> First, to halt this offensive build up, a strict quarantine of all military equipment
> under shipment to Cuba is being initiated. . . . Second, I have directed the
> continued and increased close surveillance and its military buildup. . . . Third, it
> shall be the policy of this nation to regard any nuclear missile launched from Cuba

against any nation in the Western Hemisphere as an attack by the Soviet Union on
the United States, requiring a full retaliatory response on the Soviet Union. (Chang
and Kornbluth 1993, pp. 160–64)

The ensuing days saw a number of tense moments. Soviet ships tested but
did not breach the quarantine line. An American U-2 spy plane had strayed into
Soviet air space off western Alaska, prompting both sides to despatch their
fighter planes—fortunately the U-2 left Soviet air space in time. Another U-2
was shot down over Cuba by a surface-to-air-missile. This turned out to be the
action of a Soviet commander in Cuba and not a planned escalation of the confrontation. Finally, on October 28, Khrushchev announced the decision to dis-
mantle the missiles and return them to the Soviet Union. Why did the Soviet
Union withdraw the missiles? Allison and Zelikow (1999) make the following
conclusions:

> In sum, the blockade did not change Khrushchev's mind. Only when coupled with
> the threat of further action . . . did it succeed in forcing Soviet withdrawal of the
> missiles. Without the threat of air strike or invasion, the blockade alone would not
> have forced the removal of the missiles already present. . . . Khrushchev's belief
> [was] that he faced a clear, urgent threat that America was about to move up the
> ladder of escalation. In this ladder, America benefited from its advantages in both
> its nuclear and conventional forces. (Allison and Zelikow 1999, pp. 128, 129)

If we set aside temporarily the anxiety and tension generated in the Cuban
Missile Crisis, we may discern five important features of organizational decision
making. First, decision making is concerned with *attention:* How do we recognize or frame a situation as calling for decision? What is going on here? Who are
the actors and their relationships? What are the cause-and-effect connections? In
the missile crisis, the first challenge for the decision makers was developing
hypotheses that could make sense of an unexpected and dangerous situation.
Understanding the history and the geopolitical context as well as the linkages
between interests all help to fix an underlying logic that provides a plausible narrative explaining the situation. The process of allocating attention also involves
defining the qualities of desirable alternatives ("In view of our understanding of
the situation, what would constitute a desirable outcome?") as well as the information that needs to be obtained and the facts that need to be established ("What
information do we need in order to make a decision?"). Recognizing and framing a decision situation is an important first step of the decision process, and it
can vary from perceiving very quickly a familiar problem (such as hiring a new
employee) to wrestling with enormous uncertainty to understand an unprecedented situation (as in the missile crisis).

Second, decision making is about *search:* finding alternatives and elaborating them in some detail so that they can be differentiated and compared. In
the missile crisis, much of the time and energy of the decision makers were
consumed in looking for and developing alternatives. The information search
was extensive and intensive, involving consultations with a large number of
experts with contrasting perspectives and lengthy discussions to dissect and

dispute the information put forward. Janis (1982) described the information seeking thus:

> To broaden the scope of information available to the core group of decision makers, departmental spokesmen and outside experts were invited to give their views and then were carefully questioned about the grounds for their conclusions. With an eye to obtaining fresh points of view, new advisers were brought in periodically. Recognizing the usual tendency for visitors to remain silent, members of the group deliberately asked them to give their reactions during the discussions. (Janis 1982, pp. 141–42)

In most consequential decisions, much of the time, energy, and resources are expended in information-search activities, and indeed, the quality of the information obtained has a huge impact on the quality of the decision made, as was the case in the Cuban Missile Crisis. For more-routine decisions, organizations avoid the need for extensive search by following policies and procedures that predetermine what specific information is needed, where it should be obtained, and how it should be processed.

Third, decision making is about *choice,* and making a choice is generally what comes to mind when we say we are making a decision. As we shall see later in this chapter, there are in fact many ways by which a choice can be made. A decision maker may rely on personal judgment based on experience and intuition. Formal, perhaps quantitative analysis may have been done to compare alternatives. Different groups or individuals may have tried to influence the selection of preferred options. An important dynamic of choice making in extended decision processes is that participants do change their minds:

> The views of ExComm members, of course, shifted, evolved and even reversed direction in response to the changing diplomatic, political and military situation, their own beliefs and values and the arguments of their colleagues. . . . There can be no question, after listening painstakingly to these recordings, that the often rough give-and-take with the ExComm played a decisive role in continuing to shape JFK's perceptions and decisions. . . . Every major option was discussed, frequently in exhaustive and exhausting detail—providing both the context and an indispensable sounding board for the President in making his final decision. (Stern 2003, pp. 416, 423–24)

Organizational choice requires evaluating alternatives in relation to some formulation of goals and objectives. Goals may preexist in a general form, and they may need to be clarified early in the decision process so that they become specific to the problem at hand and can be elaborated into evaluation criteria. More often than not, goals are in conflict, and this leads us to the next observation.

Fourth, decision making in organizations is inherently *multilateral.* Decision making typically engages multiple groups with multiple interests, so that conflict is always latent. Conflict surfaces in decision situations when groups perceive proposed solutions differently and adopt competing positions based on their interpretations and preferences. Groups and individuals with common interests form coalitions, rally around specific choices, and use political power to influence decisions. In the Cuban Missile Crisis, the phrase "hawks and doves" was first invented to describe the groups within ExComm that pushed for and against strong military action. Thus, decisions in organizations often appear as a collage of options generated by different groups over time:

> The decision to blockade, and link the blockade to a demand for removal of missiles from Cuba backed by the threat of more direct military action, thus emerged as a collage. Its pieces included the President's initial decision that something forceful had to be done; the resistance of McNamara and others to a surprise air strike; and the constant relationship, especially for President Kennedy, between Cuba and Berlin. . . . The process by which this [decision] happened is a story of the most subtle and intricate probing, pulling and hauling, leading, guiding, and spurring. (Allison and Zelikow 1999, p. 346)

Finally, decision making should form part of an ongoing process of organizational *learning*. The experiences gained from past decisions should be evaluated in time to influence current processes. May and Zelikow (1997) noted a changed decision-making (and information-seeking) style by Kennedy and his colleagues that was fundamentally different from the methods used during the Bay of Pigs invasion a year earlier:

> The Bay of Pigs affair also had effects on Kennedy's style of decision making. Afterward, he recognized that he had not only listened to too few advisers but that he had given the issues too little time. . . . When the missile crisis arrived, Kennedy applied the lessons taught him by the Bay of Pigs affair. From the outset, he assembled a comparatively large circle of advisers, not all of whom were obvious choices. He included Treasury Secretary Dillon. He brought in State Department experts on both the Soviet Union and Latin America. To be sure that knowledge and wisdom from the past were not ignored, he also brought in Dean Acheson, Robert A. Lovett, and John J. McCloy, key figures from the Truman administration. And, . . . he squeezed from these advisers everything they could say about the options open to him. If there were flaws in Kennedy's decision-making during the missile crisis, they are the exact opposite of those in the Bay of Pigs affair. (May and Zelikow 1997, p. 28)

I. BOUNDED RATIONALITY

Imagine a decision situation in which an individual has to select a course of action. In order to make a completely rational choice, the decision maker would have to identify all available alternatives, predict what consequences would be produced by each alternative, and evaluate these consequences according to goals and preferences. The information requirements of a purely rational mode of decision making are daunting. First, information is needed about the present state—What alternatives are currently available or should be considered? Second, information is needed about the future—What are the consequences of acting on each of the various alternatives? Third, information is needed about how to move from the present to the future—What are the values and preferences that should be used to choose between the alternatives that will, according to the set criteria, best achieve the desired results? The information-seeking and information-processing demands implied here are unrealistic. In most situations, we do not have complete information about all feasible alternatives nor can we afford the time and cost of obtaining this complete knowledge. Whichever the alternative, acting on it always creates both intended and unintended consequences, and the unanticipated consequences may well turn out to be highly significant. We rarely have a well-defined or completely consistent set of preferences or criteria by which we can, for example, rank the available alternatives in order to choose the most desirable one. Herbert Simon suggests instead that humans are only "boundedly rational" so that while we may attempt to be rational, our rational behavior is bounded in at least three ways:

1. Rationality requires a complete knowledge and anticipation of the consequences that will follow on each choice. In fact, knowledge of consequences is always fragmentary.

2. Since these consequences lie in the future, imagination must supply the lack of experienced feeling in attaching value to them. But values can only be imperfectly anticipated.

3. Rationality requires a choice among all possible alternative behaviors. In actual behavior, only a very few of all these possible alternatives ever come to mind.

(Simon 1997, pp. 93–94)

As a result of bounded rationality, decision making is driven by the search for alternatives that are good enough rather than the best possible: *"Most human decision-making, whether individual or organizational, is concerned with the discovery and selection of satisfactory alternatives; only in exceptional cases is it concerned with the discovery and selection of optimal alternatives"* (March and Simon 1993, p. 162, italics in original). An alternative is considered optimal if it is superior to all other alternatives when a single, consistent set of criteria is used to compare all the available alternatives. An alternative is considered satisfactory if it meets or exceeds a set of criteria that defines "minimally satisfactory alternatives." Such a limited search for good-enough alternatives Simon and March called "satisficing." The difference between optimizing and satisficing is likened to "the difference between searching a haystack to find the sharpest needle in it and searching the haystack to find a needle sharp enough to sew with" (p. 162). For example, the owner of a retail store could set prices optimally by determining how demand would vary with price across all her potential customers, and then choosing the price which maximizes sales, or she could satisfice by applying a simple markup over cost that would provide an acceptable level of profit.

Neither satisficing nor maximizing is likely to be observed in pure form. Depending on the situation and the nature of the goals, decision makers sometimes attempt to maximize on some dimensions of the problem while satisficing on others (March 1994). When universities consider granting tenures to professors, for instance, both satisficing rules (such as "does this person meet the university's standards for satisfactory performance?") and maximizing rules ("is this person likely to be the best possible person to be found?") may be invoked at the same time. Satisficing evaluates the positions of alternatives relative to a baseline or target, while maximizing compares the positions of alternatives relative to each other. Satisficing behaviors "simplify a complex world. Instead of having to worry about an infinite number of gradations in the environment, individuals simplify the world into two parts—good enough and not good enough" (March 1994, p. 21).

Because only a limited amount of time and effort is available to find, evaluate, and select alternatives, attention becomes the scarce resource that affects the level of participation in a decision as well as the quantity and quality of information that is brought to bear on a decision:

> The information-processing systems of our contemporary world swim in an exceedingly rich soup of information, of symbols. In a world of this kind, the scarce resource is not information; it is processing capacity to attend to information. Attention is the chief bottleneck in organizational activity, and the bottleneck becomes narrower and narrower as we move to the tops of organizations. (Simon 1976, p. 294)

Thus, the decision maker may overlook some significant news, fail to be present at a decision meeting, or respond hurriedly to set deadlines and the actions of others. The capacity to attend also depends on the language or vocabulary that the organization has developed for recording, retrieving, and transferring information. An organization that emphasizes presenting a high level of service to its customers may develop a rich vocabulary for differentiating many aspects of service quality, thereby making it easier for members to attend to and to communicate about customer service dimensions that are relevant for decision making. Conversely, where service is not stressed, subtle distinctions about service are uncoded and may not be attended to at all in choice making.

To summarize, decision makers in organizations "satisfice" rather than maximize, that is, they choose an alternative that exceeds some criteria rather than the best alternative; and they follow "action programs" or routines that simplify the decision-making process by reducing the need for search, problem solving, or choice:

1. Optimizing is replaced by satisfying—the requirement that satisfactory levels of the criterion variables be attained.

2. Alternatives of action and consequences of action are discovered sequentially through search processes.

3. Repertories of action programs are developed by organizations and individuals, and these serve as the alternatives of choice in recurrent situations.

4. Each specific action program deals with a restricted range of situations and a restricted range of consequences.

5. Each action program is capable of being executed in semi-independence of the others—they are only loosely coupled together.

(March and Simon 1993, p. 191)

Satisficing is more than a rule about how decisions take place in organizations; it is also a rule about how organizations search for information. The criterion of satisficing specifies that search is often induced by failure, so that search is started when performance falls below an acceptable target level and stops or decreases when performance achieves its target. March (1994) identifies three principal features of satisficing as a theory of search. First, search is thermostatic. Search is turned on and off when performance falls below and rises above a desired level. Second, targets are considered sequentially: "A satisficing search process is serial rather than parallel; things are considered one at a time—one target, one alternative, one problem" (March 1994, p. 28). Furthermore, alternatives in the neighborhood of the problem symptom are searched first (a solution to a problem in the production department is searched first in the production department). Third, search is active in the face of adversity. When faced with a set of poor alternatives which all fail to meet the target, the satisficing decision maker will try to find better ones by changing the problem constraints, while the maximizing decision maker will select the best of the poor lot.

Since satisficing is essentially a "first-past-the-post" strategy, the criteria or standards that define minimal acceptability are not static but are adjusted over time, so that who gets to control the standards becomes an important question: "these standards go up and down with positive and negative experience. As solutions are easier to find, the standards are raised; as they are harder to find, the standards fall. *The organization can control these standards, and it defines the situation;* only to a limited extent are they up to individuals" (Perrow 1986, p. 122, italics in original).

Lindblom (1959) describes a variation of satisficing that he observed in public policy decision making. When formulating policy on a complex issue (such as controlling inflation), an administrator does not attempt to go to the root of the matter to consider the myriad economic, social, and political variables that affect and are affected by inflation. The information required would have been enormous, and even if the information were available, the administrator would have to learn and apply theoretical principles to evaluate the alternatives and outcomes. Instead, the administrator contents herself with a relatively simple goal (such as maintaining a period of stable prices), compares a limited range of already familiar alternatives, and avoids having to go back to theory. Lindblom suggests that the prevalent mode of decision making by administrators is a strategy of *disjointed incrementalism,* which is to proceed by making *successive limited comparisons.* Changes are made in small increments by processes that seem disconnected. These small changes appear to be made to move away from current ills rather than to move toward defined goals. Selection of goals and analysis of needed action are closely intertwined, so that means and ends adjust to each other, and objectives are reconciled with policies as much as policies to objectives. Choice is simplified by considering changes at the margin and evaluating few alternatives and a few outcomes of each alternative. A succession of incremental changes reduces the risks of serious mistakes. Policies are not made once and for all, but are made and remade endlessly. The result is that decision making begins to look like a "science of muddling through" (Lindblom 1959).

Cognitive Simplifications

Rationality requires looking ahead into the future, since the consequences of actions are all necessarily in the future, and in this sense all rationality is based on predictions of one kind or another (Stinchcombe 1990). Rational decisions are therefore based on beliefs and expectations about the likelihood of uncertain events or outcomes that lie in the future. In dealing with uncertainty, people rely on a limited number of heuristic principles to reduce the complex task into simpler judgmental operations (Tversky and Kahneman 1974; Hogarth and Makridakis 1981; Kahneman, Slovic, and Tversky 1982; Kahneman and Tversky 2000; Gilovich, Griffin, and Kahneman 2002). These heuristics are two-edged, for while they reduce mental effort in decision making, their use can also lead to systemic biases or errors in judgment. Tversky and Kahneman (1974) identify three sets of heuristics that are used to assess likelihoods, frequencies, and predict values: representativeness, availability, and anchoring and adjustment.

People use heuristics of *representativeness* when they are assessing the likelihood that an event or object belongs to a certain category. They do so by judging the similarity of the event or object to stereotypes that they believe to be representative of category members. Managers for example may quickly categorize a price-lowering action by a competitor as an attempt to gain market share; supervisors may select someone based on perception of certain traits that they believe to typify a desirable worker. Representativeness heuristics may capture learning from experience but can lead to systemic errors when they do not take into account the size of the sample, prior or base probabilities of the various categories in the population, the distinction between events that are independent or related, the tendency for extreme events to regress to a mean, and so on. Schwenk (1984) observed that strategic decision makers are insensitive to sample size when making predictions, especially since they are often unable to collect data on a large number of past strategies and must generalize from a small base of experience. They tend to view strategic decisions in terms of simple analogies, assuming that the analogy is representative of their decision situation and glossing over important differences between the two. They also overestimate the extent to which the past is representative of the present, including the extent to which solutions used for problems in the past will continue to work for present problems.

People use heuristics of *availability* when they are assessing the likelihood or plausibility of a particular event or occurrence. They do so by recalling familiar, recent, and vivid instances. Consumers for example base their buying decisions on past satisfactory use rather than results of objective evaluations; air travelers worry for their own safety after learning about recently publicized accidents. Availability heuristics can save time and effort in searching for relevant precedents but can lead to biases when they are unduly limited to instances that are easy to recall or information that is easy to retrieve. Nisbett and Ross (1980) suggested that decision makers may give excessive weight to one or a few vividly described cases, basing their assessment of likelihood of a future event on this readily retrieved example. Thus, Schwenk (1984) noted that "a single vivid description of a new venture's failure in a particular industry may influence the decision about entering the industry more than volumes of statistical data indicating high success rates in the industry" (p. 121).

People use heuristics of *anchoring* and adjustment when they are trying to estimate value or size of a quantity. They do so by starting from an initially presented value (the anchor) and adjusting it to arrive at a final estimate. The size and direction of the adjustment depends on the locus or magnitude of the initial value. Managers for example may estimate sales and budgets for the next period by simple extrapolations of values obtained in the previous period. Anchors may also be qualitative: people form initial impressions that persist and are hard to change. Decision makers monitoring organizational strategies may accurately recognize important changes in the environment but fail to revise their strategies or performance targets sufficiently as justified by the new information. Anchoring heuristics may be useful in providing ballpark estimates but can lead to errors when the adjustment is insufficient or when the adjustment fails to consider the interdependency of related events.

While the heuristics and biases discovered by Kahneman and Tversky may appear to be signs of bounded rationality, it is important *not* to equate bounded rationality with irrationality and to re-emphasize that heuristics often work quite well as mental shortcuts that provide compelling and serviceable solutions:

> Kahneman and Tversky developed their own perspective on bounded rationality. Although acknowledging the role of task complexity and limited processing capacity in erroneous judgment, Kahneman and Tversky were convinced that the processes of intuitive judgment were not merely simpler than rational models demanded, but were categorically different in kind. . . . Several aspects of this program are important to note. . . . First, although the heuristics are distinguished from normative reasoning processes by patterns of biased judgments, the heuristics themselves are sensible estimation procedures that are by no means "irrational." Second, although heuristics yield "quick and dirty" solutions, they draw on underlying processes (e.g., feature matching, memory retrieval) that are highly sophisticated. Finally, note that these heuristic processes are not exceptional responses to problems of excessive complexity or an overload of information, but normal intuitive responses to even the simplest questions about likelihood, frequency, and prediction. (Gilovich et al. 2002, p. 3)

Moreover, the research agenda of the heuristics and biases program is

> to elucidate the processes through which people make a variety of important and difficult real world judgments. Is a corporation's explosive growth likely to continue? Is a coup more likely in Ecuador or Indonesia? What is a reasonable

estimate of next year's GNP? Thus, representativeness, availability, and anchoring and adjustment were proposed as a set of highly efficient mental shortcuts that provide subjectively compelling and often quite serviceable solutions to such judgmental problems. (Gilovich et al. 2002, pp. 3–4)

Gigerenzer and associates at the Center for Adaptive Behavior and Cognition in the Max Planck Institute are pursuing a related but different research program that focuses on "simple heuristics that make us smart." Instead of viewing heuristics as unreliable decision strategies that lead to systematic biases and errors, they see "heuristics as the way the human mind can take advantage of the structure of information in the environment to arrive at reasonable decisions" and "focus on the ways and settings in which simple heuristics lead to accurate and useful inferences" (Gigerenzer et al. 1999, p. 28). Their research examines three aspects of rationality:

1. Bounded rationality, including heuristic principles for guiding information search, stopping the search, and making decisions.

2. Ecological rationality, including heuristics that exploit the ways that information is structured in different decision environments in order to enable fast, frugal, accurate decision making that is also adaptive. For example, a heuristic might make use of the cue that reputable colleges tend to have extensive research programs in order to make judgments about which colleges are active in a field of research.

3. Social rationality, including heuristics that exploit the information structure of social environments in order to enable adaptive interactions with other agents. For example, social norms and emotional responses can act as heuristic principles for search, stopping, and decision making.

From our own experiences we may recall instances when decision makers selectively attend to striking cases; pay greater attention to more recently encountered incidents that are still fresh in their minds; or overlook or forget important information because of memory overload. While the heuristics we have discussed can systematically introduce error in judgment and choice, the boundaries separating the rational and the intuitive are often not at all clear-cut. Human information processing encompasses a broad repertoire of cognitive strategies, ranging from logical, reasoning methods to intuitive, heuristic-based modes, and which approach is activated depends on the conditions of a particular decision situation.

II. MODELS OF ORGANIZATIONAL DECISION MAKING

All decisions are about finding and choosing courses of action in order to attain some goals. The difficulty of making a decision then depends on how clear the goals are and how well we know about methods that can achieve the desired

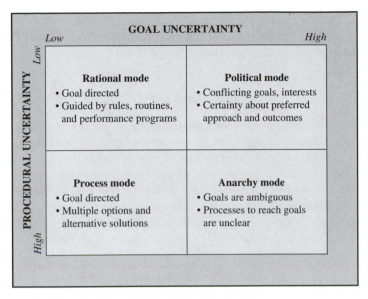

FIGURE 5.1. Four Models of Organizational Decision Making

goals. All decision situations in organizations can be characterized by these two basic dimensions: goal uncertainty and procedural uncertainty, as shown in Fig. 5.1. *Goal uncertainty* tends to be high when goals are ambiguous; when they are nonspecific and difficult to translate into concrete criteria for evaluating options; and when there is disagreement about the substance or interpretation of goals. *Procedural uncertainty* tends to be high when the problem is complex, comprising many subproblems with unclear interactions; when the problem is novel, so there is no prior experience about alternatives or even where to search for alternatives; and when the situation imposes pressures or constraints such as the need to act quickly in a crisis situation or a lack of options in a highly regulated environment.

Depending on the level of goal and procedural uncertainty, organizational decision making may be analyzed using the rational model, process model, political model, or anarchic model (Fig. 5.1). The (boundedly) rational model, as developed by Simon, March, and Cyert, conceptualizes decision making as goal directed and problem driven, where choice behavior is controlled by rules and routines. The process model, exemplified by the work of Mintzberg, Raisinghani, and Thêorét (1976), elucidates the phases and routines that give structure to apparently complex and dynamic decision-making activities. The political model sees politics as the mechanism of decision choice: different players occupy different stands and exercise different amounts of influence, so that decisions are less the result of rational choice than the pulling and hauling between competing factions. The anarchic model proposed by Cohen, March, and Olsen (1972) likens organizations to garbage cans where problems and solutions are dumped by participants, and decisions are the outcomes of the meeting of independent streams of problems, solutions, participants, and choice situations. We discuss each model in the following sections.

III. RATIONAL MODEL

When goals and methods are clear (first quadrant of Fig. 5.1), we may expect to see rational decision making. Completely rational decision making requires actors to (1) find all available alternatives, (2) evaluate alternatives according to consequences, (3) choose the alternative that best accomplishes the goal with the least amount of resources. Simon (1997) noted that this kind of maximization or optimization approach is rarely the case in organizations. The information-gathering and information-processing requirements are beyond the capacity of any individual. Instead, decision makers adopt a satisficing strategy:

> Because administrators satisfice rather than maximize, they can choose without first examining all possible behavior alternatives and without ascertaining that these *are* in fact all the alternatives. Because they treat the world as rather empty and ignore the interrelatedness of all things (so stupefying to thought and action), they can make their decisions with relatively simple rules of thumb that do not make impossible demands upon their capacity for thought. Simplification may lead to error, but there is no realistic alternative in the face of the limits on human knowledge and reasoning. (Simon 1997, p. 119)

When both the goals and the available alternatives of a decision situation are clear, the organization reduces the uncertainty of decision making by specifying decision rules and routines. Thus, although the individual's capacity for rational behavior is bounded, the organization is able to attain its goals and aspirations by "simplifying" the decision process. The classic model of the organizational decision-making process developed by Cyert and March (1992) is shown in Fig. 5.2. Beginning at the top of the flow chart, the organization observes feedback from the environment. If the uncertainty is perceived to be high, the organization negotiates with the environment to reduce uncertainty ("uncertainty avoidance"). When there is sufficient information to assess goal attainment, decision makers attend to one goal at a time and evaluate goal attainment using acceptable decision rules ("quasi-resolution of conflict"). If a goal is not being achieved, decision makers activate a problem-driven search. The search first proceeds locally, and when this is unsuccessful, the search is expanded to include more "remote" sources and alternatives ("problemistic search"). After the search is completed, the organization evaluates its search rules and decision rules ("organizational learning"). If the goal is seen as being achieved, the organization responds to the environmental feedback with standard decision rules and then evaluates its goals and attention rules. The decision-making model developed by Cyert and March is thus built on four theoretical concepts: (1) uncertainty avoidance, (2) quasi-resolution of conflict, (3) problemistic search, and (4) organizational learning.

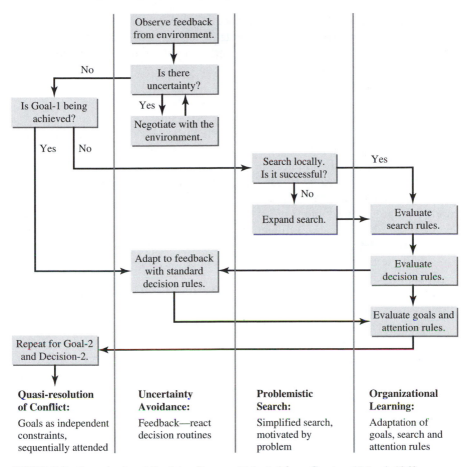

FIGURE 5.2. Organizational Decision Process (Adapted from Cyert and March 1963, Fig. 7.1, p. 175)

Organizations act to *avoid uncertainty* by focusing on the short term and attempting to control the environment. They use decision rules that emphasize short-run reaction to short-run feedback rather than try to anticipate long-run uncertain events. They arrange for a negotiated environment through the imposition of plans, standard procedures, industry traditions, and contracts on the environment (Cyert and March 1992, p. 167). For example, environmental uncertainty may be negotiated or controlled by the adoption of industry-wide practices established through trade associations, standards organizations, informal agreements, and so on. Prices, markups, costing procedures, and other variables may then be decided according to agreed-upon norms.

The goals of an organization act as independent constraints imposed by members of the organizational coalition. The organization becomes a social concourse of intersecting interests in which a number of strategies are exercised to resolve conflict. These methods may not actually achieve consensus, but they enable the organization to continue to operate despite unresolved divergences. The devices for the *quasi-resolution of conflict* are "local rationality" (whereby a subunit solves problems rationally within its own specialized domain); "acceptable level decision rules" (whereby rules that are acceptable to all interests are used, rather than rules that are optimal overall); and "sequential attention to goals" (whereby the organization attends first to one goal, then to another, in sequence).

Problemistic search is the means by which organizations determine what choices are thought to be available. Search is "motivated" in the sense that the occurrence of a problem initiates the search for ways to solve it, and that once a solution is found the search stops. Search is "simple-minded" in the sense that when a problem occurs, the search for a solution is concentrated in the neighborhood of the problem symptom and in the neighborhood of the current alternative. Search is "biased" in that it is influenced by the special training or experience of the organizational groups, the differences in the goals and aspirations of participants, and the communication biases that reflect unresolved conflict within the organization (Cyert and March 1992/1963).

Finally, *organizational learning* takes place in the decision-making process through the adaptation of goals, attention rules, and search rules. Goals are adapted by assessing past performance and experience and evaluating these results with those of other comparable organizations. Attention rules are adapted as the organization learns to pay greater notice to some aspects of its environment, and so to attend more closely to some criteria and to ignore some other criteria. Search rules are adapted when the organization fails to find a viable solution using a certain search strategy or, conversely, when it discovers an attractive alternative by searching a particular way.

The model developed by Cyert and March (1992) show how organizations rely heavily on rules and procedures for making decisions. For them, rules and procedures are the memory of the organization that provides stability and direction for the execution of recurring activities and decisions. Decision rules and procedures are based on three general principles. First, avoid uncertainty. The organization minimizes the need for predicting an uncertain future by adopting methods such as using short-term feedback to trigger action and enforcing standardized decision rules. Second, maintain the rules. The organization tends to retain a set of decision procedures for as long as it can, to shun the complex task of process redesign. Third, use simple rules. Simple rules are often elaborated by individuals using their judgment to take into account the conditions and requirements of specific cases or problems.

Organizations embed decision rules in standard operating procedures. Cyert and March (1992, pp. 122–33) discuss in some detail four types of procedures, two of which are directly concerned with information management: task performance rules, continuing records and reports, information-handling rules, and plans and planning rules. *Task performance rules* specify methods for accomplishing the tasks assigned to a member or a group. Task performance rules are invoked at many levels of the organization and are just as likely to regulate the decision making of engineers and managers as the choice behavior of operators and counter staff. Cyert and March observe that in most organizations, strategic decisions about pricing, output, inventory, and sales are fixed by simple operating rules, so that complex decisions involving great uncertainty are reduced to simple problems with minimum uncertainty. Task performance rules are important because they encode past organizational learning, and because they help to ensure that the activity of each subunit is consistent and coordinated with the work of the other subunits.

Records and reports are maintained by the organization for the purposes of control and prediction (Cyert and March 1992, p. 125). Records such as financial statements or cost reports have a control effect because organizational members assume that the records are being kept for a purpose and that someone will review or check the records at some stage. Records are also used as a database of past events, performance, and results to predict the future, making the simplifying assumption that cause-effect relations interpreted for the past will also hold for the future. Records also reflect the organization's model of the world, so much so that what records are maintained influence what aspects of the environment the organization notices and what alternatives will be considered by the organization.

Information-handling rules define the organization's communication system, "in order to provide reasonable certainty that relevant information will be available at the proper place at the proper time" (Cyert and March 1992, p. 123). Information-routing rules specify who will communicate to whom about what and often define "proper" channels of information flow that reflect the administrative hierarchy and technical specialization of the organization. Information-filtering rules specify what information is to be generated and transmitted, which are based again on the specialization and point of view of the particular member or group and can significantly influence the formation of organizational expectations.

Plans and planning rules serve the general purpose of deriving an intended allocation of resources among the alternative activities of the organization, typically presented in the form of budgets or expenditure statements. Because a plan is simultaneously a goal, a schedule, a theory (of relationships between input factors and outcomes), and a precedent (for continuing existing decisions), a plan, like other standard operating procedures, helps to reduce the uncertainty of dealing with a complex world (Cyert and March 1992, p. 132).

Cyert and March (1992) summarize their analysis of organization decision making thus:

> Most of the developments described thus far are built on a conception of decision
> making that is consequential and—within the limits imposed by information
> constraints and conflict—intendedly rational. That is theories of limited rationality
> are, for the most part, theories of rational decision making by organizations with
> consistent preferences. . . . Much of the decision making behavior we observe
> reflects the routine way in which people do what they believe they are supposed to
> do. Much of the behavior in an organization is specified by standard operating

procedures, professional standards, cultural norms, and institutional structures. Decisions in organizations, as in individuals, seem often to involve finding "appropriate" rules to follow. (Cyert and March 1993, p. 230)

IV. PROCESS MODEL

When goals are clear (lower left-hand quadrant of Fig. 5.1) but the alternatives to achieve these goals are not, we may expect to see decision making unfold as a process that involves a significant amount of searching for and evaluating options. Process models focus on the stages, activities, and dynamics of search and choice behaviors. One of the best-known decision process models is that developed by Mintzberg et al. (1976), based on their analysis of 25 strategic decision processes in various commercial and government organizations. The decisions ranged from an airline choosing new aircraft to a hospital introducing a new form of treatment. Although all the decisions were characterized by high levels of ambiguity, novelty, and movement, Mintzberg and associates were able to discern the phases and routines that form the underlying structure of the decision-making process. Reflecting the complexity and open-endedness of strategic decisions, the model has a large number of elements: three central decision phases, three decision support routines, and six sets of dynamic factors.

Decision Phases

The three central decision phases are identification, development, and selection (Fig. 5.3). The *identification phase* recognizes the need for decision and develops

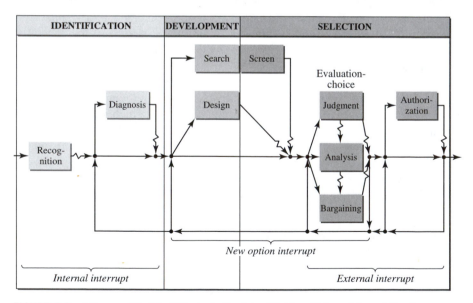

FIGURE 5.3. A Process Model of Strategic Decision Making (Adapted from Mintzberg et al. 1976)

an understanding of the decision issues. Identification consists of decision recognition routines and diagnosis routines. In the decision recognition routine, problems, opportunities, and crises are recognized and initiate decisional activity. The need for a decision is defined as an information need: "a difference between information on some actual situation and some expected standard" (Mintzberg et al. 1976, p. 253). These standards are based on past experience, projected trends, standards used in comparable organizations, people's expectations, and theoretical models. Mintzberg and associates suggest that stimuli accumulate in the minds of decision makers until they reach a threshold for action or decision. The amplitude of each stimulus depends on the individual's assessment of the source, interest level, perceived payoff, workload, and so on. In the diagnosis routine, management seeks to comprehend the stimuli-initiating decision as well as the cause-effect relations relevant for the decision situation. It is primarily an information-seeking activity involving "the tapping of existing information channels and the opening of new ones to clarify and define the issues" (Mintzberg et al. 1976, p. 254).

The *development phase* leads to the development of one or more solutions to a problem or crisis or to the elaboration of an opportunity. Development consists of search routines that look for ready-made, off-the-shelf solutions and design routines that seek to create custom-made solutions. Four types of search routines can be activated: memory search by scanning the organization's existing memory; passive search by waiting for unsolicited alternatives; trap search by activating search generators (such as letting suppliers know what the firm is planning to buy); and active search by directly seeking information about alternatives. Thus, search appears to be hierarchical, progressing from local source to remote sources, proceeding from memory and passive search to trap search and active search (Mintzberg et al. 1976). Design routines involve either developing a custom-made solution or modifying an existing ready-made alternative. Designing a custom-made solution tends to be a complex and iterative process by which vague starting ideas gradually converge on a specific solution. Whereas organizations attempting a custom-made solution focus on developing one alternative, those choosing ready-made solutions typically keep multiple alternatives in view.

The *selection phase* evaluates the alternatives and chooses a solution for commitment to action. Selection consists of screen routines, evaluation-choice routines, and authorization routines. Screen routines eliminate what is infeasible, thereby reducing the number of alternatives to be considered. Evaluation-choice routines use judgment, bargaining, or analysis to arrive at a choice. In judgment, an individual makes the choice in her own mind based on her experience and intuition. In analysis, alternatives and their consequences are evaluated against a set of criteria so as to determine the best-performing option, and the final choice is made by judgment or bargaining. In bargaining, choice is made by a group of decision makers with conflicting goals and interests, with each participant exercising judgment. Authorization routines define a path through the organizational hierarchy for a decision to obtain internal and external approval and to secure resources for implementation.

The simplest decision could just involve two routines: recognition and then evaluation-choice, as shown on the horizontal axis in Fig. 5.3. Most decisions require the development phase, during which ready-made solutions (modified) are searched or custom-made solutions are designed. Development typically takes up the bulk of the time and resources of the decision process and tends to be iterative, going through multiple search and design cycles. While selection may be the final phase, it is not uncommon for new cycles back to the development or identification phase to be restarted from the evaluation-choice or authorization routines. This could happen when, for example, a better alternative is desired or a redefinition of the decision situation is necessary.

The most prominent feature of strategic decision processes is their dynamic, open-ended character. A number of dynamic factors continuously change the tempo and direction of the decision process: "They delay it, stop it, restart it. They cause it to speed up, to branch to a new phase, to cycle within one or between two phases, and to recycle back to an earlier point in the process . . . the process is dynamic, operating in an open system where it is subjected to interferences, feedback loops, dead ends, and other factors" (Mintzberg et al. 1976, p. 263). Six sets of *dynamic factors* influence the decision process—interrupts, scheduling delays, feedback delays, timing delays and speedups, comprehension cycles, and failure cycles. As shown in Fig. 5.3, three types of *interrupts* are important. Internal interrupts occur when there is internal disagreement about the need to make a strategic decision. New option interrupts occur when a new alternative is introduced, perhaps in the form of a new leader, technology, or regulatory requirement. External interrupts occur when outside stakeholders or groups block the selection of a solution that has been worked out.

Scheduling delays are deliberately introduced by managers to separate and slow down the activities of the decision process so that they may have the time to attend to a variety of other tasks. *Feedback delays* arise when decision makers await the results of or feedback on actions previously taken. *Timing delays and speedups* are used by managers to time decisions so that they can tie in with or take advantage of some other circumstance or event. *Comprehension cycles* are sometimes needed to grapple with complex issues—managers cycle between routines in order to better understand a problem, assess the available alternatives, and reconcile multiple goals and preferences. *Failure cycles* happen when an acceptable solution could not be found, in which case the decision maker may cycle back to the development phase, relax the evaluation criteria, or delay the decision.

Undergirding the entire decision process are three *decision support routines:* decision control routines, decision communication routines, and political routines (Mintzberg et al. 1976). *Decision control routines* guide the decision process and consist of decision planning, which determines the boundaries of the decision space, selection of participants, scheduling constraints, resource commitments, and so on; and switching, which directs the decision maker's attention to the next step or the appropriate routine to activate. *Decision communication routines* gather as well as distribute information as part of the decision process. They consist of exploring, or the general scanning for information and passive review of what becomes available; investigating, or the focused search and research for information on a specific issue; and disseminating, or the distribution of information about the progress of the decision process to interested parties. *Political routines* are important in strategic decision processes and can take the form of bargaining, persuasion, or cooptation. Bargaining is used among stakeholders who have some control over the choices being made to negotiate arrangements of mutual advantage. Persuasion is used to move someone over to a different position by reasoning, influence, or, as Mintzberg et al. suggest, by disseminating information early in the development and selection phases. Cooptation is used to preempt later resistance by inviting potential objectors to participate early in the decision process, such as during the development phase.

To illustrate the process model, here are two vignettes selected from the twenty-five decision cases that Mintzberg and associates analyzed (refer to Fig. 5.3 for decision routines in square brackets):

Vignette A: Purchase of aircraft by regional airline

1. A regional airline is considering acquisition of jet aircraft. [*Recognition*]
2. Search conducted to purchase aircraft, a choice was made. [*Search*]
3. A concerned board of directors brings in a new CEO. [*New option interrupt*]
4. He cancels contract and starts search again. [*New cycle*]
5. Some alternatives rejected, remaining alternatives evaluated more closely for performance and financing and for availability of used aircraft. [*Search and screen*]
6. Narrowed down to three alternatives; negotiations for financing began. [*Analysis-bargaining*]
7. Suddenly, a foreign airline went into receivership, and two used aircraft became available at desired price and with attractive financing. [*New option interrupt*]
8. President acted quickly to purchase these aircraft. [*Judgment*]

Vignette B: Selection of switch manufacturer by telecommunications firm

1. A telecommunications company found it necessary to automate one of its switching functions. [*Recognition*]
2. Requirements were drawn up. [*Diagnosis*]
3. Two broad options considered: electromechanical, computerized. [*Search*]
4. Fifteen manufacturers contacted, and 13 were eliminated. [*Search and screen*]

5. The 2 qualifying manufacturers then developed specific systems and bids. [*Design*]

6. One was selected. [*Analysis*]

7. Decision was authorized at three successive levels of the hierarchy. [*Authorization*]

The process model makes clear how the way a decision is framed (recognized and diagnosed in the identification phase) and how the alternatives are searched or designed (in the development phase) have a major impact on the quality of the decision outcome. Mintzberg et al. point out that the bulk of the resources in a decision process is typically expended in the development phase, but relatively little research has focused on the search and design of alternatives. More generally, the value of the process model is in defining the phases and activities that lend structure to the apparent chaos that characterizes strategic decision processes. The process model provides a framework for organizations to better manage the dynamic, open-ended flow of decision activities and to anticipate or even exploit the interruptions, delays, and appearance of new options that are inherent features of strategic choice making.

V. POLITICAL MODEL

The upper right-hand quadrant of Fig. 5.1 shows the situation where goal uncertainty is high but procedural uncertainty is low. This situation can arise when decision making involves multiple groups that perceive different interests and adopt different positions with respect to the problem at hand. Between the groups, then, there is goal conflict and uncertainty about which goals are most salient. At the same time, each group is clear about its preferred outcomes and the methods that can best accomplish these outcomes—in this sense, each group sees procedural certainty. Nevertheless, no single group has all the resources or expertise to go it alone, and so no single group can completely determine the organizational agenda. *Goal conflict* is consequently a fundamental cause of the exercise of power in decision making.

Goal conflict and thus political decision making is more likely when the organization is experiencing high levels of (1) environmental uncertainty, (2) resource dependency, and (3) task interdependency. *Environment uncertainty* is high when a large number of external actors and forces have a major influence on the organization's work but the organization has limited control over these elements. Uncertainty is high when the environment is complex, changing rapidly, and cause-effect relationships are hard to discern. The general effect may be that decision makers in the organization feel vulnerable and exposed to changes in the environment. *Resource dependency* is high when the organization relies to a significant degree on external resources. These resources may be tangible or intangible, and could include, for example, fuel, raw materials, components, as well as information, sanctions, and legal rights. Resource dependency is high when the resources are vital to the organization, when its supply is limited, when the number of suppliers is small, and when there are no readily available substitutes. The general effect may be that organizations are sensitive to the need to ensure stable, ongoing relationships that underwrite the supply of key resources. *Task interdependency* is high when the ability of groups in the organization to complete their work effectively is linked to a large extent to the performance and cooperation of other groups. Interestingly, as groups specialize in their functional areas, they also become increasingly dependent on each other. Task interdependency may be high when work activities are specialized and yet highly coupled, when the need for coordination is great but the channels for communication are constrained. The general effect may be that each group develops its own view of the world and regards its interests and goals as being more important than those of other groups (Pfeffer 1992). The cumulative effect of high levels of environmental uncertainty, resource dependency, and task interdependency is a higher probability of goal conflict in decision making.

Organizations respond to goal conflict in two generic ways: they behave as coalitions; and they pursue procedural rationality (Fig. 5.4). *Coalition behavior* begins when groups assess each others' positions and preferences in relation to the decision being worked on. Groups with common interests form alliances and coalitions in order to strengthen their ability to push for preferred outcomes. They may also negotiate pacts or treaties with opposing groups to reduce the amount of resistance. Coalitions may be ad hoc and temporary—they are created around specific issues, and they last for the duration that the issue is being worked on. Another type of coalition, the dominant coalition, is a small, active group that is able to largely determine the goals of the organization through internal bargaining (Cyert and March 1993). As was noted earlier in this chapter, goal conflict is not actually resolved or eliminated. Instead, groups treat the

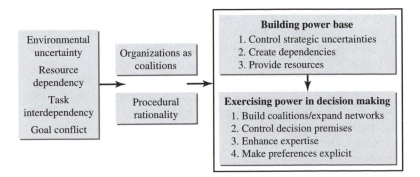

FIGURE 5.4. Political Model of Organizational Decision Making

multiple goals as constraints, seek rationality locally, use acceptable decision rules, and attend to goals sequentially (Cyert and March 1993).

The second generic response is that organizations pursue *procedural rationality* instead of goal rationality. Pursuing substantive, goal-oriented rationality would have required constructing new goals that include and satisfy the objectives and interests of all groups. On the other hand, pursuing a process-based procedural rationality involves creating procedures and forums that are perceived to be fair, and then working through these procedures to find a mutually acceptable solution. These forums and procedures typically allow interested groups to have a formal voice in the decision process: to present positions, ask and answer questions, seek assurances, and suggest alternatives.

In the political decision arena that includes coalitions, factions, procedures, and forums, groups build their power base and exercise their power (Fig. 5.4). A group can build or expand its power base by controlling strategic uncertainties, creating dependencies, and acquiring resources. A group that has the capability to control an uncertainty that is highly strategic to the firm (e.g., ensure an ongoing supply of a critical resource or develop a long-term contract with a major customer) is likely to be perceived as being powerful (Hickson et al. 1971). This is more so when the group's capability is nonsubstitutable, and when its activities are central to many other groups' functions. A group is perceived to possess power over another unit when the latter depends on the former. Here power is the property of a social relationship between two actors, and the greater the dependency of one group over another, the greater the power that the second party has over the first (Emerson 1962). Again, this power dependence is proportional to the importance of the goals being pursued, and inversely proportional to whether the goals can be achieved through alternative means or relationships. Finally, a group that acquires or provides for a significant proportion of an organization's resources is likely to be seen to have power. For example, the faculty of medicine in a university that secures the bulk of research funding or the product division that generates much of the revenues may be perceived as having power to influence decisions.

Fig. 5.4 shows four examples of ways that power may be exercised to influence decision making. First, groups can attempt to expand existing coalitions or social networks. Trusted allies may be appointed to or placed in positions of power. Dissidents may be included in committees to preempt opposition. Second, groups can try to control decision premises. They may try to select, define, or weight value premises so that their preferred alternatives are evaluated more favorably. They may also control factual premises by gatekeeping, filtering, or highlighting information selectively. Third, groups can enhance their perceived expertise. They may claim they have experience or they may vaunt past accomplishments, and outside experts or consultants may be hired to support their claims. Finally, groups make as strong a case as they can for their preferred alternatives. They may try to present a clear, reasoned case supported by data that are hard to challenge. They may try to deploy persuasive arguments by employing metaphors and analogies that resonate with decision makers and stakeholders.

Allison and Zelikow (1999) describe the dynamics of political decision making as game playing, in which players with positions, stands, and influence make their moves according to rules and their bargaining strengths. Actions and decisions may then be analyzed by answering four questions:

1. Who are the players?
2. What are the players' stands?
3. What are the players' relative influence?
4. How are the players' stands, influence, and moves combined to yield decisions and actions?

Who are the players? They are the individuals whose interests and actions have an impact on the organizational decision-making process. Individuals become players by occupying positions that provide them with the authority and access to channels that can produce significant action. Players occupy positions that give access to action channels, but positions also define what the players are allowed to do and what they are obliged to do. Positions can confer advantages as well as handicaps, and positions can also impose obligations for the performance of certain tasks.

What are the players' stands? Each player's stand is determined by her perceptions of an issue; her goals, interests, and stakes; and her reactions to deadlines and events. What the players perceive as desirable outcomes is influenced by personal, departmental, and organizational goals and interests. Organizational members may come to believe that the health of their own group is vital to the organization, and the health of the group depends on maintaining influence and securing the necessary resources and support. The overlapping of organizational, group, and personal interests constitute the individual's stakes for which the decision "game" is played, and it is these stakes that define the individual's stand on the issue. Deadlines and events such as budgets or policy changes often bring issues to a head and require busy players to take stands. Players see different faces of an issue, depending not only on their goals and interests, but also on situational elements such as deadlines and the channels in which an issue is raised.

What are the players' relative influence? This is a question of power, which Allison believes is the consequence of the individual's bargaining advantages, her skill and will in using bargaining advantages, and other players' perception of the first two elements (Allison 1971; Allison and Zelikow 1999). The sources of bargaining advantages include

> formal authority and responsibility (stemming from positions); actual control over resources necessary to carry out action; expertise and control over information that

enables one to define the problem, identify options, and estimate feasibilities; control over information that enables chiefs to determine whether and in what form decisions are being implemented; the ability to affect other players' objectives in other games, including domestic political games; personal persuasiveness with other players (drawn from personal relations, charisma); and access to and persuasiveness with players who have bargaining advantages drawn from the above. (Allison and Zelikow 1999, p. 300)

How are the players' stands, influence, and moves combined to yield decisions and actions? In order to assert influence, players have to be connected to action channels, which are the formal, routinized means of taking action on a specific kind of issue. Issues are typically identified and framed within an established action channel, and action channels then structure the decision game by determining which players can play, their points of entrance, and their relative advantages and disadvantages for that game. Rules define how the game is played in three ways. They establish positions, the power of each position, and the action channels. They limit decisions and actions, disallowing some forms of behaviors. They legitimize certain moves such as bargaining, persuading, or forming coalitions, while disapproving other moves. In the political model, actions and decisions are produced as political resultants— "political" because decisions and actions emerge from the bargaining by individual members along regularized action channels; and "resultants" because decisions and actions are outcomes of the compromise, conflict, and confusion of players with diverse interests and unequal influence (Allison and Zelikow 1999).

VI. ANARCHIC MODEL

The lower right-hand quadrant of Fig. 5.1 shows the situation where both goals and alternatives are unclear. This can happen when the decision situation is highly ambiguous and unfamiliar to the organization—it is not clear what ought to be done, and there is no prior experience to draw upon. As the organization tries out ideas and actions to discover goals and alternatives, the decision-making activity can appear to be random and disconnected. Cohen et al. (1972, p. 2) draw the contrast between the anarchic model and the other models in earlier sections:

> Although organizations can often be viewed conveniently as vehicles for solving well-defined problems or structures within which conflict is resolved through bargaining, they also provide sets of procedures through which participants arrive at an interpretation of what they are doing and what they have done while in the process of doing it. From this point of view, an organization is a collection of choices looking for problems, issues and feelings looking for decision situations in which they might be aired, solutions looking for issues to which they might be the answer, and decision makers looking for work.

Cohen et al. (1972) suggest that organizations behave as *organized anarchies* when three conditions apply: preferences are problematic, technology is unclear, and participation is fluid. First, the *preferences* used in decision making are ill-defined and inconsistent, comprising more a loose collection of ideas than a structured set, in which preferences may have to be discovered rather than being known beforehand. Second, the organization's *technology* is unclear in that its processes and procedures are not well understood by its members and the means of achieving desired ends are not readily identifiable. Third, *participation* is fluid as people vary in the amount of time and effort that they give to different activities. These features are present to an extent in any organization at least part of the time, but Cohen and associates suggest that they are most evident in public, educational, and "illegitimate" organizations.

Within an organized anarchy, decisions are the outcomes of four relatively independent streams of problems, solutions, participants, and choice opportunities (Fig. 5.5). *Problems* are points of dissatisfaction with current activities or performance that require attention. *Solutions* are products or ideas proposed by somebody (or a group) for adoption—or, as Cohen and associates put it, they are answers actively looking for a question. Solutions exist independently of problems. Members may be attracted to an idea and push for it as a logical choice regardless of the problem. *Participants* come and go in a decision situation, depending on other demands on the participants' time. Participants also bring

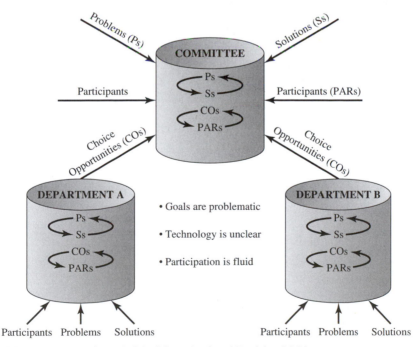

FIGURE 5.5. Garbage Can Model of Organizational Decision Making

along with them their own preferences and perceptions about how to recognize or define a problem or solution. *Choice opportunities* are occasions when an organization is expected to make a decision, such as when awarding contracts, hiring staff, and allocating budgets. Choice opportunities provide a setting for the streams of problems, solutions, and participants to meet up. Cohen et al. (1972) suggest that "one can view a choice opportunity as a garbage can into which various kinds of problems and solutions are dumped by participants as they are generated. The mix of garbage in a single can depends on the mix of cans available, on the labels attached to the alternative cans, on what garbage is currently being produced, and on the speed with which the garbage is collected and removed from the scene" (p. 2).

A decision situation is like a *garbage can* into which various kinds of problems and solutions are dumped by participants as they are generated. A decision then happens when problems, solutions, participants, and choices coincide. When they do, solutions are attached to problems, and problems to choices by participants who happen to have the time and energy to do it. Which solutions are attached to which problems is a matter of chance and timing, depending on which participants with what goals happen to be on the scene, when the solutions and problems are entered, as well as "the mix of choices available at any one time, the mix of problems that have access to the organization, the mix of solutions looking for problems, and outside demands on the decision makers" (Cohen et al. 1972, p. 16).

In an interesting study of editors in the college textbook publishing industry, Levitt and Nass (1989) concluded that the garbage can model fits well with many aspects of the decision behavior observed. Interviews with editors of the ten best-selling introductory textbooks in physics and sociology found the editors consistently describing their work in gambling terms ("a lottery with bad odds," "a crapshoot") and that decision making was best described as "guesswork, intuition, and opinion." A sociology editor expresses this feeling of ambiguity and confusion: "Editors can become schizophrenic. You think a manuscript is good and it doesn't make money. Then you get a manuscript that you think is bad, and it makes money—but not always" (quoted in Levitt and Nass 1989, p. 192). In textbook publishing, decision situations are characterized by ill-defined preferences, unclear technology, and fluid participation. Preferences are ill-defined because interpreting and differentiating between success and failure is highly equivocal and malleable. For example, one editor stated that a physics book which sold poorly was still considered a success because "it was important for the company to have an entry, any entry, in the physics market" (p. 193). The organizational technology is unclear because the connections between means and ends are unclear. There are no specifiable procedures or formula for producing a successful textbook, and editors often work in disciplines in which they are not trained. Participation is fluid because editors change departments and publishing houses relatively frequently. Levitt and Nass observed that "it is part of the occupational culture of editors that being fired (even more than once) is no indication of incompetence" (p. 195). Besides, the gestation period of textbooks is three to five years, with projects often being handed down to new successors. As predicted by the garbage can model, timing is an important element in deciding about projects. For example, introductory texts sell better in their second or later editions, but the decision to do this depends on whether the publisher is planning a new entry into that market segment. Serendipitous or random events often play a significant part in the acquisition of manuscripts, so that textbook editors recognize the importance of maintaining strong links with academics. Problems, solutions, and participants also track each other through time, as, for example, when academics in the artificial intelligence field claim that they would teach introductory AI courses if there were a suitable text, while editors counter that such texts would be produced if there were courses (Levitt and Nass 1989). Despite the disorderly decision process, the textbooks produced as outcomes show significant levels of homogeneity in terms of the ordering of contents and topics. It was as though a lid was being placed on the garbage can. Levitt and Nass (1989) showed that textbook homogenization was the result of the forces of coercive, mimetic, and normative isomorphism (DiMaggio and Powell 1983). Thus, established paradigms define the essential contents and topics that should be included (normative isomorphism); editors imitate successful textbooks produced by others (mimetic isomorphism); and the organizational structure of publishing houses often mirror that of the higher education institutes who are their customers (coercive isomorphism).

Cohen and associates suggest that in the garbage can model, decisions are made in three different ways: by resolution, by oversight, and by flight. *Resolution* is decision making to resolve problems by working on them over time. Resolution is the standard mode of choice behavior according to rational principles. *Oversight* occurs "if a choice is activated when problems are attached to other choices and if there is energy available to to make the new choice quickly" (Cohen et al. 1972, p. 8). In oversight, a choice is adopted quickly and incidentally to other choices being made. Decision by *flight* occurs when the problems leave the choice—the original problem has flown away, as it were, leaving a choice that can now be made, but the decision resolves no problems. In organized anarchies, choice by flight and oversight may be more common than decision by resolution. For example, Cohen and associates observe that university decision making often does not resolve problems but choices are made by flight or oversight. A university unable to deal with an unproductive faculty member who is protected by tenure may one day find that the problem has disappeared because the member has decided to relocate to another city (decision making by flight). Again, a department struggling to recast its role finds the decision made by oversight when it is merged with a larger department and its purpose is then defined as a component of the new parent's mission. Cohen et al. (1972) stress this relative independence of problems and solutions:

> A major feature of the garbage can process is the "partial decoupling" of problems and choices. Problems are worked upon in the context of some choice, but choices

are made only when the shifting combinations of problems, solutions, and decision
makers happen to make action possible. Quite commonly this is after problems
have left a given choice arena or before they have discovered it (decisions by flight
or oversight). (p. 16)

Although an anarchic model of decision making may seem unproductive,
the garbage can process is not dysfunctional, for it can produce decisions under
uncertain and conflictual conditions when goals are ambiguous, problems are
poorly understood, and decision makers vary in the amount of time and energy
they give to issues. Cohen and March (1986) present several case studies of
decision making mainly at educational institutions in Denmark, Norway, and the
United States which illustrate many of the ideas in the garbage can model. These
studies include the location decisions of a new Norwegian medical school, reorganization in the University of Oslo, ideology and management of a Danish free
school, and structural changes at a medium-size American university. Other
researchers have also analyzed government organizations using the garbage
can model, including Sproull, Weiner, and Wolf (1978), Pinfield (1986), and
Kingdon (1984/1995).

Sproull et al. (1978) found the organized anarchy model useful in analyzing
the early years of the new National Institute of Education (NIE), created within
the U.S. Department of Health, Education, and Welfare in 1972. The NIE's
goals were ambiguous and expressed in general terms ("to seek to improve
education"); the technology was unclear—education R&D was then regarded as
one of the least mature of the social science research efforts; and participation
was fluid, with many changing sets of external and internal actors. In the three
decision processes that were analyzed (developing conceptual framework, designing a planning process, and creating an annual budget), a decision was
made only after a large number of cycles had occurred, when closure was forced
by external deadlines, with the final decision the result of a top manager making
somewhat arbitrary judgments: "As decision processes continued without closure, they became receptacles into which were dumped the latest important
issues. Attempting to resolve the latest issue within the particular process inevitably changed the focus of the decision. Certain issues were never resolved. . . .
They tended to appear and reappear in all the decision contexts" (Sproull et al.
1978, p. 200).

Pinfield (1986) found the garbage can model helpful in understanding the
decision-making process of the Canadian federal government as it worked toward a set of policies to manage its corps of senior governmental executives. The
model elucidated the sequence of events, the effects of changes in participants,
the evolution of problems, and the timing of these changes, but neglected to address how the content of issues can link decision streams and how participation
is channeled by hierarchy and specialization.

Kingdon (1984/1995) analyzed policy making in the areas of health and
transportation at the U.S. federal government level and found the garbage can
model useful in describing the process. Policy making may be conceived as "three

process streams flowing through the system—streams of problems, policies, and politics. They are largely independent of one another, and each develops according to its own dynamics and rules. But at some critical junctures ['policy windows'] the three streams are joined, and the greatest policy changes grow out of that coupling of problems, policy proposals, and politics" (Kingdon 1995, p. 19).

The anarchic model suggests that decision making in organizations is ecological: there is random variation in the ideas and solutions that are put forward; selection of ideas by individuals who connect solutions to problems; and retention of solutions in the minds of decision makers. More generally, organizations are seen to behave as ecologies or collections of choices and decisions that are being worked upon, with decision makers allocating their attention unequally between decisions and varying significantly in the amount of search effort they expend.

Decision-Making Dynamics

Although we discussed each of the four models independently, it is clear that many decisions change their character as the decision-making activity unfolds. This can happen for example when new goals are added, perception of goals changes, new alternatives are introduced, or implications of alternatives become better understood. Fig. 5.6 illustrates the dynamic, evolving nature of decision making with a few possible pathways. We could imagine a decision situation that is initially following rational rules and procedures (such as a staff promotion decision) becoming highly politicized when, for example, it sets a precedent seen as undesirable by others (path 1 in Fig. 5.6). Similarly, a process mode to decide

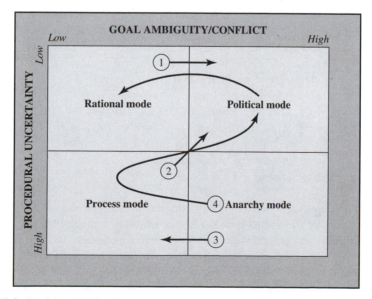

FIGURE 5.6. Decision-Making Dynamics

about whether and how to outsource a service may lead to a conflict of goals (path 2). A firm that is applying new technology to enter a new market may initially operate in an anarchy mode: goals are problematic, technology is unclear. As goals become better defined, the firm might shift to a process mode to develop alternatives and decide which segments of the market to target, what product features to prioritize (path 3). Yet another variation might be that as the options for a new project take shape, different stakeholder groups diverge in their preferences, leading to the political mode. Assuming that these differences are worked out in some way and the project is able to move into the implementation stage, it might then be following rules and routines in a rational mode (path 4 in Fig. 5.6).

VII. INFORMATION NEEDS, SEEKING, AND USE IN DECISION MAKING

In this section, we elaborate on the gathering and use of information that lies at the heart of organizational decision making. Once again we will apply the framework developed in Chapter 2 to analyze information needs, seeking, and use in terms of cognitive needs, affective responses, and situational dimensions. A summary of the ensuing discussion is in Table 5-1.

Information Needs. Organizational decision making requires information to reduce uncertainty in at least three ways. First, information is needed to *frame* a choice situation. Boundaries are drawn to delimit a problem space in which solutions are to be searched, stakeholders are to be identified, and influence is to be wielded. The framing of a problem to a large extent determines the types and content of information that would be needed in order to be able to make a decision. Second, information is needed to *define preferences* and to *select rules*. Multiple goals and interests are clarified, prioritized, and expressed as choice criteria. Decision rules are activated by matching information about the current situation with categories of problems that the organization has learned to deal with. Third, information is needed about available *courses of action* and their projected outcomes. In some modes of decision making, a great part of the information-seeking effort is on identifying, developing, and evaluating alternative courses of action. Information needs then depend on whether alternatives already exist, whether existing solutions may be customized or modified, or whether new solutions have to be discovered.

Information Seeking. Individual information seeking is shaped by the habits and *heuristics* that the decision maker has acquired as a result of training, education, or experience. At the same time, organizations design and institutionalize rules and routines to structure search behaviors based on premises derived from goals and experience. Information seeking is therefore a function of individual preferences, institutional values, and the decision situation's attributes. As an activity, information seeking is *problem-driven*—it begins when a problem

TABLE 5-1. Information needs, seeking, and use in decision making.

	Information Needs	*Information Seeking*	*Information Use*
Decision Making	• *Determine problem frame and boundaries* • *Clarify preferences and rule appropriateness* • *Information about alternatives, outcomes, preferences*	• *Guided by heuristics, habits* • *Search is problem driven* • *"Satisficing" strategy*	• *Limited by human information processing* • *Structured by rules and routines* • *Many issues compete for attention*
Cognitive Needs	• Needs vary in phases of decision making • Identification and development needs	• Multiple managerial decision roles • High-velocity decision making	• Cognitive simplifications • Selective information processing
Affective Responses	• Stress due to complexity, risk, interests, aspirations • Affective factors in problem formulation	• Stress in a conflict model of decision making • Avoiding information seeking	• Groupthink, group polarization • Overcommitment in escalation situations
Situational Dimensions	• Programmed and non-programmed decisions • Tactics to frame decision problems	• Information seeking varies by decision mode • Structure, incentives, and information access	• Information use varies by decision mode • Information-handling rules

(including the problem of how to exploit an opportunity) is attended to and recognized as requiring decision and action. Search seems to respect a hierarchy of information sources in which more accessible and familiar sources are searched first. Information search is *satisficing:* it stops when the first good-enough solution is found (rational decision model), or when ample evidence is gathered to support a preferred option (political decision model), or when courses are developed or investigated sufficiently to be presented for final evaluation (process decision model). In the anarchic decision model, information is continually generated and dumped into decision situations, but they are initially uncoupled from the problems being considered. Interested participants may then attach information about solutions or problems to choice situations, but which solutions become linked to which problems depend on factors such as temporal sequence, individual interest, and the current mix of solutions and problems.

Information Use. Decisions are made by individuals or groups of individuals. Although *human information processing* has attained a high degree of adaptive versatility by applying rules of thumb that reduce mental effort, these same shortcuts can systematically limit and bias information processing in some situations. Moreover, humans seek to maintain order, consistency, and self-esteem when evaluating choices, and this may lead them to avoid, hide, or discount information that does not support their beliefs or preferences. Decision making in groups can introduce additional social forces, including pressures to conform to group norms or to preserve group cohesiveness, which when accentuated can warp information use. The situation is exacerbated when decision makers carry heavy work and information loads and try to juggle multiple demands and agendas at the same time. Many simultaneous, competing claims on their *attention* weaken their ability to allocate time and energy according to some objective appreciation of the relative importance of issues. Organizations attempt to compensate for limitations in human information processing by establishing decision *rules and routines* that define what information and values are important (factual and value premises) for a type of problem.

Information Needs in Decision Making

Information Needs and Cognitive Needs

Information needs in decision phases. Information needs vary according to the *phases of decision making*. Simon (1977) identifies four phases: intelligence, design, choice, and review. The *intelligence phase* involves searching the environment for conditions calling for decision, where "executives and their staff spend a large fraction of their time surveying the economic, technical, political, and social environment to identify new conditions that call for new actions" (Simon 1977, p. 40). Research has found that environmental scanning by business organizations tends to be focused on market-related sectors of the environment. Information about customers, competitors, and suppliers are the most intensively gathered. In industries where other environmental forces such as technology, demographics, or regulatory policies have a strategic impact on the industry, scanning these sectors also becomes a high priority (Choo 2002). The *design phase* involves seeking information in order to invent, design, or develop courses of action that can address a decision situation. Here the information needs are to locate, elaborate, and analyze alternatives in terms of their outcomes and contributions to organizational objectives. The *choice phase* is when a particular course of action is selected from the courses that have been developed. Choice may be influenced by information about the context in which the decision is to be taken, such as the mix of other decisions being considered at the same time and forthcoming events that may affect the success or perception of the decision. The *review phase* involves "assessing the outcomes of past actions as part of a repeating cycle that leads again to new decisions" (Simon 1977, p. 40). Learning from past actions requires having the information to infer cause-effect relationships between decisions and outcomes that may be separated in time and space.

Identification and development needs. Simon's first three phases are the precursors of the identification, development, and selection phases derived by Mintzberg et al. (1976) from their field study of strategic decision processes. The *identification phase* is similar to Simon's intelligence activity. For Mintzberg and associates, it is information need that drives the decision need, so that decision making is initiated by a difference between information on some actual situation and some expected standard. The scope and content of information need depend on whether the decision situation is perceived as a problem, opportunity, or threat. Problem decisions typically require information from multiple sources and stimuli, in order to enable decision makers to read the situation and weigh the options before taking action. Opportunity decisions generally attempt to take advantage of some particular idea or innovation or some set of circumstances so as to improve on an already secure position. The idea may have been nestling in the decision maker's mind for some time, waiting for an appropriate time and setting to be translated into action. Crisis decisions, on the other hand, are reactive, requiring decision makers to respond to some pressing, threatening event. Information needs and information seeking may be narrowly pursued to enable prompt and effective measures to be taken. After a decision situation is recognized as a problem, opportunity, or crisis, the next step is "the tapping of existing information channels and the opening of new ones to clarify and define the issues" (Mintzberg et al. 1976, p. 254). Each decision situation is unique and has to be diagnosed on the basis of information that describes the situation's more pertinent dimensions. In the *development phase* information is required about possible solutions. Mintzberg and associates categorize solutions as being ready-made solutions, custom-made solutions, and solutions modified from ready-made options. Information to identify and evaluate a ready-made solution is typically more structured and better defined than the broader, more tentative information required to develop a new solution or modify an existing one. In the *selection phase,* information is required to compare the relative values of the various developed alternatives. Additional information may be necessary to answer specific concerns or fill in particular information gaps. Where such concerns are not adequately met, the selection phase may define new information needs and initiate a new cycle of identification and development activities.

Information Needs and Affective Responses

Stress due to complexity, risk, interests, aspirations. At least four aspects of organizational decision making can evoke strong affective responses in participants. First, the *complexity* of the problem and the lack of clarity about its structure (that is, the alternatives, outcomes, and preferences) induce uncertainty leading to feelings of doubt and confusion. Second, most consequential decisions involve an amount of *risk* because of the inability to control or predict the future. The larger this perception of risk, the greater the feeling of stress. Where the risks are seen as necessary or worth taking, information may be sought on how better to manage or limit these risks. However, if the decision maker is risk averse, uncertain options might be discounted or avoided altogether. Third, organizational choice typically faces a *multiplicity of interests* and stakeholders, requiring bargaining, coalition building, and negotiation among interested parties. When political "pulling and hauling" is intense or confrontational, feelings of frustration or impotence may lead decision makers to steer away from unpleasant or conflict-laden situations and outcomes. Fourth, a gap between *personal aspirations* or values and those set by the organization may generate feelings of dissatisfaction or frustration. For example, a decision maker disagreeing with organization-defined premises may feel that having to abide by them would compromise personal integrity.

Affective factors in problem formulation. The process by which a problem situation is formulated in initial decision stages affects the ensuing information seeking and processing. *Problem formulation* is sensitive to the perceptions and affective responses of individual decision makers participating in the process. An analysis of strategic problem formulation by upper-level managers of *Fortune* 500 companies in six industries found that managers used three sets of subjective criteria to form their attitudes as well as affective and cognitive responses to the formulation process (Lyles 1987). These subjective criteria are clarity, politicality, and complexity. *Clarity* refers to the managers' perception that the problem formulation process is clear and understandable. The analysis found that a clear process was perceived to be one in which several views were debated followed by a synthesis that is approved by consensus. *Politicality* "represents an affective side of the process which suggests that the process is pleasant when it is relaxed and apolitical" (Lyles 1987, p. 271). Where the process involves strong debate between opposing values or gathering support of the powerful, the process would be perceived as "tense, unpleasant, and political." A similar study conducted earlier (Lyles and Mitroff 1980) had found that fear and political power were recurring themes affecting how individuals formulated problems. Specific causes included the fear of retaliation by the politically powerful (for example, the fear of uncovering an error by senior management), the desire for the acquisition of power, and the use of political power to influence problem formulation. *Complexity* "represents a view of a complex process that is dynamic, tense and emotional because the problem is important and has widespread consequences" (Lyles 1987, p. 271). A process is perceived as complex when participants hold different views of the problem situation and there is a continued disagreement about the nature of the problem.

Information Needs and Situational Dimensions

Programmed and nonprogrammed decisions. Simon (1977) places decisions along a continuum between two polar decision-types—*programmed and non-programmed decisions*. This range may also be used to differentiate decision situations and their information-processing needs. Decisions are programmed to the extent that they are repetitive and routine, so that a definite procedure has been worked out for handling them. The decision situation is simplified by a set of common expectations, a system of subgoals, and well-defined information requirements and channels for processing the decision. Programmed decisions lend themselves to decision support technologies such as computer-based transaction processing and mathematical modeling. Decisions are nonprogrammed to the extent that they are novel, unstructured, and unusually consequential. The decision situation is ill-structured and requires participants to exercise judgment, intuition, and creativity. Nonprogrammed decisions tend to be made using rules of thumb or learned heuristics, both of which are influenced by individual training and experience. Simon's separation of decision types may be amplified by the problem dimensions proposed by Taylor (1986). Just as decisions fall between programmed and nonprogrammed, their problem dimensions would fall between the well-structured and ill-structured, simple and complex, specific goals and amorphous goals, initial state understood and not understood, assumptions agreed and not agreed upon, assumptions explicit and not explicit, and familiar pattern and new pattern. Each dimension implies information needs, so that, for example, well-structured problems may require hard, quantitative data; specific goals require data for monitoring and measurement; and familiar pattern problems are handled with procedural and historical information.

Tactics used to frame decision problems. The perception of information needs depends on how the decision problem is initially framed. While we looked at the effects of individual attitudes earlier, the application of specific types of tactics creates a broader context by introducing external ideas, targets, and new norms. From an analysis of 177 decision cases collected from mostly high-level managers in organizations across the United States and Canada, Nutt (1992) concluded that the types of *tactics used to frame decision problems* not only shaped information needs and sources but also influenced decision success. Four problem-framing tactics emerged from the study: idea tactics, problem tactics, target tactics, and reframing tactics. *Idea tactics* were the most frequently used, where an idea from outside the decision process is introduced into a decision situation as a solution. Ideas may originate from "the decision maker's visions and beliefs, educational activities, the media, the literature, vendors, joint venture opportunities, the notions of key people, and staff proposals" (Nutt 1992, p. 527). These ideas are then elaborated, tested, and refined through the decision process. *Problem tactics* begin by identifying the problem and, based on this identification, exploring and analyzing the problem's distinctive features in order to develop a remedy. *Target tactics* specify desired objectives or directions expressed as performance improvements, cost reductions, and so on. Subsequent decision making then searches for alternative solutions and selects the solution most likely to meet the target. *Reframing tactics* highlight the need for action by introducing new norms that magnify the problem and amplify the importance of acting to rectify it. New norms may be derived from "the experiences of competitors, breakthroughs by innovation, developments described in the literature, and in other ways" (Nutt 1992, p. 529) and are justified by citing their origins. The study also found that reframing, although the least frequently used, was the most successful tactic in that using the tactic led to all of the decisions being implemented, in the shortest average time, with the best results. Conversely, idea tactics were more frequently used but much less successful. Nutt (1992) suggests that decision makers preferred idea tactics because they reduced uncertainty, because decision makers believed that implementing their own visions constituted good leadership, and because the tactic was economical as "time and money was not spent in idea finding, just idea testing" (Nutt 1992, p. 537).

Information Seeking in Decision Making

Information Seeking and Cognitive Needs

Multiple managerial roles. How managers seek information in decision making depends on the roles the manager plays in an organization. From a study of managerial work based on direct observation, Mintzberg (1973) developed three sets of *managerial roles:* interpersonal, informational, and decisional roles. The manager plays three *interpersonal roles.* Because of the formal authority invested in him, he takes on the role of a figurehead, representing his organization in formal and social matters. As a leader, he defines relationships with his subordinates through staffing, motivating, and so on. Finally, as a liaison, he interacts with peers and external persons to gain information and favors. The interpersonal roles give the manager access to many internal and external sources of information, and he becomes the nerve center of organizational information. He acts in three *informational roles.* As monitor, he seeks and receives information about the organization and the environment. As disseminator, he transmits special information into the organization. As spokesman, he disseminates the organization's information out to the environment. The unique information access combined with status and authority place the executive at the focal point of the organization where decisions are made. Four *decisional roles* are discerned. As entrepreneur, the executive searches for problems and opportunities and uses information to initiate and design controlled change through "improvement projects" that exploit an opportunity or solve a problem. As disturbance handler, the executive deals with unexpected but important events for which there is no clear programmed response. Such stimulus may arise from conflicts between subordinates, loss of resources, and difficulties between one organization and another. As resource allocator, the executive controls the distribution of all forms of organizational resources by scheduling time, programming work, and authorizing decisions made by others. Finally, as negotiator, the executive engages in major, nonroutine negotiation and communication activities with other organizations or individuals. Negotiation is regarded as "resource trading in real time" in which someone in authority commits the quantity of resources at stake. The three sets of ten managerial roles form an integrated whole, where "the manager is an input-output system in which authority and status give rise to interpersonal relationships that lead to inputs (information), and these in turn lead to outputs (information and decisions). One cannot arbitrarily remove one role and expect the rest to remain intact. . . . It is the manager's informational roles that tie all managerial work together—linking status and the interpersonal roles with the decisional roles" (Mintzberg 1973, pp. 58, 71).

High-velocity decision making. Time scales have shrunk in today's environments. Technologies and market forces now compel organizations to respond in hours and days where before they had weeks and months. How do managers seek and use information in such *high-velocity environments?* Eisenhardt (1989, 1990) studied the information behaviors of top management teams in 12 microcomputer firms that were operating in "high-velocity" environments where the market and technology were moving so rapidly that information available was poor, mistakes were costly, and recovery from missed opportunities was difficult. In such dynamic environments, the ability to make fast decisions was found to be linked to strong performance. Contrary to expectations that fast decision makers would limit their information gathering and analysis to save time, the study found that fast managers used as much, and sometimes more, information as did their slower counterparts. However, fast managers concentrated on real-time information about current operations and current environment which was reported with little or no time lag, whereas slow decision makers relied on planning and future-oriented information. Real-time information is gathered in several ways: fast managers tracked operational measures of performance, shared information in frequent operational meetings, and sought advice from experienced, trusted managers. Again surprisingly, fast managers used the information to develop a larger number of alternatives than the slower decision makers. However, they analyzed the information quickly by comparing alternatives with each other rather than examining each alternative in depth. Fast managers adopted information strategies that accelerated their decision making without compromising decision quality.

Information Seeking and Affective Responses

Conflict model of decision making. Janis and Mann (1977) maintain that decisional conflicts are likely whenever consequential choices are made, and they arise because the decision maker simultaneously experiences the opposing tendencies to accept and reject a course of action. Decisional conflicts are sources of stress, which vents itself in feelings such as apprehensiveness, a desire to escape from the choice situation, and self-blame. Janis and Mann develop a *conflict model of decision making* that examines the distinctive patterns by which individuals cope with the stress of decision situations. The model is based on a series of questions that are raised in sequence by every decision maker. Faced with information suggesting a need for change, the decision maker asks herself these four questions:

1. Are the risks serious if I do not change?
2. Are the risks serious if I do change?
3. Is it realistic to hope to find a better solution?
4. Is there sufficient time to search and deliberate?

(Janis and Mann 1977)

If the risks of not changing are not serious (1), the individual behaves as before with no sense of conflict (unconflicted adherence). In this case, the individual
is indifferent toward information, taking only casual notice of messages about an
unworrisome issue. If the no-change risks are or may be serious, then the second
question asks what are the risks of taking on change (2). If the risks of effecting
change are not serious, then the individual will carry out the change action again
with no feeling of conflict (unconflicted change). As before, the individual is non-
chalant about information, since change is uncontentious. However, if the risks of
effecting change are or may be serious, the individual becomes emotionally
aroused as she starts to search earnestly for information about solutions or ways
to avoid making a choice. The next question asks, for each of the contemplated
alternatives, if there is hope of finding a better solution by furthering the information search (3). If it is unrealistic to hope for a better solution, and if the present
alternatives are unacceptable or unsatisfactory, the individual will cope by avoiding cues that aggravate anxiety or other painful feelings about being trapped in a
hopeless situation (defensive avoidance). The individual thus becomes close-
minded and biased in her information seeking. However, if it is realistic to hope
to find better solutions, the next question asks whether there is sufficient time to
search and deliberate (4). If there is too little time available to search for a better
solution that exists, as when the individual is given a deadline that it too tight
or she can see the danger closing in, the individual enters a state that Janis and
Mann call "hypervigilance," a feeling of being trapped with little time left to find
a safe way out. An extreme form of hypervigilance is panic, in which the individual makes a snap decision, often by simply following what others are doing. The
individual shows indiscriminate openness to all information, failing to discern the
relevance of messages and eventually becoming overloaded by information.
However, if there is sufficient time to search and deliberate, the individual feels
confident about finding a safe or workable solution and exercises care and dis-
criminating openness in her information seeking (vigilance). The model therefore
implies that vigilant information seeking and processing requires four conditions
to be met: awareness of serious threat if no change is taken; awareness of serious
risk in acting to change; hope or confidence that a satisfactory solution can be
found; and sufficient time to search and evaluate (Janis and Mann 1977).

Avoiding information seeking. Johnson (1996) finds that there may be as many,
if not more, reasons for not seeking as for seeking information. He identifies six
reasons to *avoid information seeking*. First, managers avoid information that
would force them to have to make a decision. Avoiding decision making can
mean not being exposed to the risk of culpability and accountability. Second,
ignorance can be used as a justification for inaction, as when a manager says that
"I cannot do anything until I know more about the problem." Third, asking for
information can imply a lack of trust. A specialist might suggest that a manager
should trust the former's actions without having to require information about
reasons and risks. Fourth, not seeking information is often a way of avoiding
conflict. This may be especially true when the information is negative or likely to

harm or embarrass some party. In contentious situations, agreement is often assumed without detailed probing. Fifth, not seeking information can allow a comfortable status quo to continue. Finding new information may require action to learn more or to change from a familiar to an unfamiliar state. Sixth, the very act of seeking information can imply revealing or admitting one's ignorance. Allen (1977) found that engineers preferred not to lose self-esteem in the eyes of colleagues by seeking information from them. Blau (1954) found that advice seeking in a government bureaucracy was associated with perceived status: a person's status would be lowered by the constant seeking of information from higher-status members, especially when the latter did not in turn ask the person for information.

Information Seeking and Situational Dimensions

Information seeking and decision modes. Information seeking in decision making varies according to the task and organizational demands that constrain or direct the process. From a database of 136 strategic decisions, Hickson et al. (1986) categorized decisions based on process variables which included information-seeking attributes. These attributes concerned the number of sources used, variability in the quality of information, use of external sources, and the amount of effort spent in acquiring information. (Other process variables described the nature of interaction, flow disruptions and impedances, process and gestation time, and the authority level at which decision ends.) The analysis showed that there were three *kinds of decision processes:* sporadic processes, fluid processes, and constricted processes (Hickson et al. 1986). *Sporadic decision processes* are protracted, informal, and spasmodic, taking over a year or two to come to a conclusion, but not before they have come up against many obstacles and disruptions that delay progress. Work is concentrated in short bursts of activity, and information gathering is characterized by the use of multiple sources, variability in information quality, and informal personal contacts. In sporadic processes, decision makers will find that "not all the information they get can be relied upon, so they and their staff will have to sift out that which they feel they have confidence in, and that which is better ignored. They will be drawn into bursts of activity in corridors and offices, in between the delays, when the matter is on everyone's mind and answers to questions are demanded there and then, until the excitement dies down as other things become even more pressing" (Hickson et al. 1986, p. 118). In contrast, *fluid decision processes* move along swiftly at a steady pace and make use of formal channels. Work is handled by committees and project groups, requiring decision makers to attend a greater number of meetings, but "far from getting in the way, these formally-arranged proceedings seem to facilitate a rapid conclusion" (p. 120). In fluid processes, fewer sources of expertise are consulted, and there is also less variability in the level of confidence of participants. *Constricted decision processes* are more narrowly channeled and are more restrained than the other two processes. Meetings and committees are still the mode, but there are fewer of them. Information seeking still involves multiple sources, but less effort is expended in acquiring information. These processes do not generate as much bustle because there is clarity about what information is required and how that information may be found.

The four *models of decision making* presented in this chapter are also characterized by distinctive approaches in information seeking. We show this in Fig. 5.7, which compares the *intensity* of information seeking across the four modes. By intensity we mean the depth and breadth of the information seeking, as well as the effort and resources that are consumed in the process. In the *rational mode,* information seeking is relatively low in intensity since it is guided by rules and routines that are designed to simplify the search process. Seeking is limited to local searches in the neighborhood of symptoms or recent experience and is driven by the appearance of well-defined stimuli or problems. In the *process mode,* information seeking is probably the most intense, mainly because there is little prior knowledge about available alternatives, or even about where to look for possibilities. Information gathering is spread out over time and iterates through many cycles, with a substantial amount of effort being expended during the development phase of the process. In the *political mode,* information seeking intensifies in order to gather and select information that supports a position or some preferred option. This may require a broad scan covering a number of sources, including expert or well-regarded sources. Moreover, information may need to be verified to ensure that it can withstand adversarial scrutiny. Information seeking may be selective and biased in favor of information that supports preferred options. In the *anarchy mode,* information seeking in the form of purposeful search is at a low level in the sense that solutions and alternatives are uncoupled from problems, and information leaves or enter decision situations with a certain degree of randomness.

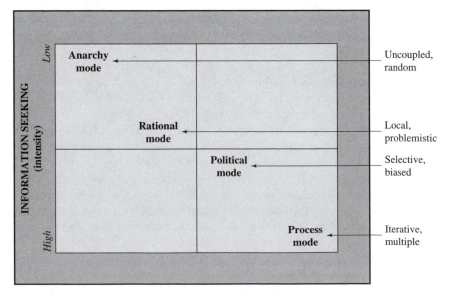

FIGURE 5.7. Information Seeking in Organizational Decision Making

Structure, incentives, and information access. Information availability and *access* is influenced by many institutional characteristics, notably the *organizational structure* that regulates information flow and *incentive systems* that reward the pursuit of certain goals and information. Hierarchy and specialization is a traditional means for organizations to increase their information-processing capacity to match task performance requirements (Galbraith 1973), but in some situations, hierarchy and specialization may impede or distort information flow. In a well-known study, Pettigrew (1972) described how a senior manager occupying a strategic position in the organizational structure was able to influence the board of directors' decision to purchase a large computer system through artfully gatekeeping the information reaching the directors. Besides structure, incentive systems influence information use by encouraging the transmission of certain types of information while discouraging the transmission of other types. Incentive systems also draw decision makers' attention to a few highly rewarded outcomes while excluding other important, possibly superior alternatives (O'Reilly, Chatman, and Anderson 1987). For example, O'Reilly et al. (1987) observed that "subordinates attempt to present themselves in a favorable light to those above them in the hierarchy and are willing to suppress certain important pieces of information while transmitting unimportant information if it reflects favorably on themselves" (p. 612).

Information Use in Decision Making

Information Use and Cognitive Needs

Cognitive simplifications. In an earlier section, we contrasted two views of *cognitive simplifications* that people use in making judgments and decisions. The heuristics and biases school found that people use mental shortcuts to reduce cognitive effort, but these heuristics can lead to errors and biases. Thus, decision makers may over-rely on the use of stereotypes, information that is easy to recall, and initial impressions or estimates (Tversky and Kahneman 1974; Gilovich et al. 2002). Many of these biases may be amplified in organizational decision situations, as when the subject matter is complex, the information is ambiguous, or time pressure or information overload forces decision makers to curtail their analysis. Another view believes that simple heuristics do in fact work well in enabling individuals to arrive at reasonable decisions (Gigerenzer et al. 1999). These heuristics exploit the ways that information is structured in different environments in order to find and use information cues that seem to work well for the problem at hand.

Eisenhardt and Sull (2001) studied dozens of firms that operated in turbulent, unpredictable environments and found many that made use of a few simple rules to decide what action to take. For example, when Cisco first moved to an acquisitions-led strategy, its rule was that it could acquire companies with at most 75 employees, 75 percent of whom would be engineers. In the mid-1980s, when Asian chip manufacturers were disrupting world markets, Intel followed a simple rule: allocate manufacturing capacity based on a product's gross margin.

At the Danish hearing-aid company Oticon, executives would pull the plug on a product in development if a key team member left for another project. Where do these rules come from? The study suggested that many grew out of experience, including mistakes. Here are two examples:

> Take Yahoo! and its partnership-creation rules. An exclusive joint venture with a major credit card company proved calamitous. The deal locked Yahoo! into a relationship with a particular firm, thereby limiting e-commerce opportunities. After an expensive exit, Yahoo! developed two simple rules for partnership creation: deals can't be exclusive, and the basic service is always free. . . . eBay, for example, started out with two strong values: egalitarianism and community— or, as one user put it, "capitalism for the rest of us." Over time, founder and chairman Pierre Omidyar and CEO Meg Whitman made those values explicit in simple rules that helped managers predict which opportunities would work for eBay. Egalitarianism evolved into two simple how-to rules for running auctions: the number of buyers and sellers must be balanced, and transactions must be as transparent as possible. (Eisenhardt and Sull 2001, pp. 110–11)

Selective information processing. Besides heuristics and shortcuts, human decision makers in organizational settings are also biased by their tendency to selectively seek out and use information that confirms their beliefs or supports their desired outcomes. This *selective processing* does not imply that decision makers abbreviate their information search, but rather decision makers seek more information than is required and use this information to increase their confidence in their choices (O'Reilly 1983). In organizational decision situations surrounded by high levels of uncertainty, "preferences for outcomes may be the least ambiguous component of the decision process, more certain than the definition of the problem, the range of feasible alternatives, or the probabilities associated with various alternatives" (O'Reilly 1983, p. 109). Decision makers may therefore reduce uncertainty by focusing on information that helps them to achieve preferred outcomes.

In public policy decisions, it is not uncommon for preferred outcomes to be selected first, and then for information to be gathered and presented to justify the desired alternative and outcome. Meltsner's (1976) study of policy analysts found two categories of information sought by decision makers: information used to *make* decisions and information used to *support* decisions that have already been made (pp. 72–79). Thus, decision makers would hire external consulting groups to do evaluation studies not for the purpose of discovering better alternatives but to garner expert support for options already chosen. A different situation is when information is *not used* in policy decision making. Based on research by herself and others, Feldman (1989) observes that "bureaucratic analysts work in a situation characterized most of the time by a lack of attention by decision makers or policy makers. Many reports they write are not read; many contracts they set up are not used; much expertise they acquire is not called upon. Decisions about policies seem to be made on the basis of politics and personal loyalties rather than the information and expertise that the analysts have to offer" (p. 93).

Information Use and Affective Responses

Groupthink and group polarization. Based on his analysis of well-documented fiascoes in policy decision making (including the Bay of Pigs invasion, the attack on Pearl Harbor, and the escalation of the Vietnam War), Janis (1982) attributed the errors to a tendency of people working in highly cohesive groups to seek concurrence to such an extent that it interferes with the vigilant processing of information. Janis (1982) coined the term *groupthink* to refer to "a mode of thinking that people engage in when they are deeply involved in a cohesive in-group, when the members' strivings for unanimity override their motivation to realistically appraise alternative courses of action" (p. 9). The symptoms of groupthink are divided into three types. First, group members share a feeling of invulnerability which leads to optimism and a willingness to take risks. Second, group members are close-minded, collectively rationalizing or discounting aberrant information and maintaining stereotyped views of opposing parties as weak and ineffectual. Third, group members press toward uniformity, sustaining a shared impression of unanimity through self-censorship as well as direct pressure against dissenting views. As a result of these affective illusions of invulnerability and solidarity, the group's seeking and use of information is compromised, and decision making becomes defective. Specifically, members fail to survey alternatives and objectives adequately; do not examine risks of preferred choice or reappraise alternatives that were initially rejected; search for information poorly; process information in a biased, selective way; and do not make contingency plans (Janis 1982). Groupthink is more likely when decision makers are members of a cohesive group, when organization structure insulates the group or lacks norms to require methodical procedures, and when the decision situation is highly stressful due to external and internal threats. Threats can cause the group to close ranks and rely on each other for social and emotional support, thereby heightening the desire to seek concurrence and consensus.

Groups can tend to make more-extreme decisions than individuals working alone. During group discussion we compare our decisions with the decisions of others. Initially we may think of ourselves as being fairly risk taking, especially when this is considered a valued trait in the organization or society. As discussion proceeds, we may realize that we are not particularly risk seeking compared to others in the group. We then increase the level of risk of our decision when asked to remake the decision. A reverse cautious shift (toward greater risk aversion) can occur in situations where caution rather than risk is the socially valued norm (Stoner 1968). This *group polarization* can be the result of informational factors and reputational factors (Sunstein 2003). The informational influence arises because people respond to arguments made by other people, and the argument pool in any group with some predisposition in one direction would be skewed in that direction. If a number of people seem to believe that some proposition is true, there is reason to believe that the proposition is in fact true. Most of what we know comes not from firsthand knowledge but from what we learn from what others do and think. The reputational influence arises because people want to be perceived favorably by others in the group and also to perceive themselves favorably. There is a pervasive human desire to enjoy the good opinion of others: if a number of people seem to believe something, there is an incentive not to disagree with them, at least not in public.

The relationship between group diversity and group performance is complex. Jehn, Northcraft, and Neale (1999) conducted a field study of 92 workgroups in one of the top three firms in the household goods moving industry. They analyzed the influence on workgroup performance of three types of diversity: social category diversity (sex, age), value diversity (goals, beliefs), and *information diversity*, which refers to differences in knowledge and perspectives that members bring as a function of differences in education, experience, and expertise. Information diversity is found to be more likely to lead to improved performance when tasks are nonroutine. Their general conclusion is that

> For a team to be effective, members should have high information diversity and low value diversity. For a team to be efficient, members should have low value diversity. For a team to have high morale (higher satisfaction, intent to remain, and commitment) or to perceive itself as effective, it should be composed of participants with low value diversity. What these consistent findings suggest is the value, for most measures of group performance, of low value diversity among members. (Jehn et al. 1999, p. 758)

Overcommitment in escalation situations. In some situations, decision makers become increasingly locked into failing courses of action. Decision makers continue to positively evaluate and pursue a course of action even when objective facts indicate withdrawal is necessary to reduce further losses. Our past decisions become what economists term *sunk costs*—old investments of time or money that are now irrecoverable. We know, rationally, that sunk costs are irrelevant to the present decision, but nevertheless they prey on our minds, leading us to make inappropriate decisions (Arkes and Blumer 1985). Organizations often find themselves in *escalation situations*, "where things have not only gone wrong, but where potential actions aimed at curing the problem can actually deepen or compound the difficulty" (Staw and Ross 1987, p. 40). A classic example of escalation is when an organization continues to pour resources into an ailing project rather than pulling the plug. (Two real-world case studies on escalation situations concern the world exposition [Expo 86] in Vancouver [Ross and Staw 1986], and Long Island Lighting Company's decision to build a nuclear power plant [Ross and Staw 1993].) Staw and Ross (1987) identify a number of psychological, social, and organizational factors that can induce escalation and overcommitment. An important psychological factor is the need for self-justification: in order to protect our own self-esteem, we may hang on or even allocate further resources to "prove" that the project is a success. Another psychological factor is biased information use. If facts challenge project viability, managers try to find reasons to discredit the information sources or the quality of the information. If the information is ambiguous, managers may only make use of favorable facts that support the project. In terms of social factors, managers persist in a project because they do not wish to expose their mistakes to others. They continue a project in order to justify the decision to others, to save face, and to avoid public admission of poor judgment. Culturally, we associate persistence with strong leadership, as implied in exhortations such as "staying the course," "weathering the storm," and "sticking to your guns." Persistence and determination is seen as a sign of leadership and withdrawal as a sign of weakness. An important organizational factor is administrative inertia. A decision to cancel a major project can be disruptive and expensive: it may require changing rules and policies, moving or firing people, litigating, or compensating for cancelled contracts, so much so that "killing a project is as costly as saving it." Another organizational factor is institutional embeddedness, which can happen if a long-standing project or line of business becomes closely identified with the organization. Stakeholder groups develop vested interests in the project. Reputations become tied to the project. In this case, decision makers may believe that "killing the project is like killing the very purpose of the organization."

Information Use and Situational Dimensions

Information use varies by decision mode. The four *models of decision making* presented in this chapter are also characterized by distinctive approaches in information use. We show this in Fig. 5.8, which compares the degree of *control in information use* across the four modes. By control we mean the effort that is expended in attempting to direct or influence the use of information. In the

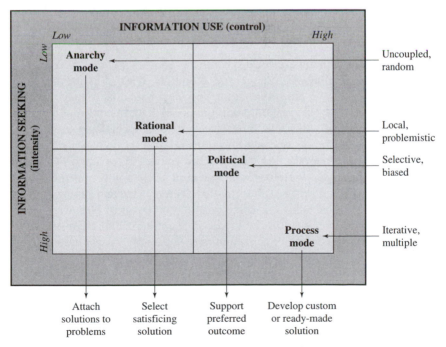

FIGURE 5.8. Information Use in Organizational Decision Making

rational mode, information use is relatively controlled, being guided by the principle of selecting an alternative that is good enough to pass acceptable criteria. In the *process mode,* information use is focused as repeated cycles of information processing converge on a solution which is a specific answer to a specific problem, and which has to be presented to and authorized by upper management. In the *political mode,* information use is highly controlled and directed as a political tactic to justify preferred outcomes. Information is selectively processed, so that information that contradicts assumptions or expectations is ignored or reinterpreted. In the *anarchic mode,* information use is uncontrolled, as solutions are attached to problems through happenstance and individual interest, and decisions are made by flight and oversight more often than by rational resolution.

Information handling rules. An important category of any organization's standard operating procedures is its *information-handling rules.* These rules direct and constrain the flow and use of information. In particular, information-handling rules define the characteristics of the input information taken into the organization; the rules for distributing and condensing the input information; and the characteristics of information leaving the organization (Cyert and March 1992, p. 127). As a result of these rules, not everyone in the organization seeks or receives all of the information the organization uses. The choice of who is to gather which information can be significant because the individual who encounters the information initially may also be the first to evaluate its relevance, determine its routing, and in general screen, condense, or highlight the information or some aspect of it. Cyert and March make clear that standard operating procedures direct information flow by setting *routing rules* and *filtering rules.* In routing information, many organizations follow the principle that "it is appropriate to process information through the hierarchy defined in terms of task specialization" (p. 129), since information needs are presumably tied to task specialization. In filtering information, each functional department (finance, personnel, production, sales) will select information using its specialized knowledge or view of the world. Routing and filtering rules interact to affect the seeking and availability of information: "What makes the routing rules important is their linkage with filtering at various communication relay points and the fact that there are dead ends in the routes. Information is condensed and summarized as it goes through the organization and some information never reaches some points" (Cyert and March 1992, p. 130). The increasing summarization of information as it travels up the levels of an organization is a well-known phenomenon. March and Simon (1993) call this *uncertainty absorption,* where "inferences are drawn from a body of evidence and the inferences, instead of the evidence itself, are then communicated. The successive editing steps that transform data obtained from a set of questionnaires into printed statistical tables provide a simple example of uncertainty absorption" (p. 186). While uncertainty absorption may reduce information load, the recipient is generally unable to judge its correctness but must trust the source and transformation process. As March and Simon quipped, the "facts" communicated may be disbelieved, but they can only rarely be checked (p. 187).

A different view of decision making is adopted in the research on *naturalistic decision making (NDM),* which focuses on decision making by skilled professionals such as firefighters, critical care nurses, pilots, nuclear power plant operators, and military personnel:

> The study of NDM asks how experienced people, working as individuals or groups in dynamic, uncertain, and often fast-paced environments, identify and assess their situation, make decisions and take actions whose consequences are meaningful in them and to the larger organization in which they operate. (Zsambok 1997, p. 5)

NDM analyzes real-world decision making in situations with these characteristics: problems are ill-structured; environment is uncertain and dynamic; goals are shifting, ill-defined, or competing; decisions are ongoing with action and feedback; time available is limited; stakes are high; multiple players are involved; and organizational goals and norms form the context. An important result of NDM is *recognition-primed decision making.* The model combines two processes: the way decision makers size up the situation to recognize which course of action makes sense, and the way they evaluate that course of action by imagining it (Klein 1998, p. 24). The basic strategy is that decision makers recognize the situation as typical and familiar; they understand what types of goals would make sense, which information cues are important to attend to, what to expect next, and the typical ways of responding in a given situation, including a course of action that is likely to succeed. Thus, decision makers do not start with goals and expectations and then analyze the situation. Instead, the recognition of goals, cues, expectancies, and actions is part of what it means to recognize a situation (Klein 1998, p. 25). Courses of action are quickly evaluated by imagining how they will be carried out, and not by formal analysis and comparison. By imagining the course of action, they can spot weaknesses and find ways to avoid these, thereby making the option stronger.

VIII. SUMMARY

- The ability of individuals in organizations to behave rationally is limited by their cognitive capacities, information constraints, and differences between personal values and organizational goals. The concept of *bounded rationality* is fundamental in the study of organizational decision making.

- Decision makers *"satisfice"* rather than maximize, that is, they choose an alternative that exceeds some criteria rather than the best alternative. They follow rules and routines that simplify the decision-making process by reducing the need for search, problem solving, or choice.

- All decisions are about finding and choosing courses of action in order to attain goals. The difficulty of making a decision then depends on how clear the goals are and how well we know about methods that can achieve the desired goals. All decision situations in organizations can be characterized by these two basic dimensions: *goal uncertainty* and *procedural uncertainty.*

- Depending on the level of goal and procedural uncertainty, organizational decision making may be analyzed using the rational model, process model, political model, or anarchic model.

- In the *rational model*, when both goals and available alternatives are clear, the organization reduces the uncertainty of decision making by specifying decision premises, rules, and routines (March and Simon 1993).

- The *process model* identifies the phases and activities that form the structure of many strategic decision processes. The quality of a decision process depends on the way a decision is framed and the way alternatives are developed (Mintzberg et al. 1976).

- Goal conflict is a fundamental cause of the exercise of power in decision making. In the *political model,* organizations respond to goal conflict in two generic ways: they behave as coalitions, and they pursue procedural rationality.

- In the *anarchic model,* a decision situation is like a garbage can into which various kinds of problems and solutions are dumped by participants as they are generated. A decision happens when problems, solutions, participants, and choices coincide (Cohen et al. 1972).

- *Information needs.* Organizational decision making requires information to reduce uncertainty in at least three ways: (1) to *frame* a choice situation, (2) to *define preferences* and to *select rules,* and (3) to identify available *courses of action* and assess their projected outcomes.

- *Information seeking.* Search is *satisficing* (March and Simon 1993): it stops when the first good-enough solution is found (rational decision model), or when ample evidence is gathered to support a preferred option (political decision model), or when courses are developed or investigated sufficiently to be presented for final evaluation (process decision model).

- *Information use.* Organizations guide the use of information by establishing decision *premises, rules, and routines* for different types of decision situations. Premises and rules define what information to attend to and what values to apply in evaluating alternatives (Simon 1997).

6

A TALE OF TWO ACCIDENTS

Oh! I have slipped the surly bonds of Earth
And danced the skies on laughter-silvered wings;
Sunward I've climbed, and joined the tumbling mirth
Of sun-split clouds, — and done a hundred things
You have not dreamed of — wheeled and soared and swung
High in the sunlit silence. Hov'ring there,
I've chased the shouting wind along, and flung
My eager craft through footless halls of air. . . .

Up, up the long, delirious burning blue
I've topped the wind-swept heights with easy grace
Where never lark, or ever eagle flew—
And, while with silent, lifting mind I've trod
The high untrespassed sanctity of space,
Put out my hand, and touched the face of God.
        —*John Gillespie Magee, Jr. (Pilot, Royal Canadian Air Force)*

The three preceding chapters looked at sense making, knowledge creation, and decision making. This chapter will consider how the interactions between the domains of meaning, knowing, and acting can both bolster and block learning in organizations. We start with a short statement of the dynamics between sense making, knowledge creation, and decision making, as shown in Fig. 6.1.

Sense making begins when organizations enact or bracket a significant change in the environment. Making sense of new signals is driven by the beliefs as well as the past actions and interpretations of the organization. The outcome of sense making is the perception of a problem (or opportunity), set against a flow of current and past constructions of meaning and purpose that are related to the perceived change. It is the combination of foreground problems and background meanings that forms the context for organizational action and reflection. *Knowledge creation* is set in motion when organizations face a consequential "knowledge gap" that needs to be filled or when new knowledge is needed to address a novel problem. Knowledge creation and use is an interplay of tacit and

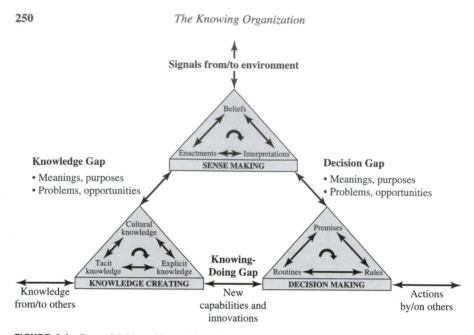

FIGURE 6.1. Sense Making, Knowledge Creating, and Decision Making in the Knowing Organization

explicit knowledge, situated in and shaped by shared norms and assumptions about what new information or knowledge would be worthwhile for the organization to pursue. The result of knowledge creation is new insight that can help the organization to make sense of a problem or new capabilities that enable decision makers to adopt a course of action. *Decision making* occurs when organizations are required to choose between courses of action—the organization faces a "decision gap." Decision making is both about respecting rules and premises that contain what has been learned from past experience and about recognizing situations where old assumptions no longer apply and new rules need to be constructed. The outcome of decision making is commitment to a course of action. Part of this commitment must rest on a shared understanding of the reasoning, interpretation, and knowledge that supports the selected option. Where this commitment is missing due to lack of trust and understanding, it becomes hard to act on the new knowledge, and we see a "knowing-doing gap."

In the following sections, we will use this framework to reflect on the two accidents that destroyed the space shuttle *Challenger* and *Columbia*. In many ways, we admire NASA as a learning organization par excellence—an organization with its accomplishments has demonstrated a prodigious capability to manage innovation and change. At the same time, the accidents, and how similar they appear to be, suggest a certain weakness in the capacity to learn. This weakness is not unique to NASA and may be an inherent element of all organizations characterized by complex structures, deeply held histories and cultures, and compartmentalized knowledge. We will take a detailed look at each accident, focusing on the interactions between meaning, knowing, and acting that can enable as well as impede learning. We will consider information-seeking and -use processes that underlay the construction of meaning and action and witness how structure, culture, politics, and human fallibility set the stage for the drama of organizational learning.

I. SPACE SHUTTLE *CHALLENGER* (1986)

On January 28, 1986, at 11:38 A.M. EST, the space shuttle *Challenger* (Flight STS 51-L) was launched from Cape Canaveral, Florida. The mission ended 73 seconds later when the *Challenger* disintegrated in a billowing cloud of fire and smoke. All seven crew members, including Christie McAuliffe ("America's teacher in space"), were killed in the explosion. The Presidential Commission investigating the accident subsequently determined that *Challenger* was destroyed after hot propellant gases flew past the aft joint of the shuttle's right solid rocket booster, burning through two synthetic rubber seal rings called O-rings and vaporizing the seal. The problems with the O-rings were not new. They had been known as early as 1977 and had been formally classified and documented as a critical, life-threatening problem for many years. NASA had in place a multi-level system of rules and routines, checks and balances to assess risk and control launch decisions. On the eve of the last flight of *Challenger,* concerns were raised repeatedly and vocally about the safety of the mission. Why was it that, despite the elaborate procedures and standards that had been put in place, the availability of information about the technical problems that caused the explosion, and the warnings and objections about the risks presented by the conditions of the launch, the mission was allowed to proceed?

The Commission concluded that "the decision to launch the *Challenger* was flawed." Specifically, it identified "failures in communication that resulted in a decision to launch 51-L based on incomplete and sometimes misleading information, a conflict between engineering data and management judgments, and a NASA management structure that permitted internal flight safety problems to bypass key Shuttle managers" (Presidential Commission 1986, p. 82). The U.S. House of Representatives conducted its own hearings and also concluded that "the fundamental problem was poor technical decision-making over a period of several years by top NASA and contractor personnel" (U.S. Congress 1986).

We suggest that the *Challenger* accident was more than a case of flawed decision making. In order to understand why the accident occurred, we need also to analyze how participants made sense of the stream of events and outcomes that preceded the launch, and why information and knowledge that could have averted the accident were not able to exercise their influence.

In 1973, Morton-Thiokol, Inc., won the bid to develop a solid rocket motor for NASA's space shuttle program. Thiokol then engineered the space shuttle's solid rocket booster (SRB) based on the Air Force's *Titan III* design because of its reliability. The SRB's steel case was divided into segments that were joined

The *Challenger* sits atop the eternal tank, flanked by solid rocket boosters (NASA Johnson Space Center STS51L(S)154 http://images.jsc.nasa.gov/lores/STS51L(S)154.jpg)

A side view, with the segmented solid rocket booster in the foreground (NASA Johnson Space Center S85-40032 http://images.jsc.nasa.gov/lores/S85-40032.jpg)

FIGURE 6.2. Space Shuttle *Challenger*

and sealed by rubber O-rings (Fig. 6.2). Although the *Titan*'s O-rings had occasionally been eroded by hot gases, the erosion was not regarded as significant. A second, redundant O-ring was added to each joint to act as backup should the primary O-ring fail. As early as 1977, a test of the SRB case showed an unexpected rotation of the joints which decompressed the O-rings, making it more difficult for them to seal the joints. In 1980, a review committee concluded that safety was not jeopardized and the joints were classified as Criticality 1R, denoting that joint failure could cause loss of life or shuttle (the 1 in the rating) but that the secondary O-rings provided redundancy (the R in the rating). In 1983, the SRBs were modified to use thinner walls, narrower nozzles, and more-powerful fuel, which worsened the joint rotation. Tests showed that the rotation could be so large that a secondary O-ring could not seal a joint and provide redundancy. The R rating was consequently removed from the joints' criticality classification. However, many NASA and Thiokol documents produced over the next three years continued to list the criticality as 1R and seemed to suggest that neither NASA nor Thiokol management had thought that a secondary O-ring could really fail to seal a joint (Starbuck and Milliken 1988b).

Closer to the time of Flight 51-L, the incidence of heat damage at the SRB joints was growing—three of the five 1984 flights showed heat damage, followed by eight of the nine 1985 flights, and the flight on January 12, 1986, just two weeks before the *Challenger* accident. In spite of these signals, the management of the SRB project at Marshall Space Flight Center and at Thiokol remained confident that the erosion was "allowable" and an "acceptable risk." The April 1985 flight

(STS 51-B) showed significant damage at one primary O-ring, with a substantial amount of hot gas blowing by this ring, which in turn eroded the secondary O-ring. This was the first instance of an erosion in a secondary O-ring: "What Thiokol found was alarming. The primary O-ring seal had been compromised because it eroded .171 inches and it did not seal. The secondary O-ring did seal, but it had eroded .032 inches [The diameter of each O-ring was .28 inches]" (Presidential Commission 1986, v.1, p. 137). Lawrence Mulloy (manager, Solid Rocket Booster Project at Marshall) said "this erosion of a secondary O-ring was a new and significant event . . . that we certainly did not understand. . . . here was a case where the primary O-ring was violated and the secondary O-ring was eroded, and that was considered to be a more serious observation than previously observed" (p. 137).

In view of the primary O-ring failure observed in STS 51-B, Mulloy placed a "launch constraint" on all subsequent flights, acknowledging that a problem of Criticality 1, 1R, 2, or 2R might occur. Nevertheless, the Commission found that: "After the launch constraint was imposed, Project Manager Mulloy waived it for each Shuttle flight after July 10, 1985. . . . Mulloy and Wear [solid rocket motor manager at Marshall] both testified that the constraint was still in effect and waived for *Challenger*'s flight" (pp. 137, 138). Mulloy later explained his waiver of the launch constraint for subsequent flights as follows:

> Since the risk of O-ring erosion was accepted and indeed expected, it was no longer considered an anomaly to be resolved before the next flight . . . I concluded that we're taking a risk every time. We all signed up for that risk. And the conclusion was, there was no significant difference in risk from previous launches. We'd be taking essentially the same risk on Jan. 28 that we have been ever since we first saw O-ring erosion. (Mulloy, quoted in Bell and Esch 1987, pp. 43, 47)

On the afternoon of January 27, 1986, the eve of the launch, the weather forecast predicted unusually cold weather for Florida, with temperatures at low 20s in the early hours of January 28. Thiokol engineers expressed concern that at such cold temperatures, the O-rings would harden and not seal the joints against the hot ignition gases. Two telephone conferences were held at three sites (Thiokol in Utah, Marshall SFC in Alabama, and Kennedy Space Center in Florida) on the evening of January 27 to discuss whether the launch should be delayed. Thirty-four engineers and managers participated in the second teleconference, where Thiokol engineers warned that at the forecast temperatures, the O-rings would seal more slowly than on the coldest launch to date, a January 1985 mission when the temperature was 53°F. At that launch, a primary O-ring was eroded so that it failed to seal, allowing hot gases to "blow by" to the secondary ring. Although the secondary ring did seal the joint then, the engineers argued that a more extensive blow-by could damage the secondary ring so that it would not seal. Someone at the teleconference then pointed out that one of the Thiokol data points showed blow-by at 75°F, suggesting that temperature was not the only factor. Roger Boisjoly, a Thiokol staff engineer specializing in O-rings, was asked what evidence existed to show that O-ring damage was the result of cold temperatures. Boisjoly replied that he could not quantify his concerns, that he had no data to quantify it, but that he knew "it was away from goodness in the current database" (Presidential Commission 1986, v. 4, p. 791).

Lawrence Mulloy asked Thiokol management for a recommendation. Thiokol's Joe Kilminster (vice president, Space Booster Programs) replied that he could not recommend a launch at any temperature below 53°F. Mulloy said that since booster joint temperatures had never been set as launch criteria, Thiokol was effectively trying to create new launch commit criteria on the eve of the launch. He then exclaimed, "My God, Thiokol, when do you want me to launch, next April?" (Presidential Commission 1986, v. 5, p. 843). George Hardy, Marshall's deputy director of science and engineering, added that he was "appalled" at the Thiokol recommendation, that the data presented did not con-clusively support a correlation between temperature and O-ring erosion, but that he would not agree to a launch against Thiokol's recommendation. The chal-lenges from both Mulloy and Hardy, worded in strong language, put pressure on the Thiokol engineers. Kilminster then asked for permission for Thiokol engi-neers and managers to go offline for a few minutes.

All participants who were asked why the offline caucus was called thought that it was because Thiokol's engineering analysis was weak:

> Thiokol's recommendation for 53°F as the baseline temperature for decision making was central to the controversy. . . . In the absence of a formalized, test-derived rule about O-ring temperature that also took into account pressure and sealing time, uncertainty prevailed. Thiokol created a rule, using the experience base: do not launch unless O-ring temperature is 53°F or greater. But people at Marshall and Kennedy were surprised at the choice of this number. First, it was contradicted by data from tests done at 30°F presented in Thiokol's own charts. . . . Second, it contradicted other temperature guidelines. There were serious differences about which ones applied. (Vaughan 1996, pp. 308, 309)

During the caucus, which lasted for about half an hour, Thiokol's senior vice president Jerald Mason stated that the possibility of blow-by and erosion had al-ways been present in the earlier flights and had been considered as acceptable risks. They should therefore consider the temperature issue separately on its own. Mason reaffirmed the belief in redundancy, that the primary O-ring would perform properly, but if it sealed slowly and blow-by occurred, then the sec-ondary O-ring would be in position and would seal. Boisjoly and another engi-neer (Arnold Thompson) defended the engineering position that based on the data they had, they did not know what the secondary O-ring would do in these cold temperatures. After several minutes of discussion Mason noted that they were starting to go over the same ground over and over again and said, "Well, it's time to make a management decision." Jerald Mason, Joe Kilminster, Calvin Wiggins (vice president and general manager, Space Division), and Bob Lund (vice president, Engineering) then conferred among themselves, effectively excluding the engineers from the decision making. Mason, Kilminster, and Wiggins supported a launch recommendation, but Lund hesitated. Mason said to Lund, "It's time to take off your engineering hat and put on your management hat." Lund then voted with the rest. When they were later asked why they had reversed their initial recommendation and changed their minds about the danger of a low-temperature launch, "all said that they were influenced by facts not taken into account before their initial recommendation. These facts supported redundancy: thus, they believed that the secondary would seal the joint" (Vaughan 1996, p. 319).

When the teleconference resumed, Kilminster summarized Thiokol's position. Although temperature effects were a concern, the data predicting blow-by were inconclusive. Erosion tests had indicated that the primary O-ring could sustain three times more erosion than that experienced in the previous worst case. Furthermore, even if the primary failed, the secondary as backup would still seal the joint. Stanley Reinartz (manager, Shuttle Projects Office at Marshall) then asked all participants of the teleconference whether there were disagreements or comments about Thiokol's recommendation. No one said anything. The teleconference ended at about 11:15 P.M. As part of normal NASA procedures, Mulloy asked Kilminster to fax a copy of the flight-readiness rationale and recommendation to Marshall and Kennedy. At 11:38 A.M. the following morning, the *Challenger* was launched. The ambient temperature was 36°F. Seconds later, the shuttle exploded, killing all on board.

Sense Making in the *Challenger* Case

In our discussion of sense making in Chapter 3, we noted that organizational sense making is driven more by beliefs than by evidence, so much so that information that is incompatible with deeply held beliefs is disadvantaged.

At NASA, the *Apollo* era and the achievement of putting the first man on the moon had instilled in the organization a "can do" self-image, a belief that NASA can accomplish any challenge that is put to it. The technical culture inherited from the *Apollo* era espoused the beliefs that NASA was committed to research, to in-house technical capability, to the acceptance of risk and failure; that NASA was staffed with exceptional people; and that it pursued a "frontiers of flight" mentality (McCurdy 1989). In this context, information suggesting catastrophic failure would be inconsistent with NASA's beliefs in its "can-do" image and "frontiers of flight" mentality and would in fact undermine NASA's perception of its identity, purpose, and record of achievements. It is also in this context that the fact that the shuttle had flown successfully 24 times becomes highly salient. Although some of these missions did show incidents of O-ring erosion, these flights had nevertheless returned safely.

There was a second set of beliefs shared by both NASA and Thiokol about the engineering design of the shuttle's solid rocket booster. The SRB is made up of three assemblies: the nose cone, the solid rocket motor, and the nozzle assembly (Fig. 6.2). Each solid rocket motor consists of four casting segments into which the propellant is poured (or cast). Casting segments are shipped in pieces by rail from Thiokol to Kennedy Flight Center, where the four segments are then assembled. Joints between the segments are called field joints. Joint sealing is

provided by two rubber O-rings with diameters of 0.28 inches which are installed, as received from Thiokol, during motor assembly (Presidential Commission 1986). The shared belief was that in the event of the first O-ring failing, the
second ring would provide full backup: "The Air Force's *Titan III* segmented
solid-fuel rocket inspired the Thiokol design for field joints on the space shuttle
booster. . . . While the *Titan* joint has one O-ring, the shuttle's joint has two—
a redundancy that left NASA and Thiokol confident that one, at least, would
seal" (Bell and Esch 1987, p. 42). It may be important to pause and consider the
robustness of this assumption, since we might expect that conditions leading to
failure in one O-ring would also bring about failure in the second.

In Weick's (1979b) model, sense making is precipitated by an ecological
change or a change in the environment—in this case, the unprecedented cold
temperatures on the morning of the launch. The sense making question here is
then, "What does the cold temperature mean for the shuttle mission and its
safety?" Sense making begins with enactment, as people selectively bracket and
notice information in order to make sense of it. On the eve of the launch, the teleconference group wanted to understand if there was a relationship between cold
temperatures and O-ring erosion. To focus the discussion, data from a number of
past flights sustaining O-ring damage were bracketed and isolated for closer
analysis: "The managers compared as a function of temperature the flights for
which thermal stress of O-rings had been observed [Fig. 6.3]. . . . In such a comparison, there is nothing irregular in the distribution of O-ring 'distress' over the
spectrum of joint temperatures at launch between 53 degrees Fahrenheit and
74 degrees Fahrenheit. When the entire history of flight experience is considered,
including 'normal' flights with no erosion or blow-by, the comparison is substantially different [Fig. 6.4]" (Presidential Commission 1986, p. 145). In Fig. 6.3,
the data on flights with O-ring erosion showed no obvious relationship between
temperature and ring erosion. However, in Fig. 6.4, the inclusion of data on
flights with no ring erosion provided a baseline, a context for making sense of the
data that did show erosion. While we still cannot say whether O-ring erosion
is related to cold temperatures, we can say that all no-incident flights were

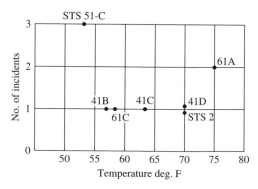

FIGURE 6.3. Plot of Flights with O-ring Damage (Presidential Commission 1986, Fig. 7,
p. 146)

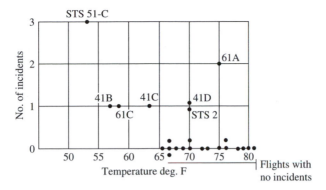

FIGURE 6.4. Plot of Flights with and Without O-ring Damage (Presidential Commission 1986, Fig. 7, p. 146)

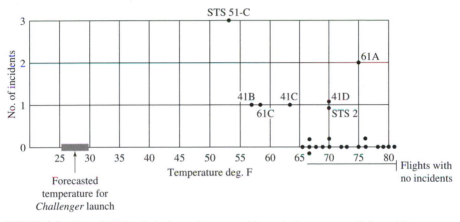

FIGURE 6.5. Plot of Flights Relative to Forecasted Launch Temperature (Adapted from Tufte 1997, p. 45)

launched at warmer temperatures. In Fig. 6.5, Tufte (1997) shows vividly how the predicted cold launch temperature is outside of NASA's experience base.

Knowledge Creation in the *Challenger* Case

The Presidential Commission investigating the *Challenger* accident concluded that "neither Thiokol nor NASA responded adequately to internal warnings about the faulty seal design. Furthermore, Thiokol and NASA did not make a timely attempt to develop and verify a new seal after the initial design was shown to be deficient. Neither organization developed a solution to the unexpected occurrences of O-ring erosion and blow-by even though this problem was experienced frequently during the Shuttle flight history. Instead, Thiokol and NASA management came to accept erosion and blow-by as unavoidable and an acceptable flight risk" (Presidential Commission 1986, p. 148).

The findings of the Commission beg the question why NASA and Thiokol did not attempt to change the design of the booster joints knowing that there were problems with the sealing action at the joints. The shuttle booster's joint was based on a reliable *Titan III* rocket design used by the Air Force for many years. It employed the same synthetic rubber (Viton) as the *Titan,* and it had essentially the same cross-sectional size. In the shuttle design, a second O-ring was added to back up the first, thereby providing redundancy. It was assumed that the shuttle joint would behave like the similar joint on the *Titan* boosters. Thiokol's Joe Kilminster expressed the feeling that

> In an overall sense, the comfort zone, if you will, was expanded because of the
> fact that the shuttle joint was so similar to the *Titan* joint, and its many uses
> had shown successful operation. That's why a lot of—I guess "faith" is the right
> word—was based on the fact that the *Titan* had had all these tests and successful
> experience. . . . We felt we could only be in a more safe condition having two
> O-rings there than with a single O-ring. (Kilminster, quoted in Bell and Esch
> 1987, p. 44)

On the tenth shuttle flight (STS 41-B, February 3, 1984), O-rings on both nozzle joints of the solid rocket motor showed erosion. The problem was reported at an early flight readiness review for the next flight. The problem assessment system at Marshall reported that no remedial action was required but noted that the possibility existed for some O-ring erosion on future flights. Thiokol ran a computer analysis that showed the O-rings would still seal even if they eroded by as much as 0.09 inch, or nearly a third of the O-ring diameter (0.28 inch). Thiokol concluded that this was not a constraint to future launches. These findings led Lawrence Mulloy to introduce the idea that a certain amount of erosion was "acceptable" since the O-rings contained a margin of safety (Bell and Esch 1987, p. 42).

In 1985, some Thiokol engineers grew increasingly concerned about the frequency of O-ring erosion, especially after the results of STS 51-B (April 29, 1985), which showed damage in both primary and secondary O-rings. An unofficial group at Thiokol was instructed to resolve the O-ring problems in July. This group came up with a number of new designs for the joints to deal with the sealing problem. In August, Thiokol formally instituted a Nozzle O-ring Investigation Task Force. By October, however, one task force member was dismayed enough to write a note to Allen McDonald (director, Solid Rocket Motor Project at Thiokol): "Help! The seal task force is constantly being delayed by every possible means. . . . This is a red flag." Roger Boisjoly also went to Joe Kilminster "pleading for help" but found that "Kilminster just didn't basically understand the problem. We were trying to explain it to him, and he just wouldn't hear it. He felt, I guess, that we were crying wolf" (Bell and Esch 1987, p. 45).

In Chapter 4, we discussed the role of cultural knowledge in knowledge creation. Cultural knowledge consists of the organizational assumptions and beliefs that influence the perception of knowledge gaps and determine the importance

3 assumptions ✓

and value of new information. Thiokol and NASA's interpretation of the O-ring problems seemed to have been shaped by the assumptions that (1) the O-ring design was derived from a tried-and-true model, (2) the addition of a second O-ring provided full redundancy, and (3) a certain amount of distress in the O-ring was an acceptable risk. These assumptions appeared to be behind the failure to fully and expeditiously address the O-ring erosion problem as a recurrent issue that was poorly understood.

During the teleconference on the eve of the *Challenger* launch (January 27, 1986), engineers familiar with O-ring erosion raised their objections: they were worried about how the low temperatures anticipated at launch time would affect the ability of O-rings to seal properly. Although they felt strong strongly about this risk, they were unable to articulate their tacit fears and concerns in a form that was meaningful, understandable, and persuasive to the managers taking part in the teleconference. In a testimony to the Commission, Roger Boisjoly (member, Seal Task Force, Thiokol) expressed his recollection of the second teleconference on January 27:

> I was asked, yes, at that point in time I was asked to quantify my concerns [about temperature effects on O-ring ability to seal properly], and I said I couldn't. I couldn't quantify it, but I did say I knew that it was away from goodness in the current database. Someone on the net commented that we had soot blow-by on SRM 22 [Flight 61-A, October 1985] which launched at 75 degrees. . . . I then said that SRM-15 [Flight 51-C, January 1985] had much more blow-by indication and that it was indeed telling us that lower temperature was a factor. This was supported by inspection of flown hardware by myself. I was asked again for data to support my claim, and I said I have none other than what is being presented. . . .
>
> Others in the room presented their charts, and the main telecon session concluded with Bob Lund, who is our Vice President of Engineering, presenting his conclusions and recommendations. . . .
>
> The conclusion was we should not fly outside our database, which was 53 degrees. Those were the conclusions. And we were quite pleased because we knew in advance, having participated in the preparation, what the conclusions were, and we felt very comfortable with that. (Presidential Commission 1986, v. 1, pp. 89–90)

Others in the teleconference were not as pleased with the conclusions and recommendations. Technical arguments in flight readiness reviews were supposed to be rigorous and quantifiable. Subjective assessments were untested hypotheses that required lab work and tests before they were admitted as evidence. Vaughan (1996) summarized the situation as follows: "Thiokol was trying to establish a correlation based on observed blow-by on two missions. The basis of Boisjoly's argument was that the *quality* of the damage was worse on the January 1985 launch because the *putty looked different* than in other instances of blow-by. Not only was this an intuitive argument according to NASA standards (because it was based on observation), but Thiokol's comparison of SRM-15 and SRM-22—the linchpin of their position—did not support a correlation: blow-by occurred on the one motor at 53 deg. F and on the other at 75 deg. F"

(Vaughan 1996, p. 355, italics in original). At the teleconference, Thiokol was seen as trying to create a new launch commit criterion at the last moment. Mulloy had exclaimed, "My God, Thiokol, when do you want me to launch, next April?"

Applying the knowledge conversion model of Nonaka and Takeuchi (1995), the teleconference exchanges suggest that the engineers most knowledgeable about O-rings were not able to convert their tacit knowledge into a more explicit form that could influence decision making. Managers, on the other hand, were demanding formal, hard, quantitative data to a problem that was not well understood. During the teleconference, engineers were being put in unusual position of having to prove that the shuttle was unsafe. Boisjoly and a colleague felt that

> This was a meeting where the determination was to launch, and it was up to us to prove beyond a shadow of a doubt that it was not safe to do so. This is the total reverse to what the position usually is in a preflight conversation or a flight readiness review. It is usually exactly opposite that. (Presidential Commission 1986, v. 1, p. 93)

[handwritten marginal note: should have proved safe to launch]

Decision Making in the *Challenger* Launch

The SRB workgroup of engineers and managers from Thiokol and NASA repeatedly used a decision-making sequence to develop rules and premises that supported their central belief about redundancy and allowed them to reinterpret information that deviated from an acceptable standard (Vaughan 1996). The decision routine consisted of five steps:

1. Signals of potential danger
2. Official act acknowledging escalated risk
3. Review of evidence
4. Official act indicating the normalization of deviance: accepting the risk; and
5. Shuttle launch.

(Vaughan 1996, p. 65)

This decision sequence had been used many times before to deal with O-ring problems in the past. Each time, the shuttle had returned safely, even though on some flights O-ring damage had been observed. This repeated use of the decision routine created precedents. These precedents turned a recurring problem into an acceptable risk. Bell and Esch (1987) observed that flight readiness briefings throughout 1984 and 1985 showed Thiokol and NASA becoming more and more sanguine. At the level I review for the 13th flight (STS 41-G) on September 26, 1984, management referred to "allowable erosion." At a meeting on February 12, 1985, NASA and Thiokol personnel spoke of the observed blow-by in two field joints in STS 51-C as an "acceptable risk." Over time, a decision premise was established to proceed with the launch while acknowledging a known risk.

On January 27, 1986, the five-step decision sequence was enacted once again. The predicted cold weather was a signal of potential danger, creating uncertainty about the relationship between O-ring resiliency and redundancy. Arranging the teleconference was an official act of acknowledging escalated risk. There followed a review of the evidence, culminating in an official act indicating the normalization of deviance: accept risk. The decision was followed by the destruction of STS 51-L. (Vaughan 1996, p. 379)

Thus, the danger signals (cold temperatures and O-ring erosion) were registered but reperceived as allowable risk, because the shuttle had flown successfully even with signs of O-ring damage. Over the experience of several successful shuttle flights, the group had become desensitized and had grown to see O-ring damage not as a recurrent problem but as an allowable risk that was not a threat to safety.

Vaughan (1996) believed that routines can normalize potentially dangerous signals as "normal acceptable risk" in highly innovative projects. She did not think that people had necessarily done their jobs improperly or violated NASA procedures. Rather, Vaughan saw a flawed decision culture in which most participants gradually demoted their concerns, causing major problems to devolve into lower-level issues. There was an "incremental descent into poor judgment." This gradual lowering of standards of acceptable risk is reminiscent of the satisficing behavior in organizational decision making described by March and Simon (1993). The Rogers Commission concluded that NASA and Thiokol had accepted escalating risk apparently because they "got away with it last time." Richard Feynman (member of the Commission) noted that the decision making was

a kind of Russian roulette. . . . [The shuttle] flies [with O-ring erosion] and nothing happens. Then it is suggested, therefore, that the risk is no longer so high for the next flights. We can lower our standards a little bit because we got away with it last time. (Presidential Commission 1986, p. 148)

This drift of decision behavior toward satisficing is abetted by forces in the NASA decision environment due to the growing pressures for bureaucratic and political accountability (Vaughan 1996). After Ronald Reagan became U.S. president, NASA, along with other government agencies, was urged to increase its use of external business contractors. This required NASA to create and expand administrative structures to coordinate and control complicated contractor relationships, causing NASA to acquire the characteristics of *bureaucratic accountability*. At about the same time, *political accountability* became necessary to garner support for funding the space shuttle program. The program was approved on the promise of providing economical, routine spaceflight, and the program was to be developed on a commercial, pay-its-own-way basis. In the ensuing years, NASA continued to push a production schedule that perpetuated this promise, although a wide gap separated this vision and the realities of the program's technical uncertainty and rising costs. The workload increased with the number of launches per year and made the goals of the original technical culture more difficult to realize. The overall effect was that the decisions from 1977 to

1985 were, "to those in the work group making the technical decisions, normal within the cultural belief systems in which their actions were embedded. Continuing to recommend launch in FRR [Flight Readiness Review] despite problems with the joint was not deviant; in their view, their conduct was culturally approved and conforming" (Vaughan 1996, p. 236).

Looking at the history leading up to *Challenger*'s last flight, our analysis suggests that to understand the decision to launch the shuttle is to understand how that decision was buttressed by a cumulative infrastructure of beliefs, interpretations, knowledge, and norms that had taken root at Thiokol and NASA. We noted that with its can-do self-image, NASA believed it could surmount any technical challenge that was put to it. Both NASA and Thiokol believed that the two O-rings in the rocket booster provided safe redundancy. O-ring erosion was known as early as 1977 and was classified as a critical and life-threatening issue, but a solution to the problem was not found. Although the recurring problem was not well understood, the shuttle had flown and returned safely on all prior occasions, and this formed the premise for making launch decisions. On the eve of the launch, we saw how engineers were unable to convert their tacit concerns into explicit messages that could influence decision making. At one level, there was the recognition that *risk was inherent* in the type of pioneering, innovative work that NASA was doing. At another level, *risk was being routinized* through the repeated use of premises and rules that became normal practice. It was not managers breaking rules that brought about the tragedy. Rather, it was the stabilization of a pattern of beliefs and understandings about the identity and history of the organization, what knowledge it was applying, what knowledge it needed to pursue, and the nature of the risks and uncertainty that accompanied launch decisions:

> It can truly be said that the Challenger launch decision was a rule-based decision.
> But the cultural understandings, rules, procedures, and norms that always had
> worked in the past did not work this time. It was not amorally calculating
> managers violating rules that were responsible for the tragedy. It was conformity.
> (Vaughan 1996, p. 386)

Information Seeking and Use

The Rogers Commission noted a lack of communication between Thiokol engineers doing technical work and top NASA managers who made launch decisions. "This breakdown meant that no information flowed on known problems with booster joints—not only during the decision to launch Challenger, but also during the entire design and development process" (Bell and Esch 1987, p. 49). An example of information not being shared is in the following testimony from Mulloy about not seeing Boisjoly's letter warning of O-ring failure:

> DR. WALKER [Arthur Walker, Jr., member of the Commission]: Mr. Mulloy,
> yesterday there was a letter which was made public, which was written by
> Mr. Boisjoly to his superiors, which predicted that unless the seal problem was

addressed a catastrophe was possible. And it's my impression that Mr. Boisjoly is the most knowledgeable engineer at Thiokol in regard to the seals. Now, was any warning or flavor of that very serious letter transmitted to anyone at NASA, to your knowledge?

MR. MULLOY: No, sir, not that letter. And I guess I wouldn't have expected it to be. That is a correspondence that occurs between an engineer and perhaps his section chief, and I wouldn't expect that type of correspondence to go up the line.

GENERAL KUTYNA [Donald Kutyna, another Commission member]: Larry, I have a problem with that. You had a briefing in July that talks about resiliency, you've got a briefing in August at NASA headquarters that talks about resiliency of those seals as a number one concern. Now, how can you say that wasn't transmitted to NASA?

MR. MULLOY: The memo.

GENERAL KUTYNA: I know the memo. But his concern is what Dr. Walker was asking.

DR. WALKER: Or the flavor of that.

MR. MULLOY: Yes, sir. I have looked back at that briefing. That is one of the things on the title sheet.

GENERAL KUTYNA: It's on the conclusion sheet: "Conclusions: primary concerns, resiliency."

MR. MULLOY: Yes, sir. And what I have looked at in that report is for the substance behind that, and I can't find it.

(Presidential Commission 1986, v. 5, pp. 1548–49)

Information seeking and use appeared to have been influenced by a differentiation between engineering roles and management roles, which in turn created a division of information roles. This was made most evident during the offline caucus at Thiokol, when Jerald Mason said to Bob Lund and others present that "Well, it's time to make a management decision. . . . It's time to take off your engineering hat and put on your management hat." Roger Boisjoly at Thiokol, Ben Powers at NASA, and other technical staff saw themselves as loyal employees, believing in the chain of command. Ben Powers had said in an interview: "You don't override your chain of command. My boss was there; I made my position known to him; he did not choose to pursue it. At the point it's up to him; he doesn't have to give me any reasons; he doesn't work for me; it's his prerogative" (Bell and Esch 1987, p. 49). At least two others asked by the Rogers Commission why they did not voice their concerns to someone other than their immediate superior replied, "That would not be my reporting channel." The engineering profession had institutionalized the norms of the legitimacy of bureaucratic authority, conformity to rules, and the need for compromise between administrative and technical constraints. To a degree, the SRB engineers adhered to the strict reporting procedures of the Flight Readiness Reviews that spanned four levels of project management and recognized that the balancing of cost, schedule, and safety was a necessary criterion by which NASA would approve change processes.

In her extensive analysis of the accident, Vaughan (1996) concluded that a major organizational factor was the hiding of information about the seriousness of the O-ring problem through *structural secrecy,* which she defines as the way that patterns of information, organizational structure, processes, and transactions systematically undermine the attempt to know and interpret situations in all organizations (Vaughan 1996, p. 238). Structural secrecy implies that "(a) information and knowledge will always be partial and incomplete, (b) the potential for things to go wrong increases when tasks or information crosses boundaries, and (c) segregated knowledge minimizes the ability to detect and stave off activities that deviate from normal standards and expectations" (Vaughan 1999, p. 277). At NASA, structural secrecy affected information use by three groups: the SRB workgroup, NASA top management, and the safety regulators.

For the *SRB workgroup members* (NASA and Thiokol managers and staff), the repetition of the five-step decision process in dealing with anomalies meant that signals initially seen as deviant were reinterpreted in the context of past decision streams which had construed similar signals as acceptable risks. Vaughan noted that these signals accumulated incrementally over time, and their significance was unclear because the signals were mixed, weak, and repeated so that they became routine.

For NASA's *top managers,* information was systematically censored through the effects of official organizational practices, specialization, and the reliance on signals. It was the official practice to progressively reduce the package of data charts and materials for management review as it worked its way through the four levels of Flight Readiness Review (FRR)—typically, the package first presented to level IV FRR would be about a half-inch thick, but this would be shrunk to 10–15 pages when it reached level I FRR (Vaughan 1996). For the information that did get through, the ability of level II and I administrators to interpret the information was constrained by the fact that though they were also trained as engineers, they now had broad administrative responsibilities that were more administrative than technical. While the information had been condensed, time available to read the packages was limited, and some level II and I administrators relied totally on oral presentations and the signals they received during the FRR sessions themselves.

The third group affected by structural secrecy were the *safety regulators.* NASA had both internal and external safety units. Internal units relied on NASA for staff, information, and resources, and this dependence diminished their ability to monitor and surface safety problems. Of the two internal regulators, NASA cut 71 percent of the staffing of one unit between 1970 and 1986 and discontinued the other unit when the space shuttle became operational. The external advisory panel consisted of nine aerospace industry leaders who theoretically would have been able to assess safety issues with autonomy. Unfortunately, the panel's breadth of responsibilities and lack of time meant that it could not be expected to uncover all potential problems.

Our discussion here suggests that organizational structure, a division of information roles, a reliance on reporting channels, and the compartmentalization of knowledge are all important elements of NASA's information environment. While these features can promote efficiency and coordination, in this case they also blocked information flow and attenuated signals about the O-ring problem, hiding and diluting information so that the signals of potential danger lost their ability to overturn the dominant belief about redundancy.

Summary

Fig. 6.6 shows the dynamics of sense making, knowledge creation, decision making, and information use in the *Challenger* case. In sense making, NASA and Thiokol engineers and managers maintained a self-image and a dominant ideology that allowed them to continue to select and retain schemas and rules that enacted interpretations which were no longer valid. With 24 successful shuttle launches behind them, the belief that the secondary O-rings provided redundancy seemed sufficiently vindicated. On the eve of the launch, a specific problem was bracketed—the exceptionally cold temperatures forecasted for the following morning and the impact on O-ring performance. NASA and Thiokol were confronted with two sets of uncertainties: (1) Will the O-rings fail to seal properly? (knowledge gap) (2) How do we make the right decision in the light of this new risk? (decision gap).

Although the O-ring problem had been recognized for many years, there was no concerted effort to fully analyze and address all of the contingencies that

uncertainties [handwritten annotation in right margin]

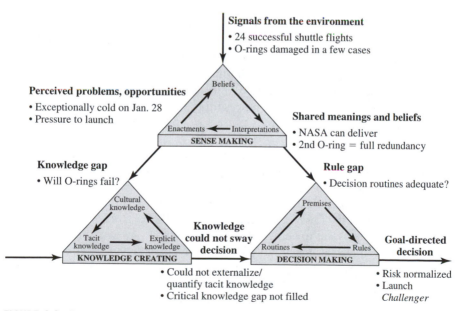

FIGURE 6.6. Sense Making, Knowledge Creating, and Decision Making in the *Challenger* Accident (1986)

could lead to a failure of the O-rings. On the eve of the launch, there was no data to quantify the concerns about ring behavior in cold temperatures. Roger Boisjoly, a staff engineer knowledgeable about the O-rings, had warned that the quality of the damage on the January 1985 launch was severe but he could not quantify his concerns. NASA management heard this as an intuitive argument that was not substantively supported. Because of the inability to convert this tacit knowledge, the warning signals remained weak and confused and could not challenge the prevailing belief about O-ring redundancy. In decision making, the process was dominated by rules, norms, and precedents that allowed engineers and managers to routinize warning signals as acceptable risks. Through a repetitive pattern of decision and rule making, engineers and managers reconstructed their decision premises of what constituted acceptable risks. Information flow was blocked and information was concealed as a consequence of the organization's structural attributes, including the bureaucratic decision and review procedures that stressed conformity and compromise and the functional specialization that limited information flow between administrators and engineers.

II. SPACE SHUTTLE *COLUMBIA* (2003)

On February 1, 2003, 17 years after the loss of *Challenger,* the space shuttle *Columbia* (Flight STS-107) developed a series of problems on its left wing while re-entering the atmosphere. Soon after 8:45 A.M., the shuttle broke up over Texas, killing all seven astronauts onboard. The *Columbia* Accident Investigation Board concluded that the physical cause of the loss of *Columbia* and its crew was a breach in the thermal protection system on the leading edge of the left wing. The breach was initiated by a piece of insulating foam that had separated from the left bipod ramp of the external tank and struck the wing 81.9 seconds after launch. During re-entry, this breach in the thermal protection system allowed superheated air to penetrate the leading-edge insulation and progressively melt the aluminum structure of the left wing, resulting in a weakening of the structure until increasing aerodynamic forces caused loss of control, failure of the wing, and breakup of the orbiter.

Dr. Sally Ride, the first American woman in space and the only member of the *Columbia* Accident Investigation Board (CAIB) who had a similar role in the *Challenger* accident, felt that she was "hearing a little bit of an echo here," that history seemed to be repeating itself (*New York Times,* April 13, 2003). Diane Vaughan, author of the *Challenger* study and a CAIB expert witness, said that the similarities became clear to her when she read reports of long-standing problems with falling foam and watched NASA officials explain at news conferences that NASA had decided the occasional foam damage was a risk NASA had grown comfortable with. The similarities between *Challenger* and *Columbia* were evident. There was a long-standing problem with a particular component: the problem of insulation foam on the external tank falling and damaging the shuttle was known as early as 1981. There were repeated warnings about significant damage

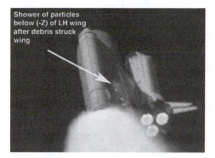

FIGURE 6.7. Foam Hits Orbiter Wing during Launch (NASA Photo KSC-03PD-0250: http://mediaarchive.ksc.nasa.gov)

FIGURE 6.8. Breach in Orbiter Wing (CAIB Photo by Rick Stiles 2003; http://www.caib.us/photos/view3ad4.html)

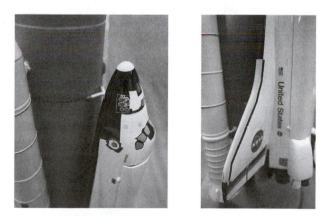

FIGURE 6.9. Model of Bipod Connecting ET and Orbiter; Left Wing of Orbiter (http://www.caib.us/photos/photo_index_itemd2ce.html)

caused by foam from a specific area of the external tank in 1983, 1990, 1992, and 2002. Engineers were highly concerned about the risk of serious damage from foam strikes but were unable to acquire or articulate the knowledge to sway decision making. Managers became desensitized about foam loss and thought of it as a maintenance issue. All these seem to suggest that not much had changed

Engineers

Managers desensitized

since the *Challenger* accident. The same questions may be asked: How does an organization make sense of mixed, ambiguous signals? How can an organization be vigilant about the way that it creates and applies knowledge? How can we learn from experience?

Sense Making in the *Columbia* Case

In this section, we discuss how (1) repeated cycles of sense making about past foam-loss problems led to the construction of beliefs about the nature of risks posed by these events; (2) the significant foam strike during the launch of *Columbia* was bracketed for further analysis; and (3) engineers and managers had formed different beliefs and expectations about the foam strike, and these fundamentally affected the ways they interpreted information about the foam strike.

Early in the Space Shuttle Program foam shedding was perceived as a dangerous problem: "design engineers were extremely concerned about potential damage to the Orbiter and its fragile Thermal Protection System, parts of which are so vulnerable to impacts that lightly pressing a thumbnail into them leaves a mark" (CAIB 2003, p. 121). Because of these concerns, the baseline design requirements of the shuttle specifically *precluded* the shedding of debris from the external tank or other parts of the shuttle. Despite these requirements, *Columbia* sustained debris damage on its inaugural flight in 1981, when more than 300 tiles had to be replaced. Foam falling from the external tank's forward bipod attachment, which connects the orbiter to the external tank, turned out to be especially worrisome, because they were some of the largest pieces of debris that had struck the orbiter. Every known instance of foam shedding from this area was examined by CAIB. Foam loss from the left bipod ramp was confirmed in 7 missions (approximately 10 percent of flights—7 events out of 72 imaged flights).

The *first* known bipod ramp foam loss occurred during STS-7 (June 18, 1983): a 19-inch by 12-inch piece of the left bipod ramp was missing, and the external tank showed a total of 65 divots in its foam covering. The foam loss was classified as an "in-flight anomaly," meaning that the problem must be resolved before the next launch. At the Flight Readiness Review for the next mission, this anomaly was "closed," or considered resolved. Although the closure documents described repairs made to the orbiter, there was no reference to foam shedding as the cause of the damage. The *second* bipod ramp foam loss occurred during STS-32R (January 9, 1990): the orbiter sustained 111 hits, 13 of which were one inch or greater in size. An in-flight anomaly was assigned and closed out at the review for the following mission. The *third* bipod ramp foam loss occurred on STS-50 (June 25, 1992): a 26-inch by 10-inch piece had separated from the left bipod ramp, causing the largest extent of tile damage in shuttle history. The foam loss was cited an in-flight anomaly by the Integration Office at Johnson Space Center *and* the External Tank Project at Marshall Space Flight Center. The Integration Office closed out its anomaly by deeming damage to the thermal protection system an "accepted flight risk." The External Tank Project closed out its anomaly stating that foam loss during ascent was "not considered a flight or safety issue" (CAIB 2003, p. 124). The *fourth* and *fifth* bipod ramp foam loss events (STS-52, October 22, 1992; STS-62, March 4, 1994) were initially undetected. They were revealed only after NASA was directed to review all available imagery for other instances of bipod foam shedding.

The *sixth* bipod ramp foam incident occurred on STS-112 (October 7, 2002): a 4- by 5- by 12-inch section of the left bipod ramp was lost, causing a 3- by 4-inch hole on the external tank attachment ring. The impact was captured by ground cameras filming the launch. The Intercenter Photo Working Group recommended that the foam loss be classified an in-flight anomaly. However, "in a meeting chaired by Shuttle Program Manager Ron Dittemore and attended by many of the managers who would be actively involved with STS-107 [*Columbia*], including Linda Ham, the Program Requirements Control Board ultimately decided against such classification. Instead, . . . [the] Chairman assigned an 'action' to the External Tank Project to determine the root cause of the foam loss and to propose corrective action. This was inconsistent with previous practice, in which all other known bipod foam-shedding was designated as In-Flight Anomalies" (CAIB 2003, p. 125). Moreover the due date for the action slipped past the launch and return of STS-107. Had the STS-112 foam loss been classified as a more serious threat, managers might have reacted differently to the foam strike in the last flight of *Columbia,* only two missions after STS-112:

> The Board wondered why NASA would treat the STS-112 foam loss differently from all others. What drove managers to reject the recommendation that the foam loss be deemed an In-Flight Anomaly? Why did they take the unprecedented step of scheduling not one but eventually two missions to fly before the External Tank Project was to report back on foam losses? It seems that Shuttle managers had become conditioned over time to not regard foam loss or debris as a safety-of-flight concern. (CAIB 2003, p. 125)

In the Flight Readiness Review of STS-113, the mission after STS-112, the foam-shedding problem was reported on. Briefing slides concluded that foam loss from the external tank had never been a "safety-of-flight" issue; that the probability of foam loss is no different than previous flights; and that **the ET is safe to fly with no new concerns (and no added risk)**" (CAIB 2003, p. 125, bold text as in original slide).

After discussion, STS-113 Flight Readiness Review participants finally agreed that foam shedding should be viewed as an "accepted risk" rather than a "safety-of-flight issue," and approved the flight readiness clearance for STS-113.

> The acceptance of the rationale to fly cleared the way for *Columbia*'s launch and provided a method for Mission managers to classify the STS-107 foam strike as a maintenance and turnaround concern rather than a safety-of-flight issue. It is significant that in retrospect, several NASA managers identified their acceptance of this flight rationale as a serious error. (CAIB 2003, p. 126)

The history of 113 missions that had flown, with foam loss in a few flights that nevertheless returned safely, combined with the precedent of labeling foam strike as an accepted risk led to the construction of the shared belief that foam strike was a maintenance issue that would affect shuttle turnaround time but not the safety of the shuttle itself.

On January 17, 2003, the day after *Columbia*'s launch, the Intercenter Photo Working Group examined film and video images of the shuttle's ascent and identified a large debris strike to the leading edge of *Columbia*'s left wing. Intercenter Photo Working Group (IPWG) members alerted senior program managers by phone and sent a digitized clip of the strike to hundreds of NASA personnel via e-mail. Group members were concerned about the size of the debris and the fact that the cameras were not able to capture a clear view of damage the strike might have caused. Bob Page, the group's chair, initiated a request to image the left wing with Department of Defense resources in order to better assess potential damage. This would be the first of three requests to secure imagery of *Columbia* on-orbit during the 16-day mission. (We discuss the imagery requests in the section below on information seeking and use.)

Also on the same day, a Debris Assessment Team was formed to analyze the strike impact. The team was co-chaired by Rodney Rocha (NASA chief engineer for the thermal protection system) and Pam Madera (United Space Alliance engineering manager), with engineers from NASA, United Space Alliance, and Boeing. According to standing procedures, such a group should have been a Mission Evaluation Room Tiger Team, with clearly defined roles and responsibilities. Although the Debris Assessment Team had the right group of engineers to work on the problem, it was not classified as a Tiger Team, and as a result, it was not "owned" or led by Shuttle Program managers, leaving it in a kind of organizational limbo (CAIB 2003, p. 142).

Already at this stage, Shuttle Program managers and working engineers were showing different levels of concern about the foam strike. Engineers in the Intercenter Photo Working Group believed that the orbiter may have been damaged. For them, it was important that on-orbit imagery be obtained to assess the damage to the left wing. Boeing and United Space Alliance engineers decided to work through the weekend (it was a holiday weekend) to analyze the strike. At the same time, Ralph Roe (head of Shuttle Program Office of Vehicle Engineering) and Bill Reeves (manager, United Space Alliance) voiced a lower level of concern: "It was at this point, before any analysis had started, that Shuttle Program managers officially shared their belief that the strike posed no safety issues, and that there was no need for a review to be conducted over the weekend" (CAIB 2003, p. 142).

In terms of Weick's sense-making process, the foam strike event was enacted— bracketed and highlighted for further sense making. A further enactment was the creation of a special group, the Debris Assessment Team, to make sense of the foam strike. Sense making by engineers and managers unfolded in two different contexts of beliefs and expectations: engineers believed that the foam could have seriously damaged the left wing of the orbiter, while program managers saw nothing to change their prior belief that foam could not cause significant damage and that foam loss was essentially a maintenance problem.

Knowledge Creation in the *Columbia* Case

In this section, we discuss how (1) the shedding of foam on the external tank was a dangerous and long-standing problem that remained poorly understood; (2) an inappropriate mathematical model was relied upon to assess damage from the foam strike; and (3) tacit concerns about the size of debris, location of strike, and uncertainties in the damage analysis were discounted by a desire to see the foam strike as not being a safety-of-flight issue.

Two of NASA's original design requirements relating to debris prevention are relevant to the *Columbia* accident. In the shuttle's "Flight and Group System Specification Book I, Requirements," there were explicit specifications that first, the external tank should not shed debris, and second, that the orbiter should not receive debris hits exceeding a trivial amount of force. Contrary to these requirements, damage caused by debris has occurred on every shuttle flight, and most missions have had insulating foam shed during ascent. Given that the shedding of external tank foam—the physical cause of the *Columbia* accident—had a long history, why did NASA continue to fly the shuttle with a known problem that violated design requirements?

Although foam-shedding from the external tank was recognized as a dangerous and long-standing problem, assessments of foam strikes were not thoroughly substantiated by engineering analysis. Despite numerous changes in foam design and application in the 25 years that the external tank has been in production, the problem of foam-shedding has not been solved, nor has the orbiter's ability to tolerate impacts from foam or other debris been significantly improved. Shuttle Program managers appeared to have confused the concept of foam-shedding being an "accepted risk" with foam not being a "safety-of-flight issue." The pressure to meet flight schedules seemed to have curtailed engineering efforts to resolve the foam-shedding issue. The CAIB report concluded that there were large gaps in NASA's knowledge about the nature and behavior of the complex foam material:

> NASA's lack of understanding of foam properties and behavior must also be questioned. Although tests were conducted to develop and qualify foam for use on the External Tank, it appears there were large gaps in NASA's knowledge about this complex and variable material. Recent testing conducted at Marshall Space Flight Center and under the auspices of the Board indicate that mechanisms previously considered a prime source of foam loss . . . are not feasible in the conditions experienced during tanking, launch, and ascent. Also, dissection of foam bipod ramps on External Tanks yet to be launched reveal subsurface flaws and defects that only now are being discovered and identified as contributing to the loss of foam from the bipod ramps. (CAIB 2003, p. 130)

During the weekend following the launch (January 18 and 19, 2003), Boeing engineers calculated the damage that might result from the observed debris using a mathematical model called Crater to predict the depth to which debris will penetrate a thermal protection system tile. The Crater model predicted an alarming result: that damage would be deeper than the actual tile thickness. This could expose the orbiter's underlying aluminum airframe and result in a possible burn-through during re-entry. Engineers in the Debris Assessment Team discounted this possibility for two reasons. First, Crater's calculations were conservative—they predicted more damage than would actually occur. Second, Crater did not take into account the increased density of a tile's lower layer, which was much stronger than the tile's fragile outer layer. The engineers therefore concluded that actual damage would not be as severe as Crater predicted and assumed that the foam did not break orbiter's outer skin.

A similar Crater-like algorithm was also developed and validated with test results to assess the damage caused by ice projectiles impacting the reinforced carbon-carbon panels (RCC—part of the thermal protection system) in the leading edge of the left wing. This analysis indicated that impact angles greater than 15 degrees would result in RCC penetration. A separate analysis of the path that the debris took suggested an impact angle of 21 degrees. However, because the algorithm was calibrated by impact data from ice projectiles, and since foam was less dense than ice, the analysts "used a qualitative extrapolation of the test data and engineering judgment to conclude that a foam impact angle of up to 21 degrees would not penetrate the RCC" (CAIB 2003, p. 145). Some engineers were uncomfortable with this extrapolation but no further analysis was done to assess RCC damage, probably because foam had not been believed to be a threat to RCC panels.

On January 24 (nine days after the launch), Boeing and United Space Alliance staff presented the Debris Assessment Team's findings to Don McCormack (manager, Mission Evaluation Room). So many engineers attended the session that it was standing room only, with people lining the hallway. The presentation focused on potential damage to the tiles, not the RCC panels. Five scenarios for debris damage were presented, with a sixth still uncompleted. Team members were confident that the analysis had been done properly but stressed that many uncertainties remained about where the debris had struck and the much-larger size of the debris (400 times larger than the standard in Boeing's database). The engineers ultimately concluded that their analysis, limited as it was, did not show that a safety-of-flight issue existed. Engineers present at the briefing felt that management had subsequently focused on the conclusion (no safety-of-flight issue) while overlooking the large uncertainties that should have qualified this result (CAIB 2003, p. 160).

The Crater algorithm, suitable for estimating small (on the order of three cubic inches) debris impacts, had been calibrated by the results of foam, ice, and metal debris impact testing. Until STS-107, Crater was normally used only to predict whether small debris, usually ice on the external tank, would pose a threat to the orbiter during launch. The use of Crater to assess the damage caused by foam during the launch of STS-107 was the first use of the model while a mission was on orbit. Moreover, engineers were using Crater to analyze a piece of debris that was several hundred times larger in volume than the pieces of debris used to calibrate and validate the Crater model. The use of Crater in this new and very different situation compromised NASA's ability to accurately predict debris damage in ways that Debris Assessment Team engineers did not fully comprehend.

The *Columbia* Accident Investigation Board summarized and commented on the use of the Crater model to analyze foam damage as follows:

> An inexperienced team, using a mathematical tool that was not designed to assess an impact of this estimated size, performed the analysis of the potential effect of the debris impact. Crater was designed for "in-family" impact events and was intended for day-of-launch analysis of debris impacts. It was not intended for large projectiles like those observed on STS-107. Crater initially predicted possible damage, but the Debris Assessment Team assumed, without theoretical or experimental validation, that because Crater is a conservative tool—that is, it predicts more damage than will actually occur—the debris would stop at the tile's densified layer, even though their experience did not involve debris strikes as large as STS-107's. Crater-like equations were also used as part of the analysis to assess potential impact damage to the wing leading edge RCC. Again, the tool was used for something other than that for which it was designed; again, it predicted possible penetration; and again, the Debris Assessment Team used engineering arguments and their experience to discount the results. (CAIB 2003, p. 168)

The use of the model and the interpretation of its results provide an illustration of the interplay between tacit, explicit, and cultural knowledge. The Crater model as a mathematical equation was codified, explicit knowledge. Its specific use in this case was heavily moderated by the judgment and experience of the analysts who made qualitative adjustments and extrapolations. Finally, the interpretation of the results of the calculation was influenced by the shared beliefs that foam would not seriously damage the RCC panels of the orbiter wing, and that foam loss was a maintenance issue that would not harm mission safety.

Decision Making in the *Columbia* Case

In this section, we focus on the two Mission Management Team (MMT) meetings of January 21 and 24, 2003. The MMT was the highest level at which the foam strike problem was raised, and these were the only two meetings when that problem was discussed.

January 21 Meeting of the Mission Management Team. On the morning of January 21, six days after the launch, the Mission Management Team discussed the foam strike problem for the first time. Based on information from the Debris Assessment Team, Don McCormack (chief Mission Evaluation Room manager) briefed the meeting that the orbiter had taken a foam hit somewhere on the left-wing leading edge, and that engineers were analyzing the possibility of damage as well as what could be done if *Columbia* had sustained damage. Linda Ham (chair, MMT) interjected at one point in McCormack's briefing that "And I'm really [*sic*] I don't think there is much we can do so it's not really a factor during the flight because there is not much we can do about it" (CAIB 2003, p. 147). After the meeting, Ham reviewed the rationale to continue to fly after the earlier foam loss in flight STS-112 of October 7, 2002 (see sense-making section). Later that same morning, she e-mailed to her superior Ron Dittemore (Space Shuttle Program manager) that "the rationale for flight for the STS-112 loss of foam was lousy." She had a different view of the current STS-107 (*Columbia*) situation: "Rationale states we haven't changed anything, we haven't experienced any 'safety of flight' damage in 112 flights, risk of loss of bi-pod ramp TPS [thermal protection system] is same as previous flights. . . . So ET [external tank] is safe to fly with no added risk" (Linda Ham e-mail of January 21, quoted in CAIB 2003, p. 148). The Investigation Board noted that Ham's attention had already shifted from the foam threat in STS-107 to the possibility of a delay of the next mission (STS-114) if the rationale to fly with foam loss was found to be flawed. Ham was due to serve as a launch integration manager of STS-114, and a delay in STS-114 would in turn delay the completion of International Space Station's Node 2, a "US Core Complete" status that was a high-priority goal for NASA (CAIB 2003, p. 148). Later, on January 22, Ham responded to an imaging request by expressing the concern that maneuvering the shuttle to make the left wing visible for imaging would delay the mission schedule. According to personal notes obtained by CAIB: "Linda Ham said it was no longer being pursued since even if we saw something, we couldn't do anything about it. The Program didn't want to spend the resources" (CAIB 2003, p. 154).

January 24 Meeting of the Mission Management Team. Early in the MMT meeting of January 24, before the foam strike damage assessment had been discussed, Phil Engelauf (chief of the flight director's office) reported that he had e-mailed *Columbia*'s crew informing them that were no concerns about the debris strike causing serious damage. Later in the meeting, Don McCormack (chief Mission Evaluation Room manager) briefed the MMT as follows:

> McCORMACK: We received, uh, received the data from the systems integration guys of the potential ranges of sizes and impact angles and where it might have hit, and the guys have gone off and done an analysis. They've used a tool they refer to as Crater, which is their official evaluation tool to determine the potential size of the damage. They went off and done all that work and they've done thermal analysis of the areas of where there may be damaged tiles. The analysis is not complete; there is one case yet they wish to run; but we're just kind of jumping to the conclusion, of all that they do show, obviously there's potential for significant tile damage here, but they do not indicate that—the thermal analysis does not indicate that there is a potential for a burn-through. There could be localized heating damage. Obviously there is a lot of uncertainty in all this in terms of the size of the debris and where it hit and angle of incidence, and it's difficult.
>
> HAM: No burn-through means no catastrophic damage and localized heating damage would mean a tile replacement?
>
> McCORMACK: Right. It would mean possible impacts to turnaround repairs and that sort of thing, but we do not see any kind of safety of flight issue here yet in anything that we've looked at.
>
> HAM: No safety of flight and no issue for this mission, nothing that we're going to do different, there may be a turnaround?

Mr. McCormack: Right, right. It could potentially hit the RCC [reinforced carbon-carbon panel] and we don't indicate any other possible coating damage or something, we don't see any issue if it hit the RCC. Although we could have some significant tile damage, we don't see a safety of flight issue.

Ham: What do you mean by that?

Mr. McCormack: Well it could be down through the . . . we could lose an entire tile and then the ramp into and out of that, I mean it could be a significant area of tile damage down to the SIP [strain isolation panel] perhaps, so it could be a significant piece missing but . . .

Ham: It would be a turnaround issue only?

McCormack: Right.

[At this point, Calvin Schomburg (engineer at Johnson Space Center regarded as an expert on the thermal protection system) stated his belief that no safety-of-flight issue exists.]

Ham: Okay. Same thing that you told me about the other day in my office. We've seen pieces of this size before, haven't we?

Unknown speaker: Hey, Linda, we are missing part of that conversation.

Ham: Right . . . He was just reiterating, it was Calvin, that he does not believe that there is any burn-through so no safety of flight kind of issue, it's more of a turnaround issue similar to what we have had on other flights. That's it? All right, any questions on that? O.K. . . .

Ham: All right, thanks for your support. An excellent job so far, so keep up the good work over the weekend we will meet again Monday at, uh, 8 o'clock.

(Transcript of MMT meeting on January 24, quoted in CAIB 2003, pp. 161–62)

When the official minutes of the meeting were produced and distributed, there was no mention of the debris strike. An entry in the Mission Evaluation Room console log stated: "MMT Summary . . . McCormack also summarized the debris assessment. Bottom line is that there appears to be no safety of flight issue, but good chance of turnaround impact to repair tile damage" (CAIB 2003, p. 162).

Questionable Decision Premises and Rule-Following. Over the course of 113 flights, foam impacts had come to be regarded as a maintenance issue that did not threaten vehicle or crew safety. Although the foam strike during STS-107 was outside the activities covered by normal mission flight rules, Mission Management Team members and Shuttle Program managers did not see a requirement for operational action by Mission Control. Program managers had, over the lifetime of the Space Shuttle Program, "gradually become inured to External Tank foam losses and on a fundamental level did not believe foam striking the vehicle posed a critical threat to the Orbiter" (CAIB 2003, pp. 168–69). This belief was particularly strong with regard to RCC panels—that they were impervious to foam impacts. Management continued to act on this premise even after seeing the video of *Columbia*'s debris impact, learning about the size and site of the strike, and noting that a foam hit with sufficient force could damage the thermal protection system.

The assumption expressed in the January 21 MMT meeting that nothing could have been done if damage had been sustained was also questioned by the Investigation Board and other observers (see, for example, Ferris 2004). The CAIB report presented a scenario where a rescue of the *Columbia* crew using the shuttle *Atlantis* would have been a feasible option (CAIB 2003, pp. 173–74).

Program managers and analysts diverged early in the mission in their perception of the potential severity of the foam strike. As the mission progressed, it became increasingly difficult for the Debris Assessment Team to have its fears heard by decision makers. Managers' low level of concern and desire to get on with the mission meant that the Debris Assessment Team had to prove that a safety-of-flight issue existed before Shuttle Program management would take further action. This was a reversal of the usual position of engineers having to prove that the situation was safe.

The section of the CAIB report analyzing decision making during the *Columbia* mission ended with these critical remarks:

> Management decisions made during Columbia's final flight reflect missed opportunities, blocked or ineffective communications channels, flawed analysis, and ineffective leadership. Perhaps most striking is the fact that management—including Shuttle Program, Mission Management Team, Mission Evaluation Room, and Flight Director and Mission Control—displayed no interest in understanding a problem and its implications. . . . Because managers failed to avail themselves of the wide range of expertise and opinion necessary to achieve the best answer to the debris strike question—*"Was this a safety-of-flight concern?"*—some Space Shuttle Program managers failed to fulfill the implicit contract to do whatever is possible to ensure the safety of the crew. In fact, their management techniques unknowingly imposed barriers that kept at bay both engineering concerns and dissenting views, and ultimately helped create "blind spots" that prevented them from seeing the danger the foam strike posed. (CAIB 2003, p. 170; italics in original)

Information Seeking and Use

During *Columbia*'s last flight, three requests for imagery were made to obtain additional information about the extent of damage caused by foam hitting the orbiter's wing. The *first request* was from the Intercenter Photo Working Group on the day after the launch (January 17) when group members observed a large piece of debris striking the left wing. Because of the size of the debris that had fallen off late in the ascent, and because none of the cameras working at launchtime provided a high-resolution view of the impact and potential damage, the group felt that it was important to obtain additional imagery of *Columbia*. The request was made in person by Bob Page (chair, Intercenter Photo Working Group [IPWG]) to Wayne Hale (Shuttle Program manager for Launch Integration at Kennedy Space Center), who was familiar with the process and agreed to explore the possibility.

image requests

The *second request* was made on January 21 by Bob White (United Space Alliance manager), as a result of concerns conveyed by his employees in the Debris Assessment Team. White telephoned Lambert Austin (head, Space Shuttle Systems Integration at Johnson Space Center) to ask what it would take to get imagery of *Columbia* on orbit. The *third request* was also made the same day. After a Debris Assessment Team meeting that discussed the Crater results of possible foam damage, Rodney Rocha (co-chair of the team) e-mailed Paul Shack (manager, Shuttle Engineering Office, Johnson Engineering Directorate) asking for "outside agency assistance" to get imagery that would help analysis. This request did not follow the usual chain of command of submitting it through the Mission Evaluation Room (MER) to the Mission Management Team (MMT) to the flight dynamics officer. Instead, the Debris Assessment Team had agreed that due to a lack of participation by MER and MMT managers, Rocha would channel the request through his division, the Johnson Engineering Directorate.

On the morning of January 22, Wayne Hale responded to the first request for imagery by calling a Department of Defense representative at Kennedy. The call was made without authorization from MMT chair Linda Ham. Furthermore, the Defense representative was not the designated liaison for such requests. Less than two hours later that morning, the NASA Department of Defense liaison officer formally cancelled the request for imagery. Linda Ham had called MMT members, the flight director, and the MER manager to determine the origin of the request and to confirm that there was a requirement for such for a request. The people contacted "all stated that they had not requested imagery, were not aware of any 'official' requests for imagery, and could not identify a 'requirement' for imagery. Linda Ham later told several individuals that nobody had a requirement for imagery" (CAIB 2003, p. 153). By officially ending the Department of Defense action, Ham had effectively canceled all three imagery requests. Three additional reasons were suggested for the cancellation. First, Ham was concerned that obtaining imagery would delay mission schedule. Second, Ham felt that even if damage was observed, there was nothing that could be done. Third, shuttle managers assumed that the resolution of imagery that could be obtained would not be good enough—this assumption was based on little or no knowledge about imaging capabilities that could have been made available.

At a more general level, the CAIB report noted an unofficial hierarchy among NASA programs and directorates that hindered the seeking and sharing of information. One consequence of this hierarchy effect was seen when the Debris Assessment Team chose the institutional route for their imagery request. The team had felt more comfortable with their own chain of command, given that they were acting without direction from the Mission Evaluation Room and Mission Management Team. Unfortunately this more "comfortable" route directed the request outside official Shuttle Program channels. Furthermore, Debris Assessment Team members were reluctant to be more vocal about their concerns because they felt that in questioning shuttle mission safety, they would be singled out for ridicule by their peers and managers.

On January 22, after being informed that the imaging request has been cancelled, Rodney Rocha wrote an e-mail that he did not send but had printed out and shared with a colleague:

> In my humble technical opinion, this is the wrong (and bordering on irresponsible) answer from the SSP [Space Shuttle Program] and Orbiter not to request additional imaging help from any outside source. I must emphasize (again) that severe enough damage . . . combined with the heating and resulting damage to the underlying structure at the most critical location . . . could present potentially grave hazards.
> . . . Remember the NASA safety posters everywhere around stating, "If it's not safe, say so"? Yes, it's that serious. (Rocha's unsent e-mail, quoted in CAIB 2003, p. 157)

When asked why he did not send this message, Rocha had replied that he did not want to jump the chain of command, that he would defer to management's judgment on obtaining imagery.

After the accident, program managers stated that if engineers had a safety concern, it was their responsibility to communicate this to management. The CAIB report pointed out that managers as leaders had a corresponding and perhaps greater obligation to create viable routes for the engineers to express their views as well as to receive information. The barriers to communication in this case not only blocked the flow of information to managers but also prevented the flow of information from managers to engineers, leaving Debris Assessment Team members unable to understand the reasoning behind Mission Management Team decisions (CAIB 2003, p. 169).

Summary

Fig. 6.10 shows the interplay between sense making, knowledge creation, and decision making in the *Columbia* case. In sense making, one of the messages most relevant to the foam-shedding problem was that the shuttle had flown 113 successful missions, and while foam-shedding occurred in most flights, the missions all completed safely. These repeated observations helped construct the beliefs that foam debris did not seriously damage the shuttle, and that foam loss could justifiably be regarded as a maintenance issue. These beliefs formed the context for decision making by mission control managers about the risk of falling debris. During the launch of Flight STS-107, engineers bracketed the falling of a particularly large piece of foam that struck the orbiter as a worrisome problem. The main question they sought to answer was "What was the extent and implications of the damage caused by the foam strike?"

Although the foam-shedding problem had been identified from the beginning of the Shuttle Program, there was inadequate analysis of the nature and behavior of the complex foam material that insulated the external tank. This knowledge gap was evident during STS-107, when there were large uncertainties about how to predict or assess the foam strike damage. A mathematical model was used to calculate the extent of damage, but the model was calibrated on data

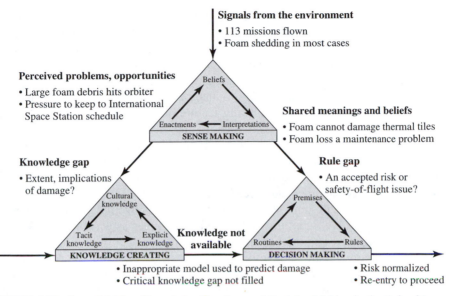

Signals from the environment
- 113 missions flown
- Foam shedding in most cases

Perceived problems, opportunities
- Large foam debris hits orbiter
- Pressure to keep to International Space Station schedule

Beliefs

Enactments ← Interpretations
SENSE MAKING

Shared meanings and beliefs
- Foam cannot damage thermal tiles
- Foam loss a maintenance problem

Knowledge gap
- Extent, implications of damage?

Cultural knowledge

Tacit knowledge → Explicit knowledge
KNOWLEDGE CREATING

Knowledge not available

Rule gap
- An accepted risk or safety-of-flight issue?

Premises

Routines ← Rules
DECISION MAKING

- Inappropriate model used to predict damage
- Critical knowledge gap not filled

- Risk normalized
- Re-entry to proceed

FIGURE 6.10. Sense Making, Knowledge Creating, and Decision Making in the *Columbia* Accident (2003)

from much smaller debris hits. The result of this flawed analysis was that there was no safety-of-flight issue. Decision makers focused on this conclusion without recognizing the limitations of the analysis and the lack of imagery data. Mindful about avoiding schedule slippages and conditioned by past experience, mission managers decided that the foam strike risk was acceptable and that the only consequence might be a longer turnaround time after the shuttle had returned.

A number of problems affected information seeking, and these were especially apparent in the attempts to obtain additional imagery to better assess the foam damage. Three separate requests were made by engineers and managers, but they were cancelled by mission management partly because the requests did not follow proper channels, and partly because management did not see a requirement for imagery. Engineers continued to be worried about the foam strike throughout the flight but did not voice their concerns because they deferred to management and did not want to jump the chain of command.

Learning from the *Challenger* and *Columbia* Accidents

Our analysis in this chapter suggests a number of common features in the loss of *Challenger* and *Columbia*. In both accidents, the danger signal (O-ring not sealing properly in *Challenger*'s booster rocket; foam falling and damaging *Columbia*'s wing) was enacted or bracketed, primarily by the engineers who had been monitoring these components. Managers found it much more difficult to see the threat. Their sense making was driven by beliefs that had formed over time about the acceptable nature of the risk that was involved, and information suggesting that there would be a catastrophic failure was incompatible with these beliefs. For both accidents, the ultimate cause was a long-standing problem that had been identified as being dangerous right from the beginning of the Shuttle Program. Unfortunately, this gap in the ability to analyze and fix the problems remained unmet until the accidents. A perplexing feature of both cases was the difficulty that engineers and technical staff had in voicing their concerns before the accidents. These concerns, based on their tacit intuition and experience, could not be easily quantified or articulated, and engineers were finally unable to influence decisions that could have avoided the accidents. Again in both cases, the repeated use of decision procedures and precedents had routinized the perception of risk so that mission and program managers became desensitized to the danger posed by a recurring problem and instead viewed this danger as acceptable risk. The Rogers Commission and the *Columbia* Accident Investigation Board both identified poor communication and information sharing as a major factor in the accidents. Information seeking and use were blocked by organizational structure and roles—people were following reviewing and reporting channels, they did not want to jump the chain of command, and they deferred to management and superiors.

Why do organizations find it so hard to learn from mistakes? What can we learn from the *Challenger* and *Columbia* tragedies? To a large extent, the answers to these questions were already in our analysis of the ways that NASA and its partner organizations perceived and interpreted their experiences, struggled with complex engineering problems, and made risky decisions in conditions of high uncertainty. By way of emphasis, we may highlight some of the more daunting challenges.

Sense making is both a way of seeing and a way of not seeing. Managers found it difficult to perceive the risks confronting them because registering them would undermine the beliefs that have formed the basis of understanding their actions and past decisions. Managers take action, and their sense making wades in the flow of actions they have taken in the past, actions they are currently working on, and actions they want to pursue in the future.

Knowledge creation and use in organizations is always a simultaneous but problematic engagement of tacit, explicit, and cultural knowing. Tacit knowledge is hard to articulate, and, as we have seen in both accidents, even harder for other persons to apprehend. Cultural knowledge, contained in beliefs about organizational identity and purpose, can influence how priorities are set about what knowledge gaps to address. Explicit knowledge is supposed to be an objective component of technical problem solving, but we have also seen how it can be a servant of personal preferences and organizational agendas.

Decision making in organizations is guided by rules and routines. Decision rules and premises capture and apply past learning and coordinate multiple sets of activities. At the same time, the repeated, unreflexive use of rules and premises can obstruct new learning. In both accidents, it was the history of rule following that created precedents and lowered the vigilance that could have averted tragic errors.

III. SUMMARY

- On January 28, 1986, the space shuttle *Challenger* disintegrated soon after launch. The accident was caused by rubber O-rings failing to seal properly in the booster rocket. This problem was known as early as 1977, and concerns were discussed on the eve of the launch.

- *Challenger—sense making.* With 24 successful shuttle launches behind them, engineers and managers believed that the use of two O-rings provided safe redundancy. On the eve of the launch, a specific problem was bracketed: Would the O-rings seal properly in the unusually cold temperatures forecasted for the following morning?

- *Challenger—knowledge creation.* Although the problem was known for many years, there was no concerted effort to analyze and fix O-ring erosion. On the eve of the launch, there was no data to quantify the concerns about ring behavior in cold temperatures. Engineers could not externalize their tacit apprehensions about possible O-ring failure.

- *Challenger—decision making.* Through a repetitive pattern of decision and rule making, engineers and managers constructed decision premises to deal with the risk of O-ring failure. Rules and precedents from past decisions had routinized O-ring erosion dangers as acceptable risks.

- *Challenger—information seeking and use.* Information seeking and use was hobbled by a hierarchical structure, a division of information roles, a reliance on reporting channels, and the compartmentalization of knowledge that were part of NASA's information environment.

- On February 1, 2003, the space shuttle *Columbia* disintegrated while reentering the atmosphere. The accident was caused by insulating foam striking the shuttle's wing. This problem was known from the first flight of *Columbia,* and foam loss had occurred in most shuttle missions.

- *Columbia—sense making.* With 113 successful missions behind them, including flights with foam loss, engineers and managers believed that foam debris did not seriously threaten the shuttle. During *Columbia*'s launch, an unusually large piece of foam was seen striking the shuttle: What was the extent and implications of the damage?

- *Columbia—knowledge creation.* Although foam loss was known from the beginning of the Shuttle Program, there was no concerted effort to analyze and fix the problem. During the *Columbia* mission, there were large uncertainties about how to assess the foam strike damage. A mathematical model was used inappropriately, resulting in a flawed analysis.

- *Columbia—decision making.* Mindful about avoiding schedule slippages and desensitized by past precedents, mission managers decided that the foam strike risk was acceptable and not a safety issue. Past decisions and precedents had routinized foam loss dangers as acceptable risks.

- *Columbia—information seeking and use.* Three requests for imagery were cancelled by mission management because they did not follow proper channels, and because management did not see a requirement for imagery. Engineers did not voice their concerns because they deferred to management and did not want to jump the chain of command.

- The *Challenger* and *Columbia* accidents illustrate the dynamics between meaning, knowing, and acting that can impede learning in any organization. *Sense making* driven by beliefs and past actions can be a way of seeing and a way of not seeing problems and risks. *Knowledge creation* can be compromised when vital tacit knowledge is not transferred and when knowledge selection and use is controlled by organizational agendas. Repeated patterns of *decision making* can entrench rules and premises, induce overconfidence, and lower decision vigilance.

7

KNOWING AND LEARNING
IN ORGANIZATIONS

It now becomes too manifest to admit of controversy, that the annihilation of
the Small Pox, the most dreadful scourge of the human species, must be the
final result of this practice.
  —*Edward Jenner, discoverer of smallpox vaccination, 1801*

The two accidents examined in the last chapter suggest that there are inherent
features in the way organizations use information to construct meaning, knowledge, and decisions that can, against the best of intentions, impede learning and
change. These challenges will loom even larger as organizations operate in
increasingly complex and uncertain environments. In this chapter, we shift our
eyes to an organization that has accomplished what might at first seem to be
an impossible task—the elimination of a deadly disease. We will work our way
toward an understanding of how organizational vision, human ingenuity, and
an openness to learning and new ideas combine to make this accomplishment
possible.

I. WHO SMALLPOX ERADICATION PROGRAM

Smallpox is the only major human disease to have been eradicated. Epidemics
of smallpox had inflicted mankind throughout history, and as recently as 1967,
some 10–15 million cases were still occurring annually in more than 30 endemic
countries (Fenner et al. 1988). Of these, some 2 million died and millions of sur-
vivors were left disfigured or even blind. Smallpox spreads by tiny droplets of
aerosolized virus that are discharged from the mouth and nose of infected victims. Within two weeks of inhaling the virus, the viremia would have caused
fever, muscular pain, infection of skin and internal organs, and the characteristic
appearance of rash on the face and body. The rash papules swell and become
filled with pus. Scabs form in the second week and leave pitted scars after they

fall off. There is no treatment for smallpox once it has been contracted. The more serious strain of the smallpox virus (*Variola major*) causes fatality of 20–40 percent among unvaccinated persons.

On January 1, 1967, the World Health Organization launched the Intensified Smallpox Eradication Programme. At that time the plan was to rely entirely on mass vaccination of susceptible persons in endemic countries—the problem was defined as one of *mass vaccination*. The mass vaccination strategy had successfully eradicated smallpox in programs in Western Europe, North America, Japan, and other areas. The WHO Expert Committee on Smallpox in 1964 had recommended that the goal should be to vaccinate 100 percent of the population, based on the observation in India that smallpox persisted in some areas despite vaccinations reported to be 80 percent or more of the population (80 percent was then assumed to be the acceptable target of a well-conducted vaccination program). A report by the WHO director-general in 1966 supported this thinking: "Eradication can be accomplished in a comparatively simple and straightforward manner by rendering immune, through vaccination, a sufficiently large proportion of the population so that transmission is interrupted. In a highly endemic area this requires almost 100 percent coverage of the population" (WHO Doc. A19/P&B/2, March 28, 1966, p. 107). In hindsight, one might have asked whether the sample size of successful vaccination campaigns was adequate to confirm this belief; whether results obtained in insulated areas (such as tests on the island of Tonga) could be replicated elsewhere; and to what extent campaigns in Europe and North America were helped by better-controlled conditions (Hopkins 1989). The same Expert Committee that had recommended total vaccination had also "ignored the information from field studies in India itself, which showed that the proportion successfully vaccinated fell far short of 80 percent because of the use of subpotent vaccines and the frequent revaccination of the most easily accessible groups" (Fenner et al. 1988, p. 484). A review of the programs conducted after 1967 suggests that mass vaccination alone could have eliminated smallpox in South America and most African countries, but not in the densely populated countries of Bangladesh, India, Indonesia, and Pakistan (Fenner et al. 1988).

A 1966 outbreak in Nigeria started the evolution of a new strategy. In western Nigeria, where over 90 percent of the population had been vaccinated, another smallpox outbreak had occurred, apparently originating in a religious group that had resisted vaccination. Vaccine supplies were delayed, forcing program staff to quickly locate new cases and isolate infected villages that could then be vaccinated with the limited supplies. A reporting network using the available radio facilities was established to locate new cases. Containment teams moved swiftly to isolate infected persons and to vaccinate susceptible villages. The Nigerian experience demonstrated that an alternative strategy of *surveillance and containment* could break the transmission chain of smallpox, even when less than half the population was eventually vaccinated (Hopkins 1989).

In 1970, a major epidemic had begun in the Gulbarga district of Karnataka in southwestern India, claiming over 1,300 victims (including 123 deaths) in more than 1,000 villages and 5 municipalities. To prevent the epidemic from spreading to more-populated areas, "prompt detection of all cases in an area of two million people was required. All available health personnel, not just smallpox health workers, were mobilized for a weeklong, house-to-house search of the area. By carefully focusing containment vaccination around each newly discovered case, they eliminated smallpox from the district within weeks" (Brilliant 1985, p. 27). The Gulbarga experience was India's first real success with surveillance-containment and showed that it could work even in a densely populated country.

The new strategy evolved gradually and was accepted slowly as local campaigns controlled outbreaks with their own variations of surveillance-containment. In India, for example, when a village-by-village search in Uttar Pradesh and Bihar in 1973 identified 10,000 new cases, surveillance first shifted to a house-to-house search, and then to market surveillance: smallpox disappeared in some 19 months before the strategy was ever fully worked out (Hopkins 1989). In Bangladesh, surveillance based on passive reporting was eventually supplemented by three systems of surveillance—market surveillance, infected village surveillance, and house-to-house surveillance. House-to-house searches were made much more effective by preceding them with presearch meetings that also examined feedback from prior searches (Fenner et al. 1988). In Nepal, surveillance teams were supervised by assessment teams who planned the itineraries, concentrating on high-risk areas, schools, tea shops, factories, brick kilns, weekly markets, fairs, and so on. As in India, "watchguards" were posted at every infected house round the clock to prevent patients from leaving the house, and monetary rewards were offered for information leading to discovery of new outbreaks (Fenner et al. 1988). Financial incentives, sometimes amounting to several months' wages, were presented in several countries to reward reporting of new smallpox cases. Even health workers were eligible for the rewards and were encouraged to bypass their superiors to report cases. Disincentives were also used to force people to receive vaccination, as in some Indian cities where people were threatened with the loss of their food ration cards or with having the names of their family members erased from the food ration registry (Hopkins 1989).

The initial definition of the problem as mass vaccination was a classic symptom of a confusion between ends and means. The goal of the program was the complete eradication of smallpox, and mass vaccination was a means to achieve that end. With the epidemiological experience available in 1966, the choice of mass vaccination as a strategy appeared rational. However, by limiting its attention on methods to vaccinate as many people as possible and by measuring performance according to how many vaccinations were given, the program was focusing on methodology and not necessarily goal-attainment. National governments also favored mass vaccination partly because it was a highly visible display of government action, and partly because of the substantial investments already made in creating the vaccination infrastructure (including jobs and salaries). Fortunately, the smallpox campaign learned quickly from its experiences in Nigeria, India, and elsewhere and was able to recast the problem and evolve a new surveillance-containment strategy through experimentation and improvisation in the field. The then director of the WHO program commented on the shift soon after it occurred: "In the development of the global program, it thus seemed more logical to reconsider the strategy in terms of the actual objective, 'eradication of smallpox,' and to determine how best to interrupt completely transmission of the disease rather than to focus attention solely on methods to vaccinate all people" (Henderson 1972, in WHO/SE/72.8, p. 1).

The process of institutional learning and local adaptation was central to the campaign's success: "*Indeed, that process, more than any other element in the campaign, is the key explanatory factor of the ultimate success of the program*" (Hopkins 1989, p. 74, italics in original). The surveillance and containment strategy was not a single policy deliberately planned for or even envisioned by WHO. Instead, it comprised a broad array of measures that emerged over time from the local practices of field teams who had to invent procedures that not only blended with local customs and conditions, but were also genuinely effective in providing early detection and enforcing isolation and control. What eventually eliminated smallpox was the combined approach of using mass vaccination to reduce disease incidence so that detection and containment could eliminate the remaining endemic foci (Brilliant 1985).

To achieve the large-scale vaccination in the program required the high-volume production of potent, reliable vaccines and an efficient, inexpensive means of delivering the vaccine. Three major technological innovations greatly facilitated the smallpox eradication program by addressing these needs. Perhaps the most significant was the development of the capacity to mass produce high-quality *freeze-dried vaccine* in many countries. Edward Jenner had discovered as long ago as 1796 that humans inoculated with cowpox became immune to smallpox. An earlier 1959 WHO smallpox program had depended on a liquid vaccine that had to be used within 48 hours and was easily contaminated. The new freeze-dried vaccine, which had the potency and stability needed for mass vaccination, was developed mainly at the Lister Institute in London using modest resources. The first apparatus for heat-sealing the ampoules of freeze-dried vaccine on a production scale was built from a child's toy construction kit (Hopkins 1989). The final production method was subsequently made freely available. Since the quality of the vaccine was crucial, WHO took the important step of establishing two regional vaccine reference centers in Canada and the Netherlands to test and ensure vaccine quality. WHO continued with many activities and services to improve vaccine quality, including organizing a vaccine production seminar, consultation, fellowship training, detailed production manuals, equipment blueprints, and so on (Hopkins 1989). Within a few years after the program started, several countries achieved self-sufficiency in vaccine production, with nearly 60 countries participating in the production of freeze-dried vaccine (Fenner et al. 1988).

Apart from the vaccine, the program also had to solve the problem of developing an efficient technique of introducing the smallpox vaccine into humans. The traditional vaccination technique was to scratch a drop of the vaccine into the superficial skin layers, employing a rotary lancet or a needle, which sometimes resulted in serious wounds. The scratch method was clearly inadequate for large-scale vaccinations that were to be accomplished in compressed time frames. Starting in 1963, the U.S. National Communicable Disease Center had led field tests of a *jet injector* that was hydraulic-powered, foot-actuated, and portable. The jet injector could do over 1,000 vaccinations in an hour, and in field tests, more than 100,000 persons were successfully vaccinated in several countries. The jet injector was deployed to good effect in West Africa but was too expensive a device for house-to-house vaccination in densely populated countries.

The third major technological innovation was the *bifurcated needle*. The new freeze-dried vaccine required a different method of presenting single doses of the vaccine. Because the vaccine had to be reconstituted each time and dispensed in tiny quantities, the traditional method of storing liquid vaccine in capillaries was no longer tenable. In developing a new solution, Benjamin Rubin of Wyeth Laboratories worked with Gus Chakros of the then Reading Textile Machine Company in needle design. It occurred to Rubin that a prolonged needle with a loop would provide both the capillarity activity and the scarification action required (Hopkins 1989). He suggested the use of a sewing needle in which the loop end was ground into a prolonged fork, creating two bifurcated prongs. A piece of wire suspended between the prongs was designed to hold a constant amount of vaccine by capillarity. By 1968, the bifurcated needle had replaced traditional methods in most countries, and by 1970 it was in use everywhere. The new needle conserved vaccine and was so easy to use that a local villager could be trained in 10–15 minutes to reconstitute vaccine and to perform effective vaccination (Fenner et al. 1988).

Although the development of the freeze-dried vaccine, the jet injector, and the bifurcated needle were milestones in the smallpox campaign, the program would not have succeeded without the ingenuity and creativity with which the field staff surmounted a host of local problems. Important innovations such as smallpox recognition cards, watchguards, rewards, rumor registers, and containment books all came from fieldworkers (Brilliant 1985). Managers and supervisors encouraged the creative solving of problems as they arose and adopted an attitude of supporting problem-oriented practical experimentation in the field. New techniques or improvements of existing procedures were then disseminated through surveillance newsletters and periodic review meetings.

Staff training was another major component of the campaign. Epidemiologists from various backgrounds and nationalities, including academic epidemiologists, had typically never worked in rural villages and so required special training. In India, part of the training program included two simulation exercises. The first was a hypothetical outbreak that required the trainee to trace the source of infection, locate all contacts, and carry out containment operations. An example scenario involved an infectious disease hospital as a source of infection. Academic epidemiologists were incredulous but realized when they reached the field that poorly guarded hospitals were notorious for spreading the disease they were trying to control. In the second exercise, the trainee played the role of the chief of a state smallpox program who had to watch against infection from

neighboring areas, investigate sources of infection, and make sense of conflicting reports. Following the exercises, the entire training group then went out to a
nearby village with a chickenpox outbreak and proceeded to vaccinate and contain the infection. The field training was highly practical and was conducted not
by a ranking administrator but by a junior paramedical assistant who had inti-
mate knowledge of village-level epidemiology.

At the strategy level, the smallpox eradication program of 1966 was guided
by a plan that linked two complementary approaches: *mass vaccination campaigns* that employed freeze-dried vaccine of assured quality to substantially reduce the incidence of smallpox in endemic areas and *surveillance systems* that
detected and reported cases early enough to permit the containment of outbreaks
and the analysis of occurrence patterns so that appropriate vaccination and surveillance activities could be taken. The WHO program functioned in a collegial
structure of many independent national programs, each developing its own administrative traditions and adapting to local social and cultural conditions. As a
result, programs differed greatly from one country to another, as well as from one
time period to another. Specific country programs were designed locally and
jointly by the country staff and their WHO counterparts, whose roles again varied somewhat from country to country. The most effective counterparts were
those who actively took part in field operations, and passive advisers who did not
travel out of the cities were encouraged to leave the program (Hopkins 1989).
The contribution of the WHO staff was significant:

> As working counterparts, WHO staff with prior experience in other smallpox
> eradication programmes transmitted confidence in the feasibility of eradication
> and were better able to introduce new methods; they frequently served to provide
> continuity and sustain momentum in programmes when the national leadership
> changed; and it was sometimes easier for them than for their national counterparts
> to approach the more senior health officials in the country to seek additional
> support or changes in policy. (Fenner et al. 1988, p. 1361)

To foster a common understanding of the principles and procedures underlying the global program, WHO produced a comprehensive manual entitled
"Handbook for Smallpox Eradication Programmes in Endemic Areas." The
handbook provided detailed information about important aspects of the campaign, including an account of the clinical features of smallpox, laboratory diagnosis methods, and the operational approaches for conducting vaccination
campaigns and containment programs.

Standards of performance were defined from the outset and refined as the
program advanced. Mass vaccination campaigns were expected to result in more
than 80 percent of the population in each area having a vaccination scar. Independent assessment teams could easily ascertain the proportion of the population
with such a scar. As campaigns improved, the target rates of coverage were
raised to 80 percent of those under 15 years old and sometimes 80 percent of
those under 5 years old. Furthermore, for primary vaccinations, a take-rate of
95 percent or better was set as the standard. Both sets of targets shared the

desirable attributes that they were attainable in well-executed campaigns under normal conditions, and that they could be easily measured and monitored soon after a campaign was concluded. From 1974, standards for surveillance and containment were added: 75 percent of outbreaks should be discovered within 2 weeks of the onset of the first case; containment of the outbreak should begin within 48 hours of its discovery; and no new cases should occur more than 17 days after containment had begun. Fenner et al. (1988) concluded that "the various standards were of the greatest value when the data were promptly collected, analysed and used as management guides for programme action. The knowledge by those collecting the information that their data were being promptly put to use contributed greatly to the development of the system and to better performance" (p. 1354). However, toward the end of the program, a proliferation of standards generated high volumes of data which could not be absorbed. It was clear that "a few indicators of overall performance, closely followed, were more valuable than a broad spectrum of indicators expressing the measure of many different aspects of programme execution" (p. 1355).

Each national program developed its own set of standard operating procedures that were adapted to the local environment. In India, Operation Smallpox Zero was launched in 1975 with a closely specified set of rules and procedures (Brilliant 1985). Village-by-village searches were changed to house-to-house. In one state capital room-to-room searches were done to prevent an epidemic from spreading. Every case of rash with fever was recorded, monitored, and treated as smallpox until proven otherwise. A rumor register was maintained at the Primary Health Center. Uncertain diagnoses were followed with containment by default. Four watchguards were posted at infected homes. All villages within ten miles of a case of known or suspected smallpox were searched. Everyone inside a one-mile radius was vaccinated. Market searches were intensified. Medical officers were posted to live in infected villages. The stringent procedures paid off. The average size of an outbreak fell to fewer than 5 cases from 7 six months before. The number of infected villages fell by 40 percent each month.

An important innovation that preceded Operation Smallpox Zero was the use of the infected rural village or urban neighborhood as an assessment index and, in effect, as a decision premise for allocating resources. A village in which any case of smallpox was recent enough to be potentially infective was labeled a "pending outbreak" and placed on the pending lists of active outbreaks maintained at the smallpox control offices. If no new cases were found at the end of the pending outbreak period (4–6 weeks), the outbreak was removed from the lists with fanfare. Brilliant (1985) wrote that pending outbreaks were

> an ideal management tool because for every outbreak, regardless of size, the same resources—a jeep, vaccine, proformae, gasoline, and containment staff—were needed to search every house in the village or mohalla [urban neighborhood]. . . . This index of program performance was the lighthouse that guided the smallpox staff through the rough and stormy seas of the smallpox cycles. Since efficient resource allocation was the most pressing management decision, the use of

pending outbreaks was an excellent management control—provided all the outbreaks were found. (Brilliant 1985, p. 54)

Throughout the program, the pursuance of clear and stringent rules and standards concerning vaccination, detection, and containment was matched by an equally fervent spirit of improvisation and experimentation in the implementation of those procedures. Many people in WHO today believe that the program had bent many rules, and indeed, many at WHO viewed the smallpox program negatively because it ran outside the regular WHO system. Hopkins (1989) recounts how one WHO official commented that if the India campaign were successful, he would "eat a tire off a jeep." When the last case was reported, Donald Henderson, director of the smallpox program, sent that person a jeep tire. There were many instances of cutting corners. Obtaining cash for the program required voluminous paperwork, and often cash flowed simply on the director's assurance that funds would be forthcoming. The regional finance officer in India often had to cover such advances but considered them as "an act of faith well justified." In Bangladesh, traditional steps in the health service hierarchy were bypassed when the mobile surveillance teams drew personnel from their other regular assignments and gave them authority and powers that exceeded their service ranks. In India, relations in the joint WHO–government of India central command became characterized by an open, informal atmosphere developed from months of working closely in the field and office. Junior staff frequently leaped over formal hierarchical levels in order to expedite action, so much so that nearly every senior Indian health official cited "level jumping" as one of the reasons for the program's success. At the core of the campaign in India (as well as many other countries) was a logic of learning by experimenting and sharing that learning quickly:

> Task implementation in smallpox was a dynamic process, constantly recycling lessons learned through hundreds of natural experiments in remote villages. As fast as these innovations could be shared at monthly progress review meetings in each state, they were disseminated at the next presearch meetings to the most peripheral PHC [Primary Health Center] levels. (Brilliant 1985, p. 92)

WHO had recognized early on the critical role of concurrently evaluating the performance of the various campaigns by independent teams so that deficiencies could be discovered and remedied while the campaigns were still active. Evaluation and assessment procedures constantly evolved in response to new experiences and lessons learned from the field. Evaluation measures were kept flexible so that they could be changed to fit each local environment. Initial output-based measures such as the number of people vaccinated proved unuseful and were replaced by outcome-based measures such as trends in the incidence of smallpox. More-specific indicators were used at lower levels. In India, for example, attention shifted to pending outbreaks (infected villages where the infection could spread) in 1974; the focus then changed to the outcome of surveillance searches in 1975; and finally search efficiency was stressed in the closing years of the campaign. A sensitive feedback and control system was thus established, relying on the extensive, accurate, and rapid collection of data from the field. Field data were rapidly analyzed and acted upon in order to influence the campaigns while they were still in progress. The smallpox program relied on careful planning and administration, creating hierarchical levels of control and reporting systems that were nevertheless simple enough for the field teams to understand. Regular feedback was provided through periodic review meetings at all levels for the analysis of failures and resolution of problems. Summaries of the program's progress also appeared regularly in the WHO weekly epidemiological record, and special papers were published on the results of research and operational methods (Hopkins 1989).

In 1977, the last case of smallpox was reported in Somalia. For the first time, a major disease had been completely vanquished. Dr. H. Mahler, WHO director-general, described the smallpox eradication program as "a triumph of management, not of medicine." It is said that at a meeting in Kenya in 1978, the then director-general, on announcing the end of smallpox, had turned to Donald Henderson, who had directed the smallpox program, and asked him which was the next disease to be eradicated. Henderson reached for the microphone and said that the next disease that needs to be eradicated is bad management (Hopkins 1989).

Our analysis of the organizational processes of the smallpox eradication program suggests that the melding of sense making, knowledge creation, and decision making into continuous cycles of interpretation, innovation, and adaptive action underpinned the program's success. In *sense making,* the program was able to unlearn its past beliefs about the nature of smallpox and to redefine the problem of eradication. Many assumptions about the epidemiological nature of smallpox were proven wrong in the field. For example, data and experience from the field showed that smallpox did not spread as swiftly as first expected, that swabbing the vaccination area was unnecessary, and that adult females were much less susceptible to the disease. The problem was poorly defined at the start of the program when the desired goal of eliminating smallpox was confused with the generally accepted means of mass vaccination. The initial belief was that smallpox could be eradicated simply by vaccinating all or nearly all persons in an endemic area. An outbreak in Nigeria where vaccine supplies were short and replenishments were delayed led fieldworkers to make do with selective vaccination, guided by detection and investigation, and followed up by isolation measures. These responses worked and showed the value of a hybrid strategy of surveillance, containment, and selective rather than comprehensive vaccination. Here was an instance of enacted learning, in which field teams acted on the environment (by locating cases and outbreaks), changed its configuration (by separating out infected homes and villages), and made it possible to deal effectively with the environment (by vaccinating and containing only the infected areas).

One of the most important elements of the program's success was its "capacity to interpret experience and to weigh evidence with the maximum degree of openness, and to respond to that experience and evidence" (Hopkins 1989, p. 127). Thus, while procedures, standards, and indicators were specified and

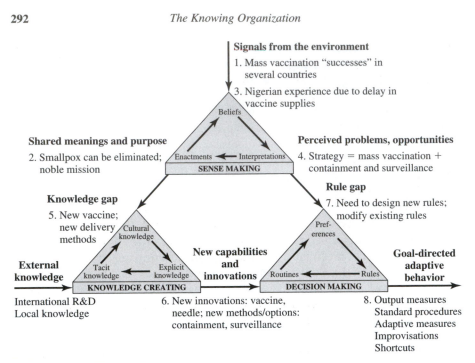

Signals from the environment
1. Mass vaccination "successes" in
   several countries
3. Nigerian experience due to delay in
   vaccine supplies

Beliefs

Shared meanings and purpose
2. Smallpox can be eliminated;
   noble mission

Enactments ← Interpretations
SENSE MAKING

Perceived problems, opportunities
4. Strategy = mass vaccination +
   containment and surveillance

Rule gap
7. Need to design new rules;
   modify existing rules

Knowledge gap
5. New vaccine;
   new delivery
   methods

Cultural knowledge

Preferences

New capabilities and innovations

External knowledge

Tacit knowledge ← Explicit knowledge
KNOWLEDGE CREATING

Routines ← Rules
DECISION MAKING

Goal-directed adaptive behavior

International R&D
Local knowledge

6. New innovations: vaccine,
   needle; new methods/options:
   containment, surveillance

8. Output measures
   Standard procedures
   Adaptive measures
   Improvisations
   Shortcuts

FIGURE 7.1. Organizational Learning in the WHO Smallpox Eradication Program

measured, the program at the same time maintained a "creative but insistent icon-oclasm," to guard against the reification of assumptions and modes of operation:

> The management of the smallpox campaign proved itself willing and able to recognize that means and ends had been confused in the original problem definition; to experiment with the new strategy of surveillance-containment and to enthusiastically adopt it as the guiding strategy; to adopt a simple technology in the form of the bifurcated needle when a more complex technology—the jet injector—could not do the job; and to constantly search for effective, direct means of assessment. (Hopkins 1989, p. 127)

As a global endeavor developing concurrently in more than 50 countries, the smallpox program evolved campaigns that were tailored to a wide range of cultures, traditions, and local practices. This diversity was held together by a unifying core of shared visions and beliefs. At the heart of the campaign was the common belief that the total eradication of smallpox was an attainable goal, that the eradication had to be done urgently, and that this was a noble, inspiring mission. One of the participants in the Indian campaign called this "management by inspiration," which was the result of

1. a common goal that was attainable in the near future;
2. a sympathetic group of co-workers who shared and encouraged belief in the goal;

3. an emergency-like work situation (the program was often referred to as being on a war footing) with the concomitant increase in output and unification that such disaster situations invoke.

(T. S. Jones 1976, cited in Brilliant 1985, pp. 141–42.)

In *knowledge creation,* the development of the freeze-dried vaccine and the methods for presenting the vaccine answered the needs of the comprehensive vaccination program. The freeze-dried vaccine was more potent, stable, and portable than the traditional liquid vaccine, was economical to administer, and could be mass produced. Vaccinating entire villages by novice or temporary fieldworkers also meant that the method of delivering the vaccine had to be efficient and easy to learn. The bifurcated needle invention scored highly on both criteria. These innovations had their beginnings in the tacit knowledge and personal creativity of individuals working with modest tools and resources. The freeze-dried vaccine ampoules were first produced using a toy construction kit. Benjamin Rubin developed the concept of a bifurcated needle from considering a sewing needle. Compared with the jet injector, the bifurcated needle was a very simple "low-tech" device, but it was the one that became universally adopted.

Just as important as the technological innovations was the ability of participants from various nationalities and backgrounds to work together in developing and adapting innovative solutions to solve problems as they arose. Knowledge transfer was a major component of the program, and cultural knowledge played an important role in this process. A notable example was the training program in India, where epidemiologists from academia, who had not worked in rural villages, underwent simulation and role-playing exercises in order to change preexisting beliefs about fighting infectious diseases in a rural environment.

Local fieldworkers drew upon their knowledge of local customs and practices to come up with practical measures that encouraged reporting and facilitated detection. Foreign staff, on the other hand, were often more effective in making contact with and persuading bureaucrats to change policies or approve resources. In India, an informal joint leadership team developed at the top management level of the campaign. Within the smallpox high command, as it was known,

> the titles and offices merged into an informal leadership partnership which, with its members trusting and liking each other, provided the impetus and the inspiration for eradicating smallpox from India.
>
> At the highest level, this shared sense of purpose expressed itself in true international collaboration. Sharing train rides together back and forth from infected areas, attending monthly progress review meetings in every state in India, jointly making plans, assessing organizational tactics and strategy, and watching the incidence of smallpox wane or wax with the success of the efforts to overcome it led to a very unusual solidarity among the central command.
>
> The organizational charts and the charts of institutional roles fail to convey the sense of personal dedication and leadership that characterized the program participants who became emotionally tied to the success of the campaign. (Brilliant 1985, pp. 96–97)

This open, two-way collaboration was possible because the participants shared the vision that they were all working toward an important, inspiring goal that was attainable but which required urgent, determined action.

Decision making in the smallpox campaign was nestled in a hierarchy of rules, routines, objectives, and indicators that became the management tools for controlling the operational strategies of mass vaccination, surveillance-containment, and assessment. A clear definition of the problem led to the development of specific operational procedures that included quantitative performance targets and unambiguous evaluation measures. For mass vaccination, the targets were to reach at least 80 percent of the population and to achieve a 95 percent take-rate. For surveillance-containment, 75 percent of outbreaks were to be detected within 2 weeks of the first case, and that containment should then begin within 48 hours.

Many of the targets were set, at least initially, based on limited information and on what was possible to achieve, and had a "satisficing" quality about them. For example, the belief that mass vaccination was the best strategy was derived less from rigorous epidemiological analysis than from a "localized search" of recent vaccination experiences which concentrated on the overall success of these experiences but ignored certain other aspects (such as their isolated locations or well-controlled conditions). The 80 percent mass vaccination target was set because it was what experience had shown that a well-run vaccination program could accomplish. Targets and indicators were continually elaborated and broken down into secondary objectives and guidelines for execution at the village or municipal level, and it was in the field that the viability of the procedures and targets was tested. Adaptive organizational learning took place whenever existing goals and targets were not being met and new searches (for solutions, not smallpox) were initiated to find out why. This would typically involve understanding the local customs or conditions that might have impeded progress or analyzing patterns and trends of disease incidence in order to improve operational planning. New procedures incorporating new rules and targets emerged, and if they proved effective, they were rapidly disseminated in the program. There were many cycles of learning and adaptation, so that standard procedures, targets, and indicators evolved continuously to fit the specifics of local conditions and often became more stringent as the programs advanced and as more experience and knowledge accumulated.

Control was central to the program: control of the quality of the vaccine; control of the operational procedures and targets to carry out mass vaccination, surveillance, and containment measures; control of the reporting procedures to ensure that reliable information was available in time to solve problems as they arose; and control of the assessment procedures to provide an independent and realistic evaluation of a campaign as it was being implemented. The specification of a structure of rules and routines that provided management control was necessary in an international program being mounted by numerous countries in very different parts of the world. One principle underlying the design of control was to seek simplicity: "Simple devices, simple procedures, and simple instructions are especially critical in programs where large numbers of people are involved in tasks that demand disciplined performance—as good epidemiology does. Uncomplicated technology and straight-forward procedures lend themselves far more effectively to success in high pressure situations under difficult conditions" (Hopkins 1989, p. 129).

Yet, paradoxical as it may seem, control was effective because it kept an open heart and an open mind. Procedures and rules, though carefully defined at a general level, were interpreted and elaborated into field tactics and targets by adjusting them to a complex variety of indigenous cultures, religions, health systems, and governmental structures (Brilliant 1985). Experimentation and improvisation were encouraged as necessary tactics of learning and getting things done. Shortcuts that bypassed standard procedures, simplifications that cut costs or saved time, and people who skipped over formal levels in the hierarchy were all tolerated and recognized as valid responses justified by their ends.

At the enabling level, the smallpox program was also a triumph of effective *information management*. The surveillance system, containment system, and assessment system, which were central to the program, were all in essence information systems. *Information needs* were derived from well-defined procedures and targets. Soon after its inception, the program avoided the trap of going only for easy-to-collect data about program inputs (such as the number of vaccinations), which would have measured effort not results, and instead moved its focus to data about program outcomes (trends of the disease incidence). The availability of high-quality information was a sine qua non, and *information gathering* in the program emphasized information quality in all its major dimensions: comprehensiveness, accuracy, timeliness. Information collection was comprehensive, involving participants at all levels of the program, including local villagers and community leaders. A long-standing problem was the gross under-reporting of smallpox cases. Incentives were offered to encourage reporting, and these were designed to capture accurate data rather than data that people thought program managers wanted to see. Since accurate and timely information reporting lay at the heart of the containment strategy, a major organizational step was the separation of the surveillance and containment functions in order to avoid a conflict of interests:

> Health workers are expected to demonstrate good results. Like all humans, they tend to find evidence which supports expectations, and to avoid evidence that doesn't. Workers responsible for controlling a disease [the containment function] will tend to understate its incidence [the surveillance function]. The separation of surveillance and control functions proved to be important. (Siffin 1977, p. 1)

Information use was swift and sophisticated. Data collected were analyzed to discern patterns of incidence and spread, sometimes employing advanced methods from operations research. Data were used to test hypotheses and to challenge existing beliefs. Where warranted by the information, shifts in strategy and operations were implemented. Significant findings and innovations were disseminated in the program through periodic review meetings, conferences, and newsletters and other publications. Effective information management was the glue that held together the cycles of interpretation, innovation, action, and feedback which moved the program toward its remarkable achievement.

Summary

The World Health Organization's smallpox eradication program exemplifies several of the major features of organizational knowing. The program continuously reappraised its beliefs based on current evidence from the field, developed innovations and new knowledge that were instrumental in allowing the program to achieve its objectives, and implemented actions and procedures that afforded a high degree of control but also allowed room for local adaptation.

In *sense making,* the program was able to revise its beliefs about the nature of smallpox and the appropriate strategy for eradicating the disease. In the field, the program enacted a new way of reconfiguring the physical environment (identifying and isolating homes and villages) in order to focus its attention and information gathering. At its core, the widely dispersed program was held together by a shared sense of purpose. The common goal of eradicating smallpox, perceived as attainable, inspiring, and urgent, unified the diversity of national and local cultures that participated in the program. These common beliefs formed the shared context for coordinated action and for determining progress. The common agenda was amplified by detailed information about the epidemiology of the disease, laboratory diagnosis methods, operational approaches for vaccination and containment, health education, and a host of related subjects, all of which were published in the WHO smallpox handbook, the program's charter.

Knowledge creation both in the research laboratories and in the field produced key innovations and new knowledge about the incidence of the disease that were pivotal to the program. One plank of the eradication strategy was mass vaccination, which required a new form of vaccine that would be potent, reliable, economical, and easy to administer. The innovations of the freeze-dried vaccine and the bifurcated needle for presenting the vaccine answered these needs. The other plank was the surveillance and containment of smallpox outbreaks, which required local knowledge about indigenous customs and practices and how these may be taken advantage of in enforcing detection and isolation. This was where the knowledge of fieldworkers was vital in coming up with innovative measures that were effective because they leveraged local cultures and customs.

The smallpox program established a system of rules, procedures, standards, and targets to regulate *decision making* in the execution and evaluation of its campaigns. At the same time, this formal system coexisted with an informal network of practices and relationships that deviated from set norms but were expedient in surmounting particular obstacles or accelerating action. The results of each campaign were objectively assessed by independent teams even as the campaign was in progress, thus providing feedback in time for corrective action. New experiences and practices learned by campaigns in other countries or regions were disseminated promptly through review meetings, conferences, and newsletters.

In the smallpox program, the cycles of adaptation and learning depended on an unimpeded flow of accurate, timely, and actionable information that brought in current news about trends of disease incidence, the effectiveness of operational approaches, and new tactics and measures discovered in the field. Information needs were well defined, information gathering was thorough and efficient, and information use was managed so that analysis and interpretation of new data were accomplished in time to influence the course of action.

II. MODELS OF ORGANIZATIONAL LEARNING

There have been many attempts to model the process of organizational learning at a general, systemic level. Two of the most influential are the models developed by March and Olsen (1976) and Argyris and Schön (1978). In this section we examine each model and relate them to the concepts of organizational knowing.

March and Olsen (1976) develop a general representation of organizational choice that has become an archetypal model of organizational learning and adaptation. The model, shown in Fig. 7.2a, shows the complete cycle of organizational choice as consisting of four connections:

1. The cognitions and preferences held by individuals affect their behavior.
2. The behavior (including participation) of individuals affects organizational choices.
3. Organizational choices affect environmental acts (responses).
4. Environmental acts affect individual cognitions and preferences.

(March and Olsen 1976, p. 13)

Looking at these connections, it is possible to suggest that individuals' cognitive development of their "models of the world" is similar or at least related to sense-making activity, while individuals participating in a choice situation leading to choices or action outcomes is in fact decision making. We label these similarities in Fig. 7.2b and propose an additional connection. As organizations

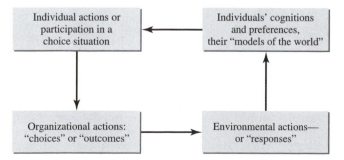

FIGURE 7.2a. Complete Cycle of Organizational Choice (March and Olsen 1976, p. 13)

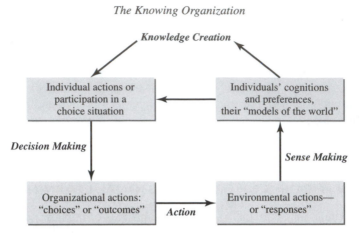

FIGURE 7.2b. Cycle of Organizational Choice (Extended)

work on novel and complex problems, they create new knowledge that introduces new options and new understandings that together form the basis on which choices can be made. We draw a new link in Fig. 7.2b to capture this notion of knowledge creation.

Although March and Olsen feel that the model is "too simple and too seductive," it does display two general structural features that are useful for subsequent model-building. First, organizational choice and adaptation takes place across multiple levels, in this case, the three levels of the individual, organization, and environment. The model shows that environmental responses are interpreted through the individuals' minds; it implies the role of action or enactment in ambiguous situations and suggests that organizational action leads to environmental response (although the same action may have different responses at different times). Second, the process is a cycle involving detection, response, feedback, and adaptation. Detection and recognition of a need for choice depends on the individuals' "models of the world" that define saliency and the allocation of attention. Response is both individual (the individual participates in a choice situation) and collective. Feedback may be unclear, since it may be difficult to trace outcomes to organizational actions. Adaptation occurs when individuals observe events, change beliefs in the light of experience, and modify behavior on the basis of this feedback.

Argyris and Schön (1978) suggest that individual and organizational behaviors are guided by a framework of goals, expectations, and learned methods, a framework that, in effect, serves as a theory of action. They define an organization's *theory of action* as including its

1. norms for corporate performance
   (for example, norms for margin of profit and for return on investment),
2. strategies for achieving norms
   (for example, strategies for plant location and for process technology), and

3. assumptions which bind strategies and norms together
(for example, the assumption that maintenance of a high rate of return on investment depends on the continual introduction of new technologies).

(Argyris and Schön 1978, pp. 14–15)

An organization's theory of action may be deduced in two ways. First, an examination of the formal documents of an organization, such as its organizational charts, policy statements, job descriptions, and archives, yields an *espoused theory* that the organization wishes to project to the outside world and to its members. Second, an observation of the actual behaviors of the organization may reveal that members act according to a different set of rules and assumptions, reflecting an alternative *theory-in-use* that may not be consistent with the espoused theory. Argyris and Schön suggest that the theory-in-use is often tacit and may remain tacit because its incompatibility with espoused theory is undiscussable, or because members are not able to articulate the elements of the theory-in-use. Nevertheless, each person in the organization constructs a partial representation of the theory-in-use of the whole, a "private image," in order to understand how her or his activity and identity relate to the overall organizational context. These private images make references to shared representations of organizational theory-in-use—"public maps," such as those depicting work flow, operating procedures, and compensation standards.

An organization learns by constructing, testing, and restructuring its theories of action. Individuals are frequently the agents of changing organizational theory-in-use:

> They act on their images and on their shared maps with expectations of patterned outcomes, which their subsequent experience confirms or disconfirms. When there is a mismatch of outcome to expectation (error), members may respond by modifying their images, maps, and activities so as to bring expectations and outcomes back into line. (Argyris and Schön 1978, p. 18)

Organizational learning takes place when members respond to changes in the environment by detecting errors and correcting the errors through modifying strategies, assumptions, or norms. The altered strategies, assumptions, or norms are then stored in the organization's memory, becoming part of the private images and public maps. Two modes of organizational learning are possible. Learning is *single-loop* when the modification of organizational action is sufficient to correct the error without challenging the validity of existing norms. In other words, the central features of the current organizational theory-in-use are preserved. It is single-loop because a single feedback loop between detected outcomes to action is adjusted so as to keep performance within the range set by organizational norms (Fig. 7.3a). The goal of single-loop learning is therefore to increase organizational effectiveness within current norms for performance (maintaining current objectives for product quality, sales, or task execution).

There are occasions when attempting to correct deviations within existing norms may not work, revealing instead conflicting requirements. Consider a firm

FIGURE 7.3a. Single- and Double-Loop Learning

whose current norms include pursuing high growth in sales and maintaining predictability in its operations. A new innovation from the research laboratory holds the promise of generating substantial sales but would require the firm to adopt new production methods and enter unfamiliar markets. A conflict arises between the existing norms of high sales and predictability. In this case, error correction requires the restructuring of the organizational norms themselves, which in turn necessitates a restructuring of strategies and assumptions associated with these norms. Learning here is *double-loop* because a double feedback loop connects error detection not only to organizational action but also to the norms (Fig. 7.3a). The goal of double-loop learning is therefore to ensure organizational growth and survivability by resolving incompatible norms, setting new priorities, or restructuring norms and their related strategies and assumptions. While single-loop learning is adaptive and is concerned with coping, double-loop learning is generative learning and creates new private images and public maps. The small-pox eradication program provides another example of double-loop learning: responding to new evidence from the field, the program restructured its norm or objective from carrying out mass vaccination to eradicating the disease itself. The new priority required new strategies and assumptions which were quickly developed (again by learning from field practices), stored in organizational memory, and disseminated (through newsletters, publications, meetings).

Looking at Fig. 7.3a, we suggest that single-loop learning is analogous to decision making, especially when that decision making is based on rule-following, and when the decision premises are taken as given. In contrast, we propose that double-loop learning is related to the activities of sense making and knowledge creation, perhaps combined together. One scenario that generates double-loop learning may be when organizations bracket or enact messages about outcomes that contradict or conflict with existing assumptions, thus precipitating new sense making and knowledge creation. If the assumptions and beliefs are modified, then new mental models or theories of action can emerge. We therefore elaborate the model in Fig. 7.3b to show that the two types of learning are related to rule-based decision making and belief-changing sense making or knowledge creation.

There are three aspects of Argyris and Schön's discussion of organizational learning that are especially germane to our conceptualization of organizational

FIGURE 7.3b. Single- and Double-Loop Learning (Elaborated)

knowing. *First, all organizations develop and subscribe to their own theories of action.* Theories of action enable organizations to accomplish complex tasks by establishing expectations of levels of performance, identifying methods and procedures to achieve those levels of performance, and postulating cause-effect relationships that in effect explain why what they are doing works.

Second, every organization maintains two versions of its theory of action. The espoused theory is that by which the organization projects and explains itself publicly to outsiders and internally to its members. It is useful for encoding past learning and experience, sustaining legitimacy, and inducting new staff. The espoused theory contains the formal, the explicit, and the codified, and is therefore related to the recorded memories, the explicit knowledge, and the written-down rules and procedures that we encountered in our discussion of sense making, knowledge creating, and decision making. The theory-in-use, on the other hand, is that which is revealed in the actions and behaviors of the organization and its members. It is important because it provides the basis for all individual action and how the action relates to that of others. The theory-in-use is inherently informal, tacit, and often uncodifiable, and is therefore related to the enactments, tacit knowledge, and heuristics that organizations employ as they make sense, make knowledge, and make decisions.

Third, each organization must continually construct, test, and restructure its theory of action if it is to learn and adapt (and thus survive) in a changing environment. Again, there are two modes of learning. In single-loop learning, the organization corrects for anomalies in performance by adjusting its actions without causing any change to its theory of action (its norms, assumptions, and strategies). In today's complex and dynamic environments, single-loop learning is insufficient, and few organizations can continue to operate by clinging on to an unchanging theory of action. In double-loop learning, adapting to anomalies involves restructuring the norms themselves, which in turn requires their associated strategies and assumptions to be modified. A new theory of action emerges. True organizational learning therefore requires members to reach back to their assumptions and beliefs, objectively appraise their content and validity in the light of current conditions and new evidence, restructure or reject norms and aspirations that are no longer viable, and reconfigure new objectives and relearn new methods to achieve them.

Furthermore, Argyris and Schön point out that while their model focuses on error detection and error correction,

> there is a domain of organizational knowing which lies, as it were, between
> error detection and error correction. In order to function as agents of
> organizational learning, individuals must set problems, construct models of
> organizational situations, and frame interpretations of error and anomaly. Their
> models, pictures, problem settings and interpretations display characteristic
> strategies for naming, framing, grouping, and describing the phenomena of
> organizational life. . . . we believe that [these] modes of organizational knowing
> are centrally inolved in processes of organizational learning. An organization's
> capacity to correct error depends, in considerable measure, on its members' ways
> of constructing the problems reflected by error. (Argyris and Schön 1978, p. 317)

III. LEARNING IN GROUPS AND IN PROJECTS

Learning in Groups: After Action Reviews

So far we have used the knowing organization framework to analyze the behavior of large organizations (e.g., NASA, World Health Organization). In this section, we look at how the processes that construct meaning, knowledge, and decisions also support learning at the group level.

One of the main messages of the knowing organization model is that learning requires the ability to collectively reflect on actions and experiences, accompanied by a willingness to modify beliefs and pursue new options when necessary. An example of a group-level learning activity that illustrates this idea would be the After Action Review (AAR) procedure, first introduced in the mid-1970s by the National Training Centers of the U.S. Army. The technique diffused slowly in the first decade and only became widely accepted after the army's AAR experiences in the Gulf War and the Haiti operations of 1994.

When U.S. troops went into Haiti (1994), AARs helped army personnel learn as they adjusted to a new and ambiguous situation. This was the first time army troops were deployed off of a navy aircraft carrier, and it was unclear if it was to be a peacekeeping or a combat mission. As the 82nd Airborne and the 10th Mountain Division arrived in Haiti, units implemented lessons learned using AARs (Baird et al. 1999). For example, one unit located on the aircraft carrier *Eisenhower* discovered an immediate problem. The hallways and stairs of an aircraft carrier were designed for efficient and quick movement of navy personnel. Army personnel with heavy packs could not move up and down the stairs easily, and it was impossible to pass in hallways. The challenge was how to quickly move thousands of troops from lower to higher decks. The solution developed in an AAR was to use the large elevators designed to raise aircraft to the upper decks to transport troops and their gear. Another unit discovered a shortage of water. The soldiers' water consumption was much higher than expected because of heat and humidity. The need for drinkable water increased dramatically. AARs developed solutions that called for supply lines to be opened and units responsible for supplying drinkable water to be moved up quickly. Another unit looked at its supply of intravenous medical equipment and projected a shortage. The heat and humidity were causing more soldiers than expected to pass out from dehydration. The standard medical supplies brought in by the troops needed to be modified. Solutions to these problems provided valuable lessons at the local level and improved operational efficiency. Lessons learned from individual units were consolidated, and higher-level solutions emerged as analysts examined all the units together and saw how the problems were related. Since soldiers were carrying 80 pounds of equipment in high temperature and humidity, they were losing more body fluid than normal. The suggested solution was to have soldiers carry only the bare essentials for a peacekeeping operation. This might reduce physical exertion enough to lower the loss of body fluid and minimize the need for water and intravenous equipment. After a successful test of this idea, orders went out to all units to minimize pack loads. Similar lessons collected during disaster assistance in the aftermath of Hurricane Andrew in Florida, Somalia, Rwanda, and Bosnia had also been disseminated by the U.S. Army and archived for future peacekeeping operations. In the corporate world, the AAR technique has been applied successfully at firms such as British Petroleum, Bechtel, Chrysler, and GTE (Gorelick et al. 2004; Dixon 2000).

The AAR is a way for a team to reflect on and learn while it is performing an activity. The purpose of the AAR is to arrive at a shared understanding of what happened in a given situation; why it happened; and what could be done differently next time. Although the process itself may be formal or informal, involve groups of various sizes, and last for minutes or hours, the discussion in an AAR is always anchored by four questions:

1. What did we set out to do? What was supposed to happen?

2. What actually happened?   *Sense making*

3. Why is there a difference?   *Knowledge creation*

4. What can we learn from this? What are we   *Decision making*
   going to do about it?

(Garvin 2000; Baird et al. 1999)

The first question (What did we set out to do? What was supposed to happen?) involves group members agreeing on the purpose of their mission and the definition of success. This then forms a baseline for evaluating performance as well as for identifying gaps or surprises that need to be better understood. The second question (What actually happened?) involves group members coming to an agreement about the events that unfolded during a mission. As we have noted in our chapter on sense making, participants bracket information differently and may notice, label, and connect events differently from each other. This part of the AAR discussion then has to deal with multiple accounts of what has happened in order to arrive at a shared reality, what the soldiers would call "ground truth." Two general approaches are applied. The first is to pool information from three sources: experienced soldiers acting as observers-controllers; instrumentation such as automated tracking and logging devices; and films made on video cameras that recorded the events. Instead of multiple sources, the second approach is to pool multiple perspectives in a facilitated discussion. The AAR is started soon after the event and includes all key participants as well as third-party observers, members from staff and support units, and even commanders. The U.S. Army found that it is critical to give sufficient time (a quarter of the time of an AAR) to addressing the first two questions, in order to develop a common understanding of the objectives and a shared interpretation of what took place.

The third question (Why is there a difference between what actually happened and what was supposed to happen?) begins the analysis of the underlying reasons for success or failure. This is typically a cause-and-effect examination that seeks an explanation of the differences between expectations and reality. Sometimes the analysis is straightforward and an outcome can be traced to a specific action. Often, problems are more complex, requiring a series of AARs to gradually tease out the factors and reasons that could account for the differences. In either case, this part of the AAR calls for problem solving, a diagnostic frame of mind, and a willingness to be honest and accept responsibility. The fourth question (What can we learn from this?) compares the current experience with past experiences, in the process forming beliefs about how to explain what was observed. The outcome may also include new ideas about how to solve a problematic aspect of the activity or how to improve performance the next time around. Taken together, dealing with the third and fourth questions is tantamount to creating knowledge that is useful to the group. The fourth question also asks "What are we going to do about it?" The natural focus here is on elements that could be improved upon, but it is also important to identify practices or procedures that should be sustained or repeated. In Haiti, where the army was undertaking an unfamiliar kind of mission, the AARs of early units were used to develop standard operating procedures for follow-on units (Garvin 2000). Importantly, the entire process is supported by a skilled facilitator and follows a number of ground rules that disallow using information in AARs to place blame, find fault, or penalize individuals.

The four questions that drive the AAR process would also drive the cycles of sense making, knowledge creation, and decision making that we believe are necessary in enabling a group to learn through action and reflection. The questions asking what happened and why there is a difference between reality and expectations are the same questions that initiate sense making in organizations. Groups negotiate this meaning collectively, taking into account the various ways that they bracket and enact events they have observed. The question of why there is a difference segues into a discussion of what can be learned from this difference. The focus shifts here to analysis and problem solving, often motivated by the desire to come up with ideas for methods that would work in similar situations. We see this brainstorming and problem solving as being analogous to knowledge creation. Finally, answering the question of what is to be done is concerned with turning lessons learned into concrete action that may be disseminated more widely or institutionalized as standard operating procedures. We see here an instantiation of decision making taking new knowledge as a potential for action and transforming it into a commitment to act.

Organizational Knowing in the Eureka Project

In chapter 4, we discussed the Eureka project at Xerox corporation that enhanced the way service technicians shared knowledge about solving tough machine problems. We now revisit the case with a different perspective. We show how Xerox as a firm had to unlearn its assumptions about the nature of field service work; how it discovered a social community of practice and supported it with appropriate technology; and how decision makers were initially skeptical and had to revise their decision premises before finally approving system deployment across the organization.

Xerox recognized that the servicing of its products at customer sites is an important means of increasing customer satisfaction and loyalty. Over time, management developed the belief that field service should follow standardized procedures laid down in the technical service manuals. This would lower costs and ensure a consistent, efficient service. These sense-making interpretations about cost-efficiency and standardization formed the premises for making decisions about field service. (The discussion of Eureka in this section is based on the account by Bobrow and Whalen 2002.)

Enactments and Belief Revision in the Eureka Project. In the early 1990s, a group in Xerox PARC saw an opportunity to apply its knowledge of expert systems to develop a system that would support field service work—work that was perceived as a well-structured task. The first enactment by the group was to develop a prototype that was demonstrated to technicians in order to determine whether such a tool would be helpful. Although impressed by the system, the technicians did not think it would be useful in the field because many products did not have service manuals, and because the hardest problems encountered in the field were those not covered in the manuals. With this feedback, the PARC group decided on a second enactment—following service technicians in their service calls so as to observe directly what they actually did during these visits. This ethnographic study found that technicians often called on a peer or an experienced person for ideas, and when unusual problems were solved they would tell stories about these successes. As a result, the PARC group constructed new interpretations about the work of service technicians: technicians solved tough, undocumented problems in the field; the new knowledge so generated is valuable and should be shared; and the creation and sharing of this knowledge depends on the shared norms and practices of the community of technicians. The PARC scientists noted that, in effect, what they had discovered was that "the community was the expert system." These new beliefs

constituted the new context for the next stage of the project—the development
of the Eureka system.

Knowledge Creation in the Eureka Project. The evolution of the knowledge-
sharing process that lies at the core of Eureka was described in Chapter 4. We
note here how tacit, explicit, and cultural knowledge are activated and combined
in Eureka. The process begins when service technicians discover workarounds
that fix tough problems based on their experience and intuition (*tacit knowledge*).
As they enter these workarounds into the pending tips database, they are starting
the process of converting their intuitions into a more explicit form. The externalization of knowledge continues when experienced field engineers and the tip
contributors converse with each other to hone these new solutions. After validation, the tips move into a formal knowledge base where they may be down-
loaded, searched, and viewed by all service technicians (*explicit knowledge*).
Technicians are willing to try these solutions because they trust the system by
which the tips are generated. They are also willing to contribute new tips because
they value the recognition of their peers. Service technicians interact with each
other as a natural community of practice. They face common work tasks, and
they can see the benefit of having the collective knowledge of the group available
as each of them works on a problem. Their knowledge sharing is supported by
social practices and norms that are based on peer recognition, trust, and cooperation (*cultural knowledge*). We may say that Eureka works because it respects
the way that tacit, explicit, and cultural knowledge are simultaneously engaged
in a natural community of practice.

Decision Making in the Eureka Project. For the firm as a whole, Eureka was
something of a radical innovation: it grew from the bottom up with little support
from top management; it purports to capture knowledge in work that was initially thought to be not knowledge-intensive; and it implicitly challenges the
authority of the product engineers who had written the service manuals in the
first place. Indeed, as we noted above, the initial premises for making decisions
about field service were based on cost-efficiency and standardization. The service organization was seen as a cost center, and management at first thought that
field service was much more of a "follow-the-manual task" than "creative problem solving." As a result, early attempts to obtain resources to support the project
proved difficult. The project group had to sometimes operate like a guerilla
group, relying on local champions who were somehow able to assemble resources and support. The project began in France and moved on to Canada before
it was considered for introduction in the United States. High-level decision
makers were still skeptical about the project and wanted to see evidence of
tangible benefits and payoffs. As the use of Eureka spread, service improvement
data became available and enthusiasm for the system grew, so that the deployment of Eureka in the United States was finally approved. The sequence of
events here is instructive. An innovation was introduced which decision makers
perceived as being risky and uncertain. Work continued under the radar, as it

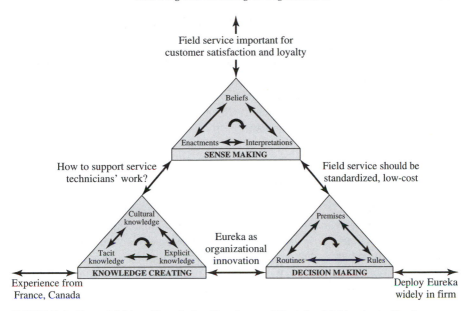

FIGURE 7.4. Sense Making, Knowledge Creating, and Decision Making in the Eureka Project

were, until a business case could be made within the existing decision rules and premises. The eventual success of the project led to a modification of the decision assumptions about the nature of field service work.

As shown in Fig. 7.4, early cycles of sense making formed management beliefs that customer field service was a standardized activity best delivered in a cost-efficient manner. Studies by PARC scientists to understand field service work constructed the new interpretations that service technicians created valuable new knowledge in their work that should be shared. This was the impetus for work to begin on a system to support the service technician community. The Eureka system that evolved recognized the intuitive, tacit nature of solving tough problems; the need to capture new ideas in a more explicit form for sharing; and the need to respect the social norms that the community had developed. It was a gradual process to get top managers to become convinced of the usefulness of Eureka as an organizational innovation. Initial resistance, typical in the face of new innovations that pose new risks and uncertainty, had to be "managed" using a number of unconventional tactics that allowed the project to grow and demonstrate its value. Eventually, the accumulation of evidence and enthusiasm led to managers changing their beliefs about the routine nature of service work and approving the deployment of Eureka widely in the firm. (For another example of the diachronic interplay between sense making, knowledge creating, and decision making, see the study by Choo and Johnston [2004] of a large Canadian foreign exchange bank that pioneered an innovative online trading system.)

IV. IMPLICATIONS FOR PRACTICE

We have applied the knowing organization as a theoretical scheme to construct narratives of organizational experience. Narratives convey something of the texture and complexity of organizational life, and they can also speak to each of us about what practical implications may be drawn for our own contexts. In this section, we discuss briefly some practical issues that may arise from our discussions in this volume. Fig. 7.5 shows three loops of learning, with each loop becoming more expansive as it connects a larger set of information activities.

Loop I Learning—Decision Making

A great deal of interest is focused on managerial decision making. Decision making is seen to be closest to action and the production of results. Many believe that the essence of management is decision making—that being decisive is a trait of a good manager, that being able to make rational decisions demonstrates competence. In decision making, the manager is motivated by questions such as what is to be done; how to meet goals; how to deliver results; and how to show competence. When we view decision making on its own, we are looking at the innermost loop of learning in Fig. 7.5, which is similar to the single-loop learning mode described by Argyris and Schön (1978), where actions are adjusted to meet current goals and targets.

Our discussions in the earlier chapters suggest that the practice of decision making may be usefully enhanced by being aware of (1) the internal structure of the decision process—the decision rules and premises that affect the quality of

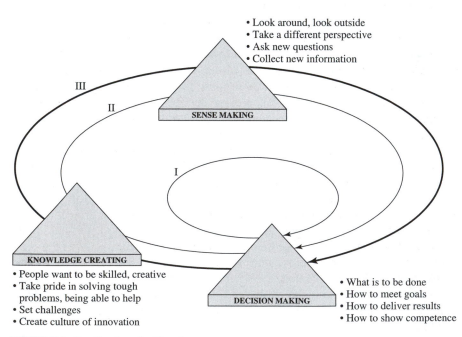

FIGURE 7.5. Implications for Practice

the process; and (2) the external context of the decision-making activity—the beliefs and knowledge that affect the quality of decisions made.

First the internal structure, and here we are concerned with the premises, rules, and routines that order organizational decision making. Among the different value premises that an organization espouses, economic or financial evaluation criteria tend to figure prominently, since most organizations aim to enlarge profits or lower costs. While financial *decision premises* are important in ensuring efficient resource allocation, allowing economic considerations to dominate decision making can disadvantage innovation and discourage risk taking. Three approaches are used to cope with financial conservatism:

- construct a business case for the innovation that takes into account both financial and nonfinancial benefits;

- create a separate business unit to pursue the innovation, and evaluate the unit on criteria different from the rest of the firm;

- grow the innovation outside the direct view of top management, until there is sufficient evidence to attest to its benefits.

Much of decision making in organizations is *rule based* and *rule following*. Some researchers believe that decision rules can block innovation. Christensen (1997, 2003), for example, argues that resources will not be allocated to disruptive innovations in decision making that is based on existing cost structures and on rules and premises that favor current customers and market segments. Others, notably Burgelman (2002), found that simple decision rules can enable strategic evolution over time. Based on an extended case study of Intel, Burgelman (2002) shows how relatively simple decision rules acted as selection mechanisms to (a) choose fittest alternatives from options generated by internal variation and (b) reveal new patterns of behavior that suggest fundamental changes in the business. Thus, Intel's adherence to set rules to allocate costly chip fabrication resources led it to make the painful decision of exiting from the computer memory market and concentrating on microprocessors—a decision that proved highly felicitous to the firm. Is there a middle ground between rules as blocking innovation and rules as enabling innovation? Ackoff has long suggested that decision support systems should be designed as learning systems that support the reflective application of decision rules (see, for example, Ackoff 1967). He developed an architecture for such a "learning and adaptation system," and systems based on the design were implemented at General Motors, Du Pont, and other firms (Barabba, Pourdehnad, and Ackoff 2002).

Decision rules and premises are embedded in organizational routines. The repeated application of standard procedures can *routinize* the way decisions are made with a number of possible consequences. Decision makers may make do with lower standards of "satisficing," good-enough solutions. They may become desensitized to warning signals or risks, and risky decision making drifts into a zone of false comfort. There may be increased inertia and resistance to change or innovation. Our analysis of the *Challenger* and *Columbia* accidents in Chapter 6 found that these tendencies contributed to the tragic results. Vaughan (1996) observed that the routinization of decision making can produce a decision culture that protects the validity of rules and premises, resulting in an inherent pressure to conform and to confirm current norms.

From the rules and routines that make up the internal structure of decision making, we move on to examine the external context of decision making. While decision making is closest to action, it is important to understand how decision making is shaped and constrained by the sense-making and knowledge-creation activities of the organization. Thus, decision premises are based on beliefs and interpretations constructed through cycles of sense making. The range of decision alternatives, as well as the quality and attainability of these alternatives, depends on the knowledge-creating capability of the firm. We amplify these ideas in the following sections.

Loop II Learning—Sense Making and Decision Making

In our model, the difference between decision making and sense making may be compared to the difference between single- and double-loop learning. Whereas decision making is often in the mode of single-loop learning (taking action to attain current goals), the approach in sense making can more resemble *double-loop learning,* especially when sense making leads to changes in the organization's governing assumptions and beliefs. In order for this to occur, organizations would need to adopt a greater openness toward information: they would view information from multiple perspectives; ask new questions; try new sources; and be willing to reconsider beliefs and assumptions. An important factor in the success of the Smallpox Eradication Program was the ability of the World Health Organization to revise and in some cases reverse its initial beliefs about the nature of the disease and the strategies to be adopted in the field.

Decision making depends on sense making. We need to know "what is going on and why" before we are able to decide "what is to be done." In a complex, dynamic world, making sense of the environment, rendering a plausible understanding of what is going on, becomes a more daunting challenge. Making sensible interpretations is as crucial as making the right moves. In Fig. 7.5, where sense making is connected to decision making, a more expansive loop of learning is at work.

Organizations are unaware of their sense making when normal conditions prevail, that is, when conditions are consistent with their mental models and expectations. Sense making becomes a conscious activity when the organization is confronted with information that is surprising, puzzling, or disturbing. Organizations need to recognize disruptive events as occasions for new learning and treat the accompanying feeling of cognitive dissonance as a signal to adopt a thinking mode that is more open, reflective, and critical. The human mind prefers stability to change, so we need to be mindful of the biases to prefer information that confirms current beliefs and the tendencies to rely on existing cognitive schemas to control sense making.

In today's networked information environment, there is a proliferation of tools and channels available to organizations to sense and enact the environment. An important component of the information competence of an organization is the ability to use these tools to widen the organization's peripheral vision, to broaden the range of signals and messages that it is attending to, without increasing information load harmfully. At the time of writing, there are commercially available software tools that are being used to track, monitor, and analyze the content of online discussions, weblogs, and other web-based communications in order to assess the reputation of an organization or the perception of a brand. An enactive organization would use communication tools and information resources to introduce new features in the environment so as to focus its sense making. For example, it might create an interactive web site with content and forums that allow it to feed information as well as to receive feedback. It might host a workshop to learn about a new technology; distribute white papers for comment; or give away a new product to find out who uses it. A proactive organization would attempt to influence the environment so that it would respond more favorably to its interests. For example, some news agencies provide a fee-based service that allows clients to preview the following day's headline stories, to introduce additional background information to these stories, or to even suggest experts who may be asked to comment on these stories.

More and more organizations recognize both the power and the vulnerability afforded by a highly networked and highly diverse information environment. Organizations realize that the enactment of favorable messages and interpretations has become a major arena for contest. This is especially so when a value-laden issue arises, and when information about the issue is mixed or confusing. Different stakeholders and observers move quickly to offer their own interpretations of events and trends. Journalists, analysts, commentators, advocacy groups, policy centers, government officials, regulators, and so on all attempt to fill a sense-making void with plausible narratives and explanations. The interpretations offered may not always be innocent—many would be aimed at securing advantage for particular groups or interests. In today's ambiguous and ambivalent environments, *sense giving* and *sense contesting* have become a new strategic element of organizational life.

Loop III Learning—Knowledge Creation, Sense Making, and Decision Making

As shown in Fig. 7.5, the most expansive loop of learning connects knowledge creation, sense making, and decision making. While organizational decision making may be routinized and sense making may be unconscious, knowledge creation at the organization level is often a deliberate, sustained activity that is driven by the need to address a problem. The creation of new knowledge can be a source of competitive advantage for the organization, particularly when it expands competencies or enables innovation. The availability of new knowledge does not necessarily imply that it will be utilized. Organizations need to make sense of the potential and implications of the new knowledge, while decision makers need to assess the risk and uncertainty of applying it. Efforts to support knowledge creation are likely to combine two complementary approaches:

- create *enabling conditions* that encourage knowledge creation, sharing, and use;
- provide *enabling tools* that support knowledge creation, transfer, and use.

Creating enabling conditions implies cultivating a culture that promotes creativity, innovation, and experimentation. A culture of innovation is built on a number of beliefs: people want to be skilled, creative; they take pride in solving tough problems; they enjoy being able to help their colleagues; they value the recognition and respect of their peers; and they find it satisfying to be able to meet challenges. Not many organizations operate based on these beliefs. One exception may be 3M (Minnesota Mining and Manufacturing Company), a firm with a track record of developing and commercializing innovative products that had not existed before. Its ideology is based on the principles of innovation ("thou shalt not kill a new product idea"); respect for individual initiative and personal growth; tolerance for honest mistakes; absolute integrity; and product quality and reliability. These principles are translated into policies. For example, technical staff are encouraged to spend up to 15 percent of their time on projects of their own choosing. Each division is expected to generate 30 percent of its annual sales from products that are introduced in the previous four years. Technology sharing awards are given to those who develop a new technology and share it successfully with other divisions (Collins and Porras 1994).

Providing enabling tools often implies using information technology to support the engagement of tacit and explicit knowledge in a work setting. Thus, there is significant interest in developing computer tools that could in some way support the use of tacit knowledge. At the time of writing, there are commercial software-based tools that automatically build expertise profiles of individuals that can then be searched. The software builds these profiles by analyzing e-mail, online discussions, documents added to or retrieved from a database, and so on. There are also interesting attempts to combine the tacit knowledge of a group through systems such as an online information aggregation market (e.g., HP has successfully used information markets to make better internal sales forecasts). Another approach is the use of case-based reasoning technology. Here, expertise is contained in a library of past cases, with each case providing a description of the problem, a solution, and the outcome. The knowledge and reasoning process used by an expert to solve a problem is not recorded explicitly but is contextualized and implicit in the description of the problem and its solution.

We may at first expect information technology to be able to support explicit knowledge effectively, given the substantial experience in applying database technology to control structured information. Unfortunately, a very significant fraction of the knowledge of an organization is in the form of unstructured information (presentations, call reports, project de-briefs, e-mail, online discussions). The management of unstructured information has become a major goal of many organizations. One approach is to create an external structure of taxonomies and controlled vocabularies to categorize, tag, and describe the unstructured content. A different approach is to generate the structure automatically on the fly, while responding to a search query, and using the generated structure to cluster search results into folders with subject headings. A third approach is to apply data-mining techniques to corpuses of text in order to extract information about entities and events (referred to as information extraction, knowledge discovery).

Knowledge sharing is an inherently social activity, supported by norms of trust and reciprocity. Communities of practice have proved to be effective because they are the social venues where members can simultaneously engage knowledge that is tacit (personal experiences), explicit (proposals, presentations), and cultural (shared values about their work). Communities of practice tend to be self-organized or to emerge naturally, and the role of information technology tools is mainly in the areas of communication and content access. For example, a typical community of practice software product would provide functions such as online discussion, chat, polling or voting, a repository of shared files, and searching for content or people. Whether choosing or developing tools to support knowledge sharing, it is worth recalling the experience of the Eureka project—that the technology works best when it respects and honors the social norms and practices that define the community of practice.

Marchand, Kettinger, and Rollins (2001, 2000) studied 983 companies operating in 22 countries and 25 industries in an attempt to answer the question "How does the interaction of people, information, and technology affect business performance?" They found that three sets of information capabilities combine together to define an organization's *information orientation,* and it is this integrative orientation that predicted business performance. The three information capabilities are (from Marchand, Kettinger, and Rollins 2001)

1. *Information technology practices:* the capability to effectively manage information technology (IT) applications and infrastructure to support operations, business processes, innovation, and managerial decision making.

2. *Information management practices:* the capability to manage information effectively over the life cycle of information use, including sensing, collecting, organizing, processing, and maintaining information. This involves scanning for information about markets, customers, competitors, and suppliers; organizing, linking, and analyzing information; and ensuring that people use the best information available.

3. *Information behaviors and values:* the capability to instill and promote behaviors and values in people for effective use of information. These values include:

   - *integrity* (information is not manipulated for personal gains);
   - *formality* (formal sources are trusted);
   - *control* (information on performance is disclosed to all employees);
   - *sharing* (information is exchanged between individuals, teams, functional areas);
   - *transparency* (members trust each other enough to talk about failures and errors);
   - *proactiveness* (members actively seek out and respond to changes in the competitive environment).

The study concluded that excellence in any one of the three areas on its own does not increase business performance. All three practices must be strong and working together to achieve superior performance: an organization must learn to manage and align its information technology, information practices, and information culture.

V. CODA

The knowing organization is a model of how organizations learn. The model focuses on the information-use activities that support learning. The three major information activities we concentrated on are sense making, knowledge creation, and decision making. Within each activity, we looked at how information needs are experienced, how information is sought, and how information is used or not used. We observed that each of these processes is deeply influenced by cognitive, affective, and situational factors that play out at the individual, group, and organizational levels. Figure 7.6a brings together these elements in a "knowing cube." Figure 7.6b "flattens" the cube to show its principal layers of analysis.

The model provides a structure and language that can be used to analyze information use in organizations. Real life itself is always richer and more complex than any of our models of it: a terrain is never the same as a map that relates to it. Even though a map is a simplified representation of reality, it does highlight key features of the terrain, show the big picture, help us see where we are, and warn us about gaps and obstacles. Although we discuss some practical

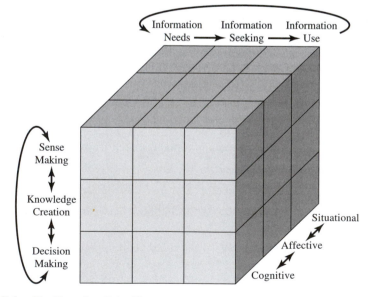

FIGURE 7.6a. The Knowing Cube (1)

	Information Needs			Information Seeking			Information Use		
	Cognitive	*Affective*	*Situational*	*Cognitive*	*Affective*	*Situational*	*Cognitive*	*Affective*	*Situational*
Sense Making Beliefs Enactments Interpretations									
Knowledge Creation Tacit Explicit Cultural									
Decision Making Premises Rules Routines									

FIGURE 7.6b. The Knowing Cube (2)

implications in the previous section, the model is more descriptive than prescriptive. Taken as a whole, the model suggests that knowing and learning in organizations is the outcome of a set of distributed but connected information activities. The model does not suggest universal solutions, but it does offer a framework that can help an organization to think through its own strategy. In the end, this is a work in progress—our goal is better understanding, as a necessary first step toward better practice.

VI. SUMMARY

- In the WHO Smallpox Eradication Program, the melding of sense making, knowledge creation, and decision making into continuous cycles of interpretation, innovation, and adaptive action underpinned the program's success.

- The smallpox program was a triumph of information management. Information needs were clearly defined, information gathering was thorough and efficient, and information use was managed so that field results were analyzed in time to influence the course of action.

- As a theoretical model, the knowing organization builds upon the classic organizational choice model of March and Olsen (1976) and the organizational learning model of Argyris and Schön (1978).

- Whereas decision making is often in the mode of single-loop learning (Argyris and Schön 1978), the approach in sense making can more resemble double-loop learning, especially when sense making leads to changes in the organization's governing assumptions and beliefs.

- Decision making depends on sense making: we need to know "what is going on and why" before we are able to decide "what is to be done." Making sensible interpretations is as critical as making the right moves.

- In a highly networked and diverse environment, where different stakeholders move quickly to offer their own interpretations of ambiguous events and issues, organizations realize that *sense giving* and *sense contesting* have become a new strategic element of organizational life.

- Efforts to support knowledge creation are likely to combine two complementary approaches: (1) creating *enabling conditions* that encourage knowledge creation, sharing, and use; (2) providing *enabling tools* that support knowledge creation, transfer, and use.

- The knowing organization is a model of how organizations learn that focuses on the information-use activities that support learning. Although the model does not prescribe universal solutions, it does offer a framework to help an organization analyze its management and use of information.

REFERENCES

Ackoff, R. L. 1967. Management Misinformation Systems. *Management Science* 14, no. 3:BB147–56.

Adler, P. S. 1993. The "Learning Bureaucracy": New United Motor Manufacturing Inc. In *Research on Industrial Behaviour,* edited by B. M. Staw and L. L. Cummings, 111–94. Greenwich, CT: JAI Press.

Aguilar, F. J. 1967. *Scanning the Business Environment.* New York: Macmillan Co.

Allen, T. 1969. Information Needs and Uses. In *Annual Review of Information Science and Technology,* edited by C. A. Cuadra, 4:2–29. Chicago: Encyclopedia Britannica.

Allen, T. J. 1977. *Managing the Flow of Technology: Technology Transfer and the Dissemination of Technological Information within the R&D Organization.* Cambridge, MA: MIT Press.

Allison, G. T., and P. Zelikow. 1999. *Essence of Decision: Explaining the Cuban Missile Crisis.* 2nd ed. New York: Addison-Wesley.

Alvesson, M. 1993. Organizations as Rhetoric: Knowledge-Intensive Firms and the Struggle with Ambiguity. *Journal of Management Studies* 30, no. 6:997–1015.

———. 2001. *Understanding Organizational Culture.* Thousand Oaks, CA: Sage.

Argyris, C. 1990. *Overcoming Organizational Defenses: Facilitating Organizational Learning.* Boston: Allyn and Bacon.

———. 1994. Good Communication That Blocks Learning. *Harvard Business Review* 71, no. 4:77–88.

Argyris, C., and D. A. Schön. 1978. *Organizational Learning: A Theory of Action Perspective.* Reading, MA: Addison-Wesley.

Arkes, H. R., and C. Blumer. 1985. The Psychology of Sunk Cost. *Organizational Behavior and Human Decision Processes* 35, no. 1:124–40.

Ashby, W. R. 1956. *An Introduction to Cybernetics.* London: Chapman and Hall.

Audi, R. 1998. *Epistemology: A Contemporary Introduction to the Theory of Knowledge.* New York: Routledge.

Auerbach Corporation. 1965. *DOD User Needs Study, Phase I.* 1151-TR-3.

Auster, E., and C. W. Choo. 1993. Environmental Scanning by CEOs in Two Canadian Industries. *Journal of the American Society for Information Science* 44, no. 4: 194–203.

Badaracco, J. L. 1991. *The Knowledge Link: How Firms Compete Through Strategic Alliances.* Boston: Harvard Business School Press.

Baden-Fuller, C., S. Pitt, J. Stopford, and D. Taylor. 1987. Sustaining Competitive Advantage Against Low Cost Imports: The Lessons from the High Quality British Knitwear Producers. Working paper, Center for Business Strategy, London Business School.

Baird, L., P. Holland, and S. Deacon. 1999. Learning from Action: Imbedding More Learning into the Performance Fast Enough to Make a Difference. *Organizational Dynamics* 27, no. 4:19–32.

Bandura, A. 1977. Self Efficacy: Towards a Unifying Theory of Behavioural Change. *Psychological Review* 84, no. 2:191–215.

Barabba, V., J. Pourdehnad, and R. Ackoff. 2002. Above and Beyond Knowledge Management. In *The Strategic Management of Intellectual Capital and Organizational Knowledge,* edited by C. W. Choo and N. Bontis, 359–69. New York: Oxford University Press.

Bartlett, F. C. 1932. *Remembering.* Cambridge, U.K.: Cambridge University Press.

Bates, M. 1971. *User Studies: A Review for Librarians and Information Scientists.* U.S. Department of Health Education and Welfare.

Bayne, R. 1995. *The Myers-Briggs Type Indicator: A Critical and Practical Guide.* London: Chapman and Hall.

Belkin, N. J. 1980. Anomalous States of Knowledge as a Basis for Information Retrieval. *Canadian Journal of Information Science* 5 (May): 133–43.

Belkin, N. J., R. N. Oddy, and H. M. Brooks. 1982. Ask for Information Retrieval: Part 1. Background and Theory. *Journal of Documentation* 38, no. 2:61–71.

Bell, T. E., and K. Esch. 1987. The Fatal Flaw in Flight 51-L. *IEEE Spectrum* 24, no. 2:36–51.

Bettis, R. A., and C. K. Prahalad. 1995. The Dominant Logic: Retrospective and Extension. *Strategic Management Journal* 16, no. 1:5–14.

Blackler, F. 1995. Knowledge, Knowledge Work and Organizations: An Overview and Interpretation. *Organization Studies* 16, no. 6:1021–46.

Blau, P. M. 1954. Co-operation and Competition in a Bureaucracy. *American Journal of Sociology* 59, no. 6:530–36.

Blight, J. G., and D. A. Welch, eds. 1998. *Intelligence and the Cuban Missile Crisis.* Cass Series, Studies in Intelligence. Portland: Frank Cass.

Bobrow, D. G., and J. Whalen. 2002. Community Knowledge Sharing in Practice: The Eureka Story. *Reflections, Journal of the Society for Organizational Learning* 4, no. 2:47–59.

Boisot, M. H. 1995. *Information Space: A Framework for Learning in Organizations, Institutions and Culture.* London: Routledge.

———. 1998. *Knowledge Assets: Securing Competitive Advantage in the Information Economy.* New York: Oxford University Press.

Borlund, P. 2003. The Concept of Relevance in IR. *Journal of the American Society for Information Science and Technology* 54, no. 10:913–25.

Bougon, M., K. Weick, and D. Binkhorst. 1977. Cognition in Organizations: An Analysis of the Utrecht Jazz Orchestra. *Administrative Science Quarterly* 22, no. 4: 606–31.

Bourdieu, P. 1988. *The Logic of Practice.* Stanford, CA: Stanford University Press.

Bowker, G., and S. L. Star. 1999. *Sorting Things Out: Classification and Practice.* Cambridge, MA: MIT Press.

Brilliant, L. B. 1985. *The Management of Smallpox Eradication in India.* Ann Arbor: University of Michigan Press.

Brockeriede, W. 1974. Rhetorical Criticism as Argument. *Quarterly Journal of Speech* 60, no. 4:165–74.

Brown, J. S. 1993. Session II—Papers submitted by, presentation by, main themes generated by John Seely Brown. In *Learning in Organizations Workshop* (Western Business School, London, Ont., Canada, June 21–23, 1992), edited by M. M. Crossan, H. W. Lane, J. C. Rush, and R. E. White, 81–115. London, Ont.: University of Western Ontario.

Brown, J. S., and P. Duguid. 1991. Organizational Learning and Communities-of-Practice: Toward a Unified View of Working, Learning, and Innovation. *Organization Science* 2, no. 1:40–57.

Brown, J. S., and E. S. Gray. 1995. The People Are the Company. *Fast Company* 1 (December): 78–82.

Burgelman, R. A. 2002. *Strategy Is Destiny: How Strategy-Making Shapes a Company's Future.* New York: Free Press.

Burt, R. S. 1992. *Structural Holes: The Social Structure of Competition.* Boston: Harvard University Press.

Campbell, D. J. 1988. Task Complexity: A Review and Analysis. *Academy of Management Review* 13, no. 1:40–52.

Caplan, N., A. Morrison, and R. J. Stambaugh. 1975. *The Use of Social Science Knowledge in Policy Decisions at the National Level.* Ann Arbor: University of Michigan, Institute for Social Research.

Case, D. O. 2002. *Looking for Information: A Survey of Research on Information Seeking, Needs, and Behavior.* New York: Academic Press.

Chang, L., and P. Kornbluth, eds. 1993. *The Cuban Missile Crisis, 1962: A National Security Archive Documents Reader.* New York: New Press.

Chang, S. J., and R. E. Rice. 1993. Browsing: A Multidimensional Framework. In *Annual Review of Information Science and Technology,* edited by M. E. Williams, 28:231–76. Medford, NJ: Learned Information.

Chatman, E. A. 1991. Life in a Small World: Applicability of Gratification Theory to Information-Seeking Behavior. *Journal of the American Society for Information Science* 42, no. 6:438–49.

———. 1992. *The Information World of Retired Women.* Westport, CT: Greenwood Press.

———. 1996. The Impoverished Life-World of Outsiders. *Journal of the American Society for Information Science* 47, no. 3:193–206.

———. 1999. A Theory of Life in the Round. *Journal of the American Society for Information Science* 50, no. 3:207–17.

———. 2000. Framing Social Life in Theory and Research. *New Review of Information Behaviour Research* 1:3–18.

Chen, C. 1982. Citizens' Information Needs—A Regional Investigation. In *Information Needs of the 80s,* edited by R. Stueart, 77–94. Greenwich, CT: JAI Press.

Chen, C., and L. B. Burger. 1984. *Assessment of Connecticut Citizens' Information Needs and Library Use Study.* Hartford: Connecticut State Library.

Chen, C., and P. Hernon. 1980. Library Effectiveness in Meeting Information Consumers Needs. In *Library Effectiveness,* edited by Library Administration and Management Association Library Research Round Table, 49–62. Chicago: Library Administration and Management Association.

Choo, C. W. 1993. Environmental Scanning: Acquisition and Use of Information by Chief Executive Officers in the Canadian Telecommunications Industry. PhD diss., University of Toronto.

————. 1994. Environmental Scanning by Canadian CEOs. *Proceedings of the 22nd Annual Conference of the Canadian Association for Information Science* (Montreal, May 25–27), edited by A. Tabah, 446–64. Montreal: Canadian Association for Information Science.

————. 1995. Information Management for the Intelligent Organization: Roles and Implications for the Information Professions. *Proceedings of the 1995 Digital Libraries Conference* (Singapore, March 27–30) 81–99. Singapore: SNP.

————. 2001. Environmental Scanning as Information Seeking and Organizational Learning. *Information Research* 7, no. 1. Available at http://InformationR.net/ir/7-1/paper112.html.

————. 2002. *Information Management for the Intelligent Organization: The Art of Scanning the Environment.* 3rd ed. Medford, NJ: Information Today.

Choo, C. W., and E. Auster. 1993. Scanning the Business Environment: Acquisition and Use of Information by Managers. In *Annual Review of Information Science and Technology,* edited by M. E. Williams, 28:279–314. Medford, NJ: Learned Information.

Choo, C. W., and N. Bontis, eds. 2002. *The Strategic Management of Intellectual Capital and Organizational Knowledge.* New York: Oxford University Press.

Choo, C. W., B. Detlor, and D. Turnbull. 2000. *Web Work: Information Seeking and Knowledge Work on the World Wide Web.* Dordrecht, The Netherlands: Kluwer Academic Publishers.

Choo, C. W., and R. Johnston. 2004. Innovation in the Knowing Organization: A Case Study of an E-commerce Initiative. *Journal of Knowledge Management* 8, no. 6:77–92.

Choo, C. W., and C. Marton. 2003. Information Seeking on the Web by Women in IT Professions. *Internet Research: Electronic Networking Applications and Policy* 13, no. 4:267–80.

Christensen, C. M. 1997. *The Innovator's Dilemma: When New Technologies Cause Great Firms to Fail.* Boston: Harvard Business School Press.

Christensen, C. M., and M. E. Raynor. 2003. *The Innovator's Solution: Creating and Sustaining Successful Growth.* Boston: Harvard Business School Press.

Clemons, E. K., and M. Row. 1988. A Strategic Information System: McKesson Drug Company's Economost. *Planning Review* 16, no. 5:14–19.

Cohen, M. D., and J. G. March. 1986. *Leadership and Ambiguity: The American College President.* Boston: Harvard Business School.

Cohen, M. D., J. G. March, and J. P. Olsen. 1972. A Garbage Can Model of Organizational Choice. *Administrative Science Quarterly* 17, no. 1:1–25.

Cohen, W. M., and D. A. Levinthal. 1990. Absorptive Capacity: A New Perspective on Learning and Innovation. *Administrative Science Quarterly* 35, no.1(March): 128–52.

Collins, H. 1998. Cultural Competence and Scientific Knowledge. In *Exploring Expertise: Issues and Perspectives,* edited by R. Williams, W. Faulkner, and J. Fleck, 121–42. London: Macmillan Press.

Collins, J. C., and J. I. Porras. 1994. *Built to Last: Successful Habits of Visionary Companies.* New York: HarperBusiness.

Collison, C., and G. Parcell. 2001. *Learning to Fly: Practical Lessons from One of the World's Leading Knowledge Companies.* Oxford: Capstone Publishing.

Columbia Accident Investigation Board (CAIB). 2003. *Columbia Accident Investigation Board Report.* Vol. 1. Washington, D.C.: Government Printing Office.

Cosjin, E., and P. Ingwersen. 2000. Dimensions of Relevance. *Information Processing and Management* 36, no. 4:533–50.

Crane, D. 1971. Information Needs and Uses. In *Annual Review of Information Science and Technology,* edited by C. A. Cuadra, 6:3–39. Chicago: William Benton.

Crawford, S. 1978. Information Needs and Uses. In *Annual Review of Information Science and Technology,* edited by M. E. Williams, 6:61–81. White Plains, NY: Knowledge Industry Publications, Inc.

Cross, Rob, A. Parker, L. Prusak, and S. P. Borgatti. 2001. Knowing What We Know: Supporting Knowledge Creation and Sharing in Social Networks. *Organizational Dynamics* 30, no. 2:100–20.

Crossan, M. M., R. E. White, H. W. Lane, and L. Klus. 1996. The Improvising Organization: Where Planning Meets Opportunity. *Organizational Dynamics* 24, no. 4:20–34.

Culnan, M. J. 1983. Environmental Scanning: The Effects of Task Complexity and Source Accessibility on Information Gathering Behavior. *Decision Sciences* 14, no. 2:194–206.

Cyert, R. M., and J. G. March. 1963. *A Behavioral Theory of the Firm.* Englewood Cliffs, NJ: Prentice-Hall.

———. 1992. *A Behavioral Theory of the Firm.* 2nd ed. Oxford: Blackwell.

Daft, R. L., and R. H. Lengel. 1986. Organizational Information Requirements: Media Richness and Structural Design. *Management Science* 32, no. 5:554–71.

Daft, R. L., and K. E. Weick. 1984. Toward a Model of Organizations as Interpretation Systems. *Academy of Management Review* 9, no. 2:284–95.

Daft, R. L., J. Sormunen, and D. Parks. 1988. Chief Executive Scanning, Environmental Characteristics, and Company Performance: An Empirical Study. *Strategic Management Journal* 9, no. 2:123–39.

Damasio, A. R. 1999. *The Feeling of What Happens: Body and Emotion in the Making of Consciousness.* New York: Harcourt Brace & Co.

———. 2003. *Looking for Spinoza: Joy, Sorrow, and the Feeling Brain.* New York: Harcourt Brace & Co.

Davenport, T. H., R. G. Eccles, and L. Prusak. 1992. Information Politics. *Sloan Management Review* 34, no. 1:53–63.

de Geus, A. P. 1988. Planning as Learning. In *Harvard Business Review* 66, no. 2:70–74.

DeLong, D., and L. Fahey. 2000. Diagnosing Cultural Barriers to Knowledge Management. *Academy of Management Executive* 14, no. 4:113–27.

Dervin, B. 1983a. Information as a User Construct: The Relevance of Perceived Information Needs to Synthesis and Interpretation. In *Knowledge Structure and Use: Implications for Synthesis and Interpretation,* edited by S. A. Ward and L. A. Reed, 153–84. Philadelphia: Temple University Press.

———. 1983b. An Overview of Sense-Making: Concepts, Methods, and Results to Date. Paper presented at the International Communication Association annual meeting, May, Dallas, TX. Available: Brenda Dervin, Department of Communication, Ohio State University, Columbus, OH 43210.

———. 1992. From the Mind's Eye of the "User": The Sense-Making Qualitative-Quantitative Methodology. In *Qualitative Research in Information Management,* edited by J. D. Glazier and R. R. Powell, 61–84. Englewood, CO: Libraries Unlimited.

———. 2003. Sense-Making's Journey from Metatheory to Methodology to Method: An Example Using Information Seeking and Use as Research Focus. In *Sense-Making*

Methodology Reader: Selected Writings of Brenda Dervin, edited by B. Dervin, L. Foreman-Wernet, and E. Lauterbach, 133–63. Cresskill, NJ: Hampton Press.

Dervin, B., and K. Clark. 1987. *Asking Significant Questions: Alternative Tools for Information Need and Accountability Assessments by Libraries.* Sacramento, CA: California State Library.

Dervin, B., and L. Foreman-Wernet, eds. 2003. *Sense-Making Methodology Reader: Selected Writings of Brenda Dervin.* Cresskill, NJ: Hampton Press.

Dervin, B., and M. Frenette. 2001. Sense-Making Methodology: Communicating Communicatively with Campaign Audiences. In *Public Communication Campaigns,* edited by R. E. Rice & C. K. Atkins, 69–87. Thousand Oaks, CA: Sage.

Dervin, B., and M. Nilan. 1986. Information Needs and Uses. In *Annual Review of Information Science and Technology,* edited by M. E. Williams, 21:3–33. White Plains, NY: Knowledge Industry Publications, Inc.

Dill, W. R. 1962. The Impact of Environment on Organizational Development. In *Concepts and Issues in Administrative Behavior,* edited by S. Mailick and E. H. Van Ness, 94–109. Englewood Cliffs, NJ: Prentice-Hall.

DiMaggio, P., and W. W. Powell. 1983. The Iron Cage Revisited: Institutional Isomorphism and Collective Rationality in Organizational Fields. In *American Sociological Review* 48, no. 2:147–60.

Dixon, N. M. 2000. *Common Knowledge: How Companies Thrive by Sharing What They Know.* Boston: Harvard Business School Press.

Donnellon, A., B. Gray, and M. G. Bougon. 1986. Communication, Meaning, and Organized Action. *Administrative Science Quarterly* 31, no. 1 (March):43–55.

Douglas, M. 1975. *Implicit Meanings: Essays in Anthropology.* London: Routledge.

———. 1986. *How Institutions Think.* Syracuse, NY: Syracuse University Press.

Douglas, P. 1999. Xerox: Documents Convey Knowledge. In *Smart Business: How Knowledge Communities Can Revolutionize Your Company,* edited by J. Botkin, 215–22. New York: Free Press.

———. 2001. Personal communication, quoted in C. Gordon, 2002. Contributions of Cultural Anthropology and Social Capital Theory to Understandings of Knowledge Management. PhD thesis, University of Toronto.

Doz, Y., and G. Hamel. 1997. The Use of Alliances in Implementing Technology Strategies. In *Managing Strategic Innovation and Change,* edited by M. Tushman and P. Anderson, 556–80. New York: Oxford University Press.

Dretske, F. I. 1981. *Knowledge and the Flow of Information.* Cambridge, MA: MIT Press.

Duncan, R. B. 1972. Characteristics of Organizational Environments and Perceived Environmental Uncertainty. *Administrative Science Quarterly* 17, no. 3:313–27.

Eden, C. 1992. On the Nature of Cognitive Maps. *Journal of Management Studies* 29, no. 3:261–85.

Eden, C., and J-C Spender, eds. 1998. *Managerial and Organizational Cognition: Theory, Methods, Research.* Thousand Oaks, CA: Sage.

Eisenhardt, K. M. 1989. Making Fast Strategic Decisions in High-Velocity Environments. *Academy of Management Journal* 32, no. 3:543–76.

———. 1990. Speed and Strategic Choice: How Managers Accelerate Decision Making. *California Management Review* 32, no. 3:39–54.

Eisenhardt, K. M., and D. Sull. 2001. Strategy as Simple Rules. *Harvard Business Review,* 79, no. 2:107–16.

Ellis, D. 1989a. A Behavioural Approach to Information Retrieval System Design. *Journal of Documentation* 45, no. 3:171–212.

————. 1989b. A Behavioural Model for Information Retrieval System Design. Special issue, *Journal of Information Science* 15, nos. 4/5:237–47.

Ellis, D., D. Cox, and K. Hall. 1993. A Comparison of the Information Seeking Patterns of Researchers in the Physical and Social Sciences. *Journal of Documentation* 49, no. 4:356–69.

Emerson, R. M. 1962. Power-Dependence Relations. *American Sociological Review* 27, no. 1:31–41.

Engeström, Yrjo. 1991. Developmental Work Research: Reconstructing Expertise Through Expansive Learning. In *Human Jobs and Computer Interfaces,* edited by M. Nurminen and G. Weir, 265–90. Amsterdam: Elsevier Science Publishers North-Holland.

Ericson, T. 2001. Sensemaking in Organisations: Towards a Conceptual Framework for Understanding Strategic Change. *Scandinavian Journal of Management* 17, no. 1:109–31.

Feldman, M. S. 1989. *Order Without Design: Information Production and Policy Making.* Stanford, CA: Stanford University Press.

————. 1991. The Meanings of Ambiguity: Learning from Stories and Metaphors. In *Reframing Organizational Culture,* edited by Peter J. Frost et al., pp. 145–56. Newbury Park, CA: Sage.

Feldman, M. S., and J. G. March. 1981. Information in Organizations as Signal and Symbol. *Administrative Science Quarterly* 26, no. 2:171–86.

Fenner, F. 1988a. Development of the Global Smallpox Eradication Programme, 1958–1966. In *Smallpox and Its Eradication,* pp. 365–419. Geneva: World Health Organization.

————. 1988b. The Intensified Smallpox Eradication Programme, 1967–1980. In *Smallpox and Its Eradication,* pp. 421–516. Geneva: World Health Organization.

Fenner, F., D. A. Henderson, I. Arita, Z. Jezek, and I. D. Ladnyi. 1988. *Smallpox and Its Eradication.* Geneva: World Health Organization.

Ferris, T. 2004. Stumbling into Space. *New York Review of Books* 51, no. 7:5–10.

Festinger, L. 1957. *A Theory of Cognitive Dissonance.* Stanford, CA: Stanford University Press.

Fidel, R., A. M. Pejtersen, B. Cleal, and H. Bruce. 2004. A Multidimensional Approach to the Study of Human-Information Interaction: A Case Study of Collaborative Information Retrieval. *Journal of the American Society for Information Science and Technology* 55, no. 11:939–53.

Finney, M., and I. I. Mitroff. 1986. Strategic Plan Failures: The Organization as Its Own Worst Enemy. In *The Thinking Organization: Dynamics of Organizational Social Cognition,* edited by H. P. Sims, Jr., D. A. Gioia, and associates, 317–35. San Francisco: Jossey-Bass.

Fiol, M. C. 1994. Consensus, Diversity, and Learning in Organizations. *Organization Science* 5, no. 3:403–20.

Fleck, J. 1998. Expertise: Knowledge, Power and Tradeability. In *Exploring Expertise: Issues and Perspectives,* edited by R. Williams, W. Faulkner, and J. Fleck, 143–72. London: Macmillan Press.

Fligstein, N. 1990. *The Transformation of Corporate Control.* Cambridge, MA: Harvard University Press.

Ford, N., T. Wilson, A. Foster, D. Ellis, and A. Spink. 2002. Information-Seeking and Mediated Searching. Part 4. Cognitive Styles in Information Seeking. *Journal of the American Society for Information Science and Technology* 53, no. 9:704–15.

Foucault, Michel. 1980. *Power/Knowledge: Selected Interviews and Other Writings, 1972–1977*. New York: Pantheon Books.

Galbraith, J. R. 1973. *Designing Complex Organizations*. Reading, MA: Addison-Wesley.

Galer, G., and K. van der Heijden. 1992. The Learning Organization: How Planners Create Organizational Learning. *Marketing Intelligence and Planning* 10, no. 6: 5–12.

Garud, R., and M. A. Rappa. 1994. A Socio-cognitive Model of Technology Evolution: The Case of Cochlear Implants. *Organization Science* 5, no. 3:344–62.

Garvey, W. D. 1979. *Communication: The Essence of Science*. Oxford: Pergamon Press.

Garvin, D. A. 2000. *Learning in Action: A Guide to Putting the Learning Organization to Work*. Boston: Harvard Business School Press.

Gerstberger, P. G., and T. J. Allen. 1968. Criteria Used by Research and Development Engineers in the Selection of an Information Source. *Journal of Applied Psychology* 52, no. 4:272–79.

Ghoshal, S. 1988. Environmental Scanning in Korean Firms: Organizational Isomorphism in Practice. *Journal of International Business Studies* 19, no. 1:69–86.

Gigerenzer, G., P. M. Todd, and ABC Research Group. 1999. *Simple Heuristics That Make Us Smart*. New York: Oxford University Press.

Gigone, D., and R. Hastie. 1993. The Common Knowledge Effect: Information Sharing and Group Judgment. *Journal of Personality and Social Psychology* 65, no. 5:959–74.

———. 1997. The Impact of Information on Small Group Choice. *Journal of Personality and Social Psychology* 72, no. 1:132–40.

Gilovich, T., D. Griffin, and D. Kahneman, eds. 2002. *Heuristics and Biases: The Psychology of Intuitive Judgment*. Cambridge, U.K.: Cambridge University Press.

Gioia, D. A. 1986. Symbols, Scripts, and Sensemaking: Creating Meaning in the Organizational Experience. In *The Thinking Organization: Dynamics of Organizational Social Cognition,* edited by H. P. Sims, Jr., D. A. Gioia, and associates, 49–74. San Francisco: Jossey-Bass.

Gioia, D. A., A. Donnellon, and H. P. Sims, Jr. 1989. Communication and Cognition in Appraisal: A Tale of Two Paradigms. In *Organization Studies* 10, no. 4:503–29.

Gioia, D. A., and H. P. Sims, Jr. 1986. Introduction to *The Thinking Organization: Dynamics of Organizational Social Cognition,* edited by H. P. Sims, Jr., D. A. Gioia, and associates, 1–19. San Francisco: Jossey-Bass.

Goldman, A. I. 1986. *Epistemology and Cognition*. Cambridge, MA: Harvard University Press.

———. 1999. *Knowledge in a Social World*. Oxford: Oxford University Press.

Goldstein, J. 1994. *The Unshackled Organization: Facing the Challenge of Unpredictability Through Spontaneous Reorganization*. Portland, OR: Productivity Press.

Gorelick, C., K. April, and N. Milton, eds. 2004. *Performance through Learning: Knowledge Management in Practice*. Boston: Butterworth-Heinemann.

Granovetter, M. S. 1973. The Strength of Weak Ties. *American Journal of Sociology* 78, no. 6:1360–80.

Grant, R. M. 1996a. Toward a Knowledge-Based Theory of the Firm. Special issue, *Strategic Management Journal* 17:109–22.

———. 1996b. Prospering in Dynamically-Competitive Environments: Organizational Capability as Knowledge Integration. *Organization Science* 7, no. 4:375–87.

————. 2002. The Knowledge-Based View of the Firm. In *The Strategic Management of Intellectual Capital and Organizational Knowledge,* edited by C. W. Choo and N. Bontis, 133–48. New York: Oxford University Press.

Haas, P. M. 1992. Banning Chlorofluorocarbons: Epistemic Community Efforts to Protect Stratospheric Ozone. In *Knowledge, Power, and International Policy Coordination,* edited by P. M. Haas 187–224. Columbia: University of South Carolina Press.

Haefliger, S., and G. von Krogh. 2004. Knowledge Creation in Open Source Software Development. In *Organizations as Knowledge Systems,* edited by H. Tsoukas and N. Mylonopoulos, 109–29. New York: Palgrave Macmillan.

Hambrick, D. C., and P. A. Mason. 1984. Upper Echelons: The Organization as a Reflection of Its Top Managers. *Academy of Management Review* 9, no. 2:193–206.

Hammond, J. S. 1973. The Roles of the Manager and Analyst in Successful Implementation. Paper presented at the TIMS XX Meeting, Tel Aviv, Israel, June 26–29, 1973.

Hansen, M. T. 2002. Knowledge Networks: Explaining Effective Knowledge Sharing in Multiunit Companies. *Organization Science* 13, no. 3:232–48.

Hardy, A. P. 1982. The Selection of Channels When Seeking Information: Cost/Benefit vs Least-Effort. *Information Processing and Management* 18, no. 6:289–93.

Harmon-Jones, E., and J. Mills, eds. 1999. *Cognitive Dissonance: Progress on a Pivotal Theory in Social Psychology.* Washington, D.C.: American Psychological Association.

Harter, S. P. 1992. Psychological Relevance and Information Science. *Journal of the American Society for Information Science* 43, no. 9:602–15.

Hayek, F. 1945. The Use of Knowledge in Society. *American Economic Review* 35, no. 4:519–30.

Haynes, R. B., K. A. McKibbon, C. J. Walker, N. C. Ryan, D. F. Fitzgerald, and M. F. Ramsden. 1990. On-line Access to MEDLINE in Clinical Settings: A Study of Use and Usefulness. *Annals of Internal Medicine* 112, no. 1:78–84.

Hedberg, B., P. C. Nystrom, and W. H. Starbuck. 1976. Camping on Seesaws: Prescriptions for a Self-Designing Organization. *Administrative Science Quarterly* 21, no. 1:41–65.

Henderson, D. A. 1972. Smallpox Surveillance in the Strategy of Global Eradication. Inter-regional Seminar on Cholera and Smallpox, Malaysia and Singapore, November 11–18, World Health Organization.

————. 1987. Principles and Lessons from the Smallpox Eradication Programme. *Bulletin of the World Health Organization* 65, no. 4:535–46.

Herner, S. 1954. Information-Gathering Habits of Workers in Pure and Applied Science. *Industrial and Engineering Chemistry* 46:228–36.

Herner, S., and M. Herner. 1967. Information Needs and Uses in Science and Technology. In *Annual Review of Information Science and Technology,* edited by C. A. Cuadra, 2:1–34. New York: Interscience Publishers.

Hewins, E. T. 1990. Information Need and Use Studies. In *Annual Review of Information Science and Technology,* edited by M. E. Williams, 25:145–72. New York: Elsevier Science Publishers.

Hickson, D. J., R. J. Butler, D. Cray, G. R. Mallory, and D. C. Wilson. 1986. *Top Decisions: Strategic Decision-Making in Organizations.* San Francisco: Jossey-Bass.

Hickson, D. J., C. R. Hinings, C. A. Lee, R. E. Schneck, and J. M. Pennings. 1971. A Strategic Contingencies' Theory of Intraorganizational Power. *Administrative Science Quarterly* 16, no. 2:216–29.

Hilsman, R. 1967. *To Move a Nation: The Politics of Foreign Policy in the Administration of John F. Kennedy.* Garden City, NY: Doubleday.

Hogarth, R. M. 1987. *Judgement and Choice: The Psychology of Decisions.* 2nd ed. New York: John Wiley & Sons.

Hogarth, R. M., and S. Makridakis. 1981. Forecasting and Planning: An Evaluation. *Management Science* 27, no. 2:115–38.

Hopkins, J. W. 1989. *The Eradication of Smallpox: Organizational Learning and Innovation in International Health.* Boulder, CO: Westview Press.

Huber, G. P. 1991. Organizational Learning: The Contributing Processes and the Literature. *Organization Science* 2, no. 1:88–115.

Huff, A. S., ed. 1990. *Mapping Strategic Thought.* Chichester, U.K.: John Wiley.

Huff, A. S., and J. O. Huff. 2000. *When Firms Change Direction.* New York: Oxford University Press.

Huizing, A., and W. Bouman. 2002. Knowledge and Learning, Markets and Organizations: Managing the Information Transaction Space. In *The Strategic Management of Intellectual Capital and Organizational Knowledge,* edited by C. C. Wei & N. Bontis, pp. 185–204. New York: Oxford University Press.

Ingrassia, P. J., and J. B. White. 1994. *Comeback: The Fall and Rise of the American Automobile Industry.* New York: Simon & Schuster.

Ingwersen, P. 1999. Cognitive Information Retrieval. In *Annual Review of Information Science and Technology,* edited by M. Williams, 34:3–52. Medford, NJ: Information Today.

Isenberg, D. J. 1984. How Senior Managers Think. *Harvard Business Review* 62, no. 2:81–90.

———. 1986a. The Structure and Process of Understanding: Implications for Managerial Action. In *The Thinking Organization,* edited by H. P. Sims, Jr., and D. A. Gioia, pp. 238–62. San Francisco: Jossey-Bass.

———. 1986b. Thinking and Managing: A Verbal Protocol Analysis of Managerial Problem Solving. *Academy of Management Journal* 29, no. 4:775–88.

———. 1987. The Tactics of Strategic Opportunism. *Harvard Business Review* 65, no. 2:92–97.

Janis, I. 1982. *Groupthink: Psychological Studies of Policy Decision.* Boston: Houghton Mifflin.

Janis, I., and L. Mann. 1977. *Decision Making: A Psychological Analysis of Conflict, Choice, and Commitment.* New York: Free Press.

Jehn, K. A. 1995. A Multimethod Examination of the Benefits and Detriments of Intragroup Conflict. *Administrative Science Quarterly* 40, no. 2:256.

Jehn, K. A., and E. A. Mannix. 2001. The Dynamic Nature of Conflict: A Longitudinal Study of Intragroup Conflict and Group Performance. *Academy of Management Journal* 44, no. 2:238.

Jehn, K. A., G. B. Northcraft, and M. A. Neale. 1999. Why Differences Make A Difference: A Field Study of Diversity, Conflict, and Performance in Workgroups. *Administrative Science Quarterly* 44, no. 1:741–85.

Johnson, J. D. 1996. *Information Seeking: An Organizational Dilemma.* Westport, CT: Quorum Books.

Johnson-Laird, P. N. 1983. *Mental Models: Towards a Cognitive Science of Language, Inference, and Consciousness.* Cambridge, MA: Harvard University Press.

Jones, G. R, and J. M. George. 1998. The Experience and Evolution of Trust: Implications for Cooperation and Teamwork. *Academy of Management Review* 23, no. 3:531–46.

Kahneman, D., P. Slovic, and A. Tversky, eds. 1982. *Judgement under Uncertainty: Heuristics and Biases.* Cambridge, U.K.: Cambridge University Press.

Kahneman, D., and A. Tversky, eds. 2000. *Choices, Values and Frames.* Cambridge, U.K.: Cambridge University Press.

Katz, R., and T. J. Allen. 1982. Investigating the Not Invented Here (NIH) Syndrome: A Look at the Performance, Tenure, and Communication Patterns of 50 R&D Project Groups. *R&D Management* 12, no. 1:7–19.

Kelly, G. A. 1963. *A Theory of Personality: The Psychology of Personal Constructs.* New York: W. W. Norton & Co.

Khrushchev, N. 1970. *Khrushchev Remembers.* Boston: Little, Brown.

Kiesler, C. A. 1971. *The Psychology of Commitment.* New York: Academic Press.

Kim, W. C., and R. Mauborgne. 1997. Fair Process: Managing in the Knowledge Economy. *Harvard Business Review* 75, no. 4:65–75.

———. 2003. Fair Process: Management in the Knowledge Economy. *Harvard Business Review* 81, no. 1:127–35.

Kingdon, J. W. 1984. *Agendas, Alternatives, and Public Policies.* Boston: Little, Brown.

———. 1995. *Agendas, Alternatives, and Public Policies.* 2nd ed. New York: Harper-Collins.

Kirton, M. J., ed. 1989. *Adaptors and Innovators.* London: Routledge.

Klein, G. 1998. *Sources of Power: How People Make Decisions.* Cambridge, MA: MIT Press.

Kleiner, A. 1989. Consequential Heresies: How "Thinking the Unthinkable" Changed Royal Dutch/Shell. Available from the author.

———. 1994. Creating Scenarios. In *The Fifth Discipline Fieldbook,* edited by P. Senge, A. Kleiner, C. Roberts, R. Ross, and B. Smith, 275–78. New York: Doubleday.

Kogut, B., and U. Zander. 1992. Knowledge of the Firm, Combinative Capabilities, and the Replication of Technology. *Organization Science* 3, no. 3:383–97.

Koplow, D. A. 2003. *Smallpox: The Fight to Eradicate a Global Scourge.* Berkeley: University of California Press.

Kornblith, H., ed. 1994. *Naturalizing Epistemology.* Cambridge, MA: MIT Press.

Kotter, J. P. 1982. What Effective General Managers Really Do. *Harvard Business Review* 60, no. 6:156–67.

Kremer, J. M. 1980. Information Flow among Engineers in a Design Company. PhD diss., University of Illinois at Urbana-Champaign.

Krohne, H. W. 1989. The Concept of Coping Modes: Relating Cognitive Person Variables to Actual Coping Behavior. *Advances in Behavioural Research and Theory* 11:235–49.

———. 1993. Vigilance and Cognitive Avoidance as Concepts in Coping Research. In *Attention and Avoidance: Strategies in Coping with Aversiveness,* edited by H. W. Krohne, Chap. 2. Seattle: Hogrefe and Huber.

Kuhlthau, C. C. 1988. Developing a Model of the Library Search Process: Cognitive and Affective Aspects. *Reference Quarterly* 28, no. 2:232–42.

———. 1991. Inside the Search Process: Information Seeking from the User's Perspective. *Journal of the American Society for Information Science* 42, no. 5:361–71.

———. 1993a. A Principle of Uncertainty for Information Seeking. *Journal of Documentation* 49, no. 4:339–55.

———. 1993b. *Seeking Meaning: A Process Approach to Library and Information Services.* Norwood, NJ: Ablex Publishing.

———. 2004. *Seeking Meaning: A Process Approach to Library and Information Services.* 2nd ed. Westport, CT: Libraries Unlimited.

Kuhn, T. S. 1970. *The Structure of Scientific Revolutions*. Chicago: University of Chicago Press.

Lakoff, G., and M. Johnson. 1980. *Metaphors We Live By.* Chicago: University of Chicago Press.

Latour, B. 1987. *Science in Action: How to Follow Scientists and Engineers through Society.* Cambridge, MA: Harvard University Press.

Lave, J., and E. Wenger. 1991. *Situated Learning: Legitimate Peripheral Participation.* Cambridge, U.K.: Cambridge University Press.

LeDoux, J. 1996. *The Emotional Brain: The Mysterious Underpinnings of Emotional Life.* New York: Simon & Schuster.

Leonard, D. 1995. *Wellsprings of Knowledge: Building and Sustaining the Sources of Innovation.* Boston: Harvard Business School Press.

Leonard, D., and W. Swap. 1999. *When Sparks Fly: Igniting Creativity in Groups.* Boston, MA: Harvard Business School Press.

Lester, R., and J. Waters. 1989. *Environmental Scanning and Business Strategy.* London: British Library, Research and Development Department.

Levinthal, D. A., and J. G. March. 1993. The Myopia of Learning. Special issue, *Strategic Management Journal* 14(Winter):95–112.

Levitt, B., and C. Nass. 1989. The Lid on the Garbage Can: Institutional Constraints on Decsion Making in the Technical Core of College-Text Publishers. *Administrative Science Quarterly* 34, no. 2:190–207.

Lin, N., and W. D. Garvey. 1972. Information Needs and Uses. In *Annual Review of Information Science and Technology,* edited by C. A. Cuadra, 7:5–37. Washington, DC: American Society for Information Science.

Lindblom, C. E. 1959. The Science of Muddling Through. *Public Administration Review* 19, no. 2:79–88.

Line, M. B. 1971. The Information Uses and Needs of Social Scientists: An Overview of INFROSS. *Aslib Proceedings* 23, no. 8:412–34.

Line, M. B., J. M. Brittain, and F. A. Cranmer. 1971. *Investigation into Information Requirements of the Social Sciences Research Report No. 2: Information Requirements of Social Scientists in Government Departments.* University Library, University of Bath, Bath, U.K.

Lipetz, B. A. 1970. Information Needs and Uses. In *Annual Review of Information Science and Technology,* edited by C. A. Cuadra, 5:3–32. Chicago: Encyclopedia Britannica.

Lord, R. G., and R. J. Foti. 1986. Schema Theories, Information Processing, and Organizational Behavior. In *The Thinking Organization: Dynamics of Organizational Social Cognition,* edited by H. P. Sims, Jr., D. A. Gioia, and associates, pp. 20–48. San Francisco: Jossey-Bass.

Lyles, M. A. 1987. Defining Strategic Problems: Subjective Criteria of Executives. *Organization Studies* 8, no. 3:263–80.

Lyles, M. A., and I. I. Mitroff. 1980. Organizational Problem Formulation: An Empirical Study. *Administrative Science Quarterly* 25, no. 1:102–19.

MacMullin, S. E., and R. S. Taylor. 1984. Problem Dimensions and Information Traits. *Information Society* 3, no. 1:91–111.

Maes, R. 2004. *Information Management: A Road Map* (PrimaVera Working Paper No. 2004-13). Amsterdam: Universiteit van Amsterdam, Department of Business Studies.

March, J. G. 1976. The Technology of Foolishness. In *Ambiguity and Choice in Organizations,* edited by J. G. March and J. Olsen, pp. 69–81. Bergen, Norway: Universitetsforlaget.

———. 1978. Bounded Rationality, Ambiguity, and the Engineering of Choice. *Bell Journal of Economics* 9, no. 2:587–608.

———. 1988. *Decisions and Organizations*. Cambridge, MA: Basil Blackwell.

———. 1991. Exploration and Exploitation in Organizational Learning. *Organization Science* 2, no. 1:71–87.

———. 1994. *A Primer on Decision Making: How Decisions Happen*. New York: Free Press.

March, J. G., and J. P. Olsen. 1976. *Ambiguity and Choice in Organizations*. Bergen, Norway: Universitetsforlaget.

March, J. G., and Z. Shapira. 1987. Managerial Perspectives on Risk and Risk Taking. *Management Science* 33, no. 11 (November): 1404–18.

March, J. G., and H. A. Simon. 1958. *Organizations*. New York: John Wiley.

———. 1993. *Organizations*. 2nd ed. Oxford: Blackwell.

Marchand, D. A., W. J. Kettinger, and J. D. Rollins. 2000. Information Orientation: People, Technology and the Bottom Line. *Sloan Management Review* 41, no. 4: 69–80.

———. 2001. *Information Orientation: The Link to Business Performance*. New York: Oxford University Press.

Marchionini, G. 1995. *Information Seeking in Electronic Environments*. Cambridge, U.K.: Cambridge University Press.

Markey, K. 1981. Levels of Question Formulation in Negotiation of Information Need During the Online Pre-search Interview: A Proposed Model. *Information Processing and Management* 17, no. 5:215–25.

Martin, J. 1992. *Cultures in Organizations: Three Perspectives*. New York: Oxford University Press.

———. 2001. *Organizational Culture: Mapping the Terrain*. Thousand Oaks, CA: Sage.

Martin, J., and D. Meyerson. 1988. Organizational Culture and the Denial, Channeling, and Acknowledgment of Ambiguity. In *Managing Ambiguity and Change,* edited by L. R. Pondy, R. J. Boland, Jr., and H. Thomas, pp. 93–125. New York: John Wiley.

Martyn, J. 1964. *Literature Searching by Research Scientists*. London: Aslib Research Department.

———. 1974. Information Needs and Uses. In *Annual Review of Information Science and Technology,* edited by C. A. Cuadra, 9:3–23. Washington, D.C.: American Society for Information Science.

May, E. R., and P. D. Zelikow, eds. 1997. *The Kennedy Tapes: Inside the White House during the Cuban Missile Crisis*. Cambridge, MA: Belknap Press/Harvard University Press.

McCall, M. W., Jr., and R. E. Kaplan. 1990. *Whatever It Takes: The Realities of Managerial Decision Making*. 2nd ed. Englewood Cliffs, NJ: Prentice-Hall.

McCaskey, M. B. 1982. *The Executive Challenge*. Toronto: Pitman.

McCurdy, H. E. 1989. The Decay of NASA's Technical Culture. *Space Policy,* November, 301–10.

McGee, J. V., and L. Prusak. 1993. *Managing Information Strategically*. New York: John Wiley & Sons.

Meltsner, A. J. 1976. *Policy Analysts in the Bureaucracy*. Berkeley: University of California Press.

Menzel, H. 1966. Information Needs and Uses in Science and Technology. In *Annual Review of Information Science and Technology,* edited by C. A. Cuadra, 1:41–69. New York: Interscience Publishers.

Merton, R. K. 1968. Making It Scientifically. *New York Times Book Review,* February 25, 41–43.

Meyer, A. D. 1982. Adapting to Environmental Jolts. *Administrative Science Quarterly* 27, no. 4 (December):515–37.

Meyerson, D., and J. Martin. 1987. Cultural Change: An Integration of Three Different Views. *Journal of Management Studies* 24, no. 6:623–47.

Meyerson, D., K. E. Weick, and R. M. Kramer. 1996. Swift Trust and Temporary Groups. In *Trust in Organizations: Frontiers in Theory and Research,* edited by R. M. Kramer and T. R. Tyler, pp. 166–95. Thousand Oaks, CA: Sage.

Mick, C. K., G. N. Lindsey, and D. Callahan. 1980. Toward Usable User Studies. *Journal of the American Society for Information Science* 31, no. 5:347–56.

Miller, S. M., and C. E. Mangan. 1983. Interesting Effects of Information and Coping Style in Adapting to Gynaecological Stress: Should a Doctor Tell All? *Journal of Personality and Social Psychology* 45, no. 1:223–36.

Mintzberg, H. 1973. *The Nature of Managerial Work.* New York: Harper & Row.

———. 1975. *Impediments to the Use of Management Information.* New York: National Association of Accountants.

Mintzberg, H., D. Raisinghani, and A. Thêorét. 1976. The Structure of "Unstructured" Decision Processes. *Administrative Science Quarterly* 21, no. 2:246–75.

Mishira, A. K. 1996. Organizational Responses to Crisis: The Centrality of Trust. In *Trust in Organizations: Frontiers of Theory and Research,* edited by R. M. Kramer and T. R. Tyler, pp. 261–87. Thousand Oaks, CA: Sage.

Mitroff, I. I., and H. A. Linstone. 1993. *The Unbounded Mind: Breaking the Chains of Traditional Business Thinking.* New York: Oxford University Press.

Morgan, G. 1986. *Images of Organization.* Newbury Park, CA: Sage.

Morris, R. C. T. 1994. Toward a User-Centered Information Service. *Journal of the American Society for Information Science* 45, no. 1:20–30.

Moser, P. K., D. H. Mulder, and J. D. Trout. 1998. *The Theory of Knowledge.* New York: Oxford University Press.

Mouzelis, N. P. 1995. *Sociological Theory: What Went Wrong? Diagnosis and Remedies.* London: Routledge.

Nahapiet, J., and S. Ghoshal. 1998. Social Capital, Intellectual Capital, and the Organizational Advantage. *Academy of Management Review* 23, no. 2:242–66.

National Library of Medicine. 1988. *Survey of Individual Users of MEDLINE on the NLM System.* Springfield, VA: U.S. Department of Commerce, National Technical Information Service.

Nelson, R., and S. Winter. 1982. *An Evolutionary Theory of Economic Change.* Cambridge, MA: Belknap Press.

Nisbett, R., and L. Ross. 1980. *Human Inference: Strategies and Shortcomings of Social Judgement.* Englewood Cliffs, NJ: Prentice-Hall.

Nishi, K., C. Schoderbek, and P. P. Schoderbek. 1982. Scanning the Organizational Environment: Some Empirical Results. *Human Systems Management* 3, no. 4: 233–45.

Noble, D. F. 1984. *Forces of Production: A Social History of Industrial Automation.* New York: Knopf.

Nonaka, I. 1994. A Dynamic Theory of Organizational Knowledge Creation. *Organization Science* 5, no. 1:14–37.

Nonaka, I., P. Byosière, C. C. Borucki, and N. Konno. 1994. Organizational Knowledge Creation Theory: A First Comprehensive Test. Special issue, *International Business Review* 3, no. 4:337–51.

Nonaka, I., and K. K. Ichijo. 1997. Creating Knowledge in the Process Organization (Commentary). In *Advances in Strategic Management.* Vol. 14, *Organizational Learning and Strategic Management*, edited by P. Shrivastava, A. S. Huff, J. E. Dutton, and J. P. Walsh, 45–52. Greenwood, CT: JAI Press.

Nonaka, I., and N. Konno. 1998. The Concept of "Ba": Building a Foundation for Knowledge Creation. *California Management Review* 40, no. 3:40–54.

Nonaka, I., and H. Takeuchi. 1995. *The Knowledge-Creating Company: How Japanese Companies Create the Dynamics of Innovation.* New York: Oxford University Press.

Nonaka, I., R. Toyama, and P. Boysière. 2001. A Theory of Organizational Knowledge Creation: Understanding the Dynamic Process of Creating Knowledge. In *Handbook of Organizational Learning and Knowledge,* edited by M. Dierkes, A. B. Antal, J. Child, and I. Nonaka. Oxford: Oxford University Press.

Normann, R., and R. Ramirez. 1993. From Value Chain to Value Constellation: Designing Interactive Strategy. *Harvard Business Review* 71, no. 4:65–77.

Nutt, P. C. 1992. Formulation Tactics and the Success of Organizational Decision Making. *Decision Sciences* 23, no. 3:519–40.

Ocasio, W. 1997. Towards an Attention-Based View of the Firm. Special issue, *Strategic Management Journal* 18 (Summer):187–206.

———. 2001. How Do Organizations Think? In *Organizational Cognition: Computation and Interpretation,* edited by T. K. Lant and Z. Shapira, pp. 39–60. Mahwa, NJ: Lawrence Erlbaum Associates.

Olsen, M. D., B. Murthy, and R. Teare. 1994. CEO Perspectives on Scanning the Global Hotel Business Environment. *International Journal of Contemporary Hospitality Management* 6, no. 4:3–9.

O'Reilly, C. A. 1983. The Use of Information in Organizational Decision Making: A Model and Some Propositions. In *Research in Organizational Behavior,* edited by B. M. Staw and L. L. Cummings, pp. 103–39. Greenwich, CT: JAI Press.

O'Reilly, C. A., J. A. Chatman, and J. C. Anderson. 1987. Message Flow and Decision Making. In *Handbook of Organizational Communication,* edited by F. M. Jablin et al., pp. 600–23. Newbury Park, CA: Sage.

O'Reilly, C. A., and J. Pfeffer. 2000. *Hidden Value: How Great Companies Achieve Extraordinary Results with Ordinary People.* Boston: Harvard Business School Press.

O'Reilly, C. A., and M. L. Tushman. 1997. Using Culture for Strategic Advantage: Promoting Innovation Through Social Control. In *Managing Strategic Innovation and Change,* edited by M. L. Tushman and P. Anderson, 200–16. New York: Oxford University Press.

Orlikowski, W. J. 1988. Information Technology in Post-industrial Organizations. PhD diss., New York University.

Orr, J. E. 1990. Sharing Knowledge, Celebrating Identity: Community Memory in a Service Culture. In *Collective Remembering,* edited by D. Middleton and D. Edwards, pp. 169–89. London: Sage.

———. 1996. *Talking about Machines: An Ethnography of a Modern Job.* Ithaca, NY: Cornell University Press.

Orton, J. D. 2000. Enactment, Sensemaking and Decision Making: Redesign Processes in the 1976 Reorganization of US Intelligence. *Journal of Management Studies* 37, no. 2:213–34.

Paisley, W. 1968. Information Needs and Uses. In *Annual Review of Information Science and Technology,* edited by C. A. Cuadra, 3:1–30. Chicago: Encyclopedia Britannica.

Pask, G. 1976. Styles and Strategies of Learning. *British Journal of Educational Psychology* 46:128–48.

Patriotta, G. 2004. *Organizational Knowledge in the Making—How Firms Create, Use, and Institutionalize Knowledge.* Oxford: Oxford University Press.

Pelz, D. C., and F. M. Andrews. 1966. *Scientists in Organizations: Productive Climates for Research and Development.* Revised ed. Ann Arbor: Institute for Social Research, University of Michigan.

Perrow, C. 1967. A Framework for the Comparative Analysis of Organizations. *American Sociological Review* 32, no. 2:194–208.

———. 1986. *Complex Organizations: A Critical Essay.* 3rd ed. New York: McGraw-Hill Publishing Company.

Pettigrew, A. M. 1972. Information Control as a Power Resource. *Sociology* 6, no. 1: 187–204.

———. 1973. The Politics of Organizational Decision Making. London: Tavistock Institute.

Pettigrew, K. E., R. Fidel, and H. Bruce. 2001. Conceptual Frameworks in Information Behavior. In *Annual Review of Information Science and Technology,* edited by M. E. Williams; 35:43–78. Medford, NJ: Information Today.

Pfeffer, J. 1992. *Managing with Power: Politics and Influences in Organizations.* Boston: Harvard Business School Press.

Pfeffer, J., and G. R. Salancik. 1974. Organizational Decision Making as a Political Process: The Case of a University Budget. *Administrative Science Quarterly* 19, no. 2:135–51.

Pinelli, T. E. 1991. *The Relationship Between the Use of U.S. Government Technical Reports by U.S. Aerospace Engineers and Scientists and Selected Institutional and Sociometric Variables.* Washington, D.C.: National Aeronautics and Space Administration.

Pinelli, T. E., J. M. Kennedy, and R. O. Barclay. 1991. The NASA/DoD Aerospace Knowledge Diffusion Research Project. *Government Information Quarterly* 8, no. 2:219–33.

Pinfield, L. T. 1986. A Field Evaluation of Perspectives on Organizational Decision Making. *Administrative Science Quarterly* 31, no. 3:365–88.

Polanyi, M. 1962. *Personal Knowledge Towards a Post-critical Philosophy.* Chicago: University of Chicago Press.

———. 1966. *The Tacit Dimension.* London: Routledge and Kegan Paul.

Popper, K. R. 1979. *Objective Knowledge: An Evolutionary Approach.* Oxford: Clarendon Press.

Porac, J. F., J. R. Meindl, and C. Stubbart. 1996. Introduction to *Cognition Within and Between Organizations,* edited by J. R. Meindl, C. Stubbart, and J. F. Porac, ix–xxiii. Thousand Oaks, CA: Sage.

Porac, J. F., H. Thomas, and C. Baden-Fuller. 1989. Competitive Groups as Cognitive Communities: The Case of Scottish Knitwear Manufacturers. *Journal of Management Studies* 26, no. 4:397–416.

Porter, M. E. 1985. *Competitive Advantage: Creating and Sustaining Superior Performance.* New York: Free Press.

Powell, W. W., and P. J. DiMaggio, eds. 1991. *The New Institutionalism in Organizational Analysis.* Chicago: University of Chicago Press.

Prahalad, C. K., and R. A. Bettis. 1986. The Dominant Logic: A New Linkage Between Diversity and Performance. *Strategic Management Journal* 7, no. 6:485–501.

Pratt, D. 1999. Lessons for Implementation from the World's Most Successful Programme: The Global Eradication of Smallpox. *Journal of Curriculum Studies* 31, no. 2:177–94.

Presidential Commission on the Space Shuttle Challenger Accident. 1986. *Report to the President by the Presidential Commission on the Space Shuttle Challenger Accident.* Vols. 1–5. Washington, D.C.: Government Printing Office.

Quine, W. V. 1969. *Ontological Relativity and Other Essays.* New York: Columbia University Press.

Quinn, J. B., P. Anderson, and S. Finkelstein. 1996. Managing Professional Intellect: Making the Most of the Best. *Harvard Business Review* 74, no. 2:71–80.

Reich, Robert. 1991. *The Work of Nations: Preparing Ourselves for 21st Century Capitalism.* New York: Simon Schuster.

Rogers, E. M. 1983. *Diffusion of Innovations.* 3rd ed. New York: Free Press.

———. 1995. *Diffusion of Innovations.* 4th ed. New York: Free Press.

Rosell, S. A., et al. 1992. *Governing in an Information Society.* Montreal: Institute for Research on Public Policy.

Rosenberg, V. 1967. Factors Effecting the Preferences of Industrial Personnel for Information Gathering Methods. *Information Storage and Retrieval* 3, no. 3: 119–27.

Rosenbloom, R. S., and F. W. Wolek. 1970. *Technology and Information Transfer: A Survey of Practice in Industrial Organizations.* Boston: Division of Research, Graduate School of Business Administration, Harvard University.

Ross, J., and B. M. Staw. 1986. Expo 86: An Escalation Prototype. *Administrative Science Quarterly* 31, no. 2:274–97.

———. 1993. Organizational Escalation and Exit: Lessons from the Shoreham Nuclear Power Plant. *Academy of Management Journal* 36, no. 4:701–32.

Roth, G., and Kleiner, A. 1999. *Car Launch: The Human Side of Managing Change.* New York: Oxford University Press.

Rousseau, D. M., S. B. Sitkin, R. S. Burt, and C. Camerer. 1998. Not So Different after All: A Cross-discipline View of Trust. *Academy of Management Review* 23, no. 3:393–404.

Ruddy, T. 2001. Personal communication, quoted in C. Gordon, 2002. Contributions of Cultural Anthropology and Social Capital Theory to Understandings of Knowledge Management. PhD thesis, University of Toronto.

Sabel, C. F. 1982. *Work and Politics: The Division of Labor in Industry.* Cambridge, U.K.: Cambridge University Press.

Sackmann, S. A. 1991. *Cultural Knowledge in Organizations: Exploring the Collective Mind.* Newbury Park, CA: Sage.

———. 1992. Culture and Subcultures: An Analysis of Organizational Knowledge. *Administrative Science Quarterly* 37, no. 1:140–61.

Salancik, G. R. 1977. Commitment and the Control of Organizational Behavior and Belief. *In New Directions in Organizational Behavior,* edited by B. M. Staw and G. R. Salancik, pp. 1–54. Chicago: St. Clair.

Salancik, G. R., and J. Pfeffer. 1978. A Social Information Processing Approach to Job Attitudes and Task Design. *Administrative Science Quarterly* 23, no. 2:224–53.

Sanchez, R. 2002. Modular Product and Process Architectures: Frameworks for Strategic Organizational Learning. In *The Strategic Management of Intellectual Capital and Organizational Knowledge*, edited by C.W. Choo and N. Bontis, 223–32. New York: Oxford University Press.

Saracevic, T. 1970. The Notion of "Relevance" in Information Science. In *Introduction to Information Science,* edited by T. Saracevic, pp. 111–51. New York: R. R. Bowker Co.

———. 1975. Relevance: A Review of and a Framework for the Thinking on the Notion in Information Science. *Journal of the American Society for Information Science* 26, no. 6:321–43.

———. 1996. Relevance Reconsidered '96. Paper presented at CoLIS 2: Second International Conference on Conceptions of Library and Information Science, Copenhagen, October 13–16, 1996.

———. 1997. The Stratified Model of Information Retrieval Interaction: Extension and Applications. Paper presented at the Annual Meeting of the American Society for Information Science, Washington, D.C., Nov. 1–6, 1997.

Saracevic, T., et al. 1988a. A Study of Information Seeking and Retrieving. Parts I: Background and Methodology. *Journal of the American Society for Information Science* 39, no. 3:161–76.

———. 1988b. A Study of Information Seeking and Retrieving. Part II: Users, Questions, and Effectiveness. *Journal of the American Society for Information Science* 39, no. 3:177–96.

———. 1988c. A Study of Information Seeking and Retrieving. Part III: Searchers, Searches, and Overlap. *Journal of the American Society for Information Science* 39, no. 3:197–216.

Schamber, L. 1994. Relevance and Information Behavior. In *Annual Review of Information Science and Technology,* edited by M. E. Williams, 29:3–48. Medford, NJ: Learned Information.

Schein, E. H. 1985. *Organizational Culture and Leadership.* San Francisco: Jossey-Bass.

———. 1991. What Is Culture? In *Reframing Organizational Culture,* edited by P. J. Frost, L. F. Moore, M. Reis Louis, C. C. Lundberg, and J. Martin, pp. 243–53. Newbury Park, CA: Sage.

———. 1992. *Organizational Culture and Leadership.* San Francisco: Jossey-Bass.

———. 1997. *Organizational Culture and Leadership.* 2nd ed. San Francisco: Jossey-Bass.

Scherer, K. R., and V. Tran. 2001. Effects of Emotion on the Process of Organizational Learning. In *Handbook of Organizational Learning and Knowledge,* edited by M. Dierkes, A. B. Antal, J. Child, and I. Nonaka, pp. 369–92. Oxford: Oxford University Press.

Schön, D. A. 1983. *The Reflective Practitioner: How Professionals Think in Action.* New York: Basic Books.

Schumpeter, J. A. 1934. *The Theory of Economic Development.* Cambridge, MA: Harvard University Press.

Schwartzman, H. B. 1987. The Significance of Meetings in an American Mental Health Center. *American Ethnologist* 14, no. 2:271–94.

———. 1989. *The Meeting: Gatherings in Organizations and Communities.* Vol. 56. New York: Plenum.

Schwenk, C. R. 1984. Cognitive Simplification Processes in Strategic Decision-Making. *Strategic Management Journal* 5, no. 2:111–28.

Shrivastava, P., I. Mitroff, and M. Alvesson. 1987. Nonrationality in Organizational Actions. *International Studies of Management and Organization* 17, no. 3:90–109.

Shrivastava, P., and S. Schneider. 1984. Organizational Frames of Reference. *Human Relations* 37, no. 10:795–809.

Siffin, W. J. 1977. *Problem Analysis: Lessons from a Case of Smallpox.* Bloomington, IN: Program of Advanced Studies in Institution Building and Technical Assistance Methodology.

Simon, H. A. 1957. *Models of Man: Social and Rational.* New York: John Wiley.

———. 1976. *Administrative Behavior: A Study of Decision-Making Processes in Administrative Organization.* 3rd ed. New York: Free Press.

———. 1977. *The New Science of Management Decision.* Revised ed. Englewood Cliffs, NJ: Prentice-Hall.

———. 1987. Making Management Decisions: The Role of Intuition and Emotion. *Academy of Management Executive* 1, no. 1:57–64.

———. 1997. *Administrative Behavior: A Study of Decision-Making Processes in Administrative Organization.* 4th ed. New York: Free Press.

Sims, H. P., Jr., D. A. Gioia, and associates, eds. 1986. *The Thinking Organization: Dynamics of Organizational Social Cognition.* San Francisco: Jossey-Bass.

Singley, M. K., and J. R. Anderson. 1989. *The Transfer of Cognitive Skill.* Cambridge, MA: Harvard University Press.

Skelton, B. 1973. Scientists and Social Scientists as Information Users: A Comparison of Results of Science User Studies with the Investigation into Information Requirements of the Social Sciences. *Journal of Librarianship* 5, no. 2:138–56.

Smircich, L. 1983. Organizations as Shared Meanings. In *Organizational Symbolism,* edited by L. R. Pondy, P. J. Frost, G. Morgan, and T. C. Dandridge, pp. 55–65. Greenwich, CT: JAI Press.

Smith, D. K., and R. C. Alexander. 1988. *Fumbling the Future: How Xerox Invented, Then Ignored, the First Personal Computer.* New York: William Morrow.

Snyder, M. 1984. When Belief Creates Reality. In *Advances in Experimental Social Psychology,* edited by L. Berkowitz, pp. 248–305. Orlando: Academic Press.

Solomon, P. 1999. Information Mosaics: Patterns of Action That Structure. In *Exploring the Contexts of Information Behaviour,* edited by T. D. Wilson and D. K. Allen, pp. 150–175. London: Taylor Graham.

Sonnenwald, D. H. 1999. Evolving Perspectives of Human Information Behaviour: Contexts, Situations, Social Networks and Information Horizons. In *Exploring the Contexts of Information Behaviour,* edited by T. D. Wilson and D. K. Allen, pp. 176–90. London: Taylor Graham.

Sonnenwald, D. H., B. M. Wildemuth, and G. L. Harmon. 2001. A Research Method to Investigate Information Seeking Using the Concept of Information Horizons: An Example from a Study of Lower Socio-economic Students' Information Seeking Behaviour. *New Review of Information Behaviour Research* 2:65–86.

Spender, J. C. 1989. *Industry Recipes.* Oxford: Basil Blackwell.

———. 1998. The Dynamics of Individual and Organizational Knowledge. In *Managerial and Organizational Cognition: Theory, Methods and Research*, edited by C. Eden and J.-C. Spender, 13–39. Thousand Oaks, CA: Sage.

Spink, A., T. Wilson, N. Ford, A. Foster, and D. Ellis. 2002. Information-Seeking and Mediated Searching. Part 1. Theoretical Framework and Research Design. *Journal of the American Society for Information Science and Technology* 53, no. 9:695–703.

Sproull, L. S., S. Weiner, and D. Wolf. 1978. *Organizing an Anarchy: Belief, Bureaucracy and Politics in the National Institute of Education.* Chicago: University of Chicago Press.

Star, S. L., and J. R. Griesemer. 1989. Institutional Ecology, "Translations," and Boundary Objects: Amateurs and Professionals in Berkeley's Museum of Vertebrate Zoology, 1907–1939. *Social Studies of Science* 19, no. 3:387–420.

Starbuck, W. H. 1992. Learning by Knowledge-Intensive Firms. *Journal of Management Studies* 29, no. 6:713–40.

Starbuck, W. H., and F. J. Milliken. 1988a. *Challenger:* Fine Tuning the Organization until Something Breaks. *Journal of Management Studies* 25, no. 4:319–40.

———. 1988b. Executives' Perceptual Filters: What They Notice and How They Make Sense. In *The Executive Effect: Concepts and Methods for Studying Top Managers,* edited by D. C. Hambrick, pp. 35–65. Greenwich, CT: JAI Press.

Staw, B. M., and J. Ross. 1987. Knowing When to Pull the Plug. *Harvard Business Review* 65, no. 2:68–74.

Stein, E. W. 1995. Organizational Memory: Review of Concepts and Recommendations for Management. *International Journal of Information Management* 15, no. 2:17–32.

Stern, S. M. 2003. *Averting "The Final Failure": John F. Kennedy and the Secret Cuban Missile Crisis Meetings.* Stanford, CA: Stanford University Press.

Stinchcombe, A. L. 1990. *Information and Organizations.* Berkeley: University of California Press.

Stoner, J. 1968. Risky and Cautious Shifts in Group Decision: The Influence of Widely Held Values. *Journal of Experimental Social Psychology* 4:442–59.

Streatfield, D. R., and T. D. Wilson. 1982. Information Needs in Local Authority Social Services Departments: A Third Report on Project INISS. *Journal of Documentation* 38, no. 4:273–81.

Suchman, L. A. 1987. *Plans and Situated Actions: The Problems of Human Machine Communication.* Cambridge: Cambridge University Press.

Sullivan, P. H., ed. 1998. *Profiting from Intellectual Capital.* New York: John Wiley.

Sunstein, C. R. 2003. *Why Societies Need Dissent.* Cambridge, MA: Harvard University Press.

Sutcliffe, K., and K. Weber. 2003. The High Cost of Accurate Knowledge. *Harvard Business Review* 81, no. 5:74–82.

Sutton, S. A. 1994. The Role of Attorney Mental Models of Law in Case Relevance Determinations: An Exploratory Analysis. *Journal of the American Society for Information Science* 45, no. 3:186–200.

Sveiby, K. E. 1996. *Tacit Knowledge.* Available from the author at http://www2.eis.net.au/~karlerik/Polanyi.html.

Swanson, E. B. 1987. Information Channel Disposition and Use. *Decision Sciences* 18, no. 1:131–45.

Taylor, R. S. 1968. Question-Negotiation and Information Seeking in Libraries. *College and Research Libraries* 29, no. 3:178–94.

———. 1986. *Value-Added Processes in Information Systems.* Norwood, NJ: Ablex Publishing Corp.

———. 1991. Information Use Environments. In *Progress in Communication Science,* edited by B. Dervin and M. J. Voigt, pp. 217–54. Norwood, NJ: Ablex Publishing Corp.

Thomas, J. B., S. M. Clark, and D. A. Gioia. 1993. Strategic Sensemaking and Organizational Performance: Linkages among Scanning, Interpretation, Action, and Outcomes. *Academy of Management Journal* 36, no. 2:239–70.

Thomas, J. B., S. W. Sussman, and J. C. Henderson. 2001. Understanding "Strategic Learning": Linking Organizational Learning, Knowledge Management, and Sensemaking. *Organization Science* 12, no. 3:331–45.

Trevino, L. K., J. Webster, and E. W. Stein. 2000. Making Connections: Complementary Influences on Communication Media Choices, Attitudes, and Use. *Organization Science* 11, no. 2:163–83.

Tsoukas, H. 1996. The Firm as a Distributed Knowledge System: A Constructionist Approach. Special issue, *Strategic Management Journal* 17:11–26.

————. 2003. Do We Really Understand Tacit Knowledge? In *The Blackwell Handbook of Organizational Learning and Knowledge Management,* edited by M. Easterby-Smith and M. Lyles, 410–27. Malden, MA: Blackwell.

Tsoukas, H., and E. Vladimirou. 2001. What Is Organizational Knowledge? *Journal of Management Studies* 38, no. 7:973–93.

Tucker, J. B. 2001. *Scourge: The Once and Future Threat of Smallpox.* New York: Grove Press.

Tufte, E. R. 1997. *Visual Explanations: Images and Quantities, Evidence and Narrative.* Cheshire, CT: Graphics Press.

Tushman, M. L., and T. J. Scanlan. 1981. Boundary Spanning Individuals: Their Role in Information Transfer and Their Antecedents. *Academy of Management Journal* 28, no. 2:289–305.

Tversky, A., and D. Kahneman. 1974. Judgment under Uncertainty: Heuristics and Biases. In *Judgement under Uncertainty: Heuristics and Biases,* edited by D. Kahneman, P. Slovic, and A. Tversky, pp. 3–20. Cambridge, U.K.: Cambridge University Press.

U.S. Congress, House of Representatives. 1986. *Investigation of the* Challenger *Accident.* House Report 99-1016. Washington, D.C.: Government Printing Office.

Utterback, J. M. 1994. *Mastering the Dynamics of Innovation: How Companies Can Seize Opportunities in the Face of Technological Change.* Cambridge, MA: Harvard Business School Press.

Vakkari, P. 1998. Growth of Theories on Information Seeking: An Analysis of Growth of a Theoretical Research Program on the Relation Between Task Complexity and Information Seeking. *Information Processing and Management* 34, no. 3: 361–82.

van der Heijden, K. 1994. Shell's Internal Consultancy. In *The Fifth Discipline Fieldbook,* edited by P. Senge, A. Kleiner, C. Roberts, R. Ross, and B. Smith, pp. 279–86. New York: Doubleday.

————. 1996. *Scenarios.* New York: John Wiley.

van der Wyck, R. W. A., and P. G. M. Hesseling. 1994. *Scenario Planning as Learning: "Metanoia."* Rotterdam: Faculty of Economics, Department of Business Organization.

Vaughan, D. 1996. *The* Challenger *Launch Decision: Risky Technology, Culture and Deviance at NASA.* Chicago: University of Chicago Press.

————. 1999. The Dark Side of Organizations: Mistake, Misconduct, and Disaster. *Annual Review of Sociology* 25:271–305.

Vidaillet, B. 2001. Cognitive Processes and Decision Making in a Crisis Situation: A Case Study. In *Organizational Cognition: Computation and Interpretation,* edited by T. K. Lant and Z. Shapira, pp. 241–69. Mahwah, NJ: Lawrence Erlbaum Associates.

von Hippel, E. 1988. *The Sources of Innovation.* New York: Oxford University Press.

————. 1994. "Sticky Information" and the Locus of Problem Solving: Implications for Innovation. *Management Science* 40, no. 4:429–39.

Von Krogh, G. 1998. Care in Knowledge Creation. *California Management Review* 40, no. 3:133–53.

Von Krogh, G., K. Ichijo, and I. Nonaka. 2000. *Enabling Knowledge Creation: How to Unlock the Mystery of Tacit Knowledge and Release the Power of Innovation.* New York: Oxford University Press.

Vygotsky, L. S. 1978. *Mind in Society.* Cambridge, MA: Harvard University Press.

Wack, P. 1985. Scenarios: Uncharted Waters Ahead. *Harvard Business Review* 63, no. 5:72–89.

Wagner, J. A., III, and R. Z. Gooding. 1997. Equivocal Information and Attribution: An Investigation of Patterns of Managerial Sensemaking. *Strategic Management Journal* 18, no. 4:275–86.

Walsh, J. P. 1995. Managerial and Organizational Cognition: Notes from a Trip down Memory Lane. *Organization Science* 6, no. 3:280–321.

Walsh, J. P., and G. R. Ungson. 1991. Organizational Memory. *Academy of Management Review* 16, no. 1:57–91.

Wathne, K., J. Roos, and G. von Krogh. 1996. Towards a Theory of Knowledge Transfer in a Cooperative Context. In *Managing Knowledge: Perspectives on Cooperation and Competition,* edited by G. V. Krogh and J. Roos, pp. 55–81. London: Sage.

Weick, K. E. 1979a. Cognitive Processes in Organizations. In *Research in Organizational Behavior,* edited by B. M. Staw, pp. 41–74. Greenwich, CT: JAI Press.

———. 1979b. *The Social Psychology of Organizing.* 2nd ed. New York: Random House.

———. 1995. *Sensemaking in Organizations.* Thousand Oaks, CA: Sage.

———. 1996. Prepare Your Organization to Fight Fires. *Harvard Business Review* 74, no. 3:143–48.

———. 2001. *Making Sense of the Organization.* Oxford: Blackwell.

Weick, K. E., and R. L. Daft. 1983. The Effectiveness of Interpretation Systems. In *Organizational Effectiveness: A Comparison of Multiple Models,* edited by K. S. Cameron and D. A. Whetten, pp. 71–93. New York: Academic Press.

Weick, K. E., D. P. Gilfillan, and T. Keith. 1973. The Effect of Composer Credibility on Orchestra Performance. *Sociometry* 36:435–62.

Wenger, E. 1998. *Communities of Practice: Learning, Meaning and Identity.* Cambridge, U.K.: Cambridge University Press.

Westrum, R. 1992. Cultures with Requisite Imagination. In *Verification and Validation of Complex Systems: Human Factors Issues*, edited by J. A. Wise, V. D. Hopkin, and P. Stager, 401–16. Berlin: Springer-Verlag.

Wikström, S., and R. Normann. 1994. *Knowledge and Value: A New Perspective on Corporate Transformation.* London: Routledge.

Wilensky, H. 1967. *Organisational Intelligence: Knowledge and Policy in Government and Industry.* New York: Basic Books.

Wilson, P. 1973. Situational Relevance. *Information Storage and Retrieval* 9, no. 8:457–71.

Wilson, S. R., M. D. Cooper, and N. Starr-Schneidkraut. 1989. *Use of the Critical Incident Technique to Evaluate the Impact of MEDLINE.* Palo Alto, CA: American Institutes for Research in the Behavioral Sciences.

Wilson, T. D. 1997. Information Behaviour: An Interdisciplinary Perspective. *Information Processing and Management* 33, no. 4:551–72.

———. 1999. Models in Information Behaviour Research. *Journal of Documentation* 55, no. 3:249–70.

———. 1981. On User Studies and Information Needs. *Journal of Documentation* 37, no. 1:3–15.

———. 1994. Information Needs and Uses: Fifty Years of Progress? In *Fifty Years of Information Progress: A Journal of Documentation Review,* edited by B. C. Vickery, pp. 15–51. London: Association for Information Management.

———. 2002. The Nonsense of "Knowledge Management." *Information Research* 8, no. 1. Available at http://InformationR.net/ir/8–1/paper144.html.

Wilson, T. D., N. Ford, D. Ellis, A. Foster, and A. Spink. 2002. Information-Seeking and Mediated Searching. Part 2. Uncertainty and Its Correlates. *Journal of the American Society for Information Science and Technology* 53, no. 9:704–15.

Wilson, T. D., and D. R. Streatfield. 1977. Information Needs in Local Authority Social Services Departments: An Interim Report on Project INISS. *Journal of Documentation* 33, no. 4:277–93.

———. 1981. Structured Observation in the Investigation of Information Needs. *Social Science Information Studies* 1, no. 3:173–84.

Wilson, T. D., D. R. Streatfield, and C. Mullings. 1979. Information Needs in Local Authority Social Services Departments: A Second Report on Project INISS. *Journal of Documentation* 35, no. 2:120–36.

Wilson, T. D., and C. Walsh. 1995. *Information Behaviour: An Inter-disciplinary Perspective.* Sheffield, U.K.: University of Sheffield, Department of Information Studies.

Winter, S. G. 1987. Knowledge and Competence as Strategic Assets. In *The Competitive Challenge: Strategies for Industrial Innovation and Renewal,* edited by D. J. Teece, pp. 159–84. Cambridge, MA: Ballinger Publishing.

Witkin, H. A., and D. R. Goodenough. 1981. Cognitive Styles: Essence and Origins, Field Dependence and Field Independence. *Psychological Issues* 14, no. 51:whole issue.

World Health Organization (WHO). 1966. Official records 151. A19/P&B/2, dated March 28.

———. 1980. *The Global Eradication of Smallpox—Final Report of the Global Commission for the Certification of Smallpox Eradication.* Geneva: World Health Organization.

Zack, M. H. 1998. A Strategic Model for Managing Intellectual Resources and Capabilities. Paper presented at the 2nd World Congress on the Management of Intellectual Capital, McMaster University, Hamilton, Ontario, January 21–23, 1998.

Zsambok, C. E., and G. A. Klein, eds. 1997. *Naturalistic Decision Making.* Mahwah, NJ: Lawrence Erlbaum Associates.

Zuboff, S. 1988. In *the Age of the Smart Machine: The Future of Work and Power.* New York: Basic Books.

Zucker, L. G. 1983. Organizations as Institutions. In *Research in the Sociology of Organizations,* edited by S. B. Bachrach, pp. 1–47. Greenwich, CT: JAI Press.

INDEX

The letters *t* and *f* following entries denote table and figure respectively.